All

A Carpenter and Philly Novel

(Fifth in a Series)

Ken Behar

All
(Fifth in a Series)

978-0-9961462-6-5 (paperback)
978-0-9961462-7-2 (eBook)

Library of Congress Control Number: 2019919016

Published by: Ken Behar
Lexington, Massachusetts

Cover design by Angela Valenti
Cover photograph © Will McKee

To

David
Chris
Paul
Jeff
Jon
Dolores
Donna
Katie
Barbara
Gail

Also by the author:

Ghosts Can Only Go Straight
(Turn of the Century Tales)

Not Too Shabby
(Barrister Tales from Ed's Breakfast Emporium)

HOOPS

Carpenter and Philly Novels:
Turn The Page
No Right Answers
Coin Flips
Full Circles
All

Contents

January

Philly's Untitled Playlist

The Catalyst

Linkin Park

1

A High School Teacher
A High School Soccer Coach

For a brief time, white, glaring sunlight had streamed through the living room window, but by one o'clock in the afternoon the sun had moved and both the glare and its illusion of warmth were gone. In the Brighton house that Philomena Piper owned and shared with an engaged couple, Raul and Isabella, Philly positioned her six-month old daughter, Daisy, on her stomach on the hardwood living room floor. Then she moved several yards to Daisy's toy chest and set it on its side with the opening facing her daughter. "Go," she urged and stepped back to watch the show.

The developmental books said that on average, crawling began at seven months, usually after a baby had mastered sitting up on her own. Philly had yet to observe Daisy sitting up on her own but here she was, not exactly crawling, but moving toward her toys in a herky-jerky motion, her right arm and right leg alternating movements with her left arm and left leg. A higher developmental stage of crawling involved alternate hand and leg movements that Daisy hadn't mastered. Yet Daisy was probably ahead in the developmental game because from the time she was weeks old, Paul's favorite activity with Daisy was to turn her on her stomach, press his hand against her feet, and urge her on as her legs pushed against his hand and propelled her forward. Daisy's progress to her toy chest was erratic but effective. When she reached the open chest, she reached for a red Elmo puppet and pulled it onto the hardwood floor. Soon other Sesame Street characters littered the floor.

Single Ladies blared from her boom box at high volume, and Philly pictured the video, Beyoncé and the two dancers with her moving as one finely tuned machine. She scooped up Daisy. So what if she wasn't a leggy dancer? So what if she was a short, solidly built attorney with time on her hands, a skewed sense of rhythm, and a baby to keep an eye on! She had the house to herself and began to move to the song's beat, singing along off key, holding Daisy close against her. Daisy wriggled with delight, her fine, black hair flying about, her blue eyes—her father Philip's gift to her—sparkling. Philly wanted to put a ring on the moment. She gripped Daisy under her arms and set her daughter's feet on the floor, moving Daisy back and forth in what she hoped was a vague approximation of the correct rhythm.

Philly became aware of the telephone ringing in her second-floor office. Hoisting Daisy and turning off the boom box in one practiced motion, she unlatched the gate to the stairs, and sprinted to the landing. Her voice mail was set to pick up after eleven rings and she reached her phone on nine. "Philomena Piper," she said breathlessly.

"It's Daniel Spring. I hope I didn't catch you at a bad time."

Philly brought her breathing under control. She was out of shape. Her New Year's resolution to get some exercise had been a recurring, idle thought she kept ignoring. "No time is a bad time when you call," she said. Daniel Spring was a teacher's union representative who had referred a number of cases her way. She wasn't about to disabuse him of his mistaken notion that she was expert in legal matters involving schools.

"I've given your name to a teacher who needs a lawyer," Spring said. "His name is Michael Waters. He's in a messy situation."

"Can you fill me in a bit?"

"The short version is that he teaches English and creative writing at James Madison High School in Boston. He reported his concern that a junior in one of his writing classes was a suicide risk. The girl claims that she was reported because she rejected his sexual advances."

Philly plopped a squirming Daisy on the floor next to a pile of toys and handed her baby a cloth doll. "Why was Mr. Waters concerned the student was a suicide risk?" Philly asked as Daisy began to suck on the doll's ear.

"He should be the one to tell you, but I understand it had to do with a short story the girl wrote for his writing class. He said it was pretty graphic. A teacher is a mandated reporter. Waters believed that the fictional story pointed to the girl being at risk. He reported the girl to his principal."

The doll's entire head was now covered in drool. "How can a mandated reporter be sued?" Philly asked. "If a teacher is required to report his suspicions, wouldn't he be protected for doing so?"

"As long as the report is made in good faith, the mandated reporter *is* protected," Spring explained. "You really need to have Waters give you the full story."

Philly wondered whether Michael Waters had the means to pay a lawyer. Teachers were constantly complaining about being underpaid. "Thank you very much for mentioning my name. If Mr. Waters reaches out to me, I'll be sure to let you know."

It hadn't been a long conversation, but Philly saw that Daisy was now collapsed on her stomach, asleep. Deciding to take advantage of her daughter's ability to conk out without warning, Philly turned on her computer and connected to a Massachusetts legal website she had found useful. The mandatory reporting statute required a teacher to report a reasonable suspicion that a student was a suicide risk, or an abuser of drugs or alcohol. A teacher reporting on these events was granted immunity from suit unless the teacher's report was made in bad faith, a term that lawyers would have a field day debating, since the concept had both a subjective and objective element.

Daisy suddenly wriggled and, although she didn't wake, let out a short, piercing wail. Startled, Philly nearly hit the delete key on her computer. "Next time you want to express yourself," Philly whispered, "give me a heads up."

A dozen miles away, at the office suite that Philly shared on Milk Street in Boston, Carpenter sat at his desk and for a moment envied Philly having to look after her kid. He wished he also had a built-in excuse to blow off work because there was really no work to do. His cupboard was bare and so was Philly's. The two younger lawyers they were collaborating with—Simon Jefferies and Rachel Boyle—had found themselves some short-term filler work but those engagements would soon be concluded. Carpenter was dismayed at giving serious consideration to the unthinkable, cutting out of work early.

Idleness had another drawback, Carpenter reflected. It gave him more time to think about his cancer. Currently, he was symptom free and his chronic lymphocytic leukemia required no medical intervention. But the CLL was there, biding its time, and the more he wasn't engaged in his legal practice, the more he thought about his disease. Last year, at the suggestion of a rabbi, he had named his cancer Fred and from time to time engaged Fred in dialogue. Well, not dialogue exactly. The conversations were one-sided and repetitive. Fred never said anything and Carpenter, for the most part, addressed Fred with profane invectives. But the rabbi was a smart man so, if the rabbi said to give his cancer a name and talk to it, Carpenter felt he was inviting disaster if he didn't follow those directives. Not that these chats with Fred had produced any revelation. There was some momentary satisfaction after leveling one of his vitriolic, one-sided harangues at Fred. But invariably the moment was fleeting.

And then there was the oddity that Carpenter couldn't talk to Fred unless he was regarding the photograph of a black man that hung on the wall facing his desk. The photograph had been a present from Philly more than three years ago. The man's head shot revealed the most unforgiving stare Carpenter had run into. Yet for some reason, whenever he talked to Fred, Carpenter believed that the man's gaze became marginally less hostile.

"Tell you what, Fred," Carpenter directed to the photograph. "Let's call it a day. I can't bear to be around this place when I've got nothing to do. I'm going to cut out early and would be honored if you joined me."

Carpenter started to rise when his phone rang. "Carpenter," he said, hoping that it would be Maxine on the line.

"This is Richard Morgan. Do you remember me?"

Carpenter drew a blank. The voice was familiar, but no name or face came to mind.

"You represented my son, Derek."

"Right!" Carpenter exclaimed, grateful that senility hadn't totally taken hold. He had sued a sports agent on Derek's behalf. "The pitcher. How's he doing?"

"Derek's good. He's pitching for the Mets' triple A affiliate. I think he'll be called up this spring."

"Good for him."

"Yeah," Morgan said. "But that's not why I called. You probably don't remember this, but Derek pitched for Middlemarch High School. It's in Kingsbury outside Worcester. Derek's younger sister, Fran, played soccer for the high school and was an all-star. Fran graduated two years ago. She plays varsity for Mountain View College where Derek went."

"That's up around UMass-Amherst if I remember," Carpenter said, as he settled into his desk chair.

"That's right. Anyway, Fran called me to let me know that her high school soccer coach got fired. She's not going to coach in the spring. The coach's name is Alison Lind."

"What happened?"

"Most of what I'm going to tell you comes from Fran. Fran was close to her coach and called Lind when she heard the news of the firing. Fran said that Lind was angry and wanted to sue to get her job back. Lind thinks she was discriminated against."

"Why does she think she was discriminated against?" These days, anybody booted out of a job immediately thought of a discrimination angle to either get the job back or recover money.

"According to Fran, male coaches weren't fired for doing the very things Lind was fired for: swearing, punishment drills, team discontent, parent complaints, and for taking her partner along to an out-of-state tournament game last school year that had an overnight."

Carpenter focused on the word partner. "Is Lind a lesbian?"

"Yeah, she is."

"You must have gotten to know Lind when your daughter played for her. What was she like?"

"I could see where she might rub people the wrong way, but I liked her. She doesn't take shit from anyone. She's one of those coaches who's a drill sergeant. And yeah, she swears like a trooper and she wouldn't take kindly to a parent who complained her kid wasn't getting enough playing time. Anyway, Lind told Fran that she wanted to sue, and Fran asked me if I knew any lawyer who could help her. I thought of you."

"That's very kind. Especially since I recall we had our disagreements when I was representing Derek."

"Maybe I'm mellowing," Morgan said. "You and that young lady you had working with you stood up to me. And the way things have worked out for Derek, I've got no complaints."

"That's good to hear. I'm interested in the case."

"Good. I'll call Fran and give her your number. She'll pass it on to Lind."

"I appreciate this." Maybe January wouldn't be completely bleak after all.

2

The temperature today was in single digits, mounds of snow from the most recent storm were everywhere, and there was a biting wind coming off the Boston waterfront. Yet Michael Waters wore no overcoat to the meeting at the Milk Street office. He was dressed in layers: a gray wool sports jacket covered a red vest which in turn covered a dress white shirt. As he sat at the conference room table, he unwound a red wool scarf that Philly guessed was over six feet long. If Waters was chilled, he didn't show it.

It was hard to tell under all those layers, but Philly pegged Waters as a fit and trim forty-year old. He had long, wavy, reddish brown hair and hazel eyes that lingered for a moment on the room's faded Japanese prints before focusing on the four lawyers who sat across from him. Waters was good looking in a professorial way. Philly imagined high school girls of a certain type developing a crush on him.

"I wasn't expecting so many lawyers," Waters said, smiling weakly.

"This is an initial meeting," Philly responded. "The four of us collaborate on cases and, whenever possible, we all like to attend the first meeting with a potential client." As she proceeded to introduce Carpenter, Simon, and Rachel, Philly wondered whether her off-the-cuff explanation had satisfied Waters. His expression gave away nothing. "We have a general idea of your legal situation," she resumed, "but we'd like to hear from you what happened."

"I've taught English and creative writing at James Madison High School for fourteen years without incident," Waters began. "This is my career—it's what I want to do."

Philly thought he was reasonably calm considering the charge against him.

"I teach an eleventh-grade creative writing course. Each student's major project for the first semester was to complete a short story of at least ten, double-spaced typed pages, due around two weeks before the Christmas vacation. All the students submitted their stories on time, and I gave them an initial reading over the next weekend. Caroline Fine's story had me concerned."

"Do you have a copy for us to look at?" Simon asked.

"I haven't decided to hire you," Waters said.

"Fair enough," Simon came back, showing no concern with being rebuffed.

"On the Monday after I went through the stories, I asked Caroline to see me after school. She came to my classroom and I told her I had a few questions about her story. I was pretty much feeling my way. In the past, I'd only had concerns with two stories that had been submitted to me and, in each case, I felt comfortable after talking with the student that the work was made up and not an autobiographical account."

Rachel was taking copious notes. Carpenter was regarding Waters without expression, but his jaw muscles were working, the sign that he was engaged. Simon's cool appraisal of Waters was inscrutable.

"What were your concerns about this student's story?" Simon asked.

"Caroline's story was about a junior in high school, a girl who was contemplating suicide. The protagonist had made a list of pros and cons in her life. The cons outnumbered the pros. The cons included overbearing parents pressuring her to get good grades and get into a top-notch college, being dumped by a boyfriend, feelings of inadequacy because she didn't excel at anything, things of that nature. The story ended with the protagonist unscrewing the tops of prescription vials filled with barbiturates that had been prescribed for her mother. As the girl in the story swallowed the first pill, she smiled and thought, like mother like daughter." Waters paused. "There's a lot more detail in the story but that's a rough outline."

During high school, Philly had never considered harming herself. But her violent thoughts about how she would pick off the assholes on her extensive shit list were particularly vivid. Had she ever turned one of her mayhem fantasies into a story, a teacher reading the work would probably have called the police.

"Do you remember what some of the pros were?" Rachel asked.

Waters breathed deeply. "I don't recall them as vividly as I do the cons. I remember one pro. In another year, the protagonist would be going away to college and wouldn't have to live at home anymore."

"What happened when you confronted your student?" Rachel followed up.

"As I said, I tried to feel my way. I told Caroline that I had read her work and liked it. I also told her that I found the story disturbing and asked her whether there was anything going on in her personal life that she wanted to talk about. My question clearly made her uncomfortable. She was dismissive. I think she said something like, 'It's just a story so what's the big deal?'

"I explained to her that teachers were under a duty to make sure that a student was safe. She became somewhat defiant and challenged me. She said, 'So you think my story was about me?' I told her that thought had crossed my mind. She became angry which struck me as out of character. She said: 'What if the story was about me? Aren't you always telling us to write about what we know?' I took what she said as an admission that her story *was* autobiographical. I told her that I hadn't meant to upset her and that if she had any personal problem, she shouldn't hesitate to talk it out with me, if she felt comfortable doing that, or with someone else. She said, 'Like that's going to happen,' and she walked out of the classroom."

Rachel looked up from her note taking. "What happened next?"

"I decided to sleep on the situation. But the next day I was still uneasy and I decided to report my concerns to the school principal. I met with her, told her I was troubled by Caroline's story, and that I felt the most prudent thing to do was to report my concerns. The principal read the story in my presence and said that I had done the right thing and she would take over."

"Did you give your principal anything in writing?" Carpenter asked.

Waters shook his head. "Just a copy of Caroline's story."

"Go on," Carpenter prompted.

"The next day the principal, Suzanne Lacey, called me into her office. She had confronted Caroline and Caroline accused me of reporting her because she had rebuffed sexual advances I had made to her. According to Lacey, Caroline claimed that her story was purely imaginary and was not a personal account."

For a moment, the only sound in the conference room was Rachel's note taking. "When you met with Caroline, was that the only time you'd been alone with her?" Philly asked.

"No. I make it a point to meet with each of my students one-on-one to review their submissions. Before the story we're talking about, I had met with each of the students in the class twice."

"How big a class is this?" Philly asked.

"Just fifteen. The word is out I'm a demanding teacher and that seems to scare away a fair number of students."

"Is there anything that you can think of in your dealings with Caroline that could be construed as inappropriate?" Philly followed up.

"No," Waters said, not put off by the question.

"Have you met Caroline's parents?" Philly asked.

"No."

"What do you know about Caroline?"

Waters shrugged. "Not much when you come down to it. This was the first time I've had her in my class. She's participated in class discussions and the critiques that we do in class. I believe she's got some talent as a writer."

"What's your principal's next move?" Carpenter asked.

"She told me that she's obligated to investigate Caroline's allegations. Lacey intends to interview me, Caroline, and anyone else that she thinks has relevant information. I'm entitled to have a union representative with me, but I'd prefer to have my own legal representation."

"Why?" Carpenter asked.

"I'm worried," Waters said with some heat. "Besides, the union rep is no great shakes. He means well but he's somewhat of a hothead. I don't care if he sits in, but I intend to treat this seriously because it is serious, and I'd rather have a pro."

Carpenter nodded. "Fair enough," he said. "Why don't you tell us a little about yourself?"

Waters again shrugged. "There's not all that much to tell. I'm the second oldest of five children. My parents are wealthy and set up trust funds for me and my brothers and sisters. Along with one of my sisters, I declined to go into the family business. I live alone in a condo in the South End. I typically travel in Europe during the summers. I've always wanted to be a teacher and I enjoy teaching. It's been the right career move for me." Waters paused. "What else do you want to know?"

Carpenter met Waters' gaze. "Don't take this the wrong way," he said, "but is there any way your sex life can enter into this?"

Philly marveled how the geezer rarely shied away from an awkward subject or question.

"That's fairly direct," Waters said, again not appearing put off by Carpenter's bluntness. "I'm heterosexual. I date regularly. I'm not disposed to get married and I'm not interested in having children. When I do date women, I put these points forward so that there's no misunderstanding. I date women more or less my own age. I don't see how any of this is relevant to Caroline's allegations but what do I know? I've never been involved in a situation like this before."

Philly decided to move the interview along. "I'm interested in your case. If you engage me, I'll be lead counsel but I'm likely to call on my colleagues for assistance. I suggest that I send you an engagement letter so that the fees you would be charged will be spelled out and so that you get a feel for the lawyer-client relationship. If you have questions about the engagement letter, please call me. Do you have any questions for us?"

Waters stared straight ahead for a long moment. "Have you ever had a case like this?"

Philly sent a mental thank you to Daniel Spring. "No," she replied, "but I've been involved in school related litigation."

A few minutes later, when Philly returned to the conference room after seeing Walters out, Simon was checking his watch. "We get to do this again in forty-five minutes."

Philly sat down and glanced at her colleagues. They were an odd group: Carpenter, over sixty, the dour, unsmiling, gray eminence; Simon and Rachel, two recent law school graduates with the boundless energy of their relative youth; and herself, a single mom in her mid-thirties. "Do you think Waters felt ganged up on?" she asked.

"I think so," Rachel said. "It clearly was something he wasn't expecting."

With her round face, short blond hair, and blue eyes, Rachel looked like an innocent. Maybe she was but, Philly reflected, of the four of them, she might also be the smartest.

"I think it's important that we all meet with a possible client," Simon put in. "We're different and I think we each might have something to offer."

Simon was of medium height, slim to the point of frailness, and wore his dark hair slicked back. Recently he had taken to wearing rimless glasses which Philly thought made his features appear more angular. Based on Simon's performance last year, Philly and Carpenter believed he had the potential to be a superstar litigator.

"Nothing's perfect," Carpenter groused. "But I want us all to sit in when Alison Lind comes in. Since we're going to keep working together, I'm okay with greeting potential clients with a committee. That's not the way it's usually done but I think we need to stick to this approach."

But when Alison Lind arrived, she didn't seem at all put off by having four lawyers confronting her. She favored the attorneys with a hard, combative stare. She was tall, broad-shouldered, and dark haired. After introducing Philly, Simon, and Rachel, Carpenter decided to borrow heavily from Philly's approach with Michael Waters.

"The four of us collaborate on cases so that's why we're ganging up on you for this meeting. We like as many of us as possible to sit in on an initial interview with a prospective client. We've found that increases the odds we'll ask all necessary questions."

"I get it," Lind said with a belligerent edge to her voice. "You all want to size me up and check me out. That's fine with me. I don't give a shit. What I say here is held in confidence, right?"

"Right," Carpenter confirmed, making the snap judgment that any complaint raised against Lind for inappropriate swearing was probably on the money. "Mr. Morgan gave me a bare outline of your situation. Why don't you tell us what's going on?"

Lind snorted and slapped the table with an open hand. "I'm being screwed over is what's going on. I got fired because I'm a woman and because I'm a lesbian. If I was a guy, none of this shit would have happened."

"You need to start at the beginning," Carpenter requested.

"I've been teaching physical education for the girls at Middlemarch High School for eight years, and for the last seven years, I've been the girls' soccer coach. The previous girls' soccer coach was a math teacher and he was more than eager to offload the coaching job. Soccer wasn't my sport—lacrosse was—but Middlemarch is a relatively small high school and doesn't have a girls' lacrosse team. I was happy to take on the coaching gig because frankly I needed the money."

"How big a high school is it?" Rachel asked.

"Eight hundred give or take, two hundred in each grade."

"I'm not familiar with Kingsbury," Simon said. "What's the town like?"

"Upper middleclass suburb. Typically votes Republican. The high school serves Kingsbury and a bunch of other towns."

"What got you fired?" Carpenter decided to get down to business.

Lind again slapped the conference room table. "I'm so angry I don't know where to start. But if you want my opinion, this all has to do with a bunch of gutless parents and their spoiled kids."

"You need to explain that to us."

"When I took over the coaching job, I took over a team that was out of shape and unmotivated. When I played lacrosse, I wasn't the best player, but I was among the fittest. I'm a big believer in conditioning. My practices are hard. I don't think I have to apologize for that. If a girl wants to play soccer for me, she's going to get her ass in shape."

Carpenter mainly followed baseball where many players looked like a sprint around the bases would do them in.

"Over the years, girls have bitched about how hard my practices were. A lot of the seniors on the team this year are a bunch of spoiled rotten, fucking crybabies. During last fall's games, I sat down a number of these seniors and played sophomores and juniors in their place because the younger kids were putting out in practice and actually cared. Well, the seniors didn't like it and their parents liked it even less. In the past, parents have complained to the principal about me but, until I got the axe, the principal pretty much let me do my job."

"What's your team's record?" Carpenter asked.

"I've had winning seasons except for the first two years when I was just taking over. The winning seasons were nothing to write home about—I think the best record was four games over five hundred. The last school year we were two games over five hundred during the fall and spring seasons. This fall we were also two games over five hundred. But I can tell you this. If I hadn't worked the kids hard, all the seasons would have been losing seasons."

"Why exactly were you fired?" Carpenter inquired.

"I can tell you what the gutless bastard who passes as principal told me. In November, Norman Joyce called me into his office and said I needed to change my act. Earlier in the month, the seniors I demoted from the starting team wrote Joyce a letter saying they were all going to quit the team in the spring if I didn't let them start. The parents of these brats petitioned Joyce to fire me. They claimed that a coach with a more tolerant attitude would produce a team that performed better. Now there's a crock! The girls' soccer team is probably the only high school team with a winning record. The seniors and their parents claimed my practices were boot camps and that the players had nothing left for the games. They told Joyce that I belittled players, swore at them, and made players who crossed me do excessive drills as punishment." Lind paused. "Oh yeah," Lind resumed, smirking. "How could I forget? A bunch of parents complained that I took Beth to an out-of-state tournament where the team spent the night."

"Beth?" Carpenter questioned.

"Beth Finegold, my partner."

"Are the two of you married?" Rachel asked.

"No. We seem to be doing okay for ourselves and don't want to jinx anything."

Carpenter let the silence lengthen. Rachel was the only one taking notes. "What did you say to your principal when he told you to change your act?" he asked.

"I told him he was out of line," Lind answered with indignation that Carpenter found genuine. "I told him the seniors who were out to get me didn't deserve to be on the field because they goofed off during practice and were being outperformed by underclass girls. I told him I didn't give a damn if the lot of them quit the team. I told him the parents of the seniors could damn well mind their own business if they were intent on spoiling their daughters rotten."

"What about making students do drills as punishment?" Simon asked.

"I do that. From the first team meeting I make it clear that anyone not putting out or making a dumb mistake can expect to run laps or do something else that isn't fun. If a girl doesn't like that, she doesn't have to join the team."

"Do you swear at the girls?" Rachel inquired.

Lind nodded. "I've got a mouth on me and when I get angry, I sound off."

"Why did you take your partner to the tournament?" Philly interjected.

"Because I wanted to. Male coaches take their wives to away tournaments. And one time, a male coach took his girlfriend to an away meet that had an overnight. Beth and I have been together since I started teaching at Middlemarch. I didn't think it was a big deal."

Carpenter decided it was time to focus on legal rights and remedies. "Why do you believe you're being discriminated against due to your sex and sexual orientation?"

"Duh!" Lind exclaimed. "How about the fact that the guys who coach the boys' sports swear more than I do and make their players run laps? How about the fact that most of the boys' teams don't have winning records? How about the time the boys' track coach took his girlfriend when the team traveled to an out-of-state meet that had a sleepover? Nothing happened to any of those guys."

"Was there ever a situation where boys or girls on a team coached by a man threatened to quit and parents asked the principal to get a new coach?" Philly asked.

Lind glared at Philly, clenching and unclenching her fists. "What does that have to do with anything?"

"I think you know," Philly said, meeting Lind's glower. "Just answer my question."

Lind silently fumed. "No," she said after a time. "Not since I've been teaching and coaching at the high school."

Carpenter favored Philly with a slight nod. She had flushed out the school's likely defense to a discrimination claim. The school would argue that players and parents were in revolt over Lind's coaching and attitude.

"Have parents complained about other coaches?" Philly pursued.

"I'm pretty sure that's happened," Lind said in a more subdued tone. "If I had to guess, I'd say most of the complaints are about their kids not getting the playing time the parents think they should have."

"Mr. Morgan said that his daughter gave you a call of support," Carpenter said.

"Fran Morgan was probably the best player I ever coached," Lind responded. "She was tall and solidly built and she could fly. I put her at center halfback so she could control play as much as possible."

"What did you talk about?" Carpenter asked.

"She told me that if I needed someone to support her, she would get behind me."

"Is that it?" Carpenter soldiered on.

"Well, we got to talking and Fran said that now that she had graduated, she had a new appreciation of what I'd been trying to do as a coach."

Lind fell silent, and Carpenter wondered why he was having to drag helpful details out of the woman. "What did she mean?"

"She said that I was hard to take as a coach because I was very demanding. She said that she used to hate practices because I came down hard on everyone. But now that she was playing in college, she realized that what I'd put her through in high school had paid off. She said that when she got to college, she became a starter as a freshman because she was in better shape than the upperclassman and wasn't afraid to work hard."

Carpenter thought of jotting down a note but then Rachel was probably taking down every word. "Are there any other graduates who would say something like that?"

"There may be," Lind responded, after a pause. "Some of the girls I coached went on to play in college. There were two I can think of who made it a point to say hello to me when they went back to the high school for a visit."

"Who replaced you as coach?" Rachel asked.

"That math teacher I told you about. He wasn't very happy about it."

"Who did the school hire to take over your phys ed classes?" Rachel continued.

"No one. Gym classes were cut back due to budget problems. The other male phys ed teachers are taking up my classes."

Carpenter wrote *male phys ed teachers* on his notepad. "Your case is far from a sure thing," he said. "The school will say it had a nondiscriminatory reason to dismiss you. The school will point to you being abrasive and alienating the seniors on the team and their parents. The principal you mentioned will probably say that you refused to change your attitude and become more accommodating. He's likely to say that never before in the history of the school had seniors on a team declared that they would quit unless there was a coaching change. That testimony might sink your ship."

"What a crock!" Lind fumed. "Are you saying that you can't help me?

"I'm saying," Carpenter came back, "that the odds may be against you. You probably want a lawyer to take your case on a contingency basis. We've done that kind of arrangement in the past but only when we thought there was a reasonably sure chance of the plaintiff winning."

"So you don't think I can win?"

"I didn't say that. I don't think that the odds are clearly in your favor when it comes to winning, so I'm not interested in a straight contingency arrangement."

For the first time during this meeting Carpenter felt sorry for Lind. She didn't have a personality it was easy to warm to, but now she looked like his assessment of her chances had crushed her.

"I can't afford to pay a lawyer for all the time he'd have to put in," Lind said dejectedly. "I guess I'm shit out of luck."

"Am I missing something here?" Carpenter directed at Philly, Simon, and Rachel. He didn't like the idea of being contradicted in front of a potential client but had decided to risk an exception in this case.

"I don't think so," Philly said.

"How did your team play during the fall after you demoted the seniors?" Simon asked.

"We won most of our games after I made the changes."

"I think Mr. Carpenter is right about your chances," Simon said. "Your case is anything but a sure thing. There are some facts in your favor, but you might have the weaker side."

"Well this truly sucks!" Lind groused.

"Maybe we can talk and get back to Ms. Lind," Simon threw out.

Carpenter shook his head. "Here's what we'd be prepared to do," he directed at Lind. "We'll take your case on a modified contingency. What I have in mind is a nonrefundable retainer of six thousand dollars. If you win the case, the legal fees will be a third of your recovery and we'll credit the six thousand dollars to that one third. If you lose, you're out six thousand dollars."

"Six thousand dollars," Lind said without enthusiasm. "I don't know if I can afford that."

"Think about it," Carpenter said. "You don't have to make a decision immediately.

Lind's comment was predictable. "Shit!"

This time, it was Carpenter's turn to return to the conference room after showing their potential client out. Simon fired off the first question.

"Where did you come up with the six thousand figure?"

"Easy," Carpenter said. "It's divisible by four."

"That must be a corollary of the divisible by three rule," Philly said, laughing. "We'll burn through the retainer in no time," she added.

"I know," Carpenter responded. "The case is going to be a time suck but there's a chance we can pull it off."

"I agree," Rachel said. "It helps that Lind was replaced by a man. I think we can show that Lind could do her job. If a coach is doing her job, what does it matter if disgruntled players and their parents don't like her?"

"It could matter," Philly put in.

"There are a number of things we can neutralize," Rachel continued. "If male coaches swear at players, Lind is doing nothing different. If male coaches discipline players by making them run laps and do drills, Lind is doing the same thing. If a male coach got to take a girlfriend on an overnight trip without incident, then Lind shouldn't be singled out for taking her partner."

Carpenter had considered the points that Rachel had made but continued to believe that the mutiny of senior players was a factor that Lind might have trouble getting around.

"I wonder if the sophomores and juniors on the team would support Lind?" Philly contributed. "If we could get underclass girls to support Lind and bring in former graduates, a hearing officer or judge would have to take notice."

"I want to try this case," Simon declared.

"Let's not get ahead of ourselves." Carpenter cautioned. "First Lind has to hire us. Second, Lind will have to get around a motion to dismiss her case. We'll figure out who does the trial work when we reach that stage."

"Let's hope that none of the male coaches is gay," Simon added.

Life was good, Philly thought. Daisy was asleep for the night, Paul had just screwed her silly and was spending the night, and with luck she and Carpenter might land two new cases.

"It's next year," Paul whispered. "Do you remember what you were going to think about when the New Year arrived?"

"You're not going to cut me any slack, are you?"

"I don't see any reason to put it off. We need to deal with the issue."

Her sated, happy mood began to evaporate. Paul lived in Cambridge where he was a detective with the city's police department. Moving in with Paul in Cambridge wasn't an option; Paul had downsized and moved into a condo after his divorce. Philly lived in Brighton, and the Brighton house would be cramped if Paul moved in. Besides, Paul had alternate weekend custody of his ten-year-old daughter, Jenny, and there was no spare room in Brighton that Jenny could use. Also, Isabella was pregnant, due to deliver in May, and Philly owed it to her housemate to stay in Brighton through the pregnancy. Without Isabella's help, she wouldn't have survived her own pregnancy with Daisy.

"Do you know what I wish?" Philly whispered. "I wish this house was bigger so that you could live here and Jenny could bunk with Daisy when she stayed with us. I never thought I'd say this, but I like the arrangement with Isabella and Raul. I really like Isabella and I need to be here during her pregnancy and for a time after she delivers. I used to think I had to have privacy, but I like having Raul and Isabella around. I'm looking forward to their baby living here."

Paul began massaging her lower back and Philly closed her eyes thinking that if she dropped off to sleep, they could again table this discussion for another day.

"What about us?" Paul asked. "I want to wake up with you in my bed. I want to go to sleep with you in my bed. The logistics of hooking up are a pain in the ass so more often than not, we're sleeping alone."

"I know."

"We can't do this forever."

"I know."

"You're very agreeable but we're not making any progress."

Philly brought Paul's hands around to her breasts which were no longer engorged after Daisy's nighttime feeding. She didn't want to stop breastfeeding Daisy, but that was something else that was going to have to change before too long. "If the house was bigger and there was room for everyone, would you be agreeable to communal living?"

"It's not what I envisioned," Paul said softly.

"But is it something you could live with?"

Philly's eyes fluttered but when Paul's fingers gently grazed her nipples, they shot open.

"I don't know," Paul said. "Raul and Isabella seem nice, but I don't really know them."

"They are nice. What about this? What if I were to do some looking around to see whether there was a bigger house we could buy?"

"You're serious, aren't you?" Paul asked.

"I am," Philly said. "I want it all. I want you and the communal living and to make a go of my practice. I want to be around for Daisy and not shortchange her. Why don't I see what's out there? It's supposed to be a buyer's market."

"That cuts two ways," Paul said. "If I sold my place in Cambridge, I'd probably take a haircut."

"There's no harm in looking," Philly countered. "What do you say?"

Paul sighed. "You're going to do it anyway so what the hell."

"Good thinking," Philly whispered. She moved closer against Paul, and this time he let her drift off to sleep.

3

Traveling by MBTA from her Somerville studio apartment was annoying and time-consuming, but whenever the destination was Philly's house, Rachel felt her irritability dissolve and her spirits lift on arrival. An awake Daisy ensured a positive mood swing; the kid was cute, liked to be held, and liked to be "walked" on her tip toes while being gripped under her shoulders. And simply being around Philly was a major plus. Philly hadn't been practicing law all that long but, somehow, some of Carpenter's common sense had rubbed off on her. Rachel always came away from a visit feeling she had learned something new. She knew her strengths and weaknesses. She was smart and a good writer and researcher. What she was missing was street smarts and aggressiveness. If she let them, Philly and Carpenter were just the people to fill those gaps.

While Philly arrayed papers and coffee mugs on the dining room table, Rachel carried Daisy around the living room. She bent low and inhaled the baby's slightly soapy, sweaty scent. Every once in a while, Rachel felt a pang of envy. Philly was settled, had a home base that meant something. Plus, she had a man in her life. Daisy's father, Philip, had died tragically, but in no time at all, Philly was in a new relationship. The man she was now seeing was gorgeous, a tall, lithe, dark-eyed man whom she had met briefly last year. Rachel hadn't gone on a date in a little over a year, and she definitely didn't want to think about that. What did Philly have that she lacked? Philly wasn't exactly a looker, but men were drawn to her.

"She's got a new trick," Philly said. "Put her on the bare floor."

Rachel obliged and Philly moved a small toy chest about six feet from her daughter and stood the chest on its side so toys leaked out.

"Let her loose," Philly directed.

"Oh my God!" Rachel exclaimed. It didn't look like crawling, but Daisy was somehow propelling herself forward toward the toys. "When did she start that?"

"Fairly recently. She does that, and sometimes she just rolls from one place to another. But she gets to where she wants to go."

Daisy reached the toys and collapsed next to an Oscar doll. Philly turned Daisy onto her back and gave her a red plastic ring to hold.

"Let's get to work. We can keep an eye on her."

Rachel had to acknowledge that despite the chaos brought on by a baby, Philly was organized. Her first order of business was two contingency cases involving former hockey players. At the end of last year, Philly had settled a case for a hockey player who had sought workers' compensation on the theory that the player's early onset dementia was caused by concussions the player had experienced during his hockey career. The case had been difficult, but the workers' compensation insurer couldn't get the case thrown out and had opted to settle. Afterwards, the lawyer and sports agent who had referred the case to Philly had sent over two similar cases which were being handled on a straight contingency basis.

"We need to move these cases and see if we can settle them quickly," Philly said, pointing to the files. "You worked on the case we had last year. I want you to draft the claims for our new clients."

Rachel nodded. "What about witnesses?"

"There's a list in each file provided by the players' wives. There are former players and, in one case, a former coach on the list. You also need to get the doctor we used in last year's case to be on board."

Rachel remembered Dr. Nancy Corrigan. The physician believed strongly that in the absence of another likely explanation, early onset dementia in former athletes who played a contact sport was the direct result of the violence they had experienced during their playing days. Witness preparation in last year's case had been time-consuming, and she now had two cases to prepare.

Philly moved a new stack of papers in front of her. "Also, Michael Waters has signed an engagement letter. He sent us a copy of the short story written by Caroline Fine. I've read it, but I don't want my views to influence you. Call me after you've read it."

Rachel appreciated Philly's approach which was one Carpenter shared. Each lawyer was genuinely interested in what she would independently contribute to a problem.

Philly reached for the remaining stack of papers on the dining room table. "Last but not least," she said, handing over several documents. "The first year I started working seriously with Carpenter, I finally got appointed in a Suffolk Probate Court case to be a guardian ad litem for a child. I just got a call from the court clerk who sent that case my way. I've agreed to be the court appointed lawyer for a woman who has a ten-year-old daughter. The girl claims to have been molested by her father and the mother doesn't believe the father committed sexual abuse. The Department of Children and Family Services wants to try to arrange an adoption for the girl and is seeking to terminate the mother's right to consent to the adoption. There's going to be a hearing in the case at the end of next month. It's not a pleasant case."

Rachel knew Philly was gauging her reaction to the facts of the case and, the truth was, the subject matter sickened her. But she resolved not to show even a hint of her discomfort.

"The clerk who sent the case my way is Allison Cooper. I've made copies for you of the background documents she sent me. Take a look at them while I deal with the rug rat."

Philly knelt before her daughter, grabbed the ring that Daisy was still holding, and gently pulled Daisy to a sitting position that struck Rachel as decidedly unstable. Philly eased Daisy onto her back and again engaged in the gentle tug that ended with Daisy sitting up. Rachel forced herself to focus on the documents Philly had given her and to ignore the never-ending Daisy distraction.

Marilyn Storm, now ten years old, claimed she was sexually abused by her father, James Farrell, when she was eight and in third grade. Marilyn's abuse claims surfaced in a meeting with a consulting psychologist, when Marilyn described being molested two years ago, most often at night when she would be woken by her father. The consultant notified the Department of Children and Family Services; Marilyn was removed from her parents' custody, and currently was living in a temporary foster home.

Rachel read through the papers both fascinated and repelled by their content. She really had led a sheltered life, she thought. But here was a case with a subject that all too frequently made headlines and, like it or not, she'd be drawn into a young girl's nightmare. Marilyn had been examined by a physician and had no hymen. The documents provided no mention of whether the father had been charged—let alone convicted—of any crime. For a time, after Marilyn had been placed in foster care, the girl had consented to both supervised and unsupervised visits with her mother. But the mother's refusal to unequivocally tell Marilyn that she believed the accounts of abuse, had caused Marilyn to want no further contact. The mother, Heather Storm, had received counseling of her own. Currently, Heather was not living with Marilyn's father but the two were in communication and would see each other. The court clerk who had sent Philly this information, had made a note on the facsimile cover page that the court record contained copies of various sealed documents such as medical reports. As the court appointed lawyer for Heather Storm, Philly would have access to the records being kept under seal.

Rachel looked up. Philly was sitting on the floor with Daisy in her lap and was reading to her daughter in a soft voice, occasionally pointing to pictures in the book. Mother and daughter were so in tune that Rachel couldn't imagine either wanting no contact with the other.

Rachel idly flipped through the pages of Heather Storm's court papers. What if Marilyn Storm hadn't been molested by her father? Had the father denied the charges in much the same way that Michael Waters denied coming on to Caroline Fine? What if both men were innocent? Or what if both were guilty? Why would either girl make up a story that would be devastating to the person she accused?

Philly, still holding Daisy, resumed her place at the dining room table. "How's that for light reading?"

"It's depressing," Rachel owned up.

Philly nodded. "Carpenter's always going on about the importance of thinking who you would want to represent in a case. He claims it helps you get a feel for which party has the strongest case. I can tell you that I'd rather be representing the kid than either the mother or father but that's not going to happen."

Rachel silently agreed with Philly's preference. The whole case had pain and suffering written all over it.

"Here's another thing," Philly continued. "The hourly rate the court pays is miserably low. Plus, it takes forever to get paid. You need to know these facts."

"Okay," Rachel said, wondering why she was being so amenable to this court-appointed assignment with a distasteful factual background.

"It's not okay," Philly responded. "But we have free time, and my feeling is that we should fill it even if the money isn't great. It's better than nothing."

Philly had a point, but Rachel was glad she'd kept her lousy, part-time, paralegal job. As a full-fledged lawyer, she found paralegal work demeaning, but the economy was still sluggish and few firms were hiring. She and Simon had decided to hang in with Carpenter and Philly for the moment. So far, the two senior lawyers had treated them fairly.

"I spoke with Allison Cooper," Philly continued. "She knows you're working with me. I want you to go see her and look through the medical records and other documents that are under seal. You also need to set up an appointment in the Boston office so the two of us can meet with Heather Storm."

Daisy reached for the pile of documents and Philly reflexively pulled her daughter back from the table. "Make an outline of the questions we should be asking Storm. I've done some brief research. The legal standard is what is in the best interests of the child. The Department of Children and Family Services obviously thinks it's best for Marilyn to be placed for adoption and out of her mother's and father's lives."

That's harsh, Rachel thought. But it was a bad situation all around. "I'm not looking forward to this case," she admitted.

"Neither am I," Philly said. "But we'll fight like hell to get Heather Storm what she wants."

Riding the T back to Boston, Rachel extracted from her shoulder bag the short story written by Caroline Fine entitled *Dead End.* In college she'd had an ambition to be a writer. She'd taken a creative writing class and been stunned by the critiques of her work. With serious expressions, her fellow classmates described her efforts as plodding, uninspired newspaper reporting, and missing a protagonist you might actually care about. To this day the frank assessments pained her. Yet the harsh but often accurate criticism of her creative efforts was one reason she had applied to law school. She turned to the first page of *Dead End.*

Do I know this person? Carlotta Finch thought as she finished proof-reading her application to Princeton University. Do I even want to know this person? Why the hell would Princeton accept a Ms. Goody Two Shoes, an uninspired and uninspiring girl who had done more than the required community service hours to make it seem like she actually gave a shit about others, who did well on the SATs after taking two—not one—preparatory courses, and who had managed an A- average by dint of late night rote rereading of any assigned work? Carlotta knew that "be careful what you wish for" applied to any application she submitted to a top ranked college. If she was accepted, maintaining a passing grade point average would be a struggle and she would quickly be exposed as the dogged plodder she was, a girl incapable of original thought or creative imagination. If she bored herself, how would she not fail to bore others?

Carlotta wondered whether she would actually submit the required essay on the topic "Describe how someone has influenced your life, positively or negatively, and what you learned from the interaction." Of all people, she had chosen her mother which was fine as far as the choice went but was anything but fine when she lied and related how her mother was a positive influence in her life. True, there was something to admire in her mother's escaping grinding poverty, obtaining a college scholarship, and becoming a licensed psychologist. But after marrying, her mother had put her career on hold and devoted herself to being a mother, constantly wanting what she saw as the best for her two children. To her mother, a child's good grades confirmed parenting success. To Carlotta, good grades suggested the opposite and yet, unlike her brother, there was something inside her that forced her to constantly strive to live up to her mother's expectations. She couldn't adopt her younger brother's mindset. At fifteen, Brian stayed out late, smoked and drank, blew off school, and met her mother's criticism over his poor grades with responses that ranged from nasty cursing and smoldering rage to studied indifference.

Rachel's academic success had come easy to her. She was one of those students who said little in class and breezed through examinations. Teachers grading her papers probably couldn't call up an image of her. Keeping in the background suited her which was probably why last year was so difficult when Philly and Carpenter had pretty much forced her to assert herself and litigate.

Carlotta tried to think of one thing in her life that gave her joy, but nothing came to mind. Richard Parks had been a change of pace, the first boy in her class to show real interest in her. Like herself he was a loner, and at first his attentions gave her a thrill. But Richard had wanted to have sex and when she said no, he dropped out of her life without so much as a "see you later."

Carlotta considered what she would do if she could choose anything she wanted for the upcoming years. Here again she came up empty. There was nothing that captivated her, called out to her. So she might as well go to Princeton or some other Ivy League school and be exposed as the fraud she was.

The Green Line was now underground, grinding along the track that led out of Kenmore Square. Metal grated against metal and the high-pitched screech was deafening. Rachel considered *her* ideal world: she'd be practicing law with Simon and Philly and Carpenter. The practice would be busy and lucrative so that she could ditch her part-time paralegal job. She would get comfortable with litigation. She would breeze through her first jury trial with no jitters and win it decisively. And somehow she would find a man who turned her on, excited her, someone who loved her and whom she loved in turn. Then the unimaginable might be attainable—a child as adorable as Daisy.

The doors of the T car opened at Auditorium and Rachel turned her attention back to Caroline Fine's story. She slowed her reading pace when the name Marshall Watts first appeared.

"Is everything okay?" Marshall Watts inquired, setting Carlotta's story down on his desk. The English teacher's expression of concern appeared genuine, but Carlotta couldn't imagine what vibe she had sent forth that prompted his question.

"Of course, Carlotta lied effortlessly. The last thing she was going to do was admit unhappiness to a stranger. And high school teachers were strangers when you came down to it although, to be fair, Mr. Watts was approachable and he made it a point to discuss students' written assignments in face-to-face meetings.

"It's just that you seem distracted, out of sorts somehow. I don't mean to pry."

Of course Mr. Watts meant to pry. Carlotta studied her English teacher, a nondescript middle-aged man who wore his hair long probably in the foolish hope that it would make him look cool to his students.

"It's college application time," Carlotta offered, feeling obliged to say something innocuous. "It's a stressful time for juniors as I'm sure you know."

Mr. Watts nodded but, if anything, his look of concern grew more pronounced. "I can't imagine you'd have any difficulty getting into an excellent college."

Carlotta was not about to tell her English teacher that she wanted to put college on hold. Never mind that she had no clue as to what she would do if she didn't continue her education.

"Are you worried about getting into college?"

"I'm not worried about anything," Carlotta snapped. She pointed to the story she had written. "Can we finish up? I need to get going."

"Of course." Mr. Watts pointed to his next marginal note in red ink and Carlotta immediately tuned him out. She continued the mental list of negatives in her life that she had begun to compose before the start of her meeting with Mr. Watts. No outside interests that turned her on. No close friends to speak of. No hope of a boyfriend. No desire to go to college. The fear of going to college and being exposed as a poseur, an imposter. All of which made her wish that she could press a pause button so that her life would hover in limbo, neither moving forward nor drifting back. The idea of stopping everything was so inviting that she smiled. Mr. Watts saw her change of expression and, totally misunderstanding it, nodded approvingly.

"So, to continue," Mr. Watts said. "Good to see you cheering up."

Rachel considered what she had read so far. The protagonist was a thinly disguised alter ego of the author. Mr. Watts had to be Michael Waters, but why Caroline Fine had chosen that particular teacher to include in her story remained unclear. Carlotta Finch was not attracted to the fictional Mr. Watts, was in fact turned off by his appearance.

That evening, Carlotta had the house to herself. Her parents were out at a concert and Brian hadn't even bothered to show up for dinner.

The medicine cabinet in her parents' bathroom had enough prescription medications to stock a small pharmacy. Most of the medications were prescribed for her mother. The tranquilizers were grouped together, three slender burnt orange plastic bottles with "WARNING" on each container in bold red lettering occupied the right-hand corner of the second shelf. Carlotta took her time reading the recommended doses. It was a miracle her mother wasn't a zombie if she actually took all three medications. Carlotta saw some poetic justice in what she was about to do for after all, hadn't she claimed her mother was the person who most influenced her life? Carlotta counted out pills from each vial, deciding that ten times the daily recommended number of tablets for each medication would be more than sufficient if ingested at one sitting.

Carlotta set the tablets down on her night table and decided to use her Simpsons mug for the water to wash them down. The comic touch would probably make no sense to her parents, Brian, and investigators, but so what? If she couldn't figure out her motives, why should anyone else be given a meaningful clue? Of all the members of the Simpson clan, only the thumb sucking baby had drawn her interest. From the time you took your thumb out of your mouth it was downhill from there.

Would anyone miss her when she was gone? Carlotta pictured her parents going through the motions of grief. Brian wouldn't give a shit—at most he would feel inconvenienced if he had to dress up and attend a memorial service. Maybe Mr. Watts would pause for a moment, think back to the last time he had met with her to go over her story and say to himself that he knew something wasn't quite right with the Finch girl.

Would anyone miss her when she was gone? There was only one way to find out. She put a pill in her mouth and swallowed it down. Like mother, like daughter, she thought, as she readied another pill.

Rachel couldn't imagine any objective person faulting Michael Waters for calling the girl's story to the attention of his principal. But the story provided no clue as to why Caroline Fine would level a sexual harassment charge against Waters. If anything, Watts was the only character who came across as sympathetic from the protagonist's point of view. Could Fine have been attracted to Waters?

Rachel considered what she would do to prepare Michael Waters' case. If money were no object, one approach would be to hire a private investigator to report on Caroline Fine's life. The more parallels between the lives of Fine and her fictional protagonist, the more justifiable Michael Waters' decision to report Fine's story. As to Fine's charge of sexual harassment, Waters was in a she-said, he-said situation. With what she knew so far, Rachel was inclined to believe their client.

4

A Mother

Heather Storm had arrived twenty minutes late for her appointment and the delay had put Philly in a foul mood which was understandable: she had to pay a babysitter. "You're late," Philly complained when Storm finally showed up and entered the office suite's conference room.

Storm was short, about Philly's height, and Rachel guessed she was about the same age, too—mid thirties. But there the resemblance ended. Rachel took in the client's brown hair which might have been auburn at some time but was now as dull and listless as her pinched expression, and gray eyes. Storm was also painfully thin.

"Do you understand why you've been assigned a lawyer?" Philly asked, after Storm settled in.

"I think so," Storm replied uncertainly. "I could lose Marilyn."

"That's right," Philly said. "Parental rights are important under the law. If a parent is in danger of losing her parental rights, the law finds that loss so serious that the parent is provided with a lawyer if the parent can't afford one."

"Well I sure as hell can't afford to pay a lawyer."

"Which is why I was appointed by the court to represent you," Philly explained. "Let's start by you going over what landed you in this situation."

Storm remained silent; going over her legal difficulties seemed to be the last thing she wanted to pursue. Philly must have picked up on the woman's reluctance because, "Do you want to lose your daughter?" was her next question.

"No."

"Then you need to fill us in. We can't help you if you won't help us."

"They're going to take her no matter what I do," Storm said resignedly.

"Maybe, maybe not," Philly countered. "But the chances of their taking her will increase if you don't start telling us what's going on."

Storm sighed. "Marilyn made up this story and told someone at school that James had sex with her."

"Why do you think Marilyn would make something like that up?" Philly questioned.

"I've been asking myself that," Storm said, displaying animation for the first time. "She's never liked James. I think she just wants to get him."

"Is it possible your daughter's telling the truth?" Rachel put in.

Storm shook her head. "James would never do something like that. It's pretty cruel what Marilyn's putting him through."

"Are you and James married?" Rachel asked.

"We never got around to that. I guess you could say we've got one of those common-law marriages you hear about."

"Are you and James living together now?" Rachel followed up.

"He moved out after the state people came for Marilyn. We thought it was better that way. But we still see each other. Now that Marilyn's living with this other family, James stays with me on and off."

Philly became lost in thought, so Rachel again jumped in. "Do you think that your daughter's ever been sexually active?"

"The girl's ten!" Storm said with feeling. "What kind of question is that?"

"You need to answer Ms. Boyle's question," Philly directed.

"No," Storm declared. "I don't think she's ever had a boyfriend."

"What about a girl friend?" Philly asked.

"What kind of question is that?" Storm erupted for the second time. "What kind of lawyers are you? You said you were trying to help me. That's not the way it seems to me."

"How long have you and James been together?" Philly came right back, ignoring Storm's outburst.

"About twelve years," Storm said evenly.

"Does James have his own lawyer?" Rachel asked.

"Yeah. The court gave him a lawyer too." Storm rummaged in her purse. "I wrote down what James told me. His lawyer's name is Stephen Minor." Storm spelled the last name and read off Minor's phone number.

"What does James do for a living?" Rachel inquired.

"Right now, he's sort of between jobs. He's a short order cook."

"And what about you?" Rachel continued.

"I work for a cleaning service. We clean up people's houses, mostly rich people."

"When's the last time you saw your daughter?" Philly asked.

"About six weeks ago. She doesn't want anything to do with me. She said if I didn't believe her and stood by James, she didn't want to see me."

Philly jotted a few words on her notepad. "What has James said to you about your daughter's allegations against him?"

"He said she's lying, and I believe him."

"The court papers we've been given say that Marilyn's seeing a psychologist," Philly said. "Do you know how that's going?"

"Not really."

"The court papers also say that you've seen a psychologist as well. How's that going?"

"I went for a month, but I stopped going. The psychologist kept trying to get me to think James had sex with Marilyn. I didn't need to listen to that garbage."

"If James approached your daughter in the night," Philly said, "would that be something you would have heard?"

Storm shrugged. "I know I'm a deep sleeper, but I think I would have heard something like that."

Philly nodded. "I'm trying to understand why a ten-year-old would come up with such a serious charge if it weren't true. It's not something that you think of a ten-year-old making up."

"Marilyn didn't like James. He was strict with her, a lot stricter than I was."

"Did he ever hit her?" Philly asked.

"He spanked her a couple of times. But I've spanked her too."

"Is your daughter a happy child?" Philly questioned.

Storm sighed. "I don't think she's been happy a lot over the last couple of years. At least she doesn't show that she's happy. But it's hard to say if she's happy. She's kind of quiet and likes to keep to herself. But when she was little, I'd say there were happy times."

"How does she do in school?" Rachel put in.

"She's kind of an average student. I'm the one who goes to the teacher conferences. All her teachers say she's real quiet and doesn't say much. I remember one of them saying that sometimes she forgot Marilyn was in her class."

"What does your daughter like?" Philly asked.

Storm frowned. "Not much I can think of. She listens to music. She's always got her music plugged in."

"I still have my music plugged in," Philly said. "I guess there are some things you never grow out of."

Philly had tried for a light tone, but Storm's dour expression remained in place.

"I think we're done for the moment," Philly said. "Thanks for coming in. Ms. Boyle is going to go to the court to look at some papers that have been locked up to protect Marilyn's privacy. I'll give you a call after we discuss what's in the papers."

Storm rose, obviously relieved the session was over. "You can look at all the papers you want," she said. "They're still going to take my daughter away from me."

"What do you think is going on with that woman?" Philly fired off when she returned to the conference room after showing Storm out.

"I think we're missing something," Rachel said, "but I can't figure out what it is."

"This girl has got to know that if she's adopted, she's going to be cut off from her parents. Her mother and father might not be given visitation rights. The kid must want to be rid of her parents. Why the hell would she want that?"

"She'd want it if the abuse allegation was true," Rachel said.

Philly nodded. "But if it's not true, the girl is making something up to cut herself off from her parents. It makes no sense."

"Marilyn has convinced the Department of Children and Family Services," Rachel observed.

"I think that's because she has no hymen," Philly said. "Without that, I wonder if the Department would be doing what it's doing."

"There are other ways besides intercourse that a girl could lose her hymen," Rachel stated the obvious. Philly gave her a look she couldn't read, and Rachel returned her gaze.

"You talk to James Farrell's lawyer," Philly directed. "Then I need you to check out the court papers that are under seal. Call me after you've talked to the lawyer."

"Sounds like a plan."

Philly checked her watch and made a beeline for the conference room door. "I'm late," she muttered as she made her escape.

Rachel reflected that of the recent cases to come their way, Storm's case loomed as the most troublesome because of its subject matter. She treated new cases with ambivalence. A law practice couldn't survive without new matters to work on; but each new client might require her to deal with something uncomfortable or force her to deal with her fears of litigation. Simon, Carpenter, and Philly were cut from a different cloth. They were fearless, loved getting their hands dirty. When it came to temperament and guts, she was the odd woman out.

"You look like you've lost weight," Maxine French observed, and Carpenter responded with what he hoped was a noncommittal shrug that would deter further questions. "It seems to me your appetite isn't what it used to be."

Carpenter shrugged again. One of the symptoms of CLL was weight loss. Loss of appetite was another. Maxine was right on both counts, but Carpenter didn't want to let on that anything was wrong. He was probably being a pigheaded asshole for not giving Dr. Specter a call but living in stubborn denial was something he took to instinctively.

"Is this something you should be talking to your doctor about?" Maxine asked, and Carpenter considered that although each woman in his life had been able to read his thoughts, Maxine had the uncanny ability to time her readings to the exact moment he was thinking about whatever she pointed out.

"I'm okay," Carpenter said, but realized immediately that he had made another mistake. Maxine picked up on his lack of conviction and was staring at him with a no-nonsense look that he suspected was close to the hard stare she gave a witness she was cross-examining. Maxine was of slight build and with her short, mostly gray hair she probably struck people as a mild-mannered, grandmotherly type. But Carpenter knew from experience that she had little tolerance for being given a song and dance.

"I want you to call your doctor," Maxine said in a tone that expected no contradiction. "Do it for me if you won't do it for yourself."

"It's not necessary," Carpenter replied with more force than the situation called for which was another mistake.

"I'm counting on you being around for a while," Maxine said. "Don't do something stupid out of stubbornness or denial. I'm not saying you're not yourself. I am saying there's something new going on that has me worried."

She was right, of course. Last night in his own condo, Carpenter had startled awake at three in the morning drenched in sweat. Night sweats were a symptom of CLL. What if he woke up in Maxine's bed a perspiring mess?

"All right, I'll call Specter."

"That wasn't so hard was it?"

Harder than you'll ever know, Carpenter thought. "When you're right, you're right," is what he said.

5

Rachel had been playing telephone tag with James Farrell's attorney, but she now had Stephen Minor on the line. Minor was a sole practitioner with an office in Chelsea. His website photograph showed a handsome man with wavy brown hair, full lips, a strong chin, and dark soulful eyes. His law school graduation date suggested that Minor had been practicing law two years longer than she and Simon. He held himself out as a general practitioner who handled probate court cases, tort claims, and business litigation.

"I thought we should touch base and perhaps exchange information," Rachel threw out once introductions had been exchanged. "May I assume that Mr. Farrell doesn't want to waive his right to consent to Marilyn's adoption?"

When Minor didn't answer right away, Rachel leaned back in the desk chair in Philly's Boston office and stared at Minor's face on her computer screen. God, the guy was good looking. He'd probably turn out to be four feet tall and weigh in at three hundred pounds. But he had that head shot going for him.

"I need this discussion to be off the record," Minor said.

"Okay," Rachel acquiesced. "That goes both ways."

"Understood. My client is conflicted. He vehemently denies abusing his daughter. But the fact that she would accuse him of abuse makes him think that he's better off with her out of his life. It's a wretched situation. Then there's the threat that criminal charges may be brought against Mr. Farrell. Frankly, I don't know why the district attorney's office hasn't at least sent the matter to a grand jury. I'm trying to figure out what they know that I don't know."

"Ms. Piper and I have been trying to figure out why Marilyn would falsely accuse your client of abuse. We've come up with nothing."

"That makes two of us. Mr. Farrell claims he has no clue."

"Do you believe him?"

Minor again paused and Rachel wondered whether he would level with her.

"I have no reason to disbelieve him. Like you, I've only been practicing a short time, but I've been lied to by clients enough not to take anything they say at face value."

So Minor had checked her website, probably while this telephone call was going on. When he saw her picture, did he think she was pretty? "Have you seen the court papers that have been sealed?" Rachel asked. "I haven't gotten around to reviewing them."

"Not yet," Minor said. "Here's a question for you. Why does Marilyn have your client's last name and not my client's last name?"

"I don't know."

"According to my client, your client made the decision in the hospital after the delivery without consulting him. Your client was the one who provided the information for the birth certificate."

"Where are you going with this?" Rachel asked.

"I'm not sure. It was just something I wondered about."

Rachel had run out of points to discuss. "Why don't you call me after you've looked at the court papers," she suggested. "Hopefully I'll have had a chance to go over them when you call."

"Okay," Minor said. "Thanks for reaching out."

Rachel turned to her website and studied her photograph. She *was* pretty, God damn it! Yet Minor had shown no interest in sweet talk or idle chitchat, had made no attempt to get to know her. True, the guy could be married or with a steady girlfriend. Still, when did that ever stop a guy from flirting?

Her website reminded her of a task she had set for herself: convincing Carpenter to get a website. Simon had one and so did Philly. Getting Carpenter to come on board would probably take an act of Congress but she was going to bug him on this point no matter how deep in the sand he tried to stick his head.

Carpenter was distracted, constantly checking his watch, which made Simon wonder whether he had an appointment to keep. They were sitting across from each other in the conference room to formulate a game plan for Alison Lind's discrimination case. Lind had signed an engagement letter and paid the retainer Carpenter had insisted on. Carpenter usually led a planning session, so Simon was a little surprised to find himself directing the discussion.

"I'm going to call Mr. Morgan's daughter, Fran," Simon said. "I'm going to ask her to reach out to former soccer players who liked Lind as a coach and have them contact me."

Carpenter nodded perfunctorily.

"Then I want Lind to give me a list of current players who might be willing to go to bat for her," Simon continued. "Maybe some of them have boyfriends who can tell us about the practices of the male coaches. I'll also ask Fran Morgan about that. Maybe she's kept up with some boys who played for coaches who swore at players and punished players who screwed up."

When Carpenter responded with another abstracted nod, Simon asked, "Are you all right?"

"Of course I'm all right. Why the hell wouldn't I be all right?"

"You seem to be off somewhere else," Simon said, deciding to confront Carpenter rather than pussyfoot around with him. Carpenter looked abashed and Simon wondered whether he had improperly crossed a line.

"I've got things on my mind," Carpenter said defensively. "Keep going."

Simon thought of Carpenter's cancer, something that would always be on his mind. It was a miracle Carpenter could think of anything else.

"I also thought of calling Mr. Morgan to see whether he'd be willing to back Lind and whether he knew of other parents who would."

"Okay," Carpenter said. "That should keep you busy for a time."

Carpenter was right, Simon reflected. The trial preparation work in Lind's case was never-ending. They had damn well better win the case because the retainer Lind had paid was a drop in the bucket.

"I'm thinking that you present Lind's case and I do the cross-examination of the school's witnesses," Carpenter proposed.

Simon would have preferred their roles to be reversed. There was something about cross-examining a witness that got his competitive juices flowing. "Okay," he said.

"That's just a suggestion," Carpenter said. "As we get into the case, we can play it by ear."

"Okay," Simon repeated. Maybe Carpenter had been engaged after all and had picked up on his lukewarm response to the roles he had assigned. "I'll get on this."

Dr. Specter reached under Carpenter's armpits to check his lymph nodes and Carpenter couldn't suppress a giggle—her touch tickled.

"That's it," Specter said. "Laugh it up."

So Carpenter laughed in earnest. He had forgotten the way Specter surprised with comments that seemed out of place for an oncologist.

"Lie down," Specter directed and Carpenter did so, the roll of waxy paper covering the examining table crinkling sharply as he lay back.

"This isn't going to hurt even for a minute," Specter said as she palpated his groin area. "Okay you can sit up. The way we're supposed to do things is I leave while you dress and then I come back after a suitable time has elapsed and talk with you. But I'm pressed for time since I had to juggle things to fit you in. If it's okay with you, I'll talk to you while you dress.

"It's okay," Carpenter said as he moved to the hooks where he had draped his clothes. It continued to take him aback how young Specter looked. With her blond curly hair, green eyes and round, open face, Specter looked like she hadn't graduated from college let alone medical school.

"I didn't feel anything out of the ordinary when I palpated your lymph nodes," Specter said as she took a seat in front of the computer station in the examining room. "Did you feel any discomfort during the examination?"

Carpenter shook his head.

Specter began typing at the computer workstation. "The results of the blood test you took this morning are back. Your white count is elevated from your last three-month test but it's not a dramatic increase. You've lost eight pounds. We both know you could stand to lose more, but an eight-pound drop when up to now your weight has held steady is something we need to pay attention to."

"What am I in for?" Carpenter asked the question he had been dreading to ask.

"I'm certainly not going to do anything different," Specter said grinning. "What were you expecting?"

"Something bad," Carpenter answered.

Specter's grin faded and she regarded him evenly. Carpenter knew that he should be feeling relieved. Nevertheless, he braced himself for something unpleasant.

"Are you under any stress?" Specter asked.

"My job is stressful, but it's always been stressful."

"Is the stressfulness different from the stressfulness in the past?"

"Somewhat different," he acknowledged.

"Explain."

Carpenter ordered his thoughts. "Until recently, I was working on cases with just one other lawyer, but she had a kid and now we've got two very young lawyers that we're collaborating with, and we all need work. The fact is that business is slow, and it's been bugging me."

"You're the senior lawyer, right?"

"Yeah," Carpenter said.

"Does that mean you think it's your responsibility to keep everyone busy?"

Carpenter saw no reason to sugarcoat the truth. "Yeah, I guess I do."

"I suggest that you change that mind set. This different kind of stress you've mentioned might be affecting your appetite and causing the night sweats you've been experiencing. I've got my own theories on whether there's a relationship between stress and white blood cell counts in people with CLL. All I'm going to say is lose the stress. These other lawyers—all of them—need to understand it's not solely your problem if business is down."

"Easier said than done," Carpenter replied.

"Don't give me that!" Specter said, her grin returning. "You can say that about anything." She looked at her watch. "We've got to stop meeting like this. Call me in a week."

Carpenter continued to dress but Specter made no move to leave the examining room; she continued to regard him from the computer workstation. "One more thing," Specter said. "I want you to exercise more."

"I do a fair amount of walking."

"I'm talking about something more rigorous. Join a gym. Have a trainer set up some exercises with weights. You also need to figure out what to do for cardio. Talk to a trainer about that. There are elliptical machines and spinning and StairMasters."

Philly had opted for spinning; Carpenter still had no idea what that was about. And what the hell was an elliptical machine? It sounded like some kind of geometrical pain inflictor. "What's the purpose of all this?"

"It's one of my other theories," Specter said. "Humor me."

"There's some medical evidence this stuff helps, right?" Carpenter asked.

"What is it with you patients?" Specter replied with mock indignation. "Now you want documentation your physician knows what she's talking about. Next, you'll probably want a cure. Where's it going to end?"

Jesus, Carpenter thought as he mustered up a smile to acknowledge Specter's light tone. Here he was having one-sided, useless discussions with his cancer and now his physician had admitted she was flying blind when it came to advice. Specter wondered where it was going to end. He decided to ignore that question.

Gerald Hatch sat on the couch in the living room and was reading to Daisy in Spanish from a picture book he had bought her, the baby rising and falling in his lap as the burly teen's right leg jiggled continuously. As far as Philly could tell, the motion had no effect on Daisy's concentration. Philly loved the rapt look on Daisy's face, her daughter's total concentration in the moment's entertainment.

Gerald had been one of Philly's clients last year when she had extricated him from a suit brought by a high school classmate accusing him of bullying and assault and battery. In the course of his visits to the Brighton house, Raul and Isabella had helped Gerald with his Spanish and the boy had developed an attachment to Daisy. The strapping teenager with an intimidating physical presence never failed to lose his volatile edge in Daisy's presence.

Isabella took the seat next to Gerald and nodded approvingly at his pronunciation. Isabella had definitely started to show. Her baby was due in May. Philly remembered being much bigger around than Isabella at the same month in her own pregnancy. At some point, Isabella was going to stop working but she had yet to say when that would be. With another grown up around during the daytime, working from home would become a less attractive option. Also, Isabella's presence would put a constraint on play with Daisy. She'd have to think twice before turning up her music and twirling Daisy about the living room floor.

"Bath time after you finish the book," Philly announced, but only Isabella gave any indication that she had heard.

Philly began to run bath water in the kitchen sink and Isabella joined her.

"I think your daughter has a boyfriend at a very young age," Isabella said.

"I love the way they get on," Philly responded. "How are you doing? You look a little tired."

"I'm exhausted. Raul has been working late. Did I tell you that his boss, Connie, is returning to the states to stay?"

Philly wondered what Carpenter's reaction would be to the return of the woman he was seeing before Maxine. He and Connie had been a couple before she moved to Rwanda. Now he was with Maxine. "Does Carpenter know?"

"I don't think so. Raul just mentioned it to me the other day in passing."

Gerald arrived at the sink with Daisy just as Philly turned off the water. "I'll take over," he said.

Gerald expertly laid Daisy down on the kitchen counter and in short order had her out of her fuzzy winter one-piece and diaper. He eased her into the sink and Daisy began kicking as soon as her feet touched the water. The sink was becoming a tight fit. Gerald reached for one of the cups in Daisy's set of bath toys and began to pour water over Daisy and a yellow rubber duck.

"What's going on with you and college?" Isabella asked Gerald.

"I've applied to a few schools. I'm going to visit them with my parents."

Philly remembered last year when it was impossible for Gerald to say a civil word to his parents.

"One, two, three," Gerald counted down and Daisy, who knew the drill, closed her eyes as Gerald poured water over her head. Streams cascaded over her face, but Gerald was ready with a washcloth to blot the wetness away.

"You're the only one she lets do that," Philly said. Gerald smiled sheepishly, plainly pleased that he had been singled out by Daisy for a special ritual.

Raul entered the kitchen and Philly noticed that he looked as tired as Isabella. Back when Philly had dated Raul, she had always been conscious of his being several years younger than she was, but he didn't seem that way now. Watching Raul embrace Isabella, holding her for a long moment, Philly knew that Paul was right; it would be nice to come home to each other.

"One, two, three."

Raul kissed Isabella on the lips and then turned to observe the kitchen sink bath. Raul was still tall and wiry with dark good looks, but Philly sensed that putting in long hours at the financial consulting firm that Connie had started had sapped some of his effervescence. Well, the law and motherhood had probably taken some of the fizz out of her, too.

"I am looking forward to the time that you will bathe our baby," Raul told Gerald. "Soon we will need to take turns at the sink."

"I can't wait," Gerald said with feeling.

Philly debated whether to bring up the subject she'd been investigating. For some things, there was no good time. "I looked at a house the other day," she said. "It's two streets over and a lot bigger than our place."

Raul's expression darkened. "We are not even here a year," he pointed out.

"I'm thinking ahead," Philly said. "Isn't that something you always told me was necessary? I think we're going to need a bigger place. Paul is now in the picture and he has a daughter."

Isabella sighed. "I don't think this is something I can deal with at the moment."

Raul nodded in agreement.

"Right now, there's nothing to deal with. But I'm looking around. Once your baby is born and settles in, I'd like you to keep an open mind on the subject."

"I know it's hard for you not to be with Paul," Isabella said. "But this is really not a good time for a major change."

Philly kept silent thinking that there was never a good time for a major change.

"One, two, three."

6

Philly was disconcerted by Carpenter's presence in her living room. His usual grumpiness was in evidence although, to be fair, it had disappeared while he had held Daisy, played peek-a-boo with her, and even tickled her under her chin. But Daisy was now napping and Carpenter's crustiness had returned.

"What brings you here?" Philly asked, assuming that something was afoot given Carpenter's dislike of driving.

"I've got some personal stuff I need to talk to you about," Carpenter said. "I didn't want to do it on the phone and that Skype business drives me fucking nuts."

Philly thought of Carpenter's cancer and wondered whether the symptoms had flared. He looked thinner.

"I went to see my oncologist the other day. I'd been having some night sweats and Maxine said I looked thinner and wasn't eating the way I used to."

She'd been right. He was one of those guys who stood to lose a few pounds but, eyeballing him, Philly was surprised that he didn't look better with some weight off. Maybe she'd gotten used to him the way he was before the weight loss. "What did your doctor say?"

Carpenter gave an impatient shrug. "She's not going to change anything medically for the moment." After a brief pause, he plowed on. "She asked me whether I was under any stress that was different from the usual stress of practicing law, and I realized that I was. I'm concerned about the lack of business and about the fact we have Simon and Rachel to deal with. My doctor made me realize that I feel responsible for keeping everyone busy. She said that the added stress of feeling responsible for work coming in wasn't good for me."

Philly knew that talking about this subject was difficult for Carpenter. "We're not exactly the kind of lawyers who get out in the community to hustle up new clients."

Carpenter nodded. "Right. I don't see either of us doing that."

"I know it will be hard for you, but you shouldn't feel everything is on you when it comes to the business."

"Yeah, well, I do feel that way. I can't help it."

"What else did your doctor say?"

"You're going to love this," Carpenter said with what passed for a smile on his part. "She said I need to do some serious exercise. She mentioned that spinning thing you do whatever the hell that is."

Philly laughed. The thought of Carpenter on a bike was beyond ludicrous.

"Do you know anything about elliptical machines?"

"Just google the damn things," Philly said.

"She wants me to join a gym, lift weights, that kind of thing."

"Then listen to her," Philly said, feeling like she was reasoning with a little kid. Carpenter sulked; he hated to do something that was helpful to him when the suggestion required him to change his routines.

"I guess I'm going to do what my doctor says about exercise," Carpenter said grudgingly. "It's the stress thing I don't know how to deal with."

"How can I help?" Philly offered.

"I wish the hell I knew. Somehow we've got to come up with more billable work."

Philly suspected that this would be a year when they would be depending on contingency cases. That would add to Carpenter's stress. And to her own. "What does Maxine have to say about all of this?"

"She said the same thing you did: I should listen to my doctor. But she has no solution to the problem of getting more business."

Philly wondered whether what she would say next would add to the geezer's stress. "I've got some news for you. Raul said that Connie's returning to the states for good."

Carpenter typically featured an unreadable expression, but his surprise was evident. Philly wondered whether he had given Connie any recent thoughts.

"When is that going to happen?"

"Raul didn't say."

"Christ! There's no let up. Life keeps throwing curveballs at you."

"What's the big deal?" Philly said. "You're with Maxine."

Carpenter became lost in thought. "You're right. It's just something else unexpected to think about. But what the hell? I could use the extra stress."

"So, feeling better now that you've got stuff off your chest?"

"Yeah, I feel fucking great. Can't you tell?"

The evening AA meeting in the basement of Saint Sebastian Church in Allston had already started when Philly arrived. She took a seat in the front row next to her sponsor, Melanie, who offered a shy smile. She was a painfully thin woman with blue eyes so washed out there were times, when the light was just so, that her eyes seemed to have no color at all.

Philly studied the group leader. Charlie would make some statements so profound that on occasion they brought you up short, and others that were so clichéd they made you wince. Philly often wondered whether he would be a more effective group leader if he didn't wear his shoulder length hair in a ponytail and didn't favor Hawaiian shirts. There was a hippy look to Charlie that made it tempting not to take anything he said seriously.

"We're all under stress," Charlie was saying, "every single one of us. What we have to learn is how to confront our stress without slipping back into self-destructive behavior. What resources can we summon when we're feeling stress?" Charlie's tone suggested he wasn't looking for an answer to his question. "I'll share something that I fall back on. When I'm feeling stressed, I think to a time when drink had overwhelmed me and I couldn't function. There were times when I couldn't get out of bed. There were times when I didn't have a bed to get out of. And I think to myself that no matter what is stressing me out, it is not anywhere as bad as what I was going through during my worst moments when I was a flat out drunk."

Charlie paused and regarded the assembled group. There were about thirty people sitting in. Charlie panned the room but seemed focused on his own thoughts, not on any of those in attendance.

"I know what some of you are thinking," he went on. "Some of you are probably thinking that all I'm saying is that there's somebody, somewhere, worse off than you. But that's not what I'm getting at. The person who is worse off than you that I want you to think about *is* the you before this. I'll tell you this: I never want to go back to the person I was when I lost control of my life."

It was odd that Charlie had brought up the subject of stress on the same day that Carpenter had raised the topic. Philly doubted there was a lesson for Carpenter in anything Charlie was saying. Carpenter's situation was the reverse of the situation Charlie was describing. The geezer's cancer and suddenly erratic law practice had made him feel he had lost control over his current life. Carpenter wanted to return to a former time when he was in charge of his life, disease free, and busy.

Philly raised her hand and Charlie acknowledged her.

"I've got this friend who has cancer. He's not experiencing any symptoms, but it weighs on him and stresses him out. He's also worried because his business is down. He's not into drugs or alcohol and I don't think he's the type of guy who would look to those things. But what can you say to a guy like that who is starting to feel overwhelmed?"

When no one responded, Charlie cleared his throat. "I'd tell a guy like that to think of a time when he was in control and not feeling stressed. I'd tell him to tune out everything else but his good feelings from that other time. Then I'd tell him to channel those good feelings when he started to feel under siege."

"You're saying he should meditate," declared a woman wearing a zipped up green ski parka. Philly wondered how the woman could breathe in the parka—it had to be eighty degrees in the basement.

Charlie nodded reflectively. "I guess I am."

Philly couldn't picture Carpenter meditating although, for a time, he had practiced breathing relaxation exercises. Besides, meditation wasn't going to bring in a new client.

"Each of us is a lot stronger than he thinks," Charlie said. "As I'm thinking about stress, I'm thinking that some former version of ourselves can help us when we're feeling stressed out. For me, thinking about what a mess I was before I got help, gets me motivated not to relapse to the person I was. But if there was a time in your life when things were going well and you were in control, maybe you can use that time as something to aspire to when you're feeling down."

Philly realized that this was one of the few times when Charlie wasn't reaching her. She didn't want to dwell on a past version of herself. She needed to chart a course for the future that would preserve and expand what she had at the moment. It came down to money if she was going to get everything she wanted. No wonder Carpenter felt stressed.

7

Philly's morning had gone well. Sarah Ferguson, her steady babysitter, was downstairs still entertaining Daisy, and Daisy had voiced no complaints in the last two hours. Philly had used part of the time to finalize the workers' compensation claim that Rachel had prepared for one of the hockey players. Rachel had interviewed witnesses, done a good job of setting forth the player's case, and had enlisted Dr. Nancy Corrigan as an expert witness. Rachel could write and was organized. The rest of the morning had been spent on the phone with Rachel strategizing over Michael Waters' case and Heather Storm's upcoming probate court hearing.

Waters' scheduled meeting with his school principal was under control. He would deny Caroline Fine's allegation of sexual harassment. Fine's story spoke for itself and Waters could hardly be faulted for concluding that the story was autobiographical. The initials of the story's characters matched those of Fine and Waters. The one detail that had yet to be tied down was finding a real-life counterpart for the fictional boyfriend, Richard Parks, who had dumped Fine's fictional alter ego, Carlotta Finch. Philly had been swayed by Rachel and was now in favor of hiring a private detective to research that matter and find out more about Fine's parents. Waters was still mulling over that plan of attack.

Rachel had also filled her in on the contents of the papers that had been kept under court seal in Heather Storm's case. Psychological evaluations of their client concluded that Heather Storm was incapable of considering the possibility that James Farrell had abused their daughter. "She won't even admit to the possibility," the child psychologist who had interviewed Storm had concluded after their final session. The evaluations of James Farrell were inconclusive. A consulting psychologist had opined that there was no objective way to determine whether Farrell's denials of abuse were credible. The psychologist who had interviewed Marilyn Storm was convinced that Marilyn had experienced trauma. The girl was withdrawn, and she exhibited fear at the mention of her father. In the psychologist's opinion, these reactions were not feigned.

Interestingly, Rachel thought a private detective would be equally useful in the Storm case. Rachel wanted a background check done on James Farrell and an investigation of Marilyn's school. But payment for a private detective would require court approval and Philly didn't think a judge would allow the expenditure. Rachel would attempt to interview Marilyn's teachers, but beyond that, they had no further plan.

Philly turned off her computer and headed downstairs to the living room. Sarah Ferguson was reading to Daisy and Daisy was following along with the intent look she displayed when she was engaged. Philly held back until Sarah had finished the book. "I'm going to feed this kid," she announced. "Then how about a walk?"

"It's freezing out," Sarah noted.

"And it will be for the next three months. Daisy and I are going out."

Sarah surprised Philly by bundling up and joining her and Daisy for some fresh air. The temperature was in the twenties, but the sun was out and making a valiant effort to dispel the gloomy, worn look of their Brighton neighborhood. Daisy was wedged into a one-piece yellow snow suit and for this outing Philly decided to carry her daughter. She wanted physical contact and decided to delude herself that contact would keep Daisy warmer than if she were pushed in a stroller wrapped up in a wool blanket.

As they passed Sarah's house, the older woman gave her front door a lingering glance before soldiering on beside Philly. Philly had a destination in mind and, walking briskly, it was a matter of minutes before they reached the sprawling three-story house that was marked "For Sale." She had toured the house a little more than a week ago. "What do you know about this place?" she asked Sarah.

Sarah unwound a red and green wool scarf to free her mouth. "It's been rented to students for a long time. There used to be a large Irish family living here but they moved out to the western suburbs."

Philly remembered her tour. In her current house, there was a separate entrance to the third-floor rooms that they rented out, but in this house the three floors were all connected. She pictured the layout. The first floor contained the kitchen, living and dining rooms, and two bedrooms, one for grownups and a smaller one for a kid. The second floor had a master bedroom for the other couple, a smaller kid's bedroom, and space for home offices for each couple. The top floor also could be used for home offices as well as for an extra bedroom. There was a basement for storage. The house would cost more than her current house. But Paul's contribution might bridge that gap as well as offset the rent that she and Raul and Isabella were now getting from their two third floor tenants. "I think we need a bigger place," Philly said.

"You'll just have to dump the policeman," Sarah replied and for a moment Philly didn't pick up on the fact that Sarah was joking. This may have been the first occasion when Sarah had kidded her.

"What are they asking?" Sarah inquired.

"Six hundred ten thousand."

"What did you pay for your current place? Low fives?"

Philly nodded, remembering her anxiety when she and Raul and Isabella had inked the mortgage.

"How many bedrooms?"

Philly replayed her house tour. "I'd say six. But some of the rooms could serve as offices or family rooms."

"How many rooms altogether?"

Philly remembered the real estate posting. "Ten with three full baths."

"I'll take a look at it for you if you want," Sarah said.

"I've already had my tour. I like the place. I'd trade up in a heartbeat."

Sarah studied the sprawling house while Daisy fidgeted. "See the big house?" Philly said pointing. To Philly's surprise, Daisy lifted a black mitten in the direction of the building. "Right," Philly said. "House."

"I may take a tour just the same," Sarah said. "Let's head on back if it's just the same to you. I'm freezing."

"House," Philly pointed again and once more Daisy raised a mitten in the direction she was pointing, strands of her daughter's soft black hair peeking out of the hood of her snowsuit, slipping down over her forehead. "I like it too," Philly whispered to Daisy.

8

Carpenter decided to go against his grain and be late for work. Since he had work to do, his opting to take Dr. Specter's advice seriously required a major shift in his priorities.

He was in a Gold's Gym in east Arlington feeling ridiculous in a gray sweat suit and trying not to gape at the finely muscled personal trainer whose job, as she had explained, was to come up with an exercise routine appropriate for his goals, needs, and lifestyle. Carpenter hadn't had the heart to tell Camellia Kim that he only had one goal—staying alive, one need—more legal business, and no discernible lifestyle.

He was seated with Kim in a small office that she shared with other personal trainers. She was reviewing the questionnaire and medical information form he had filled out. The medical form had brought him up short. For the first time in his life he couldn't check off *NO* as to each item on the long list of diseases and ailments he was asked if he had ever had. This time he'd had to check off *YES* next to cancer and had elaborated on the next line of the form by writing down

CLL. It was a sobering moment. He wondered whether he'd be better off if he had to check off heart disease, kidney disease, or lung disease instead of cancer.

Kim studied the forms he had filled out without expression. Carpenter guessed she was Korean, in her early twenties. She was tall with broad shoulders. Her short hair had a spiky look. Kim set down the forms on the desk she was seated at and regarded him with unblinking dark eyes. He wondered whether the word cancer had registered with the woman. Could she identify with a guy in his mid-sixties with a fucking fatal disease?

"You want to get in better shape," Kim said. "It's never too late to start. But perhaps you will share with me why you have suddenly decided to get in shape."

"My doctor recently suggested it," Carpenter said.

"I see," Kim said. "I'm familiar with CLL. You must excuse my forwardness. But are you experiencing symptoms?"

Kim had read what he'd written. "I've dropped a few pounds and I get night sweats, but these symptoms aren't preventing me from doing anything that I want to do."

"That's good. It sounds like you're in a holding pattern. Here's what I have in mind for you. I'd like to come up with an hour training session that you can do on your own. I propose to divide the hour pretty much in half with weight training and flexibility exercises for the first thirty minutes and aerobics for the last thirty minutes. What we're going to do this morning is try out different machines. I'll be writing down the settings and weights I think are best for you for each machine. The idea is for you to work out on your own for two weeks and then I'll observe you at your next appointment. Any questions?"

Carpenter shook his head. He couldn't ask the question that was preying on him: what was he doing here?

"You may surprise yourself," Kim said.

"What do you mean?"

"You may actually like this."

Fat chance, Carpenter thought. "I'll keep an open mind," is what he said.

Carpenter listed a little sideways as he entered the office suite conference room. Simon thought he was favoring his left leg. As Carpenter gingerly took a seat, he let out a soft, mournful sigh that seemed to have been drawn forth from a reservoir of despair.

"What the hell happened to you?" Simon queried.

"Don't ask and I won't tell," Carpenter snarled.

“Don’t take it out on me,” Simon said.

Carpenter’s irritable look softened. “Sorry,” he said in a more neutral tone.

“I’m making progress on Alison Lind’s case,” Simon reported. “Fran Morgan will go to bat for Lind and, although she’s not optimistic, she’ll try to round up one other former player who will also support Lind. Best of all, she’s put me in contact with one of the juniors on the team. I’ve got a meeting tomorrow with Brittany Stern and her boyfriend.”

“Her boyfriend?”

Simon nodded. “This could work out. Brittany Stern’s boyfriend plays on the boys’ soccer team and on the boys’ basketball team. I’m hoping he’ll say the coaches of the boys’ teams are foul-mouthed disciplinarians.”

“We can always hope,” Carpenter said.

“I can tell you this much. Over the last three years, Lind’s girls’ soccer team had a better record than the boys’ soccer team and the boys’ basketball, football, and baseball teams.”

“Then maybe we should be hoping that the boys’ team coaches are mild-mannered softies,” Carpenter said.

At first Simon thought Carpenter was joking. From the beginning, he had envisioned Lind’s case depending on coaches of boys’ teams exhibiting the same hard-nosed discipline and foul mouth that Lind displayed. But if the object of coaching was to produce a winning team, Simon realized that it might be important if the coaches of the losing boys’ teams had coaching methods that differed from Lind’s. “Let me get back to you after I hear what the Stern girl and her boyfriend say.”

Carpenter figured that the last time he’d had a bath was when he was a kid. He’d felt ridiculous easing himself over the edge of the tub and settling into the hot water. Maxine’s laughter hadn’t helped. The hot bath was her suggestion and she seemed to enjoy his discomfort as he worked his way into the tub. Still, now that he had been soaking for several minutes, he had to admit that his aches and pains were at a remove.

“You look ridiculous,” Maxine said. She was sitting on the bathroom floor next to the tub, letting her fingers trail through the soapy water. Somehow Carpenter had let her talk him into driving to her place. His condo had no tub.

“Thanks a lot.”

“Are you going to exercise again?”

Carpenter had left the gym vowing never again, Dr. Specter's instincts be damned. But the physical exertion had calmed him in a way he couldn't explain. He'd been in pain during his meeting with Simon but had also been able to concentrate during their talk.

"Am I going to exercise again?" Carpenter repeated. "I'll settle for walking naturally again."

"You need to give this a chance," Maxine said in a no-nonsense tone. "I don't know what I'd do if I didn't exercise. I think you're going to find you have more energy."

Carpenter thought back to the routine that Camellia Kim had mapped out for him. Her workout plan was accessible to him at the gym and Kim had made him a copy of the plan to study at home. She had him doing reps for his arms, shoulders, and legs and stretching exercises that involved a large blown up ball that he was supposed to lie on in different positions. He now knew what an elliptical machine was.

"When you get out of the tub, will you have energy for some action?"

Maxine had scooted around and was massaging his shoulders. He could stay in the tub forever so long as the water didn't cool. "You're assuming I can make it out of the tub."

"I'll just add cold water to help you along."

"You're forgetting shrinkage."

"You're impossible!"

Carpenter began to entertain the notion that what he wouldn't have thought possible before entering the tub, now might well be possible once he emerged.

February

Philly's Untitled Playlist

Dog Days Are Over

Florence and the Machine

9

A Hockey Player

In the Gardners' small house on the edge of Worcester, Edna Gardner sat on the front edge of a living room easy chair keeping a constant eye on her husband. She was short and trim with more black than gray in her hair, but there was a ground down air about her that Philly had noticed straightaway. Frank Gardner had settled into a matching easy chair with a blank expression. Known as "Grinder" during his hockey playing days with the Worcester Wizards, Frank Gardner's body was at odds with his vacant look; his body was in motion while his mind seemed inert. The man's right leg pumped up and down and his fingers drummed silently against the upholstered arm rests of his chair. These rapid movements had his wife on edge; maybe from experience she knew they were a prelude to some unexpected action that needed to be headed off.

"A hundred fifty thousand dollars," Edna said in a soft voice as if the sum was incomprehensible.

Philly knew that Edna would press her for a recommendation on whether to accept the settlement offer put forward by the Worcester Wizards' workers' compensation insurer. To date, Edna had managed to deal with Frank's dementia while he remained at home. Dr. Nancy Corrigan had arranged her schedule to evaluate Frank and had estimated that in about three months, Edna would need some kind of home care for her husband. The couple's house was run-down. The living room in which they were sitting needed a new paint job. The easy chairs were worn. Philly sank into the cushions of the couch she was sitting on.

"Out," Frank said suddenly, and Edna started.

"In a minute, dear."

"Out," Frank repeated.

"We usually go for a walk around this time," Edna explained. "We've fallen into a routine and Frank doesn't do well when the routine is interrupted."

"If you want, we can talk while we're walking," Philly suggested. She didn't relish the cold, but somehow the thought of staying cooped up in the living room while Frank Gardner wished to be in motion was less appealing than freezing her butt off.

"Are you sure?"

"I'm sure."

Frank led the way. He was wearing a Boston Bruins wool stocking cap pulled over his ears, a pea green army jacket that looked to Philly like a tight fit, and a Boston Bruins wool scarf wrapped twice around his neck. He leaned forward as he walked, his gloved hands sunk deep into the side pockets of his army jacket. Philly didn't think he was a defenseman like her previous hockey client, Gerard Gorman. Frank had Gorman's massive shoulders, but his legs were skinny and he wasn't as tall as Gorman.

"This is the part of the day he likes best," Edna said, keeping step beside Philly. "Sometimes when we get started on a walk, I think he'd go forever if I let him. We usually go for an hour rain or shine, but I'll try to get us back to the house in fifteen minutes so you can be on your way. We can go out again after you leave."

The sky was an angry-looking slate gray with black splotches along the underside of the cloud covering. Philly thought that she'd be frozen stiff if she stayed out in this weather for an hour. The temperature had to be in the teens.

"I've actually come to look forward to the exercise," Edna said. "It's definitely keeping my weight down."

"I've read Dr. Corrigan's evaluation," Philly steered the conversation to Frank's workers' compensation claim. "She thinks it won't be long before you're going to need help with your husband."

"I can't stand the thought of putting him in some kind of home," Edna said softly. "I know the day is coming but I can't bear to think about it. You should have seen him when he was young. Frank was fearless, a daredevil. He was always joking around. Now life's joke is on him. In a way, it's a blessing that he can't appreciate the joke."

Philly contrasted her situation with Edna's. Each of them had a baby to deal with. But Daisy was moving forward, developing skills. Frank was regressing. They would pass each other at a point where Daisy's track faced a bright horizon and Frank's approached a miserable dead end.

"If I took the offer that would get me a hundred thousand dollars," Edna said.

It was not a question, but Philly answered yes. Edna had correctly done the math by factoring in the one-third contingency fee.

"I'm trying to think what a hundred thousand dollars would buy me," Edna continued. "I could probably keep Frank at home for a longer time by bringing in home care services. I've looked into that. People say that home care services are a lot cheaper than being in some kind of home. But I have to tell you, home care services aren't cheap."

Philly remembered what Gerard Gorman's wife had said about her husband's workers' compensation recovery of $250,000. She had viewed the money as buying about five years of institutional care in an assisted living facility. If the money ran out, Gorman's wife would worry about that problem then.

"Do you think I should accept the offer?" Edna asked.

Nelson Frost, the attorney for the workers' compensation insurer, had claimed that the $150,000 offer was a take it or leave it offer. Philly didn't know Frost well enough to assess whether the man was bluffing.

"I think you should let me try to get the other side to increase the offer," Philly said. "Let me take a shot at getting the insurance company to put more money on the table and report back to you how I make out."

"Well, okay," Edna said hesitantly.

"You don't sound sure about this," Philly said.

"I don't want to lose the offer," Edna replied. "I know you have more experience than me at this sort of thing, but I can't afford to pass up that money. I could use it now. And I really don't want to go through a trial."

"I don't think the offer will be withdrawn if I try to negotiate, but I can't guarantee that. Still, I think you should let me take a run at the other lawyer."

"Okay," Edna said, nodding. "No matter what offer I accept, I can't stop myself from thinking about what I'm going to do when the money runs out. This is my one chance to make it easier for Frank and me, but I don't know what I'm going to do once I spend what they pay us."

Their words were carrying, and Frank had to be hearing what they were saying. Yet Frank gave no heed to their back and forth. He marched straight-ahead at his steady pace, his head slightly lowered, the tendrils of his Bruins scarf draped over his back. Dr. Corrigan's report had made clear that Frank's short-term memory was shot.

"Here's a horrible thought," Edna said. "Sometimes I find myself thinking it would be better for both of us if Frank were to go to sleep and not wake up. I can't believe I've been having these thoughts. We had a good marriage."

Philly noticed the past tense. Her thoughts turned to Philip, her former fiancé, and his family's painful decision to withdraw life support rather than let him persist in a brain damaged state with nothing of the man remaining except his body.

"You tell that lawyer we could use some help here," Edna said with feeling.

Carpenter had finished his tour of the weight stations Camellia Kim had assigned him. Without Kim being present to position and encourage him, he had found the exercises more difficult. In two instances, he had to cut back on the weights Kim had prescribed.

Now he was walking past the spinning room and decided to look inside. About half the bikes in the room were occupied and it looked like a class was about to start.

"Don't just stare," an instructor facing the rest of the bikes challenged him. "You're never going to know if you like spinning unless you try it."

Carpenter had resolved to put in a half hour on an elliptical machine. Didn't Philly once tell him that spinning classes were an hour? There was no way in hell he'd last an hour doing anything.

"Come on, get your ass in here," the instructor got back on his case. "If you think about it too long you won't do it."

"It's an hour right?" Carpenter asked.

The instructor nodded. She was a tall, thick set young woman whose dark hair was tied back in a short ponytail.

"Come on. Class is about to start. I just have time to get you set up. We're always looking for new converts."

Carpenter eyed the other bikers, all women except for a young guy built like a linebacker.

"You can take it easy your first time. I like to joke that spinning is the ideal sport for two-year olds. Anytime an instructor asks you to do something you can make a face and say no."

Carpenter found himself wavering. "I may have to cut out before the hour is up."

"Not a problem." The instructor was off her bike and directing him inside.

It took the instructor five minutes to get him comfortable. He sensed the rest of the class was losing patience with the delay.

"I have an extra water," the instructor said. "You're going to need it. Stay hydrated."

Carpenter's bike was in the middle of the room under a rapidly moving ceiling fan. The woman pedaling next to him was about his age. She looked like she could pedal forever.

"We're going to take five minutes to warm up. Get on a flat road. That means you want some resistance but nothing heavy."

Carpenter turned the resistance knob on his bike to the right which slowed his pace. Loud music filled the room, an instrumental with a driving beat that he couldn't keep pace with. Philly, he thought, would be laughing her ass off if she got a look at him.

"Let's do some stretching. Hands up!"

Carpenter reached toward the ceiling and kept his legs moving. Actually, the stretching felt good after his weight exercises.

"For our first working song, I want you to add a little more resistance and pedal hard for three minutes. This is not an all-out sprint. For our first-time spinner, I want you to concentrate on keeping up a pace that is slightly faster than your pace on a flat, open road. We'll begin on my count. One. Two. Three. Begin."

Carpenter picked up his cadence. He recognized *Give Me Shelter* blasting from the speakers situated in the rear of the room. There would be at least one song he knew.

There was something about moving his legs and the enveloping sound that left him clearheaded.

"Okay, good job everyone. Get some water. We're going to take it out of the saddle next. Make sure you have enough resistance. You don't want to blow out your knees. We're going to simulate a hill and increase the resistance two more times. Your hands are in position two just resting on the handlebars for balance."

Carpenter was suddenly drenched in sweat, as if his entire body was leaking uncontrollably. Other bikers had brought hand towels to the spinning class. Carpenter took off his sweatshirt to use as his towel.

"Good job everyone." A fast-paced song with a driving beat blared from the speakers. "We're going to do some thirty second sprints. That means when I give the word, I want you to give it everything you have, no holding back. But for our first-time spinner, I want you to just pedal faster than you were going."

Carpenter was not embarrassed by being singled out for easier treatment. His only goal was to get off his bike alive.

"Three. Two. One. Hit it!"

Carpenter picked up his pace. Sweat was now pouring into his eyes. It occurred to him that if he was sweating his brains out so was Fred. He was gratified that any discomfort he was experiencing was being shared by Fred.

"Hey! First time spinner! Slow down! You won't have anything left at the pace you're going."

Carpenter was taken aback to find that he was pedaling like a fiend, his heart pounding, his thighs straining in agony. He slowed his pace, giving the instructor what he hoped was an apologetic smile.

"Okay, one more sprint. After this we'll have a brief two-minute recovery and then we'll hit the hills. On my count. One. Two. Three. Thirty seconds all out!"

Carpenter reached for a slug of water and then picked up his pace. He checked the wall clock—the class had been going for half an hour. I might actually do this, he thought. Jesus H. Christ!

Paul was spending the night and every time he did Philly felt a pang of guilt that she was letting him down by not finalizing an arrangement that would keep them permanently together. At the moment, she didn't have the energy to get out of bed, get into pajamas and clean up. The sheets were a sticky mess and so were the two of them. She pulled the comforter up so it reached her chin. Somehow, she had ended up with two men who were too good to be true. She sometimes wondered what would have become of her if Paul hadn't reached out to her after Philip's death.

"What are you thinking about?" Paul whispered.

"About my good luck."

"Are we going to clean up?"

"I can't face it right now. I just want to lie here."

"I'm going to doze off."

Out of the blue Philly remembered what she needed to ask Paul. "I need a private detective," she said. "Any ideas?"

"What do you want a detective for?"

"I need someone to check out a Boston high school student. The student accused a teacher I'm representing of sexual misconduct."

Paul didn't say anything for a long time and Philly wondered whether he had dropped off.

"I've got just the guys," Paul said. "Two retired Cambridge detectives got themselves PI licenses and are in business. They're old guys but when they were on the force, they were legends. I'll e-mail you their names and phone number. They're two big guys. They'd stand out at a high school."

"I'll take what I can get," Philly said.

10

Philly remembered Nelson Frost as nondescript except for impressive black-framed glasses. Frost had been toiling in the vineyards of workers' compensation law for more than twenty years and he seemed to have total recall of every statutory provision.

"No doubt you're calling to accept my client's offer in the Frank Gardner case," Frost said when Philly's call was passed through to his office.

"I'm curious," Philly said, deliberately ignoring Frost's opening gambit. "Your offer was one hundred thousand dollars below what the Gorman case settled for. What gives?"

"Maybe the insurer settled at too high a figure in the Gorman case," Frost replied without hesitation. "There's also the factor that Gorman was in an assisted living facility while Mr. Gardner remains at home."

"Based on Dr. Corrigan's opinion, I can assure you that by the time this case goes to trial, Frank Gardner will be receiving institutional care."

"Ah, yes, Dr. Corrigan. Now there's a woman on a mission."

"Be nice," Philly said, trying for a light tone.

"You're right," Frost said. "That comment wasn't called for. You still haven't told me whether my client's offer will be accepted."

"The insurer needs to do better," Philly said, continuing to avoid rejecting the insurer's offer outright."

"I told you my client's offer is a final offer."

"You did say that," Philly acknowledged. "But I've heard that before and, often, cases settle for an amount above what was presented as a final offer."

"Do you have a demand figure?" Frost asked, and Philly took the question as an indication that Frost had been the first one to blink.

"Here's the way I want to leave it with you," Philly said. "I will recommend to my client acceptance of a two hundred fifty thousand offer. I also will tell you that I believe my client will follow my recommendation."

"I have to pass on what you said back to the insurer," Frost said, "but I can tell you now, based on my last discussion with my client, two hundred fifty thousand won't fly."

"That's extremely disappointing," Philly said. "You should see Mr. Gardner today. It's not a pretty picture, but it is a picture that a hearing officer will see firsthand. Gardner could use a little help and compassion here."

"My client's middle name is compassion," Frost rejoined.

"Very funny. Get back to me."

"Yes, ma'am." Frost rang off.

Philly assessed the concluded call. She didn't remember Frost joking around in the Gorman case—he was all business. For some reason, Frost was more confident about his chances in Gardner's case. Maybe the insurer had resolved that it was time to take a stand and try to litigate a hockey player's case. The insurer might be thinking that more hockey player workers' compensation claims were on the way. There was also the possibility that the insurer had come up with a new and helpful expert witness.

"Shit," Philly muttered. So much for quick, easy money.

Simon was borrowing Rachel's car for the day. Before his meeting with Brittany Stern and her boyfriend, he drove past Middlemarch High School. The school was a long, one-story red brick building set back off the two-lane road that was the main drag in Kingsbury. Students were milling about, and he figured he was observing a period change with the slight improvement in February weather encouraging students to get some air. Middlemarch High reminded him so much of his own high school that he felt himself tensing up. His high school days had been a nightmare. Those who said high school years were the best time in one's life hadn't considered the plight of a gay student faced with an intolerant, party-happy student body. Coming out would have made his life more of a living hell than it already was. Had he really taken a girl to his senior prom? What the hell had Stephanie Moore thought of his halfhearted goodnight kiss and hasty retreat?

A quarter mile past the high school on the way to town he passed a running track. Movable soccer goals had been positioned at opposite ends of the interior oval, an oddity, since soccer was not a winter sport even for practice. Simon continued on past the track to the bustling luncheonette where he was to meet Brittany Stern and her boyfriend.

Just when he began to think he would be stood up, two teens came in, dressed alike in blue parkas, black jeans, and stocking caps featuring the maroon and white colors of their high school. Simon waved them over, and they slid into the booth across from him. "What can I get you?" Simon offered after introductions had been exchanged.

Brittany Stern shook her head but her boyfriend, Rick Monahan, opted for a Coke and French fries. Simon rose, placed the order and returned to face the couple. Monahan looked like he wanted to be elsewhere. He was tall and thick set and his eyes kept flitting about the seating area. Stern had probably dragged her boyfriend to this meeting. With her stocking cap off she looked like a take charge girl; there was a determined set to her jaw and a no-nonsense attitude that was reinforced by the frank expression in her gray eyes. Stern was tall and solidly built and Simon wondered what position she played on the girls' soccer team.

"Thanks for seeing me," Simon began. "As you know, I'm representing Alison Lind and my purpose in meeting with you is to see if you can be of help to her. She's suing to get her job back."

"She got shafted," Brittany Stern said. "She's a little rough around the edges, but she's a great coach."

"Why do you think she got shafted?"

"Seriously?" Stern exclaimed. "The seniors on the team thought they had a right to be starters just because they were seniors. They blew off practices and were never ready for games. There are a bunch of us in my class who take soccer seriously. We put out in practices and Coach rewarded us. Now we're stuck with a math teacher who doesn't know the first thing about soccer."

Simon was relieved to hear a third-party account that backed up Lind's assessment of her predicament. "Are other sophomores or juniors willing to say what you just said?" Simon asked, as a waitress delivered Monahan's order.

"There's one other junior that might be willing to do that. I'll help Coach any way I can."

"Why only one other junior?"

"Because some of the seniors have been getting the word out that anyone helping Coach is going to regret it."

"That doesn't seem to bother you."

Stern shrugged. "It bothers me, but I'm not going to be intimidated."

"I have a dumb question," Simon said. "Why are there soccer goals set up inside the outdoor track?"

Stern smiled. "That was something Coach had always insisted on and a few of us decided to keep up the tradition even though she got fired. She'd have voluntary winter practices. She'd show up on Sunday afternoons and be there for anyone else who showed up. When it snowed, the practices were great fun. We'd be sliding around like crazy and throwing snowballs at each other. But

Coach knew what she was doing. Those crazy practices helped keep us in shape and they built up team spirit."

"I hear Coach liked to swear."

"Who the fuck doesn't," Stern said laughing. Monahan favored Stern with a quick glance that Simon couldn't read. He was attacking his French fries one by one, dipping each into a pool of ketchup before inhaling the fry.

"What do you have to say?" Simon asked Monahan before he could look away.

"What do you want to know?"

"You play soccer and basketball, right?"

Monahan nodded with little enthusiasm.

"Do your coaches for those sports swear?"

"Now and then."

"Now and then!" Stern exploded. "Coach Taylor has the biggest potty mouth I've ever heard. I've watched soccer practices. Every other word is an f-bomb."

Monahan colored. "It's like I said. My coaches swear from time to time."

"What about discipline?" Simon asked. "Do they punish the guys they coach?"

Monahan lowered his eyes. Stern was giving him a hard look.

"If we goof off, we end up doing laps or wind sprints," Monahan said.

"What about that time you told me about when Coach Taylor made you run around the track backward holding a cup of water? You told me he made you start again when you spilled a drop."

"That was one time," Monahan said defensively.

"And what about that time your basketball coach—Coach Clayton—made a guy put on a skirt because he said he was playing like a girl?"

"Coach was just kidding around."

"You told me the guy who had to wear the skirt ended up crying and quitting the team."

"The kid was a loser."

Simon was grateful he had never gone in for sports. All the macho bullshit would have sent him around the bend. During high school, the jocks were the worst of the lot when it came to anyone gay.

"Do you think your coaches—Taylor and Clayton—are good coaches?" Simon directed at Monahan.

"I guess so," Monahan replied in a way that suggested he had never before evaluated his coaches' abilities.

"Any comments on the fact that Coach Lind's teams have done better than the boys' teams?"

When it became clear that Monahan wasn't going to answer, Stern fielded the question.

"Coach Lind is hard on us and it took me a while to realize there was a method to her madness. Right now, I'm probably one of the best players on the team if not the best. But Coach was constantly driving home the message that soccer is a team game and we won or lost together. She didn't tolerate prima donnas and she treated everyone the same. She'd scream at me the same way she screamed at a sub. I think Coach Taylor and some of the other boys' team coaches have favorites and the guys know it. I think that's why the boys' teams don't do as well."

Simon believed Carpenter would have a better feel for team sports than he had. But if what Stern had said came out at a trial, the testimony would prove helpful to Lind.

"Would you be willing to testify as to what you told me about coach Taylor," Simon asked Monahan.

"I'd rather stay out of it," Monahan said, and Simon saw the disappointment in Stern's eyes.

"Why don't you think about it," Simon temporized. "Coach Lind could use some help. Nobody ever got hurt by telling the truth."

"What kind of fucking high school did you go to?" Monahan lashed out angrily.

"Not a place I care to remember," Simon said.

11

Today it was Philly's turn to be at a high school. The principal's office in James Madison High School had a worn look. The white paint on the walls had a soiled grayish tinge. The off-white blinds covering the two windows in the room were marred by black streaks and some slats were bent out of shape. The office was cramped; a small worktable took up most of the free space in front of principal Suzanne Lacey's desk. Although John Frye, the vice-principal, had repositioned the table so six people could sit in reasonable comfort, Philly directed Michael Waters to take a seat between her and Rachel and motioned for the teachers' union rep, Wayne Gordon, to sit behind her. It was a subtle but necessary bit of theater since Waters had described his union rep as a hothead.

"Thanks for coming in, Michael," Lacey began. "I know this can't be pleasant but there's a drill we have to follow."

Waters nodded. He appeared at ease, but Philly noticed tension in the rigid way he was seated. Lacey and Frye looked to be in their fifties. Lacey's expression was friendly. Frye's slightly aggressive look bothered her. Before the meeting, the union rep had described Frye as a prick, and maybe he was right.

"I think the best way to start, Michael," Lacey said, "is for you to give us your version of what happened when you met with Caroline Fine to review her story."

"Before Mr. Waters answers you," Philly broke in, "I'd like to know whether you've already met with Ms. Fine."

"We have," Lacey said, as Philly registered a hostile look from Frye.

"Sorry to interrupt. Go ahead Michael."

Waters glanced at Frye before directing his comments to Lacey. "It's pretty much as I told you. I met with each student to review the story I'd assigned. I'd read the works prior to meeting with them. I had a particular concern about Caroline's story because the protagonist was suicidal and had the same initials as Caroline. After some initial talk, I became direct with her and asked her whether there was anything in her personal life that was troubling her. She took offense. She claimed that her work was fiction and she had a right to write about anything she wanted. I explained to her that a teacher had an obligation to report a situation where he believed a student was a danger to herself. That made her angrier. She said something to the effect that even if what she wrote was true, wasn't I always telling students to write about what they know. At some point, she simply walked out. I decided to report everything to you, and you told me that I'd done the right thing."

Lacey nodded, glanced at Frye, and Philly braced herself for the bad cop to take charge.

"Let me ask you this," the vice-principal spoke for the first time. "If Ms. Fine claimed that you promised not to report the matter if she agreed to have sex with you, would she be lying?"

"Yes," Waters said simply.

"What reason would she have to make up such a fabrication?" Frye pursued.

Philly stifled the impulse to object to the question. Since this wasn't a court of law, she decided to let Waters field the question even though it was impossible to divine what motivated another person.

"You'd have to ask her," Waters said, and Philly was relieved that Waters was on his game.

"Do you have any theories?"

Waters mulled Frye's question over. Philly silently willed her client to answer the question no.

"I'd be guessing," Waters said. "Perhaps her written story was a twisted cry for help, but she may have become embarrassed and angry that I confronted her and made up her allegation."

"A twisted cry for help," Frye repeated as he wrote on his notepad. "Help with what?"

"Suicidal impulses," Waters said. "Again, I'm speculating here."

"Ms. Fine struck me as very much together," Frye said, and Philly noted the singular pronoun. Perhaps Principal Lacey had made a different appraisal of the student.

Waters said nothing, and Philly silently willed him to keep it that way. "Have you met with Ms. Fine's parents?" she asked, hoping to break Frye's rhythm.

"We have," Lacey responded.

"Does Ms. Fine's mother have barbiturates at home?"

"I'm sorry," Frye didn't bother to hide his sarcasm. "That's not something we would share with you even if we knew. This is an information gathering meeting where we get to ask the questions."

"Give it a rest," Wayne Gordon said. He was a young man, tall and thin with piercing dark eyes. Even if Gordon was the hothead Waters had described, it appeared to Philly that at least the union rep was willing to fight for an accused teacher.

Frye glared at Gordon who didn't look away.

"The reason I asked," Philly said, "is this: I'm curious whether Ms. Fine is at risk. I believe, Ms. Lacey, that you told my client he did the right thing in reporting his concerns."

"I did say that," Lacey acknowledged. "But Ms. Fine's accusation casts this situation in a new light and raises a new issue."

"What light is that?" Philly fired back.

"Ms. Fine has leveled a serious accusation against Mr. Waters, and we have to consider her claim."

"I'm not suggesting you dismiss what she said. I am suggesting that you find out whether the details of her story mesh with actual facts in her personal life. If there is a match, then Ms. Fine's motive to fabricate an allegation against Mr. Waters becomes clearer."

"That's not necessarily true," Frye responded.

"Well, if you don't do any digging," Philly came back, "you'll never know."

Wayne Gordon smirked at Frye and this time Philly wished the union rep would lose his attitude; antagonizing Frye wouldn't help Waters. Gordon's demeanor now made clear why Waters had wanted independent legal representation.

"I understand that you live alone," Frye directed at Waters.

"What does that have to do with anything?" Philly challenged the vice-principal.

"As I said, Ms. Lacey and I get to ask the questions."

"I don't mind," Waters interceded. "Yes, I do live alone. That's been the case since I started teaching."

"Are you in any kind of committed relationship?" Frye asked.

"This is total bullshit!" Wayne Gordon exploded. "I wouldn't answer any further questions."

Philly leaned toward Waters so she could whisper. They were in close quarters and she wanted to make sure she wasn't overheard. "Gordon has a point. If you want, I can put a stop to this now."

Waters shook his head and faced Frye. "I wouldn't say I'm in a committed relationship, but I have been seeing someone for a couple of months."

"Have you ever been married?" Frye asked.

"No."

"How old is the person you're currently seeing?"

"You're totally out of line," Gordon interrupted.

"I'm not going to tell you the exact age," Waters said. "That's nonc of your business. Let's just say we're about the same age."

Frye became silent and Lacey took charge. "Thank you for meeting with us, Michael. We appreciate your cooperation."

"What happens next?" Philly asked.

"Mr. Frye and I will confer, and we'll probably have some questions for the school committee's legal counsel. We hope to conclude our inquiry shortly."

"Are we done?" Gordon asked in a belligerent tone.

"I believe we are," Lacey said.

Gordon steered their group to the teachers' lounge which was empty. He was now holding court. "I swear to God, one day I'm going to take a swing at Frye."

"Thanks for sitting in, Wayne," Waters said. "I appreciate your support."

"We may file a grievance against Frye," Gordon said, his feathers still ruffled.

"Don't do anything without talking to me," Philly said, handing Gordon her card. "Our most important concern right now is Michael's situation."

"All right," Gordon said grudgingly.

"Has this matter been kept quiet or is it common knowledge at the high school?" Rachel inquired.

Waters looked to Gordon. "I'd say it's been kept quiet, but some teachers know about it," the union rep said.

"What's your read on this, Wayne?" Waters asked.

"I think Lacey is behind you," Gordon said after a long pause. "I don't think Frye wants to let this drop. If I had to guess, I'd say he's going to try to convince Lacey it's your word against the student's and there should be a formal hearing."

"What's behind your thinking?" Philly asked.

"I said it before and I'll say it again," Gordon replied scornfully. "Frye is a prick."

12

On President's Day, two former Cambridge cops were parked in Philly's living room. Apparently, when you were retired, you didn't need a day off. Paul was right when he'd said they would stand out. Barney Freedmen and Herb McCauley were huge and would never be inconspicuous. There was flab on each man, but it was hard to tell if the loose flesh camouflaged muscle. Philly suspected that it did. Freedman's buzz cut reminded her of a Brillo Pad. McCauley's hair was longer, mostly gray. Philly sat on her couch, holding Daisy. The private detectives each occupied a facing easy chair. The two men were dressed identically: blue blazers, khaki pants, dress white shirts with no ties, burnt orange, rubber-soled, ankle-high work shoes. It had to be ten degrees outside but neither man wore an overcoat.

"Thanks for coming to my home," Philly said. "With a kid, it makes it easier on me."

"Our pleasure," McCauley said. "How can we help you?"

"Why don't you tell me about yourselves first?" Philly requested.

"Paul must have told you we're former Cambridge cops," McCauley said. "We were partners, detectives, mostly homicide. We worked out of the Cambridgeport police station. We retired but we got bored and decided we needed a pastime so we got our PI licenses. It gives us something to do."

Philly figured that the men appraising her had to be around Carpenter's age. Their demeanor pretty much revealed who had been the good cop and who had been the bad cop back when they were on the force. Freedman hadn't said a word, while McCauley made funny faces at Daisy. "I've got a situation," Philly said, and she proceeded to fill them in on Michael Waters' case. While she talked, McCauley wrote feverishly on a notepad and Freedman regarded her with an expression that revealed nothing.

When she finished her account, McCauley consulted his notes. "Basically, you want us to find out about this student's home life, her mother's use of barbiturates, the existence of a boyfriend who may have dumped her, and anything else that might help your teacher client."

"That's pretty much it."

"We can do that," McCauley said. "We charge sixty dollars an hour, twenty dollars an hour for travel time. If we both go out together, we only bill for one of us."

"Those are pretty reasonable rates," Philly observed.

McCauley glanced Freedman's way before saying: "That's us, reasonable."

"May I ask you how you'll be going about this job if you're hired?"

"We've found from experience that the direct approach is best. We'll visit the high school and nose around. I'll probably take that on. Barney will check out the parents."

"How will you keep this under the radar. I don't want the Fine girl to know that she's being investigated."

"You leave that to us," Freedman spoke for the first time.

"Do you have any theories on why the student would make up a story like that?" Philly asked.

Freedman frowned. "What if it's not made up?"

"That's not an assumption I'm going to consider," Philly said.

Freedman rolled his eyes.

"There's the obvious," McCauley said. "Your client had made a connection between what this girl wrote and her having suicidal tendencies. If the girl really had thought seriously about suicide, she might not want that to get out."

Philly studied the two private detectives. There was a gruffness about Freedman that gave her concern, but McCauley seemed to balance out that trait with an open, friendly manner. Maybe that's what made them a successful team. Philly decided to trust Paul's judgment. "Okay," she said. "You're hired. Would you like some coffee?"

"I thought you'd never ask," Freedman said.

"Keep an eye on Daisy," Philly directed at McCauley as she plopped her daughter on the living room floor and moved to the kitchen.

Coffee seemed to make Freedman more voluble. Philly caught him flash a wink at Daisy and, unsolicited, he remarked that Paul was one of the rising stars of the Cambridge Police Department. "How do you know Paul?" he asked.

"We're seeing each other."

Freedman regarded her with new interest. "That tells me you've got something going for you."

"I have my moments," Philly said, secretly pleased with Freedman's comment. "As long as I've got you here, do you mind if I ask you about something totally unrelated?"

"Of course not," McCauley responded.

Keeping an eye on Daisy who was doing her odd crawling motion, Philly ordered her thoughts about Heather Storm. "I've been court appointed to represent a mother who is likely to have her kid put up for adoption without her consent," Philly began. As she provided background information, the detectives reprised their previous roles. McCauley wrote feverishly while Freeman regarded her with an unreadable look. "What do you think?" Philly concluded.

Freedman scowled, an expression she was used to from Carpenter. "Is this a case," he said, "where you have to assume the kid isn't telling the truth?"

Philly accepted the jab, thought that maybe she had it coming. "No," she said. "In this case, I'm not ruling anything out."

"What's the father's name?" Freedman asked.

"I'm court appointed," Philly reminded the detectives. "There's no money to pay you guys on this one. I was just curious what you thought."

"What's the father's name?" Freedman repeated. "We have time on our hands. We're not promising to do anything, but we might surprise you and look into it."

Philly debated only a moment. "James Farrell," she said and provided Farrell's address.

"I'd be looking at the girl," McCauley said. "Maybe something odd is going on in her life."

"This other lawyer I work with will be interviewing the child's teachers," Philly explained. "There's no question the child's hymen isn't intact."

"That doesn't mean the father did anything?" McCauley pointed out.

"Somebody did something," Philly came back.

"That somebody could have been the kid," Freedman said.

Philly had thought of that possibility but not seriously. The psychological evaluations of Marilyn Storm indicated a third party was involved. "Well, thanks for listening," Philly said. "When can I expect to hear from you on my teacher's case?"

"Soon," McCauley said.

"Or not soon," Freedman added. "By the way, we're going to need a copy of the story the girl wrote."

Philly couldn't imagine what the detectives would do with the story, but she decided not to make waves. "Watch my daughter. I've got an extra copy upstairs."

Mounting the stairs, Philly glanced back at the living room. McCauley was on the floor crawling toward Daisy. "What are you up to cutie pie," she heard the detective say.

13

Marilyn Storm's fifth grade teacher had agreed to meet with Rachel. Walking down a long corridor of the Morrisey Elementary School, Rachel marveled at the brightly colored artwork that covered nearly all available wall space. Her memory of her own grade school days was dimming, but she was reasonably certain that little or no artwork had been displayed in the halls. Margaret Fanning had agreed to stay after school for their meeting, and Rachel paused to study Marilyn's teacher through the glass panel set in the top of the classroom door. Fanning was middle-aged with brown hair that curled at her shoulders. In profile, sitting at her desk, Fanning had an intent look as she made her way through a stack of papers. When Rachel knocked on the door, Fanning looked up and motioned for her to enter.

After introductions, Fanning moved her chair to the front of her desk and fetched a straight-backed wooden chair for Rachel.

"I thought I was going to have to squeeze onto the seat of one of those kid desks," Rachel said, opting to start out on a light, friendly note.

"If you had showed up unannounced that would have been your fate. One of the perks of my job is to watch adults suffer the indignities of figuring out where to put their legs. Which assumes they can manage a soft landing for their behinds."

Rachel smiled. Fanning's humorous response predisposed her to like the teacher. "I pretty much told you on the phone why I wanted to meet with you. I also explained that you didn't have to talk to me and could stop the interview at any time. I wonder if we could start by you giving me your general impression of Marilyn."

"Marilyn is unhappy," Fanning said without fanfare. "That is my overriding impression of her. She is one unhappy little girl."

"Has that been the case for the entire year?"

Fanning took her time with the question. "Probably. But I may not have picked up on it when the school year started even though I was alerted to her unhappiness by written briefings from her previous teachers. At the end of a year, each teacher does a write up of her students that gets passed along to next year's teachers."

"Then she's been unhappy before fifth grade?"

"That's right. This seems to have started in third grade and continued in fourth grade. Each of those teachers commented on her unhappiness."

"What are the signs of her unhappiness?"

Fanning sighed. "She's withdrawn. She rarely socializes. She won't raise her hand in class. I have to call on her to get her to speak in class and sometimes, when I do call on her, she doesn't respond. She'll shake her head in this sad, resigned way and I'll end up calling on someone else."

Rachel consulted her list of questions for Fanning. "I told you on the phone about the upcoming court hearing and that a lawyer I work with is representing Marilyn's mother. Do you have any comment on the charges that Marilyn has made against her father?"

"What she's alleging would certainly explain what's going on with her."

"Do you think Marilyn's telling the truth?"

"I have no idea."

"Does anyone have any theories on what's going on with her besides the claims she's made against her father?"

"I don't," Fanning said, shaking her head. "She's been evaluated for special needs and she's met with the psychologist assigned to the school district. But nobody's been able to come up with anything concrete except for what you've said she's now claiming her father did."

Rachel took a moment to bring her note taking current with Fanning's comments. "Does she have any friends?"

"I don't believe so. She gets dropped off in the morning by the foster family she's staying with and, as I said before, she's pretty withdrawn."

"Have you met her actual parents?"

"Only her mother. Her mother came in for an evening parents' orientation after the start of the school year. I remember shaking hands with the woman but not much else."

Rachel took her time reviewing her list of questions. "It strikes me that Marilyn started to become withdrawn in third grade. Did anything out of the ordinary happen then?"

Fanning went to her desk and returned with a large file folder. She thumbed through the contents, extracted a paper and perused the document. "Grace Champion was Marilyn's third grade teacher. She noticed a change in Marilyn in April but when she asked Marilyn if she was okay, the girl nodded and wouldn't say anything more. When we're done, you might try Grace's classroom. She usually stays late."

"Is there anything else you can think of that might be helpful to me?"

Rachel was heartened to see Fanning giving her question serious thought.

"I remember one thing the special education consultant pointed out," Fanning said. "The consultant didn't think Marilyn required special education. But he did say that Marilyn wanted to go to a different school although she wouldn't say why."

Rachel made a note of the comment. She looked about the classroom taking in posters and displays covering math, geography, the American Revolution, and spelling. Several other posters caught her eye, one providing advice on dealing with strangers, another entitled, *Your Body Is Your Body.* "It looks like fifth graders get hit with a lot of difficult subjects," Rachel said, pointing toward the two posters that had caught her attention.

"At the beginning of the year we had a police officer come in and give the don't-go-anywhere-with strangers talk," Fanning explained. "That was followed up by a low-key presentation by a psychologist about inappropriate touching. You're right. It's a lot for a fifth grader to take in. But you'd be surprised at how few parents talk to their kids about these things."

Rachel suspected that her own circuits would have overloaded in fifth grade if she had been given a realistic assessment of the real-world horrors that awaited children. No doubt the pace of growing up had accelerated since then. "What room number is Grace Champion in?" she asked, and Fanning obliged with directions.

Grace Champion was in and was now listening to Rachel explain the purpose of her visit. Champion was young, in her late twenties Rachel guessed, and the attentive way she was listening suggested an infinite store of patience that had to come in handy when dealing with eight-year-olds. Rachel had opted to sit on a front row desktop rather than attempt to slide onto a seat that was too small. She had her notepad out and studied the notes she had taken during her meeting with Margaret Fanning.

"It seems that Marilyn began to become withdrawn and unhappy toward the end of the year she was in your third-grade class," Rachel started off. "Any idea what caused that change in her?"

Champion shook her head. "Not really. It was obvious that something was bothering her, but she wouldn't open up to anybody. Previously, she had been interactive with her classmates. I remember she and a little boy were inseparable. Danny Graham was his name. But then at the end of third grade, the two of them would have nothing to do with each other. I remember Marilyn asked to have her seat moved as far away from Danny as possible."

Rachel picked up her note taking. "Did you mention this to anyone?"

"I did. At the end of Marilyn's third grade year, I wrote down in my report to fourth grade teachers that Marilyn be kept apart from the Graham boy. Also, toward the end of that year, I became aware that Danny Graham and some of the girls in the class had started teasing Marilyn but nobody—and that includes Marilyn—would say a word about what the teasing was about."

"Marilyn apparently told a special education consultant that she wanted to be at another school. Do you have any idea what that could be about?" Rachel asked.

Champion shook her head. "Kids can be cruel both intentionally and unintentionally. Today we claim to be enlightened and we know that teasing can be a form of bullying. Maybe the teasing had reached an inappropriate level and Marilyn wanted to be elsewhere because she was being bullied."

Rachel wrote *teasing/bullying* on her notepad. "Did you also make this point in your report?"

Champion searched through a bottom draw of her desk and drew out a file folder which she flipped through. "Here it is. I noted that, 'Marilyn appears to be the subject of an inordinate amount of teasing from certain of her classmates.' So this must have registered with me as something out of the ordinary because there is always teasing and I rarely comment on teasing in these year-end reports."

Rachel couldn't recall any mention of teasing in Marilyn's psychological evaluations contained in the records sealed by the probate court. "Let me leave you my card. This has been very helpful. If you think of anything else, please call me anytime."

Champion took the card reflexively, her brows knitted, lost in thought. "This is all so tragic. Marilyn was a delightful little girl at the start of third grade."

"Can I ask you something? Do third graders get talks about strangers and inappropriate touching?"

"No," Champion said. "That starts in fifth grade. School districts differ on when it's appropriate to raise these issues with students. In our district, we think third graders are too young for those subjects."

14

Carpenter wondered whether he had dozed off for a moment. He had startled and sat up straight because he had the feeling he was being watched. And he was. The black man in the photograph mounted on the wall facing his desk was glaring at him. It took Carpenter a moment to get his bearings. He had been thinking—perhaps dreaming—about the actress, Jill Clayburgh, who had died three months ago from CLL. The death had caught Clayburgh's colleagues and friends by surprise. Some colleagues had remarked on working with her a few years before her death and not noticing anything that indicated she was ill. Before sitting upright, Carpenter had been thinking—or perhaps dreaming—that his own end would come without warning and catch many by surprise. In that state between wakefulness and sleep, he had been imagining a Sunday breakfast of his Barrister friends, lawyers his own age, with several of them commenting that on the preceding Sunday, he had been his usual, grouchy self.

"What?" Carpenter said to the photograph eyeing him.

But, of course, he knew what. The man was telling him to suck it up and stop feeling sorry for himself.

"It's not that easy," Carpenter complained to the photograph. "I don't think I can practice law this way."

The man's glare ratcheted up in intensity. It was easy for a fucking photograph to tell him he'd better get used to practicing law while not feeling at his best!

"You don't get it," Carpenter said. "It's bad enough going in front of a judge. But when you're feeling like shit, it's worse." The man's expression remained hostile and Carpenter realized that he'd get no sympathy from that quarter. Recently he'd had trouble sleeping which perhaps accounted for his dozing off. He would close his eyes when his head hit the pillow and drop off instantly for three to four hours. But when he'd wake, falling back to sleep was a hit or miss proposition. There were times when he'd toss and turn for hours and have to start the workday bone weary. Last night had been particularly bad. When he'd reported these latest variations on his symptoms to Dr. Specter, she'd told him to keep exercising and to try snacking on something healthful between meals. This advice struck him as inadequate. Christ, he had fucking leukemia! But Dr. Specter again had assured him that his white blood count while on the high side, was not anything unexpected. Chemotherapy would bring the white count down but was that something that he wanted to start? Had his symptoms reached a point where he couldn't function? One thing to be said for Dr. Specter when she wasn't uttering oddball comments that left him puzzled—the woman knew how to shut him up.

Maybe the black man had a point. If he didn't suck it up, Fred would win an important round. Bottom line, he wasn't about to give Fred that satisfaction.

After dinner and the washing up they were all sitting in the living room—Philly, Paul, Raul, and Isabella—while Daisy did her squirming crawl on the floor. When the doorbell rang, Raul went to the door. As Raul stood aside, Sarah Ferguson entered the front hallway and began to unwrap a red woolen scarf from around the lower half of her face, a reminder, in case anyone needed it, that February in Boston was just plain miserable. Sarah kept her winter coat on, and Philly yielded up her chair, dropping to the floor beside Daisy.

"I'm glad you're all here," Sarah said, shivering from the cold. "I have a proposal to make."

The grownups fell silent and even Daisy paused in her scrabbling, watching Sarah intently.

"I went to see that house Philly has looked at," Sarah announced. Raul's and Isabella's expressions darkened. Paul regarded Sarah neutrally.

"What if we were to go into it together?" Sarah posed. "I could live up on the third floor. I'd be a live-in babysitter. If I were to sell my house, I'd have money to contribute. I don't think you'd need tenants to make ends meet financially with me in the picture."

Philly thought of the expression often uttered when an idea received an icy reception: that went over like a lead balloon. Raul and Isabella looked ready to nix Sarah's suggestion on the spot, and Paul would likely be in their camp. But Paul surprised her. "I haven't seen the place," he said, "although Philly has described it. If you're talking three stories and living on the third floor, there would come a time when you'd have trouble managing the stairs."

"I thought of that," Sarah said. "You're probably right. But at the moment it wouldn't be a problem. I could use the exercise and it might be good for me. It might whip me into shape. I've dropped ten pounds since I started keeping after Daisy."

"Isabella and I really cannot think about a move right now," Raul said. "We are interested in staying put until well after the baby is born. We have explained this to Philly."

Sarah looked crestfallen. "I have to admit I'm being somewhat selfish," she said. "I'm tired of living alone. Babysitting Daisy has made me realize that. I would like to babysit *your* baby." Sarah paused, looking in Isabella's direction, and Philly couldn't read Isabella's expression. "I need to warn you I'm not much of a cook but, every once in a while, I get inspired and go on a cooking spree. That might come in handy for all of you."

When Daisy rolled her way onto Philly's foot, Philly picked her daughter up and settled her in her lap. Daisy was perspiring from her exertions, a wet sheen glistening on her forehead. Philly breathed in Daisy's damp, rich smell.

"Why hasn't the house sold?" Isabella asked. Philly saw that Raul was irked by her question.

"It's not a great market and maybe the seller is asking for a little too much," Sarah responded. "I have the feeling that it will sell in the spring. There may be a window right now to make a deal."

"Raul has told you how we feel about a move right now," Isabella continued. "But we will discuss what you have said."

In Philly's opinion, Raul didn't look like he was prepared to discuss the time of day.

"Take a look at the place," Sarah urged. "You won't be able to picture yourself living in the house unless you see it. It's different than this house. In a good way."

Raul sulked. Paul dropped to the floor next to Philly and Daisy. He stroked Daisy's filmy dark hair. "There's never a dull moment, is there?" he asked.

Paul's question hung in the air until Daisy squealed, the noise breaking a spell.

"I'll take that as agreement," Paul said.

15

Nelson Frost got straight to the point. "My client will increase its offer by twenty-five thousand dollars but that's a limit engraved in stone."

Philly held her phone away from her ear. The cold snap had receded temporarily and as Philly looked out the window at the neighboring house, she could see but couldn't hear the drops of water coming off the icicles pointing down from the gutters. Ice coating the window nearest to her view had begun to splinter and she wouldn't be surprised if she could actually see through the window by the afternoon.

"Any reaction?" Frost prompted.

An additional $25,000 might buy Edna Gardner another three or so months of the institutional care Frank Gardner would soon require. Frost's offer was still $75,000 less than the $250,000 figure Gerard Gorman's case had settled for. And Gorman hadn't had to pay legal fees because Philly had agreed to handle the case at a reduced hourly rate to be paid from money put up by Gorman's friends and colleagues.

"This is hard," Philly said. Carpenter had told her that there was no way to get a handle on what a good settlement was. He had stressed that Philly couldn't jeopardize Edna Gardner's instruction not to lose the settlement offer previously put on the table.

"Maybe you need to think about it and call me back."

Edna Gardner would be pleased that more money was coming her way and she might even regard Philly as having earned her fee by having the insurer throw additional money into the settlement pot. Still, if Frank Gardner lived for many years, the settlement money being offered would be long gone while Frank's medical needs were acute.

"I hate this shit," Philly vented, not caring about revealing her emotions to Frost. "I'll call you back."

When Frost rang off, Philly called Carpenter. He picked up on the first ring and she filled him in on Frost's latest proposal.

"The way you're describing this, I don't think he's going to go higher," Carpenter said.

"What would you say to reducing our contingency fee?" Philly threw out. It was a thought that had recently occurred to her and her prediction was that Carpenter would nix the idea.

"You know I don't like doing that," Carpenter said. "This could be one of those cases where we make a quick score that balance out the contingency cases where we work our asses off and end up with squat."

Philly was familiar with Carpenter's view of contingency cases. He liked having a few around because if they settled it was like getting found money. But, as they both knew from experience, a contingency case could prove to be a time suck that left you with nothing at the end of a long ordeal. "You didn't answer my question."

"I thought I did," Carpenter said. "I'd prefer not to do that. We both know that cash is going to be a struggle this year."

Carpenter was right about this year being a financial grind. Still, there was something about pocketing a legal fee in the neighborhood of $58,000 that didn't seem fair to the Gardners. Rachel had spent a fair amount of time assembling information and drafting a workers' compensation claim, but neither she nor Carpenter had expended serious time on the case. "What if we dropped our take to thirty-three grand?"

Carpenter didn't say anything. She imagined him staring at the photograph she had given him, looking for answers in the black man's merciless stare.

"This is your call," Carpenter said. "The case was brought to you. I'll go along with whatever you decide."

"Then that's what I'm going to do. Maybe we don't make this an even four-way split."

"Again, your call," Carpenter said.

"I'm going to go through all this with Edna Gardner. If anything changes, I'll call you."

Carpenter lay on his back on a mat, knees bent, his legs resting on a large rubber blue ball. He had just finished his third set of twelve crunches with his hands locked behind his head and it had been an effort. Camellia Kim knelt beside him, regarding him thoughtfully. Carpenter knew that she'd noticed his struggle. Today her short spiky hair had gold highlights at the tips and maybe it was the overhead lights that made golden flecks dance in her dark eyes.

"How are you feeling?" Kim asked.

"Not so great," Carpenter admitted.

"When we did the machines, you reduced your weights."

"I didn't think I could manage those weights," Carpenter said, wondering if Kim was now regarding him as a pathetic wimp.

"What does your doctor say?"

"She says I should keep exercising and snack between meals."

Kim nodded as if agreeing with Dr. Specter's advice. She checked the list of exercises she had mapped out. "You mentioned that you tried spinning. There's a class starting in fifteen minutes. Are you going to take it?"

"I hadn't planned on it," Carpenter said. This afternoon he couldn't face the prospect of pedaling his brains out while blaring music assaulted his ears.

"That's what you're going to do," Kim said with conviction. "I haven't spun in a while and I don't have any clients after you. I'll ride next to you."

"I'm not really up to it," Carpenter protested.

"Tough shit," Kim said grinning. "But first we're going to finish up with the ball. Grab hold with your feet and lift the ball toward your head as far as you can."

Carpenter followed Kim's instructions, feeling his abs tighten as he worked the ball up and over toward his head.

"What are you stopping for?" Kim demanded. "What's this one and done crapola. It's twelve reps or did you forget? And then we go spinning."

So far Carpenter hadn't recognized a single song that blared from the speakers in the rear of the spinning room. They had just finished a sprint and Kim's legs had been a blur. Even when he was Kim's age, Carpenter couldn't have come close to matching her tempo. He was drenched in sweat but for some reason he didn't feel as defeated as when he was going through weight and stretching routines.

"Nice job," Kim said to him as the class followed the instructor's direction to drink water before their next simulated hill challenge.

Maybe half a minute had passed before Carpenter recognized *Satisfaction* which meant this would be the second spinning session in which he'd be able to identify at least one song.

"Turn the resistance knob to the right at least three quarters of a turn," the spinning instructor directed. "This should be hard. This is what you came here for."

Carpenter suppressed a laugh. This was not what he came to the gym for. If he had his druthers, he'd be back at his condo finding something or someone to rail against.

"Stay seated. We'll come out of the saddle when we increase the resistance again."

Carpenter glanced at Kim. His trainer's legs were straining, as if she was struggling in slow motion, and he realized that she had deliberately increased the resistance beyond the level called for by the instructor.

"Everyone's looking good!"

Carpenter doubted that assertion; he suspected that he looked like a pathetic old guy trying to pretend he could keep up with young people.

"We're halfway up the hill. Two more minutes. The last thirty seconds we're going to sprint."

Speak for yourself, Carpenter silently griped as his thoughts turned to Philly. He considered the deal she was about to cut in the hockey player's case, and he had to hand it to her. Her willingness to cut their fee, something they didn't have to do, was classy; the player and his wife could use every cent they got. Philly really was good-hearted in a way he wasn't. On his own, the chances he'd have agreed to a fee cut were between slim and none. Although maybe he was selling himself short for in the past there had been occasions when he had helped a client financially.

"Thirty seconds! All out sprint! Go for it."

Carpenter willed his legs to move faster. He noticed that Kim's speed had picked up only barely; she must have loaded on so much resistance that it was impossible for her to sprint.

"All right! Back to a flat road. Get some water."

Carpenter took a slug from his water bottle. Kim leaned toward him. "Aren't you glad you did this?" she whispered.

Carpenter found himself nodding, surprised that though exhausted, he was at least for the moment not feeling sorry for himself.

"No rest for the weary," the instructor announced. "We're going to go into a serious of jumps. Make sure you have enough resistance."

"Shit!" Carpenter muttered under his breath.

March

Philly's Untitled Playlist

Sweet Surrender

Sarah McLachlan

16

Philly heard Daisy squealing with delight from the living room.

"Look at you!" Sarah Ferguson cooed. Philly guessed that Daisy was practicing her new trick of standing by the front of the couch with her hands on a seat cushion. Frequently, Daisy had to be lifted and positioned to assume that pose but, on a few recent occasions she had crawled to the sofa, gotten to her knees, placed her hands on a seat cushion, and leveraged herself to her feet.

Philly shut the door to her second-floor home office and focused on the task at hand. She reviewed the final edits to the settlement agreement in Frank Gardner's case and e-mailed the document to Edna Gardner. She had expected Edna to grab at the new settlement offer, since it was $25,000 over the initial offer that Edna had been so adamant not be lost. Instead, her reaction was, "Can we get more?" When Philly had told her no, Gardner had talked on and on about how she now thought she was making a mistake. Philly reminded her that she could elect not to settle and take the workers' compensation case to trial. That reminder silenced her. It was only when Philly had told her about the fee concession she and Carpenter were prepared to make that Gardner sighed and accepted the deal.

Philly still hadn't made up her mind how to split up the $33,000 legal fee. Recently, she and Carpenter had split two small retainers four ways. If they divided the contingency fee equally, they would be sending another message to Rachel and Simon that when it came to money, they were equal partners. The message would be direct since Simon hadn't done any work on the case. Of course, Carpenter hadn't worked much on the case either. But the geezer was different. Even though they had no formal partnership arrangement, over the past years she and Carpenter had treated each other as if such an arrangement was in place when it came to money. She thought briefly of providing different paydays for Rachel and Simon but dismissed the notion. Simon was working his ass off on Alison Lind's case and no further money would be coming in on that case unless it settled or there was a victory at trial.

Philly scribbled number combinations on her notepad. After staring at various options, she came to a decision. She and Carpenter would take home $9,500 and Rachel and Simon would each receive $7,000. She put out of mind whether the arrangement was fair. The important thing was that she had made a decision that at least for the moment, felt right.

Her office phone startled her, and she paused a moment before picking up the receiver. "Philomena Piper," she said breathlessly.

"It's Barney Freedman," a gruff voice came back at her.

"Mr. Freedman! Hi. I hope you have something to report."

"I wouldn't be calling if I didn't have anything to report," the private detective came back.

Philly smiled. It was a comment that Carpenter would have fired off. "I'm listening."

"For a short time, Caroline Fine was seeing a boy named Ronald Peterson. The Peterson kid broke things off. He said Fine was a little too weird for his tastes."

"How long were they seeing each other?"

"No more than a month. They took in a few movies, did some making out, that kind of thing."

"What did he mean by saying Fine was too weird for his tastes?"

"He wasn't real specific. He said Fine was hyper, was making more of them seeing each other than he was. He said there was something about her that made him decide to end things."

Philly finished writing down Freedman's comments. Nothing the Peterson boy had related to the detective was helpful, but Peterson's initials matched the initials of the boy in Fine's *Dead End* story—RP for Richard Parks. "What else?"

"Fine's mother has had three long-standing prescriptions for barbiturates. I'll spell the names for you."

Philly took more notes. "Do you mind if I ask you how you found out this stuff?" she said, genuinely curious.

When Freedman didn't answer right away, Philly thought detectives might be like magicians who remained closemouthed about how they did their tricks.

"Herb went to the high school administration office," Freedman said, "and asked to see the most recent yearbook. The Peterson boy was the only boy in Fine's class with the initials RP. Herb tracked him down and met with him."

"I'm surprised that the kid talked to your partner."

"Yeah, well, Herb has a way about him. Without mentioning your client's name, he hinted at a lawsuit and how the Peterson kid could be subpoenaed and how that might not be necessary if the kid talked. The kid talked."

"What about the mother's drugs? How the hell did you find out about that?"

"You don't want to know."

Philly accepted that response. "This is really helpful," she said.

"Our pleasure," Freedman replied. "There's one other thing. That name you wanted information on—James Farrell—he did time in Ohio for kiting checks. It turns out that also in Ohio, a mother filed a complaint against him to make him stay away from her daughter. I can't tell you anything more than that. According to the mother, Farrell was stalking her daughter. There was never a court order directing Farrell to keep away from the daughter."

"How old was the daughter?"

"Nine."

"Jesus Christ!"

"I thought you'd say something like that," Freedman said.

17

Rachel expected James Farrell's attorney to be nonplused at the revelation that a former Ohio girlfriend had filed for a restraining order to keep his client away from a nine-year-old girl.

"I know all about that," Stephen Minor said without hesitation or a hint of concern, "and I know about the check kiting conviction. Farrell broke off a relationship with a woman and he was immediately hit with the request for a restraining order. He had rarely seen the woman's daughter. The woman typically made sure her daughter stayed with grandparents when she had a date with Farrell. And besides, the restraining order was never issued."

Rachel was seated in Philly's Boston office and studied her notes for this call. "Is there any chance Marilyn Storm knew about this Ohio accusation against Farrell?" she asked.

"I don't know," Minor said. "But I see where you're going with this." Minor paused. "Just so you know, my client is not going to oppose the motion of the Department of Children and Family Services. Mr. Farrell is indifferent as to whether Marilyn gets adopted. Your client is upset by his position, but Farrell has made up his mind."

Rachel brought up Minor's website picture on her computer screen. No change there. The guy remained uncommonly good looking. "I met with Marilyn's teachers," she said, deciding to be forthcoming. "Something happened to Marilyn in third grade. At the end of the school year she became withdrawn and other students started to pick on her."

"Do the teachers know what brought this on?"

"No. But I'm going to explore the matter a little further. Marilyn was best friends with a little boy, and he was one of the ones to turn against her. I'm going to seek out the boy's parents."

"You're being more diligent than I am," Minor admitted.

"I'm curious," Rachel confessed. "There's something going on here that we're not seeing."

"Given Farrell's position, I get to put my curiosity on hold."

Rachel didn't have that luxury.

18

Wind whipping down Milk Street rattled the windows of the conference room where Carpenter and Simon sat. Nobody ever accused Boston of being pleasant in March. After reviewing the discrimination complaint Simon had redrafted on behalf of Alison Lind, Carpenter looked up and regarded the young lawyer. Simon had drawn on his interviews with potential witnesses and had organized the complaint paragraphs in a way that depicted Lind as a successful, superior coach in comparison to inept male counterparts. "Nice job. Send Lind a copy and ask her to comment on your draft. I think we've got a shot at this."

Simon nodded, but didn't say anything, his expression difficult to read. "Everything all right?" Carpenter asked.

Simon shrugged. "It would be nice if we were busier."

"Yeah, it would."

Simon shifted positions in his chair. Carpenter realized that he had never before seen Simon nervous. "Out with it," he prodded.

"I'm thinking of contacting that lawyer who made me a job offer at the end of last year," Simon said, meeting Carpenter's gaze. "The truth is I've had it with my part-time waiter job. I need to be practicing law full time. There doesn't seem to be enough business here for me to do that."

Although Carpenter had seen this moment coming, it was still an unpleasant jolt. "Does Rachel know what you're thinking?"

Simon nodded. "I feel bad about this. You and Philly gave us an opportunity when we had nothing. I feel like I'm betraying you both."

"Simon," Carpenter said, "I'm going to tell you the same thing I tell clients about a settlement offer: You need to do what's best for you."

"I'm torn," Simon said. "You guys have given me a lot of responsibility and freedom. I probably won't get that at a bigger firm."

There was no "probably" about it, Carpenter thought. If Simon joined a firm, he'd be monitored more closely than he and Philly would ever do. But he kept the thought to himself; he didn't want to try to sell Simon on anything. "You're not going to be betraying us," he said. "Don't ever think that way. Philly and I are the ones who are grateful to you and Rachel. You helped us out at a difficult time."

Simon offered up a weak smile. "I felt funny taking money from the hockey case that settled. I didn't do anything on the case."

"Get over it. If it will make you feel better, I didn't do a hell of a lot on the case either. But I didn't feel funny about taking a cut of the payoff. If you get a big score on the Lind case, Rachel and Philly will share in the attorney fee award. You can count on it."

Simon regarded Carpenter seriously. "The way you guys are acting, it's like we're a firm."

"Don't go there," Carpenter cautioned. "We're not a firm. Philly and I never formed a firm and you and Rachel make forming a firm more complicated. We've got a half-assed associational relationship. Damned if I know what to call it."

"Call it what it is," Simon said. "It's a firm."

Raw wind tore at Rachel's parka as she paused in front of the two-family house in Dorchester where Danny Graham and his parents lived. If it weren't for unexpected cases such as the Storm case, she realized she might have passed her entire legal career in Boston without once setting foot in some of the storied sectors of the city: Dorchester, Roxbury, Mattapan, Roslindale, South Boston, places she knew only from works of fiction, action crime stories by Higgins and Lehane. She had called ahead and although Rachel had been purposefully vague, Peggy Graham had agreed to meet with her at four in the afternoon, a time when Danny was sure to be home from school. Rachel walked up the front path, eyed the mailbox designations, and rang the bell for the door to her left.

The woman who opened the door was not what Rachel was expecting. She had anticipated being greeted by a pasty-faced, dour woman with hard eyes and an unforgiving manner. But Peggy Graham was lively, vibrant, and welcomed her inside with a genuine smile. Graham was thin and pretty, maybe in her early thirties, dressed in jeans and an MIT sweatshirt. She led the way to a small kitchen and offered coffee which Rachel accepted. Rachel remembered being told that Danny was an only child. That possibly explained why there were only three chairs set about a small circular wood table in a corner of the kitchen.

"It's only instant coffee, but on a day like this, at least it will be hot," Graham said with a smile as she turned away from a kettle that had yet to boil. "I have to say you were somewhat mysterious on the phone. You said that you were a lawyer and were representing the mother of one of Danny's classmates from third grade. I remember Marilyn Storm. She and Danny were good friends and she came over to the house to play a bunch of times. Then the friendship ended. I remember asking Danny why Marilyn hadn't been over to the house in a while and he said something like Marilyn wasn't his friend anymore."

Rachel wished Philly had taken on this assignment. She'd know what to share and what not to reveal about Heather Storm's case. Rachel decided on frankness.

"Another lawyer and I have been appointed by the probate court to represent Heather Storm, Marilyn's mother. Did you ever meet her?"

"Just to say hello when Marilyn was being dropped off here or I dropped Danny at her place."

The water started to boil. Graham spooned instant coffee into two mugs and added the steaming water. Rachel waited until she had taken a seat at the kitchen table.

"Ms. Storm might lose her daughter," Rachel explained, and she provided Graham with a brief description of Heather Storm's present legal dilemma.

"Those are very serious allegations against the father," Graham said when Rachel paused. "Poor Marilyn."

Rachel maintained eye contact with Graham so as not to lose the rhythm of their conversation.

"Something happened with, or possibly to, Marilyn at the end of third grade," Rachel said. "She became withdrawn and uncommunicative. The third-grade teacher who had Marilyn and Danny in class told me that Marilyn wanted to be seated away from Danny at the end of the school year. And she said that Marilyn became the object of some major teasing by your son and other girls in the class. I was hoping that you might have some insight as to what happened."

Graham frowned, and Rachel caught the look of worry that flitted across her face.

"You're talking about the time Danny and Marilyn stopped being friends," Graham said. "I don't recall there being any change in Danny at that time."

Rachel tried for a neutral expression, hoping to conceal her disappointment. "Is this something you could ask your son about?"

"I'll do better than that," Graham said, getting to her feet, and leaving the kitchen.

"Danny! I need you to come downstairs, please!"

Rachel registered the please. She suspected it was not a word many parents used when making a request of a child. Then she heard footsteps and after a short pause a sound of impact, as if Danny had marched down the stairs part way before leaping off and landing on the hardwood floor at the bottom.

A freckle-faced boy with sandy hair and hazel eyes entered showing no reaction to the stranger in his kitchen.

"This is Ms. Boyle," Graham said. "She's a lawyer and she's representing the mother of someone who used to be a friend of yours."

Danny stood beside his mother expressionless.

"You remember Marilyn Storm, don't you?" Graham asked.

The color drained from Danny's face. His mother couldn't have missed the change of expression.

"Why don't you join us at the kitchen table," Graham said to her son and a long moment passed before Danny moved to take the vacant chair, his head lowered.

"I remember," Graham said, "that you and Marilyn used to be good friends in third grade until the end of the year. Did something happen that ended your friendship?"

Danny shook his head. Color had returned to his face, a bright red suffusing his features.

"If something happened, it's okay to tell us about it, honey."

Danny again shook his head, looking at the tabletop.

Rachel opted for silence. Graham was more likely to obtain information from her son.

"Okay, Danny. You can run along. Thanks for trying to help."

Danny bolted from the room as if he had been given a get-out-of-jail-free card, and Rachel worked to suppress a grin.

"I'll talk to Danny," Graham said. "I might get further if you weren't around."

Rachel gathered up her belongings. “Thanks. Here’s my card. Call me whatever happens.”

19

A Golfer

Martin Hays was a large man with wavy black hair, a ruddy complexion, and broad shoulders, but these features all but disappeared as your focus was drawn to the round, black patch that covered his left eye. Carpenter lost the battle not to stare.

Hays had gotten Philly’s name from the sports agent who had sent the hockey player cases her way. This meeting was bound to be awkward—Hays had expected to meet with Philly, but Rachel was there instead.

Carpenter introduced himself and Rachel. “Ms. Piper apologizes profusely for not being able to attend today’s meeting. Her baby has a high fever and she needs to deal with the situation.”

“I understand,” Hays said. “I know what kids are like. It’s not a problem.”

Carpenter noticed that Rachel was also staring at Hays’ eye patch. Rachel, like Philly, had no interest in sports, so Philly probably should have considered Simon for this assignment, since he was the one grousing about lack of work. Still, Philly had chosen Rachel. Besides, maybe Simon also had no interest in sports.

“You got hit with a golf ball and lost an eye,” Carpenter got down to business. “I’m not minimizing your injuries, but it seems like an accident to me. Your case resembles the case of the fan who goes to a baseball game and gets hit with a foul ball.”

“There’s also the recent New York case which you may know about,” Rachel pointed out. “A golfer also lost an eye in that case. When he sued, the case was thrown out because the golfer who hit the ball wasn’t negligent by not shouting fore. The court ruled the injured golfer took the risk of an errant shot hitting him.”

Carpenter was grateful for the quick research Rachel had done.

Hays thumped the conference room table with a meaty hand. "I know all that stuff," he said with some heat. "But this is different. This happened at the Mayfair Country Club in Needham where I'm a member. There's a club rule. A golfer whose shot may cause someone risk of injury is required to shout out fore. And when you go to a baseball game, there's a warning on your ticket that you could get hit by a ball. The country club doesn't give out tickets with warnings."

At Hays' reference to a club rule, Carpenter's interest picked up. "Why don't you start at the beginning."

Hays sighed and slumped in his chair. "I'm a banker. There's this foursome I'm a part of which involves three other guys, also bankers. We're all at different banks but we know each other and like each other and it's a chance for us to shoot the shit and learn from each other. Nothing gets repeated that gets said on the course."

Carpenter gave Hays an approving nod. Hays could have been describing the Barristers, the five lawyers that he got together with for early Sunday breakfasts. The unwritten rule of those gatherings was nothing got repeated to anyone.

"We were on the seventh hole. We'd all hit our drives. My three playing partners hit the fairway, but I sliced my drive and I was off in some high, tree-shaded rough on the right-hand side of the fairway trying to find my goddamn ball. It was mid-October, the third Saturday of the month, so the leaves were still mostly on the trees. I told my playing partners to go ahead without me. So my playing partners hit their second shots and started moving ahead, not waiting for me. I finally saw my ball. I picked it up because it was unplayable. I'm walking toward the fairway where I planned to take a penalty drop and the next thing I know I'm lying on the fringe beside the fairway in incredible pain and I can't see out of my left eye."

"Who hit the ball that struck you?" Rachel asked.

"A guy named Warren Lord. He was playing in a foursome behind us."

"Is Lord a club member?" Rachel followed up.

"Yes."

"When would it have been appropriate for Lord to have hit his drive?" Rachel asked, and Carpenter began to doubt he'd get a word in edgewise while Rachel had a head of steam up.

"He should have waited until each of us in our foursome had hit our second shots and had moved on to play our third shots."

"What was par on the seventh hole?"

"Five. It's the longest hole on the course."

"What was the visibility like?"

"It was clear and sunny."

"This was last October, right?" Rachel asked.

Hays nodded. "It was chilly, but we wanted to get in a game. We figured we wouldn't have many more opportunities. A lot of people had the same idea—the course was crowded."

"When you were looking for your ball, were you visible from the tee from which Lord hit his drive?" Rachel asked.

Hays became lost in thought, as if he were picturing the layout of the seventh hole. "I may not have been when I was deep in the rough which was tree-shaded. But I had to be visible when I was nearing the fairway. Besides I had on one of those bright yellow windbreaker shells over a heavy sweater. It would have been hard to miss the yellow."

Rachel doodled on her notepad. "Would it have been reasonable for Lord's foursome to believe that your foursome had moved on?" she asked.

Carpenter studied Hays. Hays' answer to Rachel's question might well determine whether he had a case.

"If he had counted my playing partners, he would have realized there was someone missing."

"Is it customary to count like that?" Rachel asked.

Hays frowned. "To be honest, I don't always count. When you're out there playing, you kind of know when the players in front of you have cleared out."

"Where was your golf bag when you went looking for your ball?"

"I carried it into the rough."

"Was Lord's foursome behind your foursome for the previous six holes?"

"Yes," Hays said. "I think it was around the third hole when one of Lord's group gave us a shout to pick up our play. As I recall, that happened on two other holes, the fifth and the sixth. The guy who was calling out to us had leather lungs. He was kind of nasty actually. On the sixth hole, he said something about wanting to play through us if we were going to yak like a bunch of old ladies."

"Was the guy who called out Lord?"

"I couldn't tell you."

"Are you slow players?" Rachel asked.

"I don't think so. I'd say we're about average."

"Did you hear a warning shout of any kind before you were hit?" Carpenter asked, tired of sitting on the sidelines.

"No. I didn't hear a damn thing. One moment I'm nearing the fairway and the next moment I'm laid out."

"You mentioned this club rule about shouting fore," Carpenter said. "Are club members supposed to acquaint guests with the rule?"

Hays offered a wry smile. "I suppose so. But the truth is when I have guests at the club, I don't go through the rules with them. We just get out and play."

"I'm trying to picture what happened," Rachel said. "Lord must have done what you did, sliced his drive on the seventh hole. If he was tracking his shot, he would have seen it heading for where you were with your yellow shell on. He would have had time to give you a warning shout."

Carpenter smiled. Rachel had come up with a compelling way to present Hays' case. His few experiences on a golf course had been unpleasant, but he suspected that any player comfortable with the game would follow the path of a ball he had just hit.

"You must play golf," Hays said to Rachel. "I'd say you've pictured this just right."

"Actually, I don't play at all," Rachel confessed, reddening. "But my father does, and I picked his brain before this meeting. And I browsed through a book called *Golf for Dummies.* I learned about par, and hooks and slices, and golfing etiquette. It's not *that* complicated a game."

"But it can drive you nuts," Hays said. "It's a humbling game."

"Let's talk about damages," Carpenter changed the subject. "Loss of an eye is a serious injury in and of itself. How has the loss affected you?"

"Not all that much," Hays said. "I'm getting used to it."

"That won't do," Carpenter said. "I'm sure you can do better than that."

"I'll be getting one of those glass eyes," Hays said.

"I wouldn't rush that," Carpenter responded. He liked the look of Hays in an eye patch, thought it would resonate with a jury. "Right now, I wouldn't do anything. But if you hire Ms. Piper, we'll need to get a copy of the club's rules."

"Do you think I have a case?" Hays asked.

Carpenter glanced at Rachel who offered a barely perceptible nod. "Yeah, I'd say you have a case," Carpenter said. "But it's a crapshoot. I'd say the odds of your winning are a tossup. If you pressed me, I'd say you have an uphill battle given that New York case Ms. Boyle just mentioned. There's a possibility that if you file suit, a motion to dismiss your case might be allowed."

Hays drummed thick fingers on the tabletop. Carpenter pictured Hays as a golfer with a big swing and erratic aim. He didn't think the man had a delicate touch when it came to putting.

"I think you're right," Hays said. "I think it *is* a fifty-fifty proposition. But I'm going to go for it. I lost an eye for Christ's sake. Tell Ms. Piper she's hired."

Carpenter hadn't wanted a straight contingency case but there was really no other way to take on Hays' representation. If Philly asked for a retainer, Hays would more likely than not try another lawyer. So here was another case that required work with no money coming in.

Rachel was looking at him expectantly. Hays had departed and they were alone in the conference room. "I'll give you a couple of negligence complaints you can use in coming up with a draft complaint for Hays."

"Great."

"You certainly became a quick study on golf," he observed, struck by Rachel's eagerness.

"I like to learn new things," Rachel said. "I also watched some golf on TV. I can't believe there's a golf channel!"

"If you're on the other side and trying to dismiss Hays' case, what would you argue?"

"I'd probably make the point we just talked about that a golfer assumes the risk of getting hit by an errant ball."

"What else?" Carpenter prompted.

"I'd argue that an errant shot isn't negligence but just part of the game."

Carpenter nodded. "That's the point I'm worried about in this case. Even professional golfers spray balls all over the place."

Rachel became lost in thought. "Are you saying it comes down to this guy Lord not shouting out a warning?"

"It could," Carpenter said. "Which would mean the New York case could really hurt us."

"So why did we take this case on?" Rachel asked.

"Because there's a chance we can survive a motion to dismiss and because the damages are serious and clear. There's also the fact that Hays was wearing something bright yellow. You'd think this guy Lord would have seen that."

"I guess I know what to emphasize in this complaint," Rachel said.

20

Two days later, Rachel sat alone in the office suite conference room waiting for Peggy Graham, who hadn't wanted to talk on the phone, a fact had both piqued Rachel's interest and left her feeling discomforted. She couldn't believe the amount of time she was spending on Heather Storm's case. Could or would Philly bill for all of the hours she had logged? Philly hadn't seemed concerned, and just told her to do what needed to be done.

Rachel liked the responsibility Philly and Carpenter entrusted her with. Money was an issue for Simon but not a big issue for her. She could cover her basic living expenses with her half-time paralegal job. Whatever she made practicing law with Carpenter and Philly was found money. Last year, for the first time in her life, she had felt . . . not exactly rich . . . but comfortable. Today she had money in the bank and was debt free. Simon, she knew, was still paying off law school loans. After her last discussion with Simon, she was pretty certain that he would be leaving their group and joining a law firm. She couldn't blame him; Simon was talented, and it had to be demoralizing every time he reported for his part-time waiter job. For some reason, she didn't share Simon's impatience that their legal careers were not fully in high gear.

There would be a selfish benefit to Simon's leaving—more legal work would fall her way. Still, her preference was to have Simon around. She genuinely liked him, had spent more time than she wanted to think about bemoaning the fact that he was gay.

Rachel heard the office suite door open and left the conference room to greet Peggy Graham. When they shook hands, she was struck by the worried look in Graham's eyes. When Graham asked for water, it seemed to Rachel that she was playing for time.

Rachel closed the conference room door and took her seat. She smiled, hoping to lighten Graham's mood, but her visitor seemed lost in thought, not focusing on her surroundings.

"My husband and I spent a lot of time debating whether I should come and see you," Graham said. "We realize that anything we tell you is not confidential. We thought of hiring our own lawyer and getting advice. But in the end, we have information that your client needs to know. We couldn't live with ourselves if Ms. Storm lost Marilyn because we kept silent."

Rachel nodded, offered another brief smile that she hoped was reassuring and belied her own anxiety.

"I can't remember what it was like to be a third grader," Graham said. "When you're a kid, you think whatever's going on at the moment is all there is in the world. You can't imagine a time when you won't even remember what the moment was about."

Graham became teary and Rachel decided not to leave the room and return with the box of tissues that was on the unoccupied receptionist desk by the front door. Leaving the room would be like breaking a spell.

"After you left the other day, I sat Danny down for a talk. We both saw that there was something to do with Marilyn that made him uncomfortable, and I asked him to tell me what it was. At first, he wouldn't. I explained that Marilyn might be taken away from her parents and that he might have information that could prevent that from happening." Graham paused, dabbed at her eyes with a sweater sleeve. "That's when Danny said, 'I didn't mean it.'"

Rachel tried to control her breathing, felt her heart pounding.

"It sounds like a cliché, but they were playing doctor. One thing led to another apparently. Danny inserted his finger and . . . there was a time when Marilyn began to bleed."

Rachel didn't want to think of the guilt Danny Graham was dealing with.

"They both freaked out as you can imagine. That was the end of the friendship. Neither of them said anything to anybody."

Rachel willed herself to think like a lawyer in the face of Graham's pleading look.

"I know that Heather Storm will be forever grateful to you for telling me what you found out. It took a lot of courage to meet with me." Rachel paused, saw that her words were of no comfort to Graham. "I'm curious about one thing. If they kept things quiet, what was the teasing about?"

Graham's expression turned rueful. "Girls in the class had started to tease Danny. They'd ask him how come Marilyn was no longer his girlfriend. He ignored them, but one time he blurted out that Marilyn had cooties."

Rachel hadn't heard that word in years. Well, apparently, third grade boys never changed. What the hell was a cootie anyway?

"The girls in the class began to tease Marilyn. They'd tell her that Danny said she had cooties. That was when Marilyn moved her seat away from Danny."

Rachel pictured Marilyn's ostracism, her sense of abandonment with her former best friend perceived as a traitor. God only knew how the girl had dealt with her bleeding. And then there was Danny to think of. Had he felt that he had betrayed Marilyn each time she was teased?

"So now you know," Graham said.

Rachel understood that the new information was vital to Heather Storm, but she couldn't help feeling sorry for the Graham boy.

"Yeah, now I know. How's your son?"

"I don't know. At first I thought he was relieved to get this off his chest. Now I'm not so sure. Maybe he had successfully put everything out of his mind. I keep thinking that dredging this up might mean he'll end up confused and frightened when it comes to sex. It's occurred to me that he might never have a normal relationship with a woman. The whole thing makes me want to cry."

Rachel was relieved that while she felt for Graham and her son, she didn't feel guilty about opening this wound in their lives. Maybe she was more like Philly than she thought.

"What are you going to do with this information?" Graham asked, plainly fearful.

"I'm going to share it with the lawyer I work for. She's going to make the final decision on how we proceed. But I will call you and let you know what we decide." We owe you that, Rachel thought, but didn't say.

21

"We've got to stop meeting like this," Carpenter joked. Philly had parked Daisy with her babysitter and was putting in a rare appearance in her Boston office. Carpenter sat in her visitor's chair.

"If you don't mind, I'd like to start," Philly said, and Carpenter realized joking was out. "There's this court-appointed case Rachel is helping me on, and it's taken an unexpected turn."

As Philly talked about two third graders fooling around, Carpenter experienced one of those hollow feelings in his gut that came out of nowhere when a tragedy was revealed.

"What do you think I should do next?" Philly asked after finishing her narrative.

Carpenter stated the obvious. "You're going to have to use this evidence at the court hearing."

"I'm trying to think of a way not to expose the boy to testifying," Philly said. "It's a miserable situation."

"I don't see how you can avoid that, but I thought in probate court a judge could protect a child by ordering a closed-door hearing in an informal setting."

"I thought of that," Philly said. "I'm also thinking of sharing what I know with the lawyer for the Department of Children and Family Services. Maybe the Department will drop the case."

Carpenter thought through the pros and cons of such an overture. "State agency lawyers sometimes think they're on a mission and aren't receptive to common sense."

"I'm not seeing a downside to reaching out," Philly countered.

"Let me think about it. I'm going to call Weiskoff."

"One of your Barrister buddies, right?"

"Right. He specializes in probate court cases. Keep in mind that just because these two little kids fooled around in third grade doesn't mean anything the little boy did broke the little girl's hymen."

"But there was the bleeding," Philly pointed out.

"Maybe she got cut in some way," Carpenter came back.

"Shit!" Philly muttered. "I'm thinking that no matter what caused the girl's hymen to break, this evidence is going to get the father off the hook, and that's probably going to mean that the girl isn't going to get put up for adoption without my client's consent. So that's good, and I should be feeling upbeat for my client. But Rachel and I can't help feeling two kids are going to be put through hell before this case is over."

"Even if the little boy broke the girl's hymen, the father could have still abused her," Carpenter said, and Philly shook her head in disgust. "Let's move on," he suggested. "You have to use the evidence. You have a client to represent. Let the judge do the agonizing. That's what judges get paid to do."

Philly looked dissatisfied but she changed the subject. "We're about to file another workers' compensation claim for another hockey player. The facts are pretty good. It's another one-third contingency."

Carpenter immediately thought of a quick settlement that would put some money in their pockets. He didn't like thinking that way but when business was slow, he couldn't help himself. "Good. I'll look at it if you want me to."

"I'll e-mail you a copy. It's pretty much identical to the Gardner case."

Carpenter paused, wondering whether to raise a concern that was nagging at him. Why not. "Rachel seems to be doing most of the spinoff work. I think we're going to lose Simon."

Philly nodded abstractedly. She looked good, energized. Her mass of black curls sat on her head like a frizzy helmet and her deathly pale coloring should have detracted from her liveliness, but it didn't.

"I don't have an answer to the Simon question," Philly said.

"We need something big to come in soon to keep Simon. I don't fault him for looking elsewhere. Maybe you should have given him the case with the golfer."

Philly shook her head. "I played a hunch giving that case to Rachel. If Simon's still around, I'll work with him on whatever comes my way next."

"I don't want to lose him," Carpenter said.

"I don't think we have any control over the situation."

It was approaching lunchtime. In the old days, Carpenter might have suggested that they go out for a beer. He had liked those occasions when they had gotten out of the office and knocked off a brew and a sandwich. That was then. "Let's grab a sandwich," he suggested, accepting what was now. "My treat."

22

An Assisted Living Center Resident

Philly paced about the entryway of the Maple Leaf Assisted Living Center, a three-story brick building in Guilford, a town neighboring Malden. The lobby was decked out with cartoonish paper St. Patrick's Day decorations Philly guessed came from the Dollar Store, paradoxically depressing with their obviously artificial cheer. Simon was running late this morning, so Philly decided to do some exploring and check out the scene of the accident. She observed no security on the first floor. She had not been approached for identification and probably could have meandered throughout the building if she appeared purposeful and nodded a curt greeting to anyone she encountered.

She followed a sign to the dining room and looked inside. The room was large, carpeted wall to wall in gray, and contained about three dozen tables. The kitchen staff was setting the tables for the noon meal which, in facilities of this type, counted as the day's main meal, with white linen tablecloths, white linen napkins, and cut-glass water glasses. Most of the tables were round, but there were a number of square tables that seated four and a smaller number of rectangular tables that seated two.

Philly studied the entrance to the dining room. Double doors swung out into the hallway. What had Lila Gorman told her on the phone? According to Lila's third-hand account, Mary Foster had pushed open the dining room door and begun turning right as the door started to close behind her. Foster never got to complete her turn to the right. A motorized wheelchair driven by Harrison Blaine knocked her down. Foster was now hospitalized with a broken hip. There had been another motorized wheelchair behind Blaine's operated by another male resident. Neither Blaine nor his wheelchair had suffered injury. According to Lila Gorman, Mary Foster's daughter was beyond pissed off and wanted to sue anyone and everyone. Lila would be accompanying Ruth Foster to the Center this morning.

Philly wandered back to the entryway and found Simon waiting. He didn't look happy which probably meant he was agonizing about his professional future. She sympathized up to a point.

"A place like this depresses me," Simon said. "Is this how we all end up?"

"I'm not going to worry about that now," Philly replied, although she knew where Simon was coming from. On her brief scouting expedition to the dining room she had observed elderly people moving forward cautiously relying on canes, walkers, and in one case a motorized wheelchair probably similar to the one that had run Mary Foster down. There were two ways to look at the residents' efforts: in Simon's despairing way because there was something heartbreaking about watching once vigorous people inch along, or with admiration for the residents who were gutting it out, doing the best they could.

"Ms. Piper!"

It took a moment for Philly to recognize Lila Gorman, so much had she changed in the last year. The beaten down posture and hangdog demeanor were gone, the worry lines previously creasing her forehead barely in evidence. Today the middle-aged woman was smiling. Philly wondered whether the financial settlement she had reached in her husband's workers' compensation case had eased her burdens.

"This is Ruth Foster," Gorman said, and Philly exchanged a brisk, firm handshake with a woman perhaps in her early forties, dressed in worn jeans, a black down vest, and running shoes. Ruth Foster had flaming red hair that was out of control and an angry look in her piercing blue eyes.

"Ruth's husband used to play hockey and was friendly with Gerard. Ruth and I became friends and when Ruth explained what happened to her mother and how she needed a lawyer, I immediately thought of you."

"I'm grateful you thought of me," Philly said, before introducing Simon.

"I'm mad as hell," Foster let loose before Philly could inquire after Gerard Gorman's health. "I hope you're a pit bull because I want to make this place pay."

Philly wanted to escape the entryway and pointed to a library off to their right. "Let's get some privacy and discuss the situation."

They had the library to themselves. Simon sat at a reading table in the middle of the room and took out his notepad. Philly and Gorman also took seats, but Foster stayed on her feet and began pacing.

"How's your mother doing?" Philly asked.

"Shitty," Foster said. "The last thing a seventy-nine-year-old needs is a broken hip. A broken hip is the kind of injury that can set an elderly person back permanently. I'm worried about my mom. Right now, she's still doped up and in pain."

"Has a hip replacement been recommended?" Simon asked.

"It's a definite possibility," Foster said, still steaming.

Philly deliberately said nothing while Foster paced. She didn't think Foster would totally wind down, but maybe pacing would take some of the starch out of her.

"Have you ever done a case like this before?" Foster asked.

Philly picked up on the challenging tone to the question. "I'd like to make a suggestion," she said. "This meeting will be a lot more productive if you take a deep breath, calm down a little, and have a seat. We have a lot to go over."

Foster stopped pacing but continued to stand, her hands jammed into the pockets of her jeans. "I don't want to calm down!"

Philly met the woman's angry glare with what she hoped was a bland expression. "Suit yourself. The answer to your question is no, I've never handled a case of this kind before. I can also tell you that before I represented Mr. Gorman, I had never handled a workers' compensation case involving a hockey player."

"How many trials have you had?" Foster followed up, her challenging tone still in place.

"About three," Philly said. "Just so you know, I work with another litigator who's had scores of trials."

"Will you take the case on a contingency basis," Foster asked.

"Probably. But I want to hear some more background from you before I decide whether to take your mother on as a client."

Foster's jaw dropped and Philly realized that the woman hadn't considered the possibility that a lawyer might decline to represent her mother.

"You don't sound all that eager to get involved with my mother's case," Foster said. "Maybe I'm talking to the wrong lawyer."

Philly glanced at Gorman. Her former client's wife shifted uncomfortably in her chair.

"I realize you're upset," Philly directed at Foster. "Nevertheless, you need to tell us what you know about the accident."

"Upset doesn't begin to describe it," Foster replied. She sighed deeply and finally took a seat at the reading table. "I warned these assholes about wheelchairs. Wait till you meet Richard Mason. He's the useless sack of shit who's supposed to run this place. I told him if he didn't put in some rules, someone was going to get seriously injured by one of those wheelchairs. I even sent him an e-mail about it. But the asshole blew me off and did nothing."

Philly was pleased that Simon was writing. "What did you specifically ask Mason to do?" she inquired.

"I told him he damn well better get people to stop racing and slow down. We're talking about people whose reaction times are piss poor. I also told him that if he knew what was good for him, he'd have staff monitoring the hall in front of the dining room during mealtimes to direct traffic. He gave me one of those condescending looks and told me that would detract from the homelike atmosphere they were trying to achieve. What a crock!"

"How fast do these wheelchairs go?" Simon asked, looking up from his notepad. "You said people in wheelchairs were racing."

"How the hell should I know?" Foster retorted. "I'd guess five miles an hour, maybe eight or ten, but I've never taken one for a test drive."

"What did you mean by racing?" Simon pursued.

"Just what I said. Some of these idiots race against each other."

"Why did you specifically warn Mason about the dining room?" Philly asked.

"Because there's a rush to get into the dining room. For some reason, some of these people feel a need to get seated first. It's like they're afraid the place is going to run out of food. Like that's going to happen!"

Philly pictured a crush at the dining room door as elderly, infirm residents with mechanical aids jostled each other for entry. For some reason she thought of a zombie movie scene, infected creatures lurching forward in pursuit of a human yet to be infected. It was an appallingly tactless thought, and she struggled to get her mind back to Ruth Foster.

"You said your mother was leaving the dining room when she got hit," Philly directed at Foster. "Wouldn't exiting from the dining room be less chaotic than entering?"

"Apparently not. Ask my mother."

"Has the Center said anything to you about your mother since the accident?" Simon asked.

Foster emitted a guttural snort. "Mason's stayed the hell away from me. I told him he'd be hearing from my lawyer and he'd better get out his checkbook."

"What do you know about Mr. Harrison Blaine?" Simon asked.

"I know that asshole is going to be lighter in the pocketbook. My mother's never mentioned him."

"Ms. Gorman told me that there was another wheelchair behind Mr. Blaine's wheelchair," Philly said. "Do you have any information on that other wheelchair?"

"No."

Philly studied Ruth Foster. Mary Foster would be the client but there was no question that Ruth would run the show. Philly had never minded a strong-willed client. In some respects, a client who took a stance and forthrightly made her views known was preferable to one who couldn't make up her mind. But a strong-willed client who was unreasonable was another story. Carpenter preached the importance of dampening the expectations of a potential client, but Ruth Foster appeared to be a woman on whom that strategy wouldn't work. Philly foresaw Mary Foster's case going to trial because her daughter would never regard any settlement proposal, however reasonable, as sufficient.

"I'm interested in taking your case if you and your mother wish to engage me," Philly said. "I'd be prepared to do so on a one-third contingency fee basis. Your mother would be the client and would be responsible for costs. Our state supreme court has approved the standard form of contingency agreement that I use. Why don't you think it over, talk with your mother, and get back to me?"

Ruth Foster slid a business card across the table to Philly. "E-mail me the agreement you would want my mother to sign."

"Okay," Philly said. "Before we go, I need to say something to you. So far all you've heard is your mother's side of the story. Her side presents a compelling case for recovering a damage award. That said, you can count on there being another side to the story. You need to keep that in mind."

"This is an open and shut case in my opinion," Foster retorted. "But I wouldn't put it past Mason to lie through his teeth."

Philly drove, heading for Malden where she would drop Simon off to catch a bus into Boston. She resented the detour. She didn't mind paying Sarah Ferguson for watching Daisy, but she wanted to minimize the expense. Simon needed to get himself a car. But if she broached the subject, Simon would probably come back that he wasn't earning enough to buy and maintain one. Probably quite true.

Philly remembered that when she was drinking, she had little tolerance for people who irritated her. Having now stopped drinking, she expected that she'd be cutting others some slack. But to her surprise she wasn't. Now she couldn't blame her combativeness on being a bad drunk and had to face the fact that there was a volatile side to her that had nothing to do with liquor.

Philly liked Simon but she'd had it with the unspoken tension around the possibility of his leaving to join a firm. Carpenter would probably opt for not forcing the issue, and Philly understood that she should probably talk with him before giving Simon a nudge. But Mary Foster's case provided a reason to confront Simon and get him to decide what he was going to do. If Simon wasn't going to be around, she needed to get Rachel involved in Foster's case. Assuming she was hired.

"This could be a fun case to try," Philly threw out to gauge Simon's interest level. "Damages are serious and unless there's some surprise we don't know about, liability looks pretty clear. I'm thinking jury trial."

"I agree," Simon said.

"I'm thinking we both try the case, split the witnesses."

Simon was staring out the window, lost in thought. "I guess so," he said halfheartedly.

"You guess so!" Philly took several deep breaths but that didn't help her calm down. "Listen, Simon, if you're not going to be around to work on this case, Carpenter and I need to know now. I think we're going to be hired. This is going to be one of those grinding years where cash flow will be uneven because a lot of the work we're getting involves contingency cases. So, are you in or out?"

Simon didn't rattle easily, but now he blushed and looked away from her.

"I don't know," Simon said, and Philly understood he was genuinely distressed.

"I'm speaking for myself and not for Carpenter," Philly said. "But you're not knowing doesn't cut it for me. Make up your mind. Either you're in or you're out." Simon hung his head. "Trust me, you'll feel a lot better once you make a decision."

"I need to think about it some more."

Philly didn't say anything. Carpenter would be irked that she'd gone off on Simon without consulting him. But the truth was, she was tired of talking with him about Simon.

She glanced at Simon and the young lawyer was plainly downcast. No doubt he disliked being pushed, but she sure as hell felt better having done some pushing.

23

By arriving early at her paralegal job, Rachel had finished work there by eleven and now she paced the lobby of the Mayfair Country Club waiting for Martin Hays to arrive for their one o'clock meeting. She was both nervous and pleased that Philly had assigned her to meet with Hays: nervous because she really didn't know anything about golf and pleased because the task showed that Philly and Carpenter trusted her.

Mounds of dirty gray snow still surrounded the parking lot, but there were patches of brown grass showing on some of the fairways, and the temperature hovered around forty, just warm enough to have seduced Rachel to swap her parka for a lightweight wool coat.

Hays arrived out of breath, apologetic for running late. He was wearing a gray wool sports jacket, gray slacks and a black turtleneck that matched his eye patch. The total effect was appealingly rakish.

"I suppose you want to get a look at the seventh hole," Hays said.

"Actually, I'd like to start by looking at the signup list for the day you were injured."

In short order, Hays had them seated in the office of the club manager who quickly produced the signup sheet for the day of Hays' injury. Hays' foursome was the eighth group to sign up. Their signup time was eight in the morning and it was a half hour later before they teed off. Warren Lord's foursome was the next group to sign up. In addition to Lord, the group included Ryan Cannon, Jake Mobley, and Alan Atkinson.

"Who else in Mr. Lord's group was a club member?" Rachel asked the manager.

"Mr. Atkinson is a member. The other two were guests."

"Do you have any information for the guests other than their names?"

The manager consulted a file folder and extracted two forms. "Our guests complete an identification form."

"I can copy the information," Rachel said, "but it would save time if you'd make copies of these documents for me."

The manager wavered but Hays wasn't interested in delays. "I'm going to get this information eventually, so you might as well make the damn copies."

The man swallowed his discomfort and made the copies.

"Do you know the other member, Atkinson?" Rachel asked Hays.

"Not really. I've seen him around."

Rachel studied the guest sign in forms. Cannon and Mobley each listed his occupation as consultant. Each had the same business address in Atlanta, Georgia. They had included e-mail addresses in their contact information.

"Anything else?" the manager asked.

"I'd like a copy of the club rules," Rachel said, and that sent the manager in search of another file folder.

When Rachel stood next to Hays on the tee of the seventh hole, a cool, stiff breeze met them head on. Rachel pulled her overcoat closed and put on her gloves. Hays, who seemed impervious to the breeze, left his sports coat jacket unbuttoned. The day had suddenly turned blustery and overcast, and no golfers were in evidence.

"Do you see that clump of tall grass?" Hays pointed down the right-hand side of the fairway. "Further off into the rough is approximately where I found my ball. As you can see, I probably wasn't visible from the tee when I found my ball because of the trees. I picked up my ball and walked toward the fairway and I may have even been on the fairway when I was hit."

Rachel followed Hays' pointed direction and thought she had a good idea where he'd been struck. She took out her cell phone and lined up a photograph. With the low, dark cloud cover, a distance shot probably would produce little detail. But she wanted a record of the scene.

"How far do you think it is from here to where you were hit?" Rachel asked.

Hays took his time assessing the distance. "I'd guess about a hundred and eighty yards give or take."

"You said that this hole is the longest hole on the course. Does that mean someone teeing off would use a driver?"

"Yeah," Hays said nodding. "If you didn't use a driver, you really wouldn't have a chance to make par. I used a driver, but I totally mishit the ball."

"Wouldn't most drives be longer than one hundred eighty yards?"

"Generally, yes," Hays said. "But for older players or inexperienced players that might not be so."

"Was Lord an experienced player?"

"I couldn't tell you. As a club member, he probably was. Someone wouldn't join the club unless he was an avid golfer and had played the game for a while."

Rachel was tempted to walk off the distance from the tee to where Hays had been felled, but she opted to remain in place. The wind had picked up and she was already cold. From the tee to where Hays had been hit, the fairway was wide and straight. The fairway didn't begin to curve until a cluster of trees now just beginning to bud which Rachel guessed were about seventy yards beyond where Hays was struck. She pictured Hays wearing a bright yellow shell. He'd be hard to miss on a clear day.

24

A Hockey Fan

Simon had arranged for a meeting with a potential new client, but he had also requested a pre-meeting to "clear the air" as he had put it. Philly had filled Carpenter in on her previous talk with Simon. He had given her his baleful look but otherwise was remarkably restrained. He had just nodded when Philly said that Simon needed to be pushed.

In the conference room Simon slid into the chair at the head of the table appearing at ease. "I want to get something off my chest," Simon began. "I haven't been fair with you by telling you I've been thinking of leaving. I'm not leaving for the short term if you'll continue to put up with me. I won't bring up any career move for the rest of this year."

Carpenter grunted and Philly judged he was content to accept Simon's statement and move on. She was having none of that.

"What made you decide that?" Philly asked.

"It was this case we're going to hear about shortly," Simon said. "The firm I was considering couldn't take the case because of a conflict of interest. I took that to be a sign."

Philly took in this intelligence with a nagging misgiving. Simon probably would have jumped ship if there had been no conflict of interest. Which meant that his heart might not be in continuing to practice with them.

"This is not going to work if you've got underlying misgivings or are unhappy," Philly said. "We need you to be fully on board."

"I am fully on board. Do I have misgivings? Yes. It's not ideal. I'll still have to wait tables which bothers me. But I'm in."

Carpenter nodded curtly. Philly accepted the gesture as a directive to back off. "Okay," she said. "Welcome back. What's with the new case?"

"Have you ever heard of the Salem Stampede?"

Philly had never heard of the name. When Carpenter nodded, she figured it had something to do with sports.

"It's the minor league hockey team that plays out of Salem," Carpenter said.

"Right. At a home game three weeks ago, a fan fell on top of Martina Glass and broke her collarbone. Martina wants to sue. She's a friend of my parents. They suggested she call me."

"What do you mean fell on her?" Philly asked. She pictured a soused guy staggering back to his seat, clutching a beer in each hand and losing his balance.

"The guy tumbled over a railing and fell. Martina was sitting below. It was something like an eight-foot fall."

"Ouch!" Philly exclaimed.

"Martina is about a hundred pounds soaking wet. The guy who landed on her weighed about two twenty."

"How's she doing?" Carpenter asked.

"She's back home and angry. She's looking at some serious rehabilitation."

"That's how we want our prospective plaintiff clients," Carpenter said. "Pissed off and in for more misery."

Martina Glass' left arm was in a sling. Her broken collar bone had been set and the sling was part of a corset-like arrangement that kept her left arm snug against her body. Her ski parka draped over the injured limb. The friend who had driven her into Boston, Cecelia Brown, helped Glass free herself from her parka and then each took a seat at the conference room table. They were a mismatched pair, Philly thought—Glass as thin and wiry and cranky as Simon had described, Brown taller, broader, and seemingly more mild mannered than her friend. Philly figured the women to be in their fifties.

"Why don't you start at the beginning," Simon requested after introductions had been made.

"I'm a hockey nut," Martina launched her tale. "Sam—that's my husband—Sam and I try to take in the Stampede's home games. There are these seats we like and we try to get them. They're in the second tier of seats, slightly off center of the faceoff circle in the center of the ice. There's a tier above us. The night in question it's the third period and the Stampede is up a goal. There are these guys sitting above us who have been screaming their brains out all game, cussing out the other team, sounding like they'd had more than a few. They were annoying, but Sam and I had experienced worse."

Philly had heard stories of hockey fans being a boisterous, hard-drinking bunch. Martina Glass didn't seem to fit that type. Maybe she had a mouth on her.

"Out of the blue I hear one of the guys say, 'Watch it Dunnster,' and then I hear, 'Holy shit!' and this son of a bitch has fallen on me. I felt something snap in my shoulder. Sam was telling me later that it was a miracle the guy missed him."

Simon had brought in the potential case and Carpenter had been clear that he was to run this meeting. But Simon seemed uncertain how to proceed. "What's the drinking policy at these games?" Philly asked, opting to bail Simon out in case he needed help.

"They stop selling beer five minutes into the third period," Glass explained. "So what happens is, a lot of people buy a couple right after the third period starts."

"Did you get a look at the guys above you during the game?" Carpenter asked.

"There was one time I turned around and looked up. There were three of them, young burly guys in their twenties. Two of them were wearing Bruins jerseys."

"Did you see them drinking?" Carpenter followed up.

"I don't really remember," Glass said.

"What's the security like?" Simon asked.

"There are guys in uniform who patrol the stands. There's a toll-free number you can call if you see somebody getting out of hand or if another fan bothers you."

"Have you ever used that number?" Simon pursued.

"No. Sam and I mind our own business and try to keep a low profile. You're always going to run into an asshole or two at one of these games."

"Has anyone from the hockey team contacted you?" Philly asked.

"No."

Philly jotted down a list of potential defendants: the arena owner, the hockey team, the beer vendor, the guy who fell on Glass. "Do you know anything about the guy who fell on you?"

"His name is Fred Dunn," Glass replied. "The fucking asshole wasn't hurt at all."

Well, thought Philly, she was right about the mouth. She was curious. "How did you find out the guy's name?"

"A police officer interviewed me in the hospital. She gave me the guy's name."

Philly doubted criminal charges would be brought against Dunn, but stranger things had happened.

"We're interested in your case," Simon said. "We'd be willing to handle your representation on a contingency basis, but you do have the option of paying hourly rates."

Glass regarded Simon evenly, seemed to be sizing him up, probably wondering whether slight, spare Simon could hold his own with lawyers twice his size. Also, Philly figured that Glass was weighing the fact that she knew Simon's parents. Glass and Cecelia Brown exchanged whispered confidences.

"Your mother says you're a good lawyer," Glass observed.

"She's prejudiced," Simon replied with a smile.

"I'm going with mother knows best," Glass said. "I'd like to do that contingency thing you mentioned. Sam and I are not exactly rolling in it."

Inwardly, Carpenter sighed.

25

Daisy was in her highchair, banging a rattle on the tray, watching the food she, Paul, Raul, and Isabella were shoveling into their mouths. The kid loved putting stuff into her mouth, anything really, ranging from baby books to dust bunnies. Philly remembered the time she had dipped a finger into a pool of mustard and offered Daisy a lick. Daisy's features had scrunched up so tight

Philly had wondered whether they would ever return to normal. When her features relaxed, Daisy had opened her mouth and stuck out her tongue and then accepted another lick.

"I went to see that house you were talking about," Isabella filled a lull in the adult talk. "I went back later with Raul much against his will."

Paul stopped eating. Raul lowered his head and stared at his food. Isabella resumed eating, calmly scraping the skin off the fish that Raul had cooked, leaving her observation hanging in the air. Philly thought Isabella looked good. She hadn't stopped working but that time was coming. Her housemate's pregnancy seemed to have escalated in a rush. Isabella was now big, and the stairs were a challenge. Philly had again offered to switch rooms, but Isabella had said no.

"What's the house like?" Paul asked.

"It's nice," Isabella replied.

Raul looked like he had a different opinion of the dwelling. Philly suspected that if the two deadlocked, Isabella would be the one who got her way.

"Nice?" Paul repeated.

Isabella nodded. Her face was fuller. Philly couldn't predict whether she would be one of those women who quickly returned to pre-pregnancy size following delivery or carried some of the weight forever. After Daisy was born, it had taken a while to shed pounds but even now, when Philly looked at herself in a full-length mirror, she knew that she'd never again return to her former shape.

"Can you be a little more descriptive?" Paul said.

"Philly is right. There is more room and more privacy. If Sarah went in with us, that would offset the loss of rent from tenants. I'm prepared to consider a move."

Raul flushed. "We need to wait until after the baby is born."

"I'm willing to consider a move before the baby is born." Isabella grinned. "If we were to move before the baby was born, I wouldn't have to do any of the moving."

Isabella was plainly joking but Raul's expression was not amused.

"Let me ask you something, Raul," Philly intervened. "Which house would you rather be living in? Forget the hassle of moving. Which house do you prefer?"

Raul continued to color. "There is the cost to consider."

"Humor me," Philly entreated. "Forget the cost and moving. Which house do you like better?"

Raul sighed and Philly had her answer. She remembered that when she and Raul were a couple, Raul was the adventurous one, she the stick in the mud. When they were a couple, Raul acted as if he had nothing to lose. Now he seemed to be running not quite scared, but cautiously. In the presence of Isabella and Paul, it wouldn't be fair to Raul to point out his changed approach.

"Do you remember when you convinced me to buy this house with you?" Philly directed at Raul. "I'm glad you did. I couldn't ask for better housemates than you and Isabella."

Raul offered a weak smile. "You are trying to butter me up."

"Is it working?" Philly asked as Daisy hurled her rattle onto the table.

26

Carpenter had filled Philly in on what Weiskoff had to say about her court appointed case. Philly was working from home and they had activated Skype. Daisy sat in her lap, working the handle of a rattle in and out of her mouth. The baby's blue eyes showed intelligence, alertness. They were Philip Sizemore's eyes, Carpenter reflected, not for the first time.

"I suppose Weiskoff is right," Philly said morosely. "I had pretty much come up with most of what he said."

Weiskoff had stated the obvious that the incident in third grade between Danny Graham and Marilyn Storm should be a key focus of Heather Storm's case. Weiskoff's further advice had not been obvious. He recommended that James Farrell be convinced to change his position and oppose the motion of the Department of Children and Family Services that Marilyn be adopted without her parents' consent. Weiskoff further urged that Heather Storm and James Farrell aggressively seek their daughter's return now. Weiskoff's theory was that Marilyn had accused her father of molestation in order to escape from the school where she had experienced unhappiness. He felt that a united front by Marilyn's parents would help keep the focus on what happened between the two children.

"Are you going to do what Weiskoff recommended?" Carpenter asked. "I'm asking because you don't seem upbeat about this case or what he had to say."

Philly idly stroked Daisy's hair. Her daughter gurgled as she continued to mouth her rattle.

"Probably," Philly said. "I'll talk to my client and then have Rachel deal with James Farrell's lawyer."

"But something's bugging you about it?"

"Two things. First, the molestation charge. That's a hell of a thing for a kid to make up about her father."

"Maybe the daughter was feeling desperate."

"Yeah, but . . . Jesus, that's a pretty vicious accusation. I can't picture a little girl coming up with something like that unless it happened. And if it did happen, I don't like the idea of Farrell even sharing custody."

"What's the second thing?"

"I'm feeling bad for this little boy, Danny Graham, and for the daughter, Marilyn. They're going to be dragged through something very unpleasant."

In Philly's position, Carpenter didn't think he'd be experiencing her misgivings. "There's no getting around putting the kids through something unpleasant. Just do what's best for your client. Everything Weiskoff said to do will help your client get what she wants."

"You're right, I get it," Philly said. "Let's change the subject. You remember the Michael Waters case? The one about a girl writing a short story and then accusing her teacher of coming on to her? Well, James Madison High School is going to hold an investigatory hearing in the case. We just got a letter letting us know. Waters is not a happy camper and I can't say I blame him."

"Waters has a strong case."

"I know. But he's being dragged through a messy ordeal and you never know what may emerge at an investigatory hearing."

Carpenter offered no response. That life wasn't fair was an axiom he lived by.

"And by the way," Philly said. "I'm thinking of buying another house with Raul and Isabella. We need a bigger place. Both Paul and the babysitter I've been using would go in on the deal."

Carpenter laughed. "You really make an effort not to get stuck in a rut."

"I want it all," Philly said as Daisy waved her drool-soaked rattle in Carpenter's direction.

Rachel's Internet research on Warren Lord's golfing foursome revealed that Lord and Alan Atkinson were in real estate. They sought out buyers to purchase business properties. If a buyer syndicate purchased a property, Lord and Atkinson would get a percentage of the purchase price as a finders' fee. The buyer syndicate would own and manage the purchased property, and then, if things went well, sell the improved property for a profit. It seemed that Lord and Atkinson never put up any of their own money in these deals. Rather, the two acted like business brokers. Rachel figured that they had an impressive track record if investors trusted their judgment by throwing considerable dollars in the direction of projects they were touting. She wondered how Lord and Atkinson had survived the 2008 real estate collapse and general economic downturn.

The other members of the foursome, Ryan Cannon and Jake Mobley, were associated with a private investment fund based in Atlanta, Georgia. Rachel inferred that Lord and Atkinson had arranged the golfing date at Mayfair Country Club as part of a sales pitch to the two Georgians.

It wasn't clear whether Rachel's Internet research helped Martin Hays' case. Lord was certain to testify that his tee shot on the seventh hole was a poor shot that got away from him. He might even claim that he lost sight of the ball and didn't see it heading for Hays. Lord might claim that Hays' foursome had moved on down the fairway out of range of the seventh tee.

Rachel doodled on her notepad and then began to make a list.

1. *What club did Lord use to hit his drive?*
2. *What did each person in Lord's foursome observe in connection with Lord's drive?*
3. *Did anyone in Hays' foursome look back and observe Lord's drive?*
4. *Which member of Lord's foursome shouted out about the other foursome's slow play?*
5. *Would there be a need to take depositions in Georgia?*
6. *If Hays and his foursome saw nothing, did that mean Hays would have to deal with four people claiming the errant golf shot was an accident?*
7. *Was Hay's wearing a yellow shell and the failure of Lord's foursome to shout fore enough to prevent Hays' suit from being dismissed?*

Rachel couldn't even hazard a guess about what a judge would do if faced with a motion to dismiss Hays' case. Carpenter had probably correctly assessed Hays' case as less than a fifty-fifty proposition. If only they had one more fact to buttress Hays' claim! For the moment that illusive, extra fact was nowhere in sight.

Simon made it a point to arrive at the Maple Leaf Assisted Living Center before the noon meal. The snow that had been piled up in the parking lot when they last visited had been replaced by large puddles of slush, and Simon's shoes were soaked. Wet feet in March were a fact of life in the Boston area.

Philly was right about security being nonexistent. No one stopped him in the entryway, and he made a beeline for the library where the sole occupant was an elderly woman with long, straight, white hair combed back over her head. The woman was seated at the reading table in the center of the room. She looked up from her book when Simon entered, nodded his way, and then resumed reading.

Simon now wished that he had a game plan besides wanting to observe the noontime rush to the dining room. Perhaps in advance of coming to the Center he should have inquired as to Mary Foster's friends.

Simon sat across from the woman and checked his watch. A little after eleven o'clock. He understood that the dining room doors opened at eleven thirty leaving him with time to kill. He began idly scanning the titles of shelved books before becoming conscious of the woman's eyes upon him.

"You look lost," the woman said.

"That's my usual condition," Simon said, and that drew a smile from the woman.

"I haven't seen you around here," the woman observed.

"I'm just checking things out. This place is probably not for me. I'm looking for a slightly older crowd."

The woman laughed in earnest. "What are you really doing here?"

Simon studied his questioner. The woman was thin and wiry and alert looking. He glanced at the book she was reading: *The Accidental Tourist* by Anne Tyler. "I'm a lawyer," Simon said, and he proceeded to tell her exactly why he was at the Center.

"Loretta Frank," the woman introduced herself when Simon concluded his account. She offered her hand and Simon was surprised by the firmness of the grip of her bony fingers.

"I know Mary Foster by sight, but I don't know her well enough to say hello. The truth is I'm pretty much of a loner. I haven't made a lot of friends here."

"So what are *you* doing here?" Simon asked, deciding to turn Frank's question back at her.

Frank straightened in her chair. "I'm eighty-four years old. I know I don't look it," she added, smiling. "I never married but that didn't stop me from having and raising two children. They live out-of-state and they've been worried about me living alone. They've been urging me for years to move into a place like this and finally I agreed."

"What tipped the scales?"

"A number of things," Frank said with a sigh. "I hate to cook and having meals prepared for me is a big plus. Also, I'd become somewhat of a menace driving and this place has a van that can get me to where I want to go or to a connection I can use. That's another thing I don't have to worry about here."

Simon remembered his first visit to the Center and being depressed by the infirmities much in evidence. "Are you happy here?"

Frank laughed. "Let's not go overboard. Let's just say the tradeoffs that come with living here are acceptable to me for the moment. I can always change my mind and leave."

"I was hoping to get a look at Harrison Blaine," Simon said.

"I can help you with that," Frank looked at her watch. "We might want to leave now."

"Do you know him?"

"I don't know him know him, but everyone knows who he is. The man is a menace. He and his sidekick, Harry Fried, are insufferable."

"What's their problem?"

"You'll see for yourself," Frank said, moving sprightly to her feet. "They start in the C wing and head for the dining room."

"Are you saying they're still racing?"

"They're not supposed to. Someone from housekeeping is supposed to keep an eye on things but, as far as I can tell, the person is seldom there. Let's just say if there's no one from the Center around to observe, they tend to pick up speed."

Which was exactly what Simon saw.

April

Philly's Untitled Playlist

Little Lion Man

Mumford & Sons

27

Gerald Hatch was pushing the stroller. Daisy sat quietly, taking in the surroundings. The early April evening was decidedly chilly, and Philly had stuffed her daughter into her winter snowsuit to ward off the cold. Daisy's white sneakers protruded from the snowsuit. The sun had gone done but sunlight still lingered, casting the streets in a soft, burnt orange light. They were retracing the route they had typically taken during the previous summer and fall, a rectangular course that led past Sarah Ferguson's house. In another month, Sarah would likely be perched on her front steps. Being in motion reminded Philly that she was still pathetically out of shape. But walking brought her into a rhythm that cleared her head.

"What are your plans for the summer?" she asked.

"I need to find a job. My parents are paying my college tuition, but I want to contribute to my living expenses."

That scenario hadn't seemed likely when Philly had first met Gerald, a sulky, hostile boy who had beaten up a high school classmate. She had not only resolved his case but had also discovered in the boy an eagerness for new experiences. Raul and Isabella had improved his Spanish (at that time it was the only class he cared about) and Daisy had unbuttoned a tender side that no one, not even his parents, had suspected.

Gerald would be attending UMass-Amherst in the fall. Philly had written him a heartfelt letter of recommendation and had made suggestions for his college essay. "I'm really proud of you, Gerald."

"Thanks. I really think I'm going to get the Spanish award at the end of the year. I've been dreaming in Spanish. I'm fluent."

"Maybe you'll get to spend a semester in Spain. I'm sure UMass has a study abroad program."

"There's no maybe about it," Gerald said. "Junior year I'm going. I can't wait. My mom and dad are all for it."

They walked for a time in silence. The only sounds were Daisy's occasional jabbering and the wheels of the stroller grinding over the rough sidewalk. Philly found thoughts of work intruding on this end-of-day respite. She remembered Carpenter telling her that when he walked with Maxine, his thoughts gravitated to cases he was working on.

"Let me ask you something," Philly said, and in broad terms she filled Gerald in on Michael Waters' case. "What do you make of that?"

Gerald's expression grew serious. Philly remembered the first time she had asked his advice and how thrilled he had been to be consulted.

"I'd say the girl is in trouble," Gerald finally said. "It seems to me that she's alone and lonely. And whatever she does, she's digging herself in deeper. She made this very serious charge and now she's involved in a hearing. I think the idea of having to go through with the hearing would freak her out. I know the feeling."

Philly considered Gerald's observations seriously because he was close to Caroline Fine in age. She liked to think that she easily could slip into the mindset of a teen and had to continually remind herself that at well past thirty, she was nearly twice Carolyn Fine's age. Probably ancient, to Gerald.

"When I was going through that case last year," Gerald resumed, "there were a lot of times when I was close to losing it. It was a lot of pressure. I think if I'd had some other lawyer, I might not have made it through. You and Daisy helped me get through that mess."

"*You* had a lot to do with putting that case behind you," Philly said. "Don't ever forget that."

They turned the last corner and were now headed to the house. Philly signaled Gerald to stop and she unloaded Daisy from the stroller. "Watch this. It's her new trick."

Philly set Daisy down; her daughter grasped the side of the stroller and began to inch forward. Daisy looked up at Gerald with a goopy grin, and Gerald clapped in appreciation.

"Aren't you a big girl," Gerald said with admiration.

Philly thought of another big girl—Carolyn Fine. If Gerald was right, Fine was a disaster waiting to happen.

Dr. Specter wanted Carpenter to exercise and Maxine was doing the doctor's bidding. They were walking along Massachusetts Avenue toward Cambridge at a brisk pace, Maxine ensconced in her winter parka, the hood up. There was a chill in the air, but Carpenter considered the temperature mild at fifty degrees. It was past the dinner hour and there was a fair amount of foot traffic. Carpenter realized that he was breathing easily, not struggling to keep pace with Maxine. That had to be Camellia Kim's doing. When he finished his weight training exercises with her, she refused to abandon him until he had parked his ass on a spinning or exercise bike or had started in on an elliptical machine.

"Admit it, getting out like this is fun," Maxine said.

"Speak for yourself," Carpenter said without much conviction. He didn't have it in him to drift into a cantankerous mood he didn't feel.

"I'm starting to think that your weight loss has nothing to do with your CLL. I think it has to do with exercise."

Carpenter offered up a noncommittal grunt. He disagreed with Maxine on this point but didn't want to disabuse her. The weight loss had started before he'd begun to exercise. Even now, at most mealtimes, he wasn't hungry though he'd pretend to an appetite if Maxine was present. Night sweats had become less frequent, but they were still present. Fred was not about to go peacefully into the night.

"I've come to a decision," Maxine said, and Carpenter didn't like the sound of that. Decisions meant change and for the moment, he wanted the status quo.

"I'm pretty sure I'm going to retire after this school year is over. I may do some consulting but if that doesn't work out, I won't be disappointed."

Maxine had talked about retiring a while back, but she hadn't brought up the subject recently. Carpenter didn't want to show his surprise. "That's a big step," he said neutrally. "Will you be taking social security early?"

"That's my thinking. I don't see why not."

Carpenter thought of his life with Maxine around more. It had been something he'd been looking forward to back when they had discussed living together. Would it make a difference if Maxine wasn't working?

"If I'm not working, there'd be nothing to tie me to the South Shore. I could move up here."

So, not just change; big change. Carpenter thought of Philly buying a new house. Philly certainly wasn't afraid to break up her settled routine. Maybe that had to do with her being young. Had he become a stick-in-the-mud old fogey without realizing it?

"Say something," Maxine entreated.

"We could get someplace nice," Carpenter said. Living 24/7 amidst Maxine's nice furnishings would take some getting used to.

"You don't sound enthusiastic. I thought this was something you wanted."

Carpenter chose his next words carefully. He was fully capable of blowing the best thing that had happened to him in recent years. "I told you before I wanted this," he said. "But you know me. I have to get used to a new idea even if it's something I came up with."

"So get used to it."

"I will."

28

Philly now had her first look at Caroline Fine. The girl was seated between her parents in chairs placed to the right of the principal's desk. The teen was plain looking: round face, brown eyes, light brown straight hair, medium height. She was wearing brown pants with a white blouse. Sitting beside her fidgeting parents, Fine stared straight-ahead, her posture rigid, her affect stoic.

Fine's parents were short, spare, and appeared frightened. Philly had suspected that the Fine family would have a lawyer present but that wasn't the case.

Philly glanced at Michael Waters, who was regarding Caroline Fine with a neutral expression; if he harbored resentment toward the girl, he was hiding it well. Philly and Waters and Rachel had taken chairs to the left of Principal Lacey's desk. Wayne Gordon, the teachers' union representative, sat behind them. Suzanne Lacey sat behind her desk with Vice-Principal John Frye beside her. There was a tape recorder on Lacey's desk.

"Let's begin," Lacey said. "I've just turned on a tape recorder so that we have a record of today's proceeding. This is an investigatory hearing. The hearing is somewhat formal and somewhat informal. Caroline Fine has made a sexual harassment charge against Michael Waters and that will be our focus today. We're not going to swear in witnesses. We will first hear from Ms. Fine. Then Mr. Waters or his representatives may ask her questions. If either Mr. Frye or I have any questions, we will ask them. We will then repeat the process with Mr. Waters. Any questions?"

"The teachers' union objects to this entire proceeding," Wayne Gordon said forcefully. "This kind of proceeding isn't a part of the teachers' contract. This is a farce."

"Thank you, Mr. Gordon," Lacey said with an indulgent smile. "The union's position is now a matter of record. Caroline, would you please tell us the nature of your complaint against Mr. Waters."

Caroline didn't respond immediately. When her mother gave her a gentle nudge, she seemed to emerge from a trance. Her account contained no surprises. In short, clipped sentences she recounted her meeting with Waters to discuss her short story. She claimed that Waters threatened to report her as a suicide risk if she didn't agree to have sex with him.

Lacey nodded in Waters' direction and Philly asked her first question.

"Prior to your discussion with Mr. Waters about your short story, *Dead End*, had Mr. Waters ever harassed you in any way?"

Caroline Fine shook her head.

"You need to speak your answer so the tape recorder can pick it up," Philly reminded the girl.

"No."

"Have you ever contemplated suicide?"

Fine again shook her head as her parents blanched. "No," she said, seemingly unperturbed by the pointed question.

"Were you depressed or unhappy around the time you discussed *Dead End* with Mr. Waters?"

"Not particularly."

"Not particularly," Philly repeated. "What do you mean by not particularly?"

"I can't think of anything in particular I was sad or depressed about."

"Were you sad or depressed about your life?" Philly asked.

"Not particularly."

"Were you happy at the time you discussed your short story with Mr. Waters?"

"I'd say I was reasonably happy."

"Who is Ronald Peterson?"

Fine's stoic demeanor disappeared for a brief moment. Emotion—possibly anger—flashed in the girl's eyes.

"He's a boy in my class."

"Did you either date or see Ronald Peterson socially?"

"We went out a few times."

"Did he break off your seeing each other?"

Fine shifted in her chair. Philly suspected she was debating whether to lie.

"Yeah."

"Was the Richard Parks character in *Dead End* based in any way on Ronald Peterson?"

Fine shrugged. "That's possible."

"I didn't ask you whether it was possible. I asked you whether the Parks character in your story was based on Ronald Peterson. Yes, or no?"

"I think Ms. Fine has answered your question?" John Frye intervened.

"You can think what you want," Philly countered, having previously resolved to fight Frye at every turn. "Answer my question," she demanded of Fine. "Was the Parks character in your story based on Ronald Peterson?"

"Probably to some degree."

"Were you upset when Peterson broke things off with you?"

"Not particularly."

"Not particularly," Philly repeated, favoring Fine with her hard stare. "Would you have preferred that he continued to see you?"

"Since he broke things off, I don't think it would have been a good idea for us to have kept seeing each other. I mean, if that's how he felt, what would have been the point?"

"Have you had a boyfriend during high school?"

"Not really."

"Before seeing Ronald Peterson socially, had you ever gone out on a date before?"

Fine lowered her eyes. "No."

"Have you ever taken Phenobarbital?"

Fine's mother winced at the question. Her hand went to cover her mouth.

"No."

"Does anyone in your family take that medication?"

Fine seemed about to reply but stopped herself. "You'd have to ask my family," she finally said.

"I'm asking you," Philly snapped. "Answer my question."

"I fail to see the relevance of this line of questioning," Frye interjected.

"You're not a lawyer," Philly said, "so it's to be expected you would have no understanding of relevance." She heard Wayne Gordon snicker behind her. "I'll repeat my question. Does anyone in your family use Phenobarbital? Your mother for example?"

"I think she uses something. I'm not sure what it is."

Fine's mother had turned scarlet. Her father appeared to be in a daze.

"Was the Marshall Watts character in your short story modeled on Mr. Waters?"

Again Philly couldn't assess whether it was anger that flashed in Fine's eyes. Might Fine be dangerous, not someone at risk as Gerald Hatch had theorized?

"That's possible."

"I didn't ask you whether it was possible. I asked you if it were the case."

"I suppose to some degree."

"The Watts character and Mr. Waters are both English teachers, correct?"

"Yes."

"They're similar in physical appearance, aren't they?"

Fine paused. "I think so. I don't really remember. I haven't looked at the story in a while."

"Is the Carlotta Finch character in your story modeled on you?"

Fine again paused, longer this time. "I suppose parts of me might be reflected in the character."

"What parts?"

"Like we're both in the same year in high school."

"Also, you were both dropped by boys with the same initials, correct?"

"That's a coincidence."

"You were both taught by an English teacher with the same initials, correct?"

"That's another coincidence."

"Is it simply another coincidence that your fictional character and you have mothers using a barbiturate?"

"Yeah, that's another coincidence."

"Did you apply to Princeton University?"

"Yeah."

"Do you want to be accepted and attend that school?"

"Sure. Who wouldn't?"

"Perhaps you wouldn't. Do you have the same concerns about attending Princeton that your fictional character, Carlotta Finch had?"

"Not really."

"Isn't it true that you have made up your sexual harassment claim to get back at Mr. Waters for reporting you as being at risk of harming yourself?"

"No, that's not true."

Now Philly paused. Fine's denial had been immediate but had lacked force.

"Have you ever been under psychiatric care?"

"I think you've gone too far," Frye said.

"Hardly," Philly snapped. "I'm just getting warmed up," she lied. She was pretty much at the end of her questions. "Answer my question. Have you ever been under psychiatric care?"

"No."

"Did anyone ever suggest that you receive psychiatric care?"

Fine shot a fleeting glance at her mother. "No."

"Did your mother ever suggest that you see a psychiatrist or psychologist?"

Fine stared straight ahead while her mother shifted in her seat. "Not that I remember."

"Do you have any romantic feelings for Mr. Waters?"

This time Fine's anger was visible as she glared at Philly. "You've got to be kidding."

"Answer my question."

"No."

"You didn't report Mr. Waters the day you claim he proposed having sex with you, did you?"

Fine slumped in her chair. "No, it was after the weekend."

"Isn't it true you first accused Mr. Waters of proposing to have sex with you *after* Principal Lacey informed you that Mr. Waters had reported to her that he was concerned you were a danger to yourself?"

Fine sat up straighter and took a deep breath. "That's right. I brought it up after Ms. Lacey told me Mr. Waters had reported me. I was going to see her about what he had said, but I just hadn't gotten around to it."

"Isn't it true that you made up Mr. Waters proposing to have sex with you because you were angry with him for reporting that you were a risk to yourself?"

"No."

"Then explain again why you didn't immediately report Mr. Waters upon leaving his classroom following the discussion of your story."

"I just didn't get around to it. I was probably in some kind of shock over what he said."

"Shock?" Philly repeated. "Did you complain about Mr. Waters to your parents on the evening of the day you discussed your story with Mr. Waters?"

Fine regarded her parents for a brief moment. "I don't think so."

"Do you agree that Mr. Waters was correct to report you as a risk to yourself?"

"No."

"Why not?"

"I had written a made-up story," Fine said. "He was always telling us to use our imagination. I made up a story the way he told us to."

"Didn't Mr. Waters also tell you to write about what you knew?"

"Yeah."

"Isn't it true that you wrote about yourself in *Dead End* because Carlotta Finch was you?"

"Not really."

"At the end of *Dead End* did Carlotta Finch kill herself?"

"That wasn't revealed in the story."

"But Carlotta did try to take her own life, didn't she?"

"Yes."

"That *was* revealed in the story, correct?"

"I just said it was."

"Did you write an essay as part of your application to Princeton?"

"Yes."

"What was the subject of the essay?"

"My mother."

"Your mother. The same subject as Carlotta Finch's essay in your story, correct?"

"Yes."

"Did you write about your mother in your essay as a person you looked up to?"

"Yes."

"Do you look up to your mother?"

"I wouldn't have said that in my essay if I didn't."

Philly paused and took her time regarding Fine. The teen had parried many of the rough questions thrown at her. Philly couldn't decide whether Fine possessed some inner strength or was teetering on an edge where there was nothing but misery below her. She decided to change tone.

"Was Carlotta Finch, the protagonist in your story, happy?"

"If you read the story, you'd know the answer to that."

"I'm asking you, though, Ms. Fine," Philly said in a soft voice.

"No, she wasn't happy."

Philly let the silence lengthen. "How can your parents and your school help you with your own unhappiness?"

"Who said I'm unhappy?" Fine challenged.

"You did," Philly said simply. "You wrote all about your unhappiness. As you're well aware, that's really why we're here."

Philly noticed Lacey regarding Fine with a troubled look. Frye appeared loaded for bear.

"Did you make up what Mr. Waters said to you about having sex?" Frye asked.

"No."

"What possible reason would you have to make up such a thing?" Frye continued.

"None. I wouldn't make something like that up."

"Do you identify with the Carlotta Finch character in your story?"

Fine shook her head. "Not really."

Frye glanced in her direction and Philly wanted to smack the smirk off his face.

"I don't have anything else to ask Ms. Fine," Frye concluded.

"In that case," Lacey said, "we'll hear your version of events Mr. Waters."

Michael Waters' account of his meeting with Caroline Fine was consistent with the recital he had provided at his previous meeting with Lacey and Frye. He addressed his remarks to the educators but occasionally paused to regard his accuser.

"Ms. Fine, do you have any questions for Mr. Waters?" Lacey said.

"No."

"I do," her father spoke up. Philly hadn't imagined him uttering a word at this hearing.

"Why would you ask my daughter to have sex with you?" Mr. Fine said in a tortured voice.

"You need to understand something," Waters replied calmly. "I never asked your daughter to have sex with me. Ever. Your daughter is troubled. She's very unhappy. You and your wife need to take action to protect her."

"Why would she make up something like that?" Mr. Fine questioned, appearing genuinely at a loss as to his daughter's motivation.

"I can't answer you definitively," Waters said. "But I think her story was a cry for help. I heard her cry and reported my concerns about her to Ms. Lacey. I had a duty to do that. Ms. Lacey said that I did the right thing in reporting my concerns to her. And at some level, I think that's what Caroline wanted. But also, I think that when your daughter found out that I reported she was a danger to herself, she felt I had betrayed her in some way. I think she was angry at me for having shared the information, and angry with herself for writing the story so frankly. So she made up a story to get back at me, to hurt me. I'm trying to get across to you that your daughter needs help."

Mr. Fine didn't say anything. Philly thought he had run out of steam and Lacey apparently reached the same conclusion. "I have no questions for Mr. Waters," the principal said.

"I do," Frye announced. "Do you have any training as a psychologist, Mr. Waters?"

"No formal training."

"Then you're in no position to analyze Ms. Fine's mental state, are you?"

Philly had told Waters to count to ten if a question made him angry and he appeared to be going through that exercise before responding to Frye's question.

"I disagree with you, Mr. Frye. I've been teaching well over a decade. I have observed teenagers lying, making up stories, being petty and vindictive, and also showing incredible compassion. Mr. Fine asked me a question and based on my experience I answered it. I would keep a close eye on Caroline so she doesn't do something horrible that we'll all regret."

Caroline regarded Waters without expression.

"You're full of fine speeches, aren't you?" Frye challenged.

"Thank you," Waters said. "I agree that I've expressed myself well."

A smile played briefly on Lacey's lips, but the principal recovered her serious demeanor in short order.

"In the last ten years, have you ever dated a woman under twenty?" Frye asked.

"No."

"What about you, Frye?" Wayne Gordon called out. "Do you fancy teenagers?"

"That'll be enough Mr. Gordon," Lacey admonished.

"No, it's not enough. You're the goddamn principal," Gordon thundered. "How the hell can you sit there and let this jerk ask about who Mr. Waters dates?"

"You're out of order," Lacey raised her voice. "John," she said to Frye. "I think we've heard enough."

For a moment Frye seemed poised to continue with his questions. Then he nodded at Lacey.

"I want to thank everyone for coming and providing information to us," Lacey said. "We'll be conferring and advising as to next steps. We're adjourned."

After they left the office, Waters led them to a vacant science classroom and Rachel studied the posters mounted on the walls. Not much had changed since she had been in high school. She took in the periodic table, evolution timelines, and cutaway depictions of chromosomes. She had never gravitated to science, feeling more at home with words. An outburst from Wayne Gordon brought her back to the present.

"I swear to God I'm going to file a grievance against Frye. What a fucking asshole!"

"Don't do anything," Waters entreated. "Let's see what happens next. I'm hoping that Lacey puts a stop to this."

"If she had any balls, we wouldn't have had to go through the farce we just took part in. I don't trust her. You're making a mistake if you think she's going to do the right thing because it's the right thing."

Waters shrugged. Rachel thought he had acquitted himself well. He'd kept his cool and answered every question put to him. Still, it was a he-said, she-said case so no one could be sure what had transpired.

"Is this case now common knowledge at the high school?" Philly asked.

"You asked this before," Waters said. "I don't think anything's changed."

"Teachers know about it," Gordon said, glancing briefly in Waters' direction. "I think the students are in the dark, but I can't be sure. Rumors have a way of getting started."

"You did a good job today," Philly said to Waters. "Continue to go about your business in a professional way. And by the way," she continued, turning to Gordon. "Keep what happened today to yourself. I don't want students getting wind of anything so the less said the better. If a teacher asks you about what happened don't say anything."

"Michael's got no reason to be concerned if word gets out," Gordon said, somewhat defensively.

"I'm not worried about Michael. If this reaches the student body, I'd be worried about Fine."

Rachel wondered if she had misread Fine. The teen had shown some spunk at the hearing, didn't appear to be in despair although at times she seemed distant. If Fine was a suicide risk, wouldn't Marilyn Storm be one as well?

29

Philly was working from home. She closed the door to her second-floor office so she wouldn't be distracted by Daisy's squeals. Her daughter was now an expert crawler in the more traditional mode. She could even crawl upstairs and—alarmingly—downstairs, if she wasn't watched carefully. So Sarah Ferguson had upgraded the baby proofing so now the downstairs had electrical wall sockets plugged and a gate by the stairway to the second floor. Raul and Isabella were being good sports about the inconveniences.

Her phone rang. "Right on time," she said to Carpenter, after picking up.

"Where do you want to start?" Carpenter got right to the point.

"Michael Waters," Philly replied, and she gave him a recap of the investigatory hearing.

"That union rep has a point," Carpenter said. "It sounds like this vice-principal has made up his mind against Waters and the principal isn't reining him in."

"I still don't think we should do anything aggressive," Philly came back.

"Do you really think the girl is going to harm herself?"

"I think it's a possibility."

"Then you believe Waters."

"Yeah, I do. I think he's legitimately worried about the girl."

"Suppose the girl does something to herself?" Carpenter asked.

"You mean, how would it affect the case?"

"Right."

"I think it helps Waters," Philly said.

"I think so too. So maybe you want it to get out to the student body about what the Fine girl has alleged. Maybe it would push Fine to do something to herself."

"You're kidding, right?" Philly said. This wasn't the first time Carpenter had come up with a course of action that would help a client but prove nasty to a non-client.

"Yes and no. I'm just throwing this out. You and Waters are looking out for the girl. That's not *your* job. I'm not saying I wouldn't be doing what you're doing. I am saying that there's a morbid, hard-nosed way of looking at the case."

"I'd never do what you're suggesting, and I don't think Waters would either." Fortunately, Philly thought, at least up to now, Michael Waters was being a nice guy.

"I'm not suggesting you do anything. I'm just thinking out loud."

"We've got the Storm case hearing coming up," Philly changed the subject. "I'm letting Rachel do most of the heavy lifting. Rachel has asked for a pre-trial conference before the judge. She's told the father's lawyer about what happened in the third grade. I decided not to tell the Department's lawyer about it."

"Go get 'em," Carpenter said. "I'm letting Simon do the heavy lifting in the probable cause hearing in Alison Lind's case."

"Simon came up with a lot of helpful information in that wheelchair case," Philly said, and she updated Carpenter on the facts of the Foster case.

"How soon can we get a complaint together?" Carpenter asked.

"A couple of days," Philly said.

"Get Simon on it. I'm thinking that this is a case where liability is pretty much a lock. If I'm that assisted living center, I'd be thinking of making a quick payment and avoiding publicity."

Philly understood where Carpenter was heading. Their cash flow was poor, and he was looking for a quick score in a case where liability was clear. "Mary Foster may need a hip replacement, but I don't think her damages are permanent."

"Didn't you say the woman was close to eighty?" Carpenter came back. "The older you get the worse it is to break a hip. I'll find us a physician expert if her doctor isn't helpful. If the Foster woman needs a hip replacement, the damages in this case are going to be higher than you think."

"I wouldn't want to make any statements about a big damage award," Philly said, remembering her impression of Ruth Foster, Mary's daughter. "The daughter will be calling the shots and I think I mentioned to you that she's got unreasonable expectations as to a recovery."

"I get your point," Carpenter said.

"Then there's the golf case," Philly said. Rachel had come to like Martin Hays and wanted to help the man. "Remember the private detectives who helped me with Michael Waters' case?"

"Yeah. They found out some helpful information about the girl who's accusing Waters."

"Right. I want to hire one of them to go to Atlanta."

"What do you hope to get out of that?"

Philly went through her reasoning, filling Carpenter in on Rachel's visit to the country club and the club's seventh hole. "We need another helpful fact in this case," Philly concluded. "I want someone to try and interview the guys in Atlanta who were in the foursome that followed Hays and his three banker buddies."

"Why not hire someone in Atlanta?"

"I don't know anyone in Atlanta. Besides, I trust these guys. Paul was right in vouching for them."

"Will Hays pay for this?"

"He's going to have to under our agreement if he gives the okay. But I want to move on this. I'll advance the funds."

Carpenter again fell silent. Philly knew that he liked to minimize out-of-pocket expenses in any contingency case. Fine. He didn't have to agree to participate.

"Okay," Carpenter said. "We'll split the advance. Get Hays on board. That's the first thing."

"Then there's Martina Glass' case. Liability seems pretty clear—someone fell on her for Christ's sake. I'm going to get Rachel started on a complaint."

"Sure, why the hell not?"

"What's eating you?"

"I've never been involved in so many contingency cases before. I think I told you once that I like having one or two around. But contingency cases are pretty much all we've got. It's an epidemic."

"It could be worse," Philly said, knowing Carpenter liked to torture himself with worst case scenarios. "We could have no contingency cases. Then where would we be?"

30

Each time Simon handled the argument in a case and acquitted himself well, Carpenter vowed that next time he'd turn Simon loose without misgivings. But here he was, waiting for the probable cause hearing to start in Alison Lind's discrimination case, and fretting that the matter was out of his hands. True, he could whisper guidance to Simon and, if Lind's case was careening downhill, he could tell Simon to keep his seat and take over. But even with these fallback positions available, Carpenter couldn't shake his unease. Was he that much of a control freak?

Carpenter studied Darren Grayson, the opposing attorney who had filed the motion to dismiss Lind's case on the ground there was no factual basis (referred to as probable cause under the agency's regulations) for her discrimination claims. Was Maxine's assessment of Grayson contributing to his doubts about putting Simon in charge of this hearing? The attorneys representing schools and school systems were a small, tight knit group, so Maxine knew Grayson and had seen him in action once. In Maxine's opinion, Grayson was an effective litigator. The defendants' lawyer looked to be in his thirties. He was tall and thin and displayed a cockiness that Carpenter had noticed in younger litigators in recent years. At the moment, Grayson was laughing, talking to a middle-aged man who didn't seem to get the humor in what Grayson was saying. That had to be Norman Joyce, Carpenter thought. Joyce had a dyspeptic look about him and Carpenter remembered Lind describing the principal of Middlemarch High School as useless.

Anne Forrester, the MCAD hearing officer, took the chair behind the head table positioned at the front of the hearing room. Carpenter thought Lind had lucked out by having a woman hear the dismissal motion. A gay woman would have been the jackpot, but seeing Forrester's wedding ring, Carpenter figured you couldn't have everything. Then he remembered. Since 2004 in the People's Republic of Massachusetts, a wedding ring gave no indication of the sex of the ring wearer's partner.

Carpenter turned and faced the rear of the hearing room. Lind was seated with her significant other, Beth Finegold, a small mousy woman who, at the moment, seemed to have more of an edge to her than Lind. In meetings, Lind had come across as an aggressive, hard-nosed, take-no-prisoners kind of woman, but today she was subdued. It never failed, Carpenter thought. The most self-assured, cocky bastard inevitably was brought down a peg when the realization dawned that her fate was in a stranger's hands.

Forrester called the hearing to order. Carpenter guessed her age at forty. You couldn't tell by looking at her whether she had ever played sports in school. She didn't appear to have an athlete's body; Forrester was short and stocky and slightly stoop-shouldered.

"I have before me a motion by the respondents to dismiss the discrimination complaint of Alison Lind because of lack of probable cause. Ms. Lind claims that she was fired as a physical education teacher and girls' soccer coach at Middlemarch High School because of her sex and sexual orientation. Her complaint names the high school, the school district, and Mr. Norman Joyce, the high school principal, as respondents."

Joyce winced when his name was said aloud. Grayson must have been aware of his client's unease because he gave Joyce a reassuring pat on the back.

"I have before me legal memoranda from the parties. Mr. Joyce has submitted an affidavit. Ms. Lind has submitted an affidavit. On behalf of Ms. Lind, I have affidavits from Fran Morgan, Richard Morgan, and Brittany Stern. I've read all the papers. I have some questions and I'd like to start with you Mr. Grayson since you represent the moving parties."

Grayson rose smartly and favored the hearing officer with an open, expectant expression.

"Ms. Lind was fired because she swore at the girls she coached, made them do punishment drills, and took her significant other with her to an overnight tournament," Forrester catalogued. "Yet the affidavits submitted in support of Ms. Lind's position establish that male coaches engaged in similar behavior. Isn't that reason alone to deny the respondents' motion to dismiss?"

"Not at all, Your Honor," Grayson responded without hesitation. "The testimony about male coaches comes in largely through the affidavit of a student,

Brittany Stern, who repeats things that her former boyfriend allegedly told her. That is plainly hearsay and should not be considered at this hearing."

Carpenter silently acknowledged that Grayson had made a fair point. Stern's boyfriend, a Rick Monahan, had refused to provide an affidavit supporting Lind and, according to Simon, the Stern girl had broken up with him as a result.

"Also," Grayson continued, "there is another fundamental reason why Ms. Lind was discharged, a reason that has never surfaced in connection with any male faculty member. Specifically, Ms. Lind was the subject of complaints by girls on the soccer team and their parents. No other coach at the high school had lost the confidence of so many players and their parents. For that non-discriminatory reason alone, Ms. Lind's case should be dismissed because the school had every right to base its decision on team dissension."

"What do you say to that?" Forrester directed at Simon.

Simon rose and ran a hand over his already slicked down hair. "I have a lot to say about that," he began, and Carpenter wondered why he had entertained any doubts about letting Simon handle this hearing.

"As to Mr. Grayson's first point, the affidavit of Mr. Richard Morgan sets forth his first-hand knowledge that male coaches swore at their student players and employed punishment drills. Mr. Morgan's son was a star pitcher on the high school baseball team, and he was present at many practice sessions and games. Therefore, the evidence before you is not all hearsay. Even if it were, the MCAD rules permit you to consider hearsay testimony in connection with a motion to dismiss filed at this early stage of proceedings. Moreover, as Ms. Lind's pleadings set forth, she should be given a chance to engage in discovery with respect to male coaches and male players. Given Ms. Stern's affidavit and Mr. Morgan's affidavit, testimony from those sources is likely to establish that male coaches engaged in the exact same conduct that got Ms. Lind discharged but, to a man as it were, resulted in no disciplinary action whatsoever when it came to the male coaching staff. And finally, on this point, it bears emphasizing that the affidavit from the principal, Mr. Joyce, does not deny that male coaches at the high school did all the things Ms. Lind did and were not subject to discipline. Male coaches apparently are allowed, with impunity, to swear at students on their teams, subject students on their teams to punishment drills, and to take a significant other to an overnight sporting event."

Forrester was writing which Carpenter took as a good sign.

"With respect to Mr. Grayson's second point, let's make sure we assess that argument in the proper context. Ms. Lind's affidavit establishes that her girls' soccer teams fared demonstratively better than boys' teams in all major sports at the high school. Put simply, Ms. Lind is a successful coach. The male coaches at the high school are not; their teams are, we have to say, losers. The inference to be drawn from these facts, facts which principal Joyce has not rebutted, is that Ms. Lind puts on the soccer field the players who are the best on the team based on their ability, and does not play favorites or succumb to pressure from parents. In short, she plays the students on her team such as Ms. Stern who earn their playing time. The students who complained about Ms. Lind were for the most part seniors who got it into their heads that being seniors entitled them to goof off and not have to earn playing time. When Ms. Lind responded to their lackadaisical efforts by not playing them, they whined and ran to their parents, showing themselves to be the spoiled, feckless girls they were. Apparently, their parents are whiners as well. Losers often whine and blame someone else, and that's all that happened here. Simply because some students and parents have perfected the art of whining doesn't mean that their whining justifies discrimination."

Carpenter suppressed a smile. Had the word feckless ever before been used in an argument in a discrimination case? Where the hell did Simon come up with that word? He tried to remember what feckless meant. Something to do with ineffectiveness he recalled vaguely.

"Consider the affidavit of Fran Miller," Simon resumed. "She makes the point that Ms. Lind teaches her players the value of hard work and dedicated effort. These lessons are plainly lost on principal Joyce who obviously prefers to practice discrimination by hiding behind the self-serving, unfounded gripes of shirkers and complainers."

Simon took his seat but not before turning his attention to Joyce and staring at the principal until the educator looked away.

Carpenter found himself grinning. He had also lost sight of the fact that Simon loved mixing it up in legal argument.

"May I respond, Your Honor," Grayson said rising.

Forrester nodded but not before completing what she had been writing.

"Teachers are supposed to lead by example," Grayson continued. "The example set by Ms. Lind is simply a bad example that a school need not tolerate under any circumstances. Ms. Lind's excessive use of profanity cannot be excused and is a non-discriminatory reason for discharging her. Her meting out punishment has a certain vindictiveness about it that also need not be tolerated by a school. And lastly, whether Mr. Jefferies cares to recognize it or not, soccer is a team sport and a school need not turn a blind eye to the fact that a coach has alienated a substantial number of team members. A school doesn't have to put up with divisiveness caused by a coach and, the firing of a coach who is as divisive as Ms. Lind, is not a discriminatory act in any way, shape or form."

When Grayson took his seat, Forrester spent a long moment in thought, looking in the direction of Simon and Grayson. The hearing officer took a deep breath and then began reviewing the notes she had made. When she finally looked up, Carpenter was certain that she would make her ruling now.

"I'm simply not prepared to dismiss Ms. Lind's complaint at this early stage of proceedings, Mr. Grayson. You make some valid points and ultimately those points might carry the day. But the evidence is not all your clients' way—there are plainly factual disputes present here and, as you know, a motion to dismiss should not be allowed where facts are in dispute."

Carpenter noticed that Grayson was unperturbed by Forrester's ruling. Norman Joyce was another story. The despairing look on the principal's face had to have reflected the educator's realization that he was in for a protracted battle. Joyce had to be thinking that being cross-examined by Simon would not be fun.

"I expect the parties to conclude discovery promptly," Forrester said. "I'm prepared to move this case forward rapidly because I know it's important to the parties that a decision be reached quickly. I will likely set a trial date during June."

"That's agreeable," Simon said. "Thank you, Your Honor."

Grayson said nothing, having nothing to be thankful for.

"You'll receive written notice of my ruling shortly." Forrester rose. "The hearing is concluded."

Lind had given Simon an awkward hug and now stood with a sappy look on her face as she held Beth Finegold's hand. Carpenter nodded to Simon to field Finegold's question as to next steps.

"We will be filing interrogatories which are questions that Joyce will have to answer under oath," Simon explained. In the meantime, it would be helpful if we could obtain some evidence from boys who had played sports at the high school and had helpful information about male coaches."

"We'll work on that," Finegold said, and Carpenter now wondered whether Lind's partner was the dominant woman in their relationship.

"Getting other girls besides Brittany Stern to help your case would also be a help," Simon added.

Finegold nodded and made a note on a small notepad.

"There's one other thing," Carpenter interjected. "Doesn't soccer season start about now?"

"The team has played two games," Lind confirmed. "I went to both."

"Who's your replacement playing?" Carpenter asked.

"The spoiled bitches who got me fired," Lind snapped. "Who else?"

"How'd the team do?" Carpenter wanted to know.

"They lost the first two games."

"Perfect," Carpenter said. "Let's hope the team keeps up its losing ways. I know you're rooting for them but if they end up having a losing season, it can only help you."

"That sucks!" Lind exclaimed. "I want my job back and I'd like to beat the shit out of Joyce. But there's no way in hell I'm hoping the girls lose."

Spoken like a client, Carpenter mused. Where the hell was self-interest when you needed it?

31

When Philly had appeared before Judge Hannah Sturdy four years ago, the judge had struck her as old. She had expected that the passage of four years would have left the judge looking positively ancient. But now, in the flesh, Judge Sturdy looked pretty much the same. There was her curly gray hair, pale, round face, and cheeks that sagged slightly. She still sported glasses with pink tinted frames that didn't qualify as granny glasses in Philly's opinion and looked so ridiculous they couldn't be labeled hideous. Philly had reviewed her one experience before the judge with Rachel, warning her colleague not to view the judge as a warm and sensitive grandmotherly type. But the slight smile on Rachel's face suggested that the admonition had gone for naught.

The lawyers in the Storm case had taken up seats arranged in a semicircle about the desk in Judge Sturdy's chambers. Stephen Minor, the lawyer representing James Farrell, was strikingly handsome. Minor was lean and rugged looking and had dark soulful eyes. Philly noted that the lawyer representing the Department of Children and Family Services was also no slouch in the looks department. Howard Pine had a long and lanky swimmer's build and long blond hair and blue eyes that reminded her of Philip. She sighed. Probably lanky blond lawyers would always remind her of him.

"You asked for this pre-trial conference, Ms. Boyle," Judge Sturdy began, "so why don't you tell us why we're gathered together today."

Rachel seemed to be taken aback by the judge's less than friendly opening, but she quickly recovered. "Thank you, Your Honor. We're here because of evidence that has been discovered and will be presented on behalf of Heather Storm. The evidence may require testimony not only from Marilyn Storm, who is the subject of this case, but also from a former classmate of hers, a young boy who, like Marilyn, is today in the fifth grade."

Philly noticed that Judge Sturdy's expression remained a cipher as Rachel described the third-grade incident between Marilyn Storm and Danny Graham. Stephen Minor had been informed of the event and his expression also revealed nothing. But Howard Pine was staring at Rachel wide-eyed. Philly now was certain that she had made the correct decision to withhold information about Danny Graham from Pine until today.

"In conclusion, we wanted to make the court aware of the likely testimony and would ask that when it comes to both Marilyn Storm and Danny Graham, their testimony be taken in chambers and not in public. We believe that this event will be difficult for the children to talk about."

Judge Sturdy's expression suggested she'd have no difficulty in having the children testify in open court.

"We would also ask that the hearing on the merits be continued so that Heather Storm and James Farrell are given an opportunity to file motions to dismiss the Department's case based on this new evidence."

Judge Sturdy frowned and Philly remembered her court clerk's warning about Judge Sturdy's antipathy to any lawyer tactic that produced delay.

"Do you have anything you want to say?" Sturdy directed at Minor.

"I won't repeat what Ms. Boyle said," Minor responded. "My client, Mr. Farrell, has denied abusing Marilyn Storm in any way at any time. The Department has argued that Marilyn's ruptured hymen supports Marilyn's abuse allegation. Mr. Farrell disagrees with that proposition and this new evidence renders the proposition untenable. Therefore, Mr. Farrell, in particular, needs an opportunity to move to dismiss the Department's case and to clear his name."

In Philly's view, Judge Sturdy was unmoved by Minor's speech. She now leveled her gaze in Howard Pine's direction. "I'm sure the Department has an opinion here. So let's have it, Mr. Pine."

Pine was momentarily at a loss for words. "This is all new to the Department," he said. "The Department would oppose any motion to dismiss its case and would prefer to go ahead with a trial. This new evidence doesn't prove that Mr. Farrell didn't abuse Marilyn Storm. All the evidence should come in at a trial and be subject to cross-examination."

"Would you agree that the new evidence, if it unfolds as Ms. Boyle related, casts doubt on the Department's allegation against Mr. Farrell?"

Philly saw only one answer to the judge's question, but Pine didn't provide that answer.

"No," Pine said. "The Department regards Marilyn Storm as truthful. There will be no conclusive testimony that her hymen was ruptured as a result of the third-grade incident."

Pine had just made the point that Carpenter had raised. Whether Judge Sturdy was persuaded by the point was impossible to tell from her expression.

"I'm going to think about this before making any ruling," the judge said. "I'm currently inclined to deny the parents an opportunity to file dismissal motions since facts are in dispute. I'm inclined to set this matter down for a trial. At trial, I will make sure that any child's testimony is taken in as unthreatening an environment as possible." Judge Sturdy paused. "After thinking matters over, I may change my mind. Does anybody have anything else to say? In that case, this pre-trial conference is concluded."

After leaving Judge Sturdy's chambers, Howard Pine made a quick exit from the courtroom while Philly, Rachel, and Stephen Minor gathered before one of the counsel tables in front of the judge's bench.

"That's not quite how I thought things would go," Minor said. "What's with this judge's attitude?"

"She's unpredictable," Philly offered, opting for a euphemism. She was puzzled. The evidence involving Danny Graham should have had Minor more upbeat regardless of Judge Sturdy's attitude.

"With the new evidence about the Graham boy, is your client okay with regaining custody of Marilyn?" Rachel asked.

"It's a difficult situation. Marilyn has accused my client of something particularly nasty. It's understandable he remains conflicted as to what he's going to do."

"He's going to be cross-examined by Pine and probably by the judge," Philly pointed out. "My advice to you is to get him to make up his mind what he wants before this judge has a go at him."

"I pretty much figured that out after listening to the judge today."

Philly foresaw that Heather Storm would be in a precarious position if Farrell wanted nothing more to do with their daughter. If Storm wanted Marilyn back, she might have to end her relationship with Farrell.

"Damn!" Rachel said, and Philly viewed her oath as a sign that she had just gone through the same analysis.

"You need to let us know what Mr. Farrell intends to do as soon as possible," Philly said.

"Easier said than done," Minor said ruefully. "Don't be surprised if my client vacillates until the time of trial."

Philly exchanged a glance with Rachel. One of them needed to have a frank discussion with Heather Storm. Philly was prepared to nominate Rachel for that unpleasant task.

Isabella had retired early, making painstakingly slow progress up the stairs to the second floor. Philly had tensed twice when Isabella teetered in a prelude to a fall.

Now Philly sat back in the living room relaxing in one of the easy chairs after seeing to the after dinner washing up. Raul was draped in the other easy chair with his eyes closed, but Philly knew that he wasn't asleep. Daisy was down for the night and Paul had Jenny staying over at his place, a rare event for a weekday night.

It's just you and me, she thought regarding Raul. She couldn't remember a recent serious talk between them. She reflected again that Raul had changed in the four years since they briefly had been a couple. Four years ago, there had been an eccentric impulsiveness to Raul. He had been the one eager to try new things while she had been the stick-in-the-mud, obsessed with work and content to stay holed up in her apartment living on takeout food and sex. Since their joint house purchase, Raul had become less spontaneous, more serious, conservative really. His reflexive negative reaction to buying a different house was a case in point.

"Why do you look at me in that way?" Raul asked. His eyes were open and he had straightened in his chair.

"Sorry," Philly said, realizing she'd been staring. "I was daydreaming."

Raul nodded without saying anything. Four years ago, Philly reflected, it took an act of Congress to get Raul to stop talking.

"I got nervous watching Isabella go up the stairs," Philly said. "Why don't you guys reconsider and we can switch floors until Isabella delivers."

"Isabella will not hear of it," Raul said. "She says the exercise is good for her."

"Is she going to work right up to delivery?"

"No. This is her last week. She will begin her maternity leave."

Philly considered upcoming mornings. There was going to be a crowd—Daisy, Sarah Ferguson, and now Isabella.

"How are *you* doing, Raul?"

Raul seemed at a loss how to answer the question. But his uncertain look cleared. "I am doing well."

"Are you nervous about the baby?"

Raul seemed poised to deliver a pat answer, probably a denial, but he checked himself. Raul was someone she could talk to about anything but, since their breakup, Philly doubted that Raul felt the same way about her.

"Perhaps a little," Raul said. "It is sure to be a big change in our lives."

"What worries you?" Philly decided to press.

Raul chewed on his lower lip, a mannerism Philly had never seen before.

"Of course, I wish for the baby to be healthy."

Philly nodded. Raul and Isabella had stuck to their position of not learning the baby's sex in advance.

"If you must know I am worried about money once Isabella stops working."

"That's understandable," Philly said neutrally. "And I suppose I'm just adding to your worry list every time I bring up the subject of a new house."

Raul smiled weakly. "Yes, the new house is now something else I need to worry about."

Philly wondered whether Raul's and Isabella's marriage plans had become more concrete, but she held back a question on that subject.

"Do you remember when you approached me two years ago about buying a house together?" Philly asked, thinking of a way to ease into what she really wanted to say to Raul.

"Of course."

"You were so excited. Your mind was racing. I remember you were trying to do everything at once: the financing, the home inspection, dealing with the broker, thinking about tenants."

This time Raul's smile was broad. "You are right. I tend to go off in a lot of directions at once."

"But not recently, Raul. Recently, you seem more . . . I don't know . . . subdued in a way."

Raul shrugged.

"I want to see more of the Raul who once talked my ear off, the Raul who was excited about everything. Remember, I was the one who couldn't match your excitement or keep up with your interests."

Raul took a deep breath and let the air out slowly. Despite his desk job he was still dark complexioned, fit looking, and wiry. Even now his heavy-lidded soulful eyes were a turn on, one of the reasons there was a time when Philly couldn't get enough of him. Now her memories of their time together were hazy.

"Are you saying you are worried about me?" Raul asked.

"I'd say I'm puzzled," Philly replied, opting for a non-confrontational word. "Should I be worried about you?"

"I believe you have sufficient worries of your own."

Philly let Raul's non–answer slide. "Do you remember early last year when you discovered my drinking and helped me?" Raul's nod was barely perceptible. "Well, I'm always available to help *you* even if it's just to talk."

"I will keep that in mind."

"If money becomes a problem for you paying the mortgage, I can help."

Raul didn't say anything. Philly felt that she was losing him and opted to quit while she was only slightly behind. She had left the door to Daisy's room ajar and when Daisy emitted a high-pitched chirp, they both started at the noise. The interruption made Philly realize that Raul and Isabella would need a baby monitor to hear their baby from the second floor.

Philly resisted the urge to check on her daughter. Daisy had learned to settle herself unless something serious was awry.

"I wonder whether I will be a good father," Raul said softly, his eyes averted. Was impending fatherhood what had gotten Raul down?

"How am I doing as a mother?" Philly asked.

Raul now looked at her, engaged. "In my humble opinion I would say that you are a devoted and caring mother."

Philly blushed at the compliment. "Admit it, Raul. Back when we were seeing each other, would you agree that you would never have said I'd be a decent mother?"

"What is your point?"

"My point is that if I can be a halfway decent parent, you are going to be a great father. Your kid won't be able to keep up with you. I can't wait to see you and Isabella with your baby."

Raul kept silent but Philly sensed that he was buoyed by her comment.

"This weekend I would like to invite Connie and her husband for dinner," Raul changed the subject.

"Connie has a husband?"

This was news to Philly. Back when she and Raul had been a couple, so were Connie and Carpenter. That was how Raul had met Connie. Impressed by his intelligence and drive, Connie had hired him to manage her investment company stateside while from Rwanda, she focused on attracting international investors. It had worked out well. Now she was back, with a husband, and about to be coming to dinner.

"His name is Bernard,' Raul continued. "Please have Paul join us."

"Does Carpenter know that Connie is back and married?"

"I do not believe so, but I cannot be sure."

"May I tell him?"

"I will leave that up to you."

"Where is she living?"

"She and her husband have rented an apartment in Cambridge. When the lease on her condo expires and the current tenant moves out, she and her husband will move there."

Had the geezer ever wanted to marry Connie? Philly remembered him saying that Connie wanted to stay away from marriage.

"By the way," Raul said, "you were right."

"I was?"

"Yes. When we were seeing each other, I would never have said you would be a terrific mother."

Raul was smiling, offering a glimpse of the man she liked. "Well thanks a fucking lot!"

32

Barney Freedman hated to fly. He could only afford coach and the seats were too small for his large frame. If he didn't luck out with an aisle seat forget it—it would take him thirty minutes to recover the circulation in his legs when he finally got to his feet after the plane landed. When he was flying on business, one option was to ask the client to pay for an upgrade. But he seldom made the request. Somehow it didn't seem right to charge a client for avoiding an unpleasantness that he would put up with if left to himself. And when it came to a client like Philomena Piper who didn't seem flush with money, he didn't have the heart to ask her to foot an upgrade bill.

On the flight to Atlanta he had drawn the middle seat, the worst position. Pressed against the small window of an inside seat, there had been times when he'd been able to put his leg pains out of mind and doze off. Seated between two passengers, sleep was out of the question. Mercifully his neighboring passengers were silent types so he had time to review the plan he and Herb had come up with. They'd decided on the direct approach. Herb had produced a street map of the downtown Atlanta area where Ryan Cannon and Jake Mobley worked for a private investment fund. Herb had also found Barney a cheap hotel within walking distance of the investment fund's office and had downloaded pictures of the two men. Freedman had trusted Herb's instincts not to contact the men before arriving in Atlanta. Instead, on arrival, he would call one of them and try to get the guy to bite at a luncheon meeting to discuss a business matter. That line was not exactly a lie—he did want to discuss a business matter albeit one that would be of no interest to a private investment firm. The guy he reached would ask how he got their names and he'd put off an answer until they met. He'd give his real name and, if pressed for an occupation, he'd follow Cannon's and Mobley's example and say consultant.

Freedman checked into the hotel, then walked around a bit before returning to his room. You could say this for Atlanta, though: in mid-April it was paradise. Boston had a little grass and a few pushy crocuses. But Atlanta had it all—green turf, blossoming trees, and a lushly warm breeze.

When the east coast markets closed for the day, Freedman placed a call to Cannon and was passed through in moments.

"Ryan Cannon."

"Mr. Cannon, my name is Barney Freedman. I'm interested in taking you and your colleague, Mr. Mobley, to lunch tomorrow. There's a business matter I'd like to discuss with you both."

Cannon didn't respond immediately. Freedman imagined that there was a time in Cannon's life when he made cold calls to prospective clients. Now he was on the receiving end of a call that was frigid.

"How'd you get my name and what's the nature of this business matter?"

"I'd rather discuss those subjects when we're face-to-face."

"That's not going to cut it," Cannon said curtly. "Jake and I are busy guys and you'll have to give me something more."

"I understand you and Mr. Mobley are golfers," Freedman said. "The something more I can give you is that lunch would be on me and I'm looking at a hundred-dollar gift certificate for each of you for the pro shop at your country club."

"Where are you from?" Cannon asked with more warmth than he had so far displayed.

"Massachusetts."

"Jake and I were up there late last year."

"Sorry I missed you. Do we have a deal?"

"What the hell," Cannon said. "We've all got to eat."

"Excellent." Freedman passed on the name of a nearby restaurant that Herb said rated three out of four stars and set the time for noon.

Philly had just set Daisy down for the night and returned to the living room when she heard her second-floor office phone ring. Who the hell would be calling so late? she wondered, as she sprinted up the stairs. Isabella had retired to bed after dinner and the last thing Philly wanted was the phone to wake her.

"Philomena Piper," she gasped, winded by the climb.

"It's Michael Waters. I'm sorry to be calling so late."

"Not a problem. Is everything okay?"

"Caroline Fine has been hospitalized. She swallowed a bunch of pills and it was just chance that her mother found her before it was too late. She had her stomach pumped and is in intensive care."

Philly wondered whether it was a character defect that her first thought was how this development affected Waters' legal position. Shouldn't she have been more concerned with the condition of the Fine girl? She tried to put things back in the right order.

"I'm sorry to hear that, for Caroline's sake. Who told you about this?"

"Ms. Lacey just called me. She'd gotten a call from Caroline's mother."

"What else did she say?"

"Nothing else really. She just said that she wanted to let me know what she had heard."

Philly took her time thinking through the ramifications of Waters' news. The Fine girl's suicide attempt validated Waters' decision to report the girl as a danger to herself but shed no light on whether the girl's accusation of sexual misconduct was true or false. Had the informal hearing somehow pushed Fine to act on a self-destructive impulse? Philly remembered a frequently uttered Carpenter aphorism—when you don't know what to do, do nothing.

"I don't think you should act any differently because of this," Philly advised. "My advice to you is to go about your business and under no circumstances discuss this development with anybody."

"I'm trying to think what pushed Caroline to do this," Waters said in a tired voice.

"I was also trying to figure that out," Philly acknowledged. "I didn't come up with anything."

"Maybe the hearing put pressure on her," Waters speculated. "Maybe it caused her to snap in some way."

"You and I are not going to figure out what motivated her. That's partly why I think you should behave as if it were business as usual."

"I feel that I'm responsible in some way for what Caroline tried to do."

"You know that's not true," Philly quickly reassured Waters. "If you're going to start coming up with off-the-wall scenarios, I'm probably more responsible than you for what happened. I'm the one who asked her tough questions at the hearing. And as long as we're casting blame, let's hold Lacey and Frye responsible for putting her through a hearing in the first place."

"Thinking rationally, I know you're right, but there's this nagging thought I can't shake that I'm somehow to blame. Can Caroline sue me over this?"

"Anyone can sue anyone over anything," Philly said, parroting another Carpenter bit of wisdom. "But I don't think she has grounds. You have immunity for reporting her as a risk to herself so long as you acted in good faith. Her suicide attempt supports your decision and then some."

"I know you said it should be business as usual, but somehow that doesn't seem possible. This will be all over the school."

"You're probably right," Philly conceded. "And I know you're feeling uncomfortable. But my job as your lawyer is to give you this advice. Don't talk to anyone about this, and that goes for Wayne Gordon, your union rep. Talk to nobody. Get hold of Gordon and tell him to keep his mouth shut, too."

"Okay," Waters said weakly.

"How do you think Ms. Lacey and Mr. Frye are doing right now?" Philly asked.

"I don't know."

"If I'm Lacey," Philly said, "I'd be second-guessing myself on why I let Frye talk me into holding a hearing. If Lacey had told Fine that her charge had been taken seriously and thoroughly investigated but no further action would be taken, I'm betting that the Fine girl would have done nothing to herself."

"You can't know that," Waters objected.

"You're right. But that's my read on this situation."

33

Barney wouldn't have chosen the restaurant that Herb had picked out, a yuppie place that served small portions and played jazz that set his teeth on edge. But as soon as he saw the two guys who had to be Ryan Cannon and Jake Mobley, he knew that Herb had made the right choice. They were young guys, muscular, each with gelled hair, loud ties, and tailored dark suits. Cannon was distinguishable by a short, dark beard covering his chin, but they were otherwise interchangeable.

Barney had claimed a table for three if you could even call it a table. Three tall chairs with low back support and the look of bar stools were grouped around a small, raised, rectangular, marble-topped surface that confirmed there would be no large servings when it came to food. Even drinks and small plates on the surface would be a tight fit.

"First things first," Barney said, and he handed over the pro shop gift certificates he had promised Cannon. Cannon and Mobley shared an amused glance and pocketed the certificates. Barney signaled a waitress and they got drink orders out of the way. He hated the way he hesitated to order a beer after Cannon and Mobley requested club soda with a lime wedge but hell, he wanted a brew, it was warm outside, and what was the point of trying to pretend he had anything in common with two young guys who worked for a private investment fund whatever the hell that was. When the drinks were served Cannon and Mobley took small sips and settled back in their seats. Barney downed a healthy swallow of beer and took the hint.

"I said I wanted to talk to you about a business matter, but the truth is it's got nothing to do with your investment firm business. I wasn't lying. I do have a business matter to discuss with you, but I wasn't as forthright as I should have been because I wanted to make sure you'd meet with me."

Cannon's amused look remained in place, but Mobley's stare was close to hostile.

"This has to do with when you were in Massachusetts last November playing in a foursome at the Mayfair Country Club in Needham."

"What'd I tell you?" Mobley blurted out, annoyed, but as far as Barney could tell, Cannon wasn't put off by the purpose of his visit. Cannon took out his pro shop gift certificate and waved it in Barney's direction. "Was this to butter us up?" Cannon asked.

"Pretty much," Barney said. "Is it working?"

"Let's get out of here," Mobley said, but Cannon was smiling. "Who the hell are you working for?" Cannon asked.

Barney explained being hired by a Boston lawyer and he gave them Philly's name. The more he talked, the sourer Mobley's expression grew. When he got to the part about Martin Hays losing an eye, Mobley muttered, "Shit," under his breath and Cannon lowered his eyes.

"Jake's right," Cannon said when Barney had finished his account. "Maybe we should leave."

"Weren't you the guy who agreed we all had to eat?" Barney came back. "I'm still buying. I can't make you talk to me if you don't want to. But I said I'd feed you and I will."

The waitress appeared as if on cue and when Cannon placed an order, Mobley reluctantly followed suit. Barney searched in vain for a burger. He ended up settling for a club sandwich that had a name he'd never heard before.

"So why should we talk to you?" Cannon asked.

"Beats the hell out of me," Barney said, which brought back Cannon's smile. "You guys are witnesses to something that happened to a guy that cost him an eye. The guy is going to sue over this, and I want to hear what you have to say about what happened. I want to know if you can help the guy's case."

"You still haven't given us a reason to talk to you" Cannon came back.

Barney considered whether Cannon was actually searching for a reason to open up. Mobley had made clear that he wanted nothing to do with any discussion.

"I'm not a lawyer," Barney said, "although I play one on TV."

"You're a real comedian," Cannon said, smiling, but Mobley was not amused.

"The way I understand it is this: each of you guys could have his deposition taken once a lawsuit is filed in Massachusetts by the guy who got hit. It gets complicated because Ms. Piper will have to come down to Atlanta and get a court order here to take your deposition. Or maybe she'll hire a lawyer down here. So, if you can't help the guy who got hit and that's what you tell me, Ms. Piper can rule out coming down here to depose you."

"What's to stop us from lying to you by telling you we can't help the guy who got hit?" Cannon said.

"Nothing."

"We can't help the guy who got hit," Mobley said.

Cannon favored his colleague with a sharp, reproving look.

"Let's go," Mobley urged even though their orders hadn't been served.

Cannon shook his head. "You can take off if you want. I've been promised a meal and damn it, I'm going to eat it."

"Shit!" Mobley hissed, but made no move to go.

When their orders came, Barney dug in, immediately not happy with his estimate that five or six bites would demolish his sandwich. He was hungry. Watching Cannon and Mobley make small inroads on their salads, he wondered whether the guys were watching their weight. He watched his own weight which was headed in one direction—up—but he was damned if he was going to pick at salads to drop a few pounds.

They ate in silence. Barney considered his next move. He sensed that giving Cannon a hard sell would backfire. Cannon was either going to talk or not.

When Cannon finished his salad, he motioned to Mobley. "You can take off if you want. I'm going to talk to Mr. Freedman."

"I figured as much," Mobley said, resignedly. "I'll hang around."

"I'm thinking," Cannon said, "that if I was the guy who got hit, I'd want someone who saw what happened to speak up. We don't owe those two guys we were with anything."

"We don't need to get sucked into this mess," Mobley said. "If this lawyer in Massachusetts wants to know what happened, she can take the depositions of the two guys who live in Massachusetts."

"What if they lie?" Cannon said.

Mobley looked daggers at his friend.

"What do you want to know?" Cannon asked Barney.

"What brought you to Massachusetts?" Barney led off.

"We work for a private investment fund," Cannon said. "Do you know what that is?"

"No."

"We try to find attractive investments for people who have money to invest. Our firm kicks in money and we get other investors to kick in money. In the typical deal, we set up a company, buy a business, manage the business, and hopefully make the business more profitable than it was. Then if all that works, we sell at a profit and the investors and our firm make money."

Barney thought of Richard Gere in *Pretty Woman*. Until the Julia Roberts character got hold of him, the Gere character bought up businesses, carved them up, and sold off the parts for a profit.

"We were contacted by Warren Lord and Alan Atkinson," Cannon continued. "They were more or less acting like brokers and were trying to find a buyer for a small upscale shopping mall outside of Hingham. The seller was willing to take a loss on what he had paid for the property. Jake and I did some research and accepted their offer to fly us up for a site visit. They had done their homework. They knew we liked golf and promised us eighteen holes at their country club. We decided to kill a day and go. We flew up the Friday night before and were out on the course early Saturday."

Barney took out the small notepad he used when he was on a case. He'd yet to hear anything worth writing down.

"We were in the foursome behind the foursome with the guy who got hit. What was his name?"

"Martin Hays." Barney said.

"Well, there are slow players and there are slow players. Hays' group were a bunch of snails. A few times Atkinson called out to Hays' group to try to get them to speed up their play. That didn't work. Jake and I weren't in any rush and we didn't mind the slow pace. Down here people are leisurely, and we're used to biding our time. We were scheduled to see the shopping mall in the afternoon and even though it was cold for us, we were enjoying the course."

"Speak for yourself," Mobley interjected.

"Don't listen to Jake," Cannon said. "We were both having a good time. Anyway, I forget the hole Hays was on when he was hit."

"It was the seventh hole," Barney contributed.

"Whatever. Our group was at the tee. Hays must have lost his ball and been farting around in the rough trying to find it. His playing partners had moved ahead. Anyway, Hays must have found his ball because he suddenly showed up and started moving toward the fairway. You couldn't miss the guy. He was wearing this bright yellow shell. Atkinson muttered something like, 'Look at that asshole, he probably stopped to take a shit.' That's when Lord said, 'Maybe this will give him a wakeup call,' and he launched an iron shot at Hays."

Barney's note taking could barely keep up with Cannon's narrative. Cannon had verified much of what Hays had told Ms. Piper, and he'd added some facts that would help Hays.

"I was standing there with my mouth open. I couldn't believe what Lord had done. I lost track of the ball and the next thing I saw was Hays go down."

Barney finished his note taking and regarded the young men. Cannon seemed almost relieved to have delivered his account. Mobley continued to sulk.

"Did anyone call out to Hays?" Barney asked

"No," Cannon said. "I'm kicking myself over that. I froze and, like I said, I had lost track of the ball, so I had no reason to believe Hays was in any real danger."

"What happened after Hays went down?"

"He wasn't moving. Jake and I ran down to him from the tee. Jake yelled back to Lord to call the clubhouse on his cell phone and get some emergency medical people on the scene."

"Did Lord or Atkinson call for medical help?"

Cannon shrugged.

"I think so," Mobley contributed.

"We got down to where Hays was lying, and his face was a mess. He was lying partly on his golf bag. Jake and I didn't really know what to do. The guy was breathing but his face was all bloody. I remembered you weren't supposed to move somebody who had been seriously injured so I didn't do anything. Jake took off his jacket and covered the guy."

Barney took his time writing down these further details. "How long before help came?"

"I don't know," Cannon said. "It seemed like forever."

"Twenty minutes," Mobley said. "I noted the time."

"What happened when help arrived?"

"An ambulance came, and the emergency team put Hays on a stretcher and drove off with him," Cannon responded. "They threw his golf bag in the back of the ambulance."

"What did you guys do?"

"We waited for Lord and Atkinson to join us which they did. Lord wanted to go back up to the tee and finish the round, but Jake and I said no. So we called off the rest of the round. They took us to see the property and the funny thing was it had possibilities. It was the kind of property we would have considered as an investment."

Barney decided to be direct. "I'd like to get a statement from you before I leave. What would be best for me would be an affidavit."

Mobley rolled his eyes. Cannon became lost in thought.

"I think you both know that what you saw can only help Mr. Hays," Barney prodded.

"I'm not going to give you anything in writing today," Cannon said. "Here's my business card. The lawyer who hired you can draft up whatever she wants me to sign. I'll have my lawyer look it over and if it's in order, I'll probably sign."

Barney didn't like the word probably. He pictured some tight-ass lawyer telling Cannon not to sign anything. Yet if he came on too pushy or desperate, Cannon might back away from signing anything.

"That sounds fair and prudent," Barney said. "Can I get you another drink or dessert?"

"Nothing for me," Mobley said.

"That beer you had looked pretty good to me," Cannon said. "I'll have a beer."

"Christ," Mobley exclaimed, then sighed in resignation. "This is going to be one of those days where fucking nothing gets done. Make it two."

Barney started to relax. "Did you guys ever follow up on that investment that was pitched to you?"

Cannon and Mobley both laughed. Mobley, Barney observed, seemed to have sloughed off his cranky mood now that Cannon had revealed everything that happened.

"You don't get it," Mobley said. "It's not just the financial aspects of a deal that come into play. You've got to trust the people you're getting into bed with. After what happened to Hays and after Lord and Atkinson wanted to finish the round, Ryan and I wanted no part of them after that. We went to see the property just to be polite. In this neck of the woods, politeness is taken seriously."

Barney wondered why he didn't need a passport to travel to Georgia. It sounded like a foreign country. "From now on, you might think about staying south of the Mason-Dixon Line. The further north you go, the ruder people get."

34

Philly was crouched down in the living room, arms extended, holding Daisy's hands, feeling upbeat because she had settled her final hockey player workers' compensation case and the $33,000 contingency fee, again discounted to make the settlement happen, would come in handy. Pink's *Who Knew* was at high volume and Daisy sported a happy grin, two teeth, and a drool-soaked chin as Philly tried to engage her in dancing of a sort. Isabella sat in an easy chair, smiling at them, bouncing a leg to the beat of the song.

When *Glitter in the Air* came on, Philly gathered Daisy up and nuzzled her. Then she collapsed on the floor next to Isabella's chair. It was amazing how a payday could brighten her mood. She and Carpenter had agreed to divide the fee the same way as in the Frank Gardner case.

"Can I do anything to help get ready for tonight?" Philly asked as she smoothed Daisy's hair.

Isabella shook her head. "Raul is coming home early. He claims he has everything under control."

"Raul told me that you refuse to change rooms until you deliver. Is that true?"

"Yes. I don't like being treated as an invalid. Besides, it will soon be over. I can feel I'm getting close."

Philly decided to drop the subject. She had made the offer she needed to make. "I haven't seen Connie in ages."

"She's a wonderful woman. She's taken Raul under her wing. I haven't met her husband."

"Can you imagine her with Carpenter?"

Isabella laughed. "I have difficulty imagining Carpenter with anyone."

Philly's thoughts turned to Paul. She couldn't wait to see him tonight. Raul and Isabella seemed to be giving no thought to marriage even with a baby imminent. But recently Philly had been thinking of little else. After Isabella's baby was born, she'd broach marriage with Paul. If he was of a similar mind—and she thought he was—they'd have to confront in earnest the question of where to live.

Daisy wriggled free of Philly's embrace and crawled briskly to her book box. She sat with a thump, pulled out a book whose edges had been chewed, and thrust out the book in Philly's direction.

"What have we here?" Philly said, accepting the book.

Daisy wriggled her way back into Philly's lap and a thumb found her mouth.

Philly began to read. Daisy's selection was a thick-paged book about farm animals and Philly dutifully made all the animal sounds. In moments, Daisy was napping and Philly set the book aside. She stayed seated by Isabella's chair inhaling the moist sweetness of her daughter.

"By the way," Isabella said softly. "Raul is open to making a bid on the house you're interested in. But he wants a condition of the bid to be that we sell this house."

Philly made no attempt to hide her surprise at Raul's turnabout. "What made him change his mind?"

"Maybe you did," Isabella said. "He asked me whether he had become boring and it came out the two of you had had a talk."

Philly colored. She should have considered that Raul wouldn't be shy about sharing his feelings with Isabella. "I'm sorry. I think I used the work subdued."

Isabella laughed. "I have never found Raul boring. Or subdued. But there's a serious side to him that has been more in evidence since I became pregnant."

Philly should have kept her mouth shut. When was she going to learn?

"I don't mind you being frank with Raul. I would mind if you weren't."

"I have to remember to mind my own business," Philly said.

"Fat chance."

Bernard Mucowahandi was a large man with close cut salt and pepper hair, a broad chest, and an infectious laugh. He won Philly over when he stooped to shake Daisy's hand, picked her up, and spun her around which produced a healthy squeal of delight. Daisy had yet to exhibit stranger anxiety.

Connie, Philly thought, looked amazing. She had lost weight but had retained the hourglass figure that Raul had been taken with the first time the three of them had met. It struck Philly that Raul was literally walking on eggshells as if trying to be on his best behavior with his boss.

Paul had been the last to arrive coming straight from a crime scene. Philly liked the way Paul first gave her a kiss and a hug and then scooped up Daisy for a repeat performance.

When Raul announced, "Dinner is served," Philly saw to the seating, arranging Daisy's highchair next to her seat at the dining room table.

"I would like to propose a toast," Raul said, once the fish dinner had been placed on trivets. "To Connie and Bernard. I do not mean to slight Bernard, but I must give special thanks to Connie for taking me under her impressive wing and giving me responsibility in making investment decisions. She is my mentor and I appreciate the confidence she has shown in me."

Bernard clapped in appreciation and Paul joined him.

Raul urged everyone to serve themselves and once serving dishes had made a complete pass, they ate for a time in silence punctuated only by Daisy's banging on the tray of her highchair or emitting chirpy squeals.

"I also would like to propose a toast," Connie broke the silence. "This is to you Raul. In a way, you have been more responsible for the success of our business venture than I have. It's true that I recruited most of our investors from Rwanda. But you have been the one here on the ground managing the business. We have been acting as full partners, but you have not been made a partner. I propose to change that."

Raul appeared stunned, about to tear up. "I am at a loss for words," he finally managed. "I do not know what to say except thank you. I cannot imagine a better partner."

"What will you be doing here?" Paul asked Bernard.

"For the short term, I have what I believe in this country you call a gig." Philly wondered about Bernard's background. He had a deep, resonant voice and spoke with the lilting vowels and carefully articulated consonants of Africans educated in the British system, precise and rather formal. "I will be a visiting guest lecturer at Brandeis and have been assigned a seminar. I have been asked to teach about the Hutu and Tutsi tragedy that ravaged Rwanda some years ago. I have been requested to speak about how the country is trying to put the tragedy behind it."

"In my job," Paul said, "I see instances of human cruelty of a one-on-one nature. I can't imagine what a widespread, vicious rampage is like."

"It is a form of hell," Bernard supplied, simply.

Philly remembered that while Carpenter was in Rwanda, he hadn't been interested in learning about the Hutu-Tutsi violence. He'd said that tragedies on a grand scale didn't interest him as much as an immediate personal problem affecting someone he could help. Philly hadn't given much thought to the distinction he had drawn, but now realized that she shared Carpenter's view. Solving the more narrowly focused problem of a single individual held more allure for her than trying to understand a global nightmare affecting hundreds of thousands of people.

"Are you one of Connie's investors?" Philly asked.

"Yes. My brother and I have each entrusted Connie with some of our funds. But now that we are married, they are Connie's funds as well. She is now investing money that is partly hers."

"Today things are going well," Connie said, "so I'm not getting complaints. You should have heard Bernard and his brother when there were reverses."

Bernard shrugged. "It is now all a game to me. My brother and I have withdrawn our initial investments. We are now playing with the house's money as Connie likes to say. It took me a while to understand that expression."

"That's a nice position to be in," Paul commented.

"That is true," Bernard said. "Although it is less exciting. I have tried to let Connie do her job without commenting but that is not totally my nature."

"Have you seen Carpenter?" Philly directed at Connie.

"I've been putting that off," Connie admitted. "Before I left for Africa, I told him that I had no interest in marriage. I don't know how he'll take it when he learns I've married."

"I know how he'll take it," Philly replied. "He'll be curious why you changed your mind."

"I'm more concerned he'll be angry with me."

"I wouldn't worry about that. He'll be curious. Besides, he's with Maxine and they're doing well. I believe you've met Maxine."

"I did," Connie confirmed.

"So why did you change your mind about marriage?" Philly pressed.

"Bernard changed my mind. I just knew."

Philly hazarded a sideways glance at Paul. He was regarding Connie with a solemn expression. She hoped that he was thinking what she was thinking.

35

As she studied her calendar to get a feel for what May held in store, Philly wondered whether she was morphing into Carpenter. She had always regarded his fixation on his calendar as bordering on an obsession, especially the way he liked to end each month on a high note. April was not about to close on a high note and May looked like it was going to be a grind.

Judge Sturdy had ruled that she would not consider motions to dismiss filed on behalf of Heather Storm and James Farrell, and had set the case down for trial the first week of May. Rachel had let Peggy Graham know of the trial date and had reported that Danny Graham's mother was having second thoughts about getting her son involved in the case. Stephen Minor still hadn't revealed whether his client, James Farrell, wanted to have custody of Marilyn Storm. The trial before Judge Sturdy promised to be one of those cases where she and Rachel would have to wing it. At least their client, Heather Storm, knew what she wanted.

In the Waters case, the silence from Suzanne Lacey was troubling. The high school principal had not revealed whether she was going to hold a further proceeding in connection with Caroline Fine's allegation. Waters had sent Philly an e-mail stating that Fine was home from the hospital.

Rachel had drafted an affidavit for Ryan Cannon which she had forwarded to the Georgia businessman by e-mail. After Carpenter read the private investigator's report, he had sent Philly an e-mail predicting that the Martin Hays case would make their year. Philly hoped that his instincts were literally on the money.

A court complaint on behalf of Mary Foster had been filed against the Maple Leaf Assisted Living Center and against Harrison Blaine and Harry Fried, the two wheelchair racers. Simon had obtained a helpful written statement from a resident at the center, Loretta Frank.

Carpenter was in the process of making final edits to the complaint that would be filed on behalf of Martina Glass the first week in May. The Salem Stampede and Fred Dunn, the man who fell on Glass, would be answering that complaint.

Just to keep things complicated, Philly needed to contact the broker in charge of the listing of the house she was interested in. Paul had given his okay to the project. And Raul was now the eager beaver he had been when it came to buying their current house. He had already prepared a financial projection outlining how the participants in the purchase would contribute to the mortgage.

Philly turned her calendar back to April and then remembered the most important May event. Isabella was scheduled to deliver in May. No doubt her baby would be born at the most stressful, inconvenient time.

May

Philly's Untitled Playlist

When the Desert Meets the Rain

Sade

36

Outside the courthouse, the air was fresh and the day sunny. Inside, it was not. Judge Sturdy had assembled the lawyers in her chambers and was now laying out the ground rules for the hearing in the Storm case. Philly was only partly paying attention. She had gotten her first look at James Farrell and hadn't liked what she saw. He was a tall, thin man who combed his black hair straight back and sported a soul patch. He was considerably older than Heather Storm. When Stephen Minor had made the introductions, Farrell hadn't looked Philly in the eye. Minor had advised her that Farrell would not be taking the stand unless the judge insisted on his doing so, and that he was not going to take a position on the motion of the Department of Children and Family Services to dispense with parental consent for Marilyn Storm's adoption. At this news, Heather Storm's features had crumbled, and she couldn't hold back her tears. Philly had taken her aside, given her a pep talk, and Storm, to her credit, remained firm in wanting her daughter back. "I'm through with James," she had said with more determination than Philly had thought her capable of mustering.

"So to recap," Judge Sturdy said, regarding each of the assembled lawyers in turn. "We'll return to the courtroom and I'll place on the record that we'll start off hearing from Marilyn Storm in chambers and then proceed with Daniel Graham also in chambers. When the children have concluded their testimony, we'll return to the courtroom and start with witnesses from the Department. Any questions?" When silence followed, the judge gestured for the attorneys to return to the courtroom.

With two lean parents, Philly had expected Marilyn Storm to be a slip of a girl. Instead she was stout, almost chubby. The girl looked dazed—it had to be intimidating for a fifth grader to take part in a court proceeding.

Howard Pine, the DCFS lawyer, asked his questions in a direct but gentle manner that didn't come across as talking down to Marilyn. He brought out that Marilyn was happy in foster care and would welcome an adoption that would take her away from her parents. Heather Storm lowered her head at this pronouncement, but James Farrell was unmoved by his daughter's testimony and stared straight-ahead.

"Why don't you want to stay with your parents?" Pine asked.

Marilyn pointed at Farrell. "I don't like the way he touched me," she said in a soft voice.

Pine produced an anatomically correct doll and requested Marilyn to demonstrate on the doll where Farrell had touched her.

"Here," Marilyn said, first pointing to the doll's vagina and next rotating the doll and pointing to its anus. Rachel winced at Marilyn's gestures.

Pine asked the record to reflect where Marilyn had said she was touched, and Judge Sturdy honored the request.

"Did your mother know about your father touching you?" Pine next asked.

Marilyn shrugged her shoulders.

"Do you know if your mother knew about this? Pine prompted.

Another shrug from Marilyn. "I don't know."

Pine consulted his trial notebook. "I have no further questions."

"Mr. Minor," Judge Sturdy said, once Pine took his seat.

Minor rose hesitantly. "Good morning, Marilyn. I'll try to make this brief. What grade were you in when you claim your father touched you in a way you didn't like?"

For a moment, Marilyn looked confused by the question. "Third grade."

"Today you're in fifth grade, right?"

Marilyn nodded.

"May the record show that the witness nodded a yes answer to the question?"

"It may," Judge Sturdy said. "Marilyn, please try to remember to speak your answers."

"Why did you wait until fifth grade before telling someone about your father touching you?" Minor resumed.

"I don't know."

"You don't know," Minor repeated. "Isn't it true, Marilyn, that you've made up a story about your father touching you because you are unhappy at the school you're attending when you live at your mother's house?"

"I didn't make it up," Marilyn said defiantly.

"But you are unhappy at that school, aren't you?"

"I guess so."

"Why are you unhappy at that school?"

"I don't like any of the other kids."

"Do those other kids tease you?"

"Yeah."

"What do they tease you about?"

"They don't like me."

"What do they tease you about?" Minor repeated.

"They're mean. They say I've got cooties. They laugh at me."

"Isn't it true that you made up the story about your father touching you, so you could move to a new school and get away from the kids who are mean to you?"

"I didn't make it up," Marilyn repeated, this time with less force.

"Would you do pretty much anything to get away from the kids who are mean to you at school?"

"Objection!" Pine nearly shouted.

"Rephrase your question, Mr. Minor," Judge Sturdy directed.

"Do you want to get away from the kids who are mean to you?" Minor asked.

"I guess so."

"It isn't much fun to be picked on the way those mean kids are picking on you, is it?"

"No."

"If you didn't have to live at your mother's place, you wouldn't have to go to the school where kids were mean to you. Isn't that so?"

"I guess so."

"You'd do pretty much anything to get away from those kids who are mean to you, wouldn't you?"

"Objection!" Pine intervened.

"Do you understand Mr. Minor's question?" the judge asked.

"I'm not sure."

"Mr. Minor wants to know if you would do pretty much anything to get away from the kids who are mean to you. Is that true? Would you do pretty much anything to get away from those kids?"

"I guess so."

Minor took his time perusing his notes. "You said your father touched you in a way you didn't like when you were in third grade. Did he touch you in a way you didn't like in fourth grade?"

"I don't remember."

"What about fifth grade? Did he touch you in a way you didn't like in fifth grade?"

"No."

Minor turned to look at his client. James Farrell had remained staring straight-ahead not looking at his daughter or anyone else.

"I have no other questions."

"Will it be Ms. Piper or Ms. Boyle?" Judge Sturdy asked.

Rachel stood and smiled at Marilyn. "Hi Marilyn. My name is Rachel Boyle and I'm a lawyer who is here to help your mother. I have a few questions I need to ask you. If you don't understand any question I ask you, please tell me. Will you do that?"

Marilyn nodded.

"Is that a yes?"

Marilyn nodded again and Rachel laughed out loud. Rachel's amusement seemed to break the ice with Marilyn; the girl offered Rachel a weak smile.

"The record may reflect that the witness nodded yes to the last questions put to her," Judge Sturdy noted. "Please Marilyn. Try to remember to speak your answers to questions."

"Do you love your mother, Marilyn?" Rachel asked.

Marilyn had to think about her answer. "I guess so."

"Has your mother been a good mother to you?"

"I guess so."

"When you were growing up, did your mother play with you?"

"Sometimes."

"I'm curious. What kinds of things did the two of you do when you played together?"

"I like playing with dolls and she bought me a lot of dolls."

"I played with dolls when I was your age," Rachel said. "Did you and your mother play dress up?"

"Yeah. She had lots of old clothes we would put on."

"That sounds like fun. Was it fun?"

"I guess so."

Rachel regarded Marilyn with concern. Philly knew where Rachel's next set of questions were headed.

"Was Danny Graham a friend of yours in third grade?"

Marilyn recoiled at the name. Then she nodded.

"I'm sorry Marilyn," Rachel said softly. "You need to speak your answers the way the judge explained. Was Danny Graham ever a friend of yours in third grade?"

"Yes."

"At some time did you two of you stop being friends?"

"Yes."

Rachel paused. Philly assessed that she had made the right move having Rachel question Marilyn. With her blond hair, blue eyes, and open, round face, Rachel came across as non-threatening. Plus, Rachel's voice was soothing, an adjective that couldn't be applied to anything about Philly.

"Are you nervous, Marilyn?"

"Yeah, I don't like this."

"You don't like talking about Danny Graham, do you?"

"No."

"I get nervous sometimes too," Rachel said. "But I learned a trick to make the nerves go away. Do you want to know the trick I use?"

Marilyn leaned forward in her chair. "Okay."

"What I do sometimes is to close my eyes. Why don't you try it?"

Marilyn hesitated only a beat. Her eyes snapped shut as if a switch had been flipped.

"Did something happen with you and Danny that made you stop being friends?"

"Yeah."

"What happened?"

"We were playing doctor and he touched me."

"Did he touch you any place where you said your father touched you?"

"Yeah."

"Would that be the first place you pointed to on the doll?"

"Yeah."

"Did he put his finger in that place?"

Philly didn't think it was possible, but Marilyn squeezed her eyes shut more tightly. "Yeah."

"Did you notice any blood?"

Pine rose to his feet and then sat down abruptly, apparently thinking better of objecting to the obviously leading question.

"It was coming out of me."

"That must have been very scary. Were you scared?"

Marilyn slumped over. "Yeah."

Rachel took a deep breath and Philly heard the exhale.

"Marilyn, you've been very brave to come here and answer questions the way you have. You can open your eyes now. I'm sorry I had to ask you about things you didn't like talking about, but I'm all done with that. I only have a few more questions to ask you."

Marilyn opened her eyes and blinked rapidly several times.

"You're in fifth grade now, isn't that right?" Rachel resumed.

"Yeah."

"I visited your fifth-grade classroom and talked with your teacher."

Marilyn favored Rachel with a curious look.

"Your fifth-grade teacher, Ms. Fanning, told me that fifth grade is the grade where you first learn about not talking to strangers and about people not touching you in a way that is wrong. Did you learn about those things for the first time this year?"

Marilyn's expression darkened; the girl was now regarding Rachel with mistrust.

"Yeah."

"When you learned about people touching you in a way that is wrong, did that give you the idea to say that Mr. Farrell touched you in a way that was wrong?"

The courtroom became totally silent. Philly noticed that Judge Sturdy was regarding Marilyn with interest. Marilyn had turned red, her lower lip trembled for a brief moment.

"No," Marilyn said in a soft voice.

"Are you sure?" Rachel pressed.

Marilyn nodded with her head lowered. Her yes was barely more than a whisper.

"No further questions," Rachel said.

"Mr. Pine?" Judge Sturdy asked.

Howard Pine stood and regarded Marilyn for a long moment. Philly wondered whether this was a time when Pine hated his job.

"Did your father also put his finger inside you where Danny Graham did?"

Marilyn shut her eyes. "Yeah."

"Nothing further."

"Anything else for this witness?" Judge Sturdy asked.

Minor rose reluctantly.

"Did you start bleeding at any time when you say your father put his finger inside of you?"

"No."

"Nothing further," Minor said.

"You may open your eyes now," Judge Sturdy said to Marilyn. "Thank you for answering the questions you were asked. I have one question for you. Do you still wish to leave your mother and father?"

"Yes," Marilyn said in a clear voice.

"Would you want to live with your mother if your father were not around?"

"I don't want to go to that school anymore."

"Would you want to live with your mother if your father wasn't around and you didn't have to go to that school anymore?"

Marilyn took her time digesting the question. Philly wondered if it was a question Rachel should have asked.

"I guess so," Marilyn said.

"You really don't like that school, do you?" the judge followed up.

"I hate that school," Marilyn said.

"Thank you dear," the judge said. "You may leave your seat and go with my court officer who will take you to your foster mother."

"Is there any need for the Graham boy to testify?" the judge asked once Marilyn had left her lobby.

Philly had asked herself the same question. "I don't see a need," Rachel whispered, and Philly nodded her agreement.

"We don't believe that testimony from Danny Graham is necessary," Rachel said, and Minor and Pine quickly concurred.

"Let's recess for fifteen minutes," Judge Sturdy said. "Ms. Boyle, you can tell the Graham boy's mother that his testimony is no longer necessary. We'll reconvene in open court in fifteen minutes."

Rachel was feeling the same sense of relief that Peggy Graham had voiced when told that her son would not have to testify. Danny Graham's mother's eyes began to tear and she'd uttered a choked, "Thank God." Rachel had not been looking forward to conducting a direct examination of Danny. She was not quite sure how she had gotten through questioning Marilyn Storm. Even though Philly had told her that she had done a good job, she had no sense as to how she had performed. Hopefully the most difficult part of the case was behind her.

"I would like to proceed next with Mr. Farrell," the judge stated upon taking her seat. "Mr. Minor, does Mr. Farrell wish to present any evidence?"

"No," Minor said, and Rachel suppressed a smile at Judge Sturdy's astonishment. The judge quickly recovered her judicial mien. "What is Mr. Farrell's position on the Department's motion to dispense with parental consent to guardianship of his daughter?"

"Mr. Farrell has no position on the motion," Minor declared.

"No position! This is his daughter we're talking about."

Minor met the judge's penetrating gaze. Rachel would not want to be in his shoes.

"Mr. Farrell's daughter has leveled a very serious allegation against him," Minor said. "It's an allegation that Mr. Farrell denies. However, the fact that the allegation has been made and repeated in this courtroom leads Mr. Farrell to conclude, reluctantly, that his daughter does not want him in her life."

Judge Sturdy tapped her pen on her notebook and appeared uncharacteristically nonplussed.

"I'm going to ask Mr. Farrell to take the stand," Judge Sturdy declared. "I have a few questions for him, and perhaps other counsel will wish to make inquiry of him."

Minor gestured for his client to come forward and Farrell advanced hesitantly from the rear of the courtroom to the witness chair. Once he was sworn in, Farrell looked about nervously as Judge Sturdy consulted her notebook.

"Are you saying, Mr. Farrell, that you no longer wish to be Marilyn's father?"

Farrell stared at his hands. "Not after what she said I did."

"Did you do what she said you did?" the judge followed up.

"No."

"Do you have any idea why she would make up a story about what she said you did?"

"You heard her," Farrell said, with a faint note of defiance.

"What do you mean?" the judge asked.

"She's having a tough time in school and wants to leave the school. She'll say anything to make that happen."

"Then you've decided not to fight for her, is that it?" Judge Sturdy asked.

Farrell looked up, anger in his eyes. "What's the point?"

"That's for you to decide," the judge retorted with an edge to her voice. "If Marilyn is returned to her mother, are you agreeable to staying away from your daughter and Ms. Storm?"

Farrell looked at Heather Storm and Rachel found his expression impossible to read.

"If that's what she wants," Farrell said.

"If that's what who wants?" the judge followed up.

"Heather."

"Mr. Pine," the judge said. "Any questions for Mr. Farrell?"

Pine went after Farrell about the complaint that had been filed against him in Chicago; Farrell held his own. Listening to the exchange, Rachel wondered how judges and juries were able to tell whether anyone was speaking the truth. Farrell denied stalking the girl in Chicago and stuck to his story about the girl's mother making up the allegation to get back at him for dumping her. Farrell didn't seem surprised that the Chicago incident was brought up. Rather, Rachel thought, he seemed resigned to this event dogging him throughout his life.

"Ms. Boyle? Any questions for Mr. Farrell?"

Philly huddled with her and Rachel couldn't think of anything that would help Heather Storm.

Philly stood. "Not at this time. We would ask that Mr. Farrell remain in the courtroom."

"You may return to your seat, Mr. Farrell," the judge instructed. "But please do not leave the courtroom. Are we now to hear from your client, Ms. Piper?'

Philly sat and Rachel rose, gesturing for Heather Storm to take her seat in the witness chair. The woman looked so tightly wound that Rachel feared she would crack if asked a difficult question. She remembered the technique she had employed with Marilyn.

"Please close your eyes and take a deep breath," Rachel led off. Storm seemed surprised by the request, but she followed the instruction.

"Again," Rachel directed. "You don't have to open your eyes unless you want to while I ask you a few questions," she continued after Storm again breathed deeply. "Let's start simply. Do you want your daughter to be adopted?"

"Why would I want something like that?" Storm responded, her eyes still closed. "I want her back with me. It's bad enough this department took her away from me. I never treated her bad. I don't deserve this."

"If your daughter is returned to you, do you plan to continue your relationship with Mr. Farrell?"

Storm opened her eyes and searched out Farrell where he was sitting in the rear of the courtroom. "I wanted us to be together on this but since he won't join me, I won't be having him around if Marilyn comes back to me. It would be over between us."

Judge Sturdy was writing in her notebook. Rachel wondered whether the judge had an idea how she was going to rule.

"Will you be able to provide for Marilyn by yourself?"

"I think so. I think James will help me when it comes to money. I don't think he's going to like it, but I think he'll help me."

"Did you hear Marilyn say that she didn't want to go to the school she went to when she lived with you?"

"I heard her."

"What are you going to do about her school?"

Rachel was relieved to see Storm pause and gather her thoughts. They had gone over this question.

"You've been helping me look at options for Marilyn's schooling. I'd try to get her into a charter school if she keeps on with not wanting to go back to her old school. There would be a commute and it's more inconvenient, but I'd try to do that for Marilyn if that's what she really wants."

Storm had so far handled herself well, so Rachel decided to ask an open-ended question not on her testimony outline. "How would you describe your current relationship with your daughter?"

Storm seemed surprised by the question and Rachel wondered whether she had committed the cardinal lawyer sin of asking one question too many.

"I'd say the relationship is strained what with everything that's gone on. I think Marilyn feels that I let her down by doubting what she had to say about James. But I can't help that. I don't think James did what she said. He wouldn't do that. But if James isn't going to be in our lives anymore, I'm hoping we can get close again, the way we were."

"Nothing further."

"Any questions for the witness, Mr. Minor," Judge Sturdy inquired.

"No, Your Honor."

"What about you Mr. Pine?"

Pine stood and regarded Storm evenly. Rachel had grilled her client on possible cross-examination questions, but she was not about to predict whether any of the practice rounds would now serve Storm in good stead.

"Why didn't you believe your daughter's accusations against Mr. Farrell?" Pine began.

"Like I said, I don't think he could do a thing like that. I never saw him being mean to her or anything like that. Back when Marilyn said it was going on, she never acted like anything like that was happening and she didn't say anything to me."

"Did it occur to you that she might have been frightened to bring the subject up with you?"

"Did it occur to me?" Storm repeated. "I guess it didn't. She wasn't frightened to talk to people at the school, so I can't understand why she'd be frightened to talk to me. Maybe I'm not understanding what you're asking me."

"Why does Marilyn have your last name and not Mr. Farrell's?" Pine changed subjects.

"It was something I wanted to do. I told James I wanted to do that, and he didn't seem to mind. There's nothing wrong with what I did, is there? Nobody at the hospital ever said I couldn't give Marilyn my last name."

"Why didn't you and Mr. Farrell marry?"

"I guess it was just something that we didn't do. The piece of paper saying we were married wouldn't have made any difference to either of us."

"How would you describe your relationship with Mr. Farrell?"

"I've always loved him. We've had our fights, but I never stopped loving him. Even when he's not in my life I'm still going to love him. I wish it hadn't come to all this."

Pine paused and Rachel suspected he was assessing whether he was making any headway with Storm. Rachel believed her client's answers were coming across as heartfelt. But that didn't mean they were making an impression on Judge Sturdy. The judge probably didn't have a heart.

"What kinds of things did the two of you fight about?"

"Oh, you know, money, the times when one of us wasn't working."

"No further questions," Pine said, taking his seat.

"I have just a few questions for you," Judge Sturdy said, and Rachel thought, here it comes.

"Do you think your daughter is capable of deciding what's best for her?" the judge started off.

When Storm frowned, Rachel began second-guessing herself. This was not a question she had anticipated.

"She's just a kid," Storm said. "She probably thinks she knows what's best for her, but that doesn't mean it is best for her."

Rachel's tension eased slightly. Storm had come back with a sound, safe answer.

"Is it clear to you that your daughter doesn't want to stay with you if it means she will remain at the school she's been going to?"

Storm slouched in her chair. "She pretty much said that. I'm trying to deal with that situation. That's why I mentioned a charter school for Marilyn. I'm sure something can be worked out."

"Are you able to manage financially when it comes to taking care of Marilyn?"

"I'd say so. I've done right by her so far. I don't think I've ever denied her anything she really needs. Why are you asking me that?"

Judge Sturdy gave Storm a hard stare and pointedly ignored the question.

"What assurance can I have that Mr. Farrell will no longer be a part of your life if Marilyn is returned to you?"

"I already told you," Storm replied, and Rachel knew it was too much to ask that the judge hadn't picked up on Storm's annoyed tone. "I made my choice. I can't see him anymore if Marilyn is with me."

Judge Sturdy closed her trial notebook. "Does anyone have anything else to say? No? In that case I'm going to take this case under advisement. I hope to have a decision issued shortly. Court is adjourned."

In the corridor outside Judge Sturdy's courtroom, Rachel took her time answering Heather Storm's questions, making sure their client understood the potential next steps in the case. Philly was struck by how there was no way to tell whether Marilyn or Farrell was telling the truth. In that respect, this case was similar to the Waters case; either Waters or Caroline Fine was telling the truth, not both. She couldn't figure out Farrell at all. If the man had not abused his daughter, shouldn't he have fought to get Marilyn back into his life and deal later with whatever it was that had caused her to lie? Or was Marilyn's accusation so cruel that Farrell was just too angry to imagine ever having a good relationship again with his daughter? Maybe he thought fighting to be with her just wasn't worth the trouble. And then there was Marilyn. If the girl had lied about her father, would guilt someday overwhelm her and leave her dysfunctional in some debilitating way? Philly couldn't guess.

Storm walked off and Rachel came over to Philly.

"I'm going to have a cup of coffee with Minor," Rachel said, and Philly nodded, having taken note of the way Rachel had been regarding Farrell's lawyer.

"You did a good job," Philly said. "I thought that went as well as we could have hoped."

"This judge is going to screw Storm, isn't she?" Rachel came back.

"That could happen. I wouldn't predict what she'll do. But I thought Storm acquitted herself well. She surprised me actually."

"Me too," Rachel admitted. "I'm going to feel miserable if she loses her daughter."

"You and me both," Philly said. "Go get your coffee. I have a babysitter to rescue."

37

Philly had just finished energizing the broker who held the listing for the Brighton property she and her housemates were interested in. Relying on Raul's numbers, Philly had floated an offer that was twenty thousand less than the current asking price. The broker hadn't blanched at the figure. Philly had made clear that her offer was contingent on the property passing a housing inspection, and the sale of the houses and condo owned by her and Raul and Isabella, Sarah Ferguson, and Paul. She envisioned the broker with dollar signs spinning in her head at the thought of four commissions. Did real estate brokers have a regulation against playing both sides of a sale? If so, this one didn't seem troubled by it. Philly had hung up the phone confident that the broker would recommend the offer she had put on the table. A home inspection would follow in short order.

Philly stood up and stretched. She was in miserable shape. Chasing Daisy all over the first floor was exercise but not the kind that left her spent on an endorphin high. Somehow, she had to reintroduce spinning into her life. She could buy a bike for the new house but what she really enjoyed was a class with other sufferers, the loud, driving rock music, the exhortations of instructors.

Philly slit open the door to her office. She heard Daisy scooting about the living room, chirping happily, and Sarah Ferguson's deeper laugh. The two of them really got on well together. The money she was paying Sarah was money well spent.

Philly closed her office door and returned to her computer, resolved to devote the rest of the morning to Martin Hays. Rachel had forwarded copies of signed affidavits from Ryan Cannon and Jake Mobley.

Philly started with Cannon's affidavit, reading it slowly, comparing it with the draft that had been forwarded to the Georgian. For the most part, Cannon had accepted the language that she and Rachel had prepared; the word changes he or his lawyer had made weren't substantive.

The Mobley affidavit was a surprise. Barney Freedman's report had noted that Mobley had wanted no part of the case. It was shorter than Cannon's but, in some ways, more dramatic. Philly searched out Barney Freedman's contact information and punched in his cell phone number. He picked up on the first ring.

"This is Barney."

"It's Philomena Piper. You did a heck of a job down in Atlanta. I not only received an affidavit from Cannon but one from Mobley as well."

"No shit!"

"Take a listen," Philly said, and she read the Mobley affidavit through.

"I'd say you got what you needed," Freedman said after a time.

"Cannon's affidavit would have been enough," Philly said. "Maybe Mobley was feeling guilty or something."

"I think Mobley said to himself 'what the hell' after it was clear Cannon was going to help Hays."

"That's one way to look at it."

"What are you going to do with the affidavits?" Freedman asked.

"If I can, I'll sit on them until I get to take depositions of Lord and Atkinson."

"If I had to bet, I'd wager they'd lie," Freedman said.

"One can only hope. Again, thanks for everything. Send me your bill."

"That can be arranged."

Philly put down her phone and reread Mobley's affidavit. Carpenter was right. The Hays case could be big. So far, all the client contact had been handled by Rachel. One of these days she would have to meet Hays.

Carpenter finished his third rep on a machine that was supposed to build up his arm strength and when he stood up to stretch, was surprised to find Camellia Kim observing him. She must have seen him working out.

"Nice form," Kim said. "You're looking good. How are you feeling?"

Now there was a complicated question, Carpenter thought. He was experiencing night sweats just about every other night. His appetite remained off. He continued to make a show of cleaning his plate when Maxine was around but doing so was an effort. There were times when he woke in the night to take a piss and couldn't sleep when he returned to bed. "I'm feeling okay," he said.

"You don't sound convinced so you're probably feeding me a line of bullshit." Kim offered a weak smile but there was no humor in her eyes.

"I still don't have much of an appetite and night sweats are pretty frequent. Otherwise I'm having the time of my life."

"Are you going to take the next spinning class?" Kim asked.

"I'm not sure. I may decide to feel sorry for myself and skip it."

"That's not an option. Let's do the class."

Carpenter shrugged. If Kim hadn't been around, he probably would have blown off spinning. Dr. Specter and Maxine bugged him about staying physically active but there were times when he didn't see the point.

"I'll take that shrug as a yes," Kim said. "Any problems dealing with your job?"

Carpenter's thoughts turned for the umpteenth time to the lack of billable hour work. The preponderance of contingency cases kept gnawing at him because he had been around long enough to know that contingency cases were a mirage. You could see a victory down the road but oftentimes when you reached the end of the road there was nothing but dust.

"Your job," Kim prompted. "Are you able to work normally?"

"Physically, I'm okay at work. But the kind of business I'm used to is down so work is a source of stress. And for years I've practiced law alone, but now I'm hooked up with three other lawyers and I still haven't gotten used to delegating work."

Kim delivered a solemn nod, but Carpenter questioned whether she had truly identified with anything he'd said. Here was a twenty-something, powerfully built Asian woman with spiky hair who probably had never been inside a law office.

"Who are these people you work with?" Kim asked, and Carpenter provided thumbnail sketches.

"Are they competent?"

"Yeah, they are," Carpenter said, not really having to think about it. "They're all smart."

"Then you are a very fortunate man. This is an opportunity you'd be foolish to pass up. Keep delegating. Make time to get out of your office. Go to the gym more often. The weather is nice. Get outside. All of this will relieve stress."

Carpenter resisted the urge to ask Kim where she came by her advice. The woman was so earnest and sincere he resolved to keep his cynicism under wraps. For whatever reason, Kim was genuinely concerned about how he was faring.

"Let's claim our bikes," Kim said. "I'm looking forward to kicking your sorry ass."

If he could feign appetite for food in Maxine's presence, Carpenter knew he could muster up enthusiasm for an hour on a bike. "In your dreams," he said.

38

Before the phone rang, Philly had been staring out the open window of her second-floor office watching the sun play off the roof of the neighboring house.

The air was crisp and invigorating. On a day like today, she and Philip might have played hooky from work and gone on a bike ride. Paul wasn't his own boss, couldn't blow off work on a whim, and Philly realized she'd probably never ask him to do so. Suddenly her eyes smarted and she felt herself begin to tear up, consumed by a sinking feeling. She hated these moments when an overwhelming sense of loss ambushed her, and she was overcome with an endless list of possibilities that would never be realized.

And then the phone rang, and Philly took a call from Amy Huff, a lawyer representing Maple Leaf Assisted Living Center's insurance company. It was a real-world problem that would temporarily banish thoughts of Philip from her mind.

"Mary Foster's accident is a terrible tragedy," Huff began while Philly pulled herself together and began to search out Huff's firm on the internet. "Maple Leaf Assisted Living Center is hoping to resolve this matter as quickly as possible."

For four years, Huff had been an associate with a small insurance defense firm located on State Street in Boston. The firm's client list included a fair number of assisted living facilities and nursing homes. The firm had carved out a niche practice defending these health care providers against tort claims. Huff had tried numerous cases. Her photo revealed a young woman with short, dark hair, blue eyes, and a confident smile.

"That's good to hear," Philly said, waiting for the inevitable lowball offer.

"Calumet Insurance Company has authorized me to propose a fifty-thousand-dollar settlement in the case."

Philly jotted the figure down on her notepad. A settlement with the assisted living center would still permit Mary Foster to pursue claims against the wheelchair racers, Harrison Blaine and Harry Fried.

"I'll pass on your offer to my client," Philly said, already anticipating Ruth Foster's explosion of outrage at the trifling amount.

"Is my client's proposal something you'd be willing to recommend?" Huff pursued.

"I haven't decided one way or the other," Philly lied. There was no way in hell she was going to recommend accepting an initial offer. And with Ruth Foster in the picture, only God knew whether it would be possible to get authority to make a counteroffer. Philly felt out of her league. She had no feel for whether it made sense to settle quickly with one defendant or to not settle with any defendant until a global amount had been agreed to by all defendants. This is where Carpenter came in. He'd have been through this situation countless times.

"Please get back to me," Huff said. "My client would like to try to resolve this case before having to file an answer to the complaint."

"I'll keep that in mind," Philly replied. "Thank you for the proposal. It will be treated seriously." Why not another lie? She thought.

Carpenter stared at the photograph across from his desk and did his best to match the black man's unforgiving look. Which took some doing because Carpenter felt good this afternoon. He had made minor revisions to the complaint against the Salem Stampede and Fred Dunn that would be filed with the court tomorrow on behalf of Martina Glass. He'd replied to Philly's e-mailed question about how to deal with the offer made by Calumet Insurance Company on behalf of Maple Leaf Assisted Living Center. And he'd gotten his head back into Alison Lind's discrimination case.

Carpenter had advised Philly to reject the offer made by the insurance company, not make a counteroffer, and try to nudge the case forward toward trial. With multiple defendants, it was likely that each defendant would take shots at the others. The assisted living center would blame the wheelchair racers. The wheelchair racer who hadn't run into Foster would blame the wheelchair racer who did. It was probably too much to hope for, but the two wheelchair racers might blame the facility for not stopping the races when it was common knowledge races were going on. And all of that blaming and finger pointing would strengthen Mary Foster's case against all the defendants. Plus, with a hip replacement coming up, Mary Foster was going to make a very sympathetic plaintiff. This was a case that made sense to take to trial, unless the three defendants proposed a settlement that was too good to pass up. Which didn't seem likely.

Carpenter found himself grinning at the thought of three defense lawyers taking pot shots at each other and even the black man's expression lightened at that prospect. "I know," Carpenter said aloud. "The thought of defense lawyers pissing all over each other is a plaintiff's lawyer's wet dream."

This quip caused the man's expression to darken and the man's usual glower became fixed in place.

"What?" Carpenter said. "You were almost smiling a moment ago. You thought what I said was funny."

The man was no longer amused, and Carpenter realized that his change in expression was a change in subject. The man wanted to talk about Fred. Or, more to the point, the man wanted him to talk about Fred. Now there was a depressing subject.

"Some days I think Fred is getting the upper hand," Carpenter admitted grudgingly. "The fucker visits me with night sweats and has taken away my appetite." The man's brows knitted, inviting him to go on. "I'm exercising but sometimes I don't see the point—the symptoms aren't going away."

Carpenter paused. There were some things he didn't want to say aloud, even to a photograph, because he'd gotten it into his head that giving voice to a worry would mean the worry was real. But it was true that notwithstanding all the exercising he was doing, there were times when he was too tired to make love to Maxine. He had to be letting her down. Not that she'd said anything or given any indication of concern. But Maxine had to be mindful that they weren't going at it as frequently as they used to.

"Any advice, asshole?" Carpenter directed at the photograph.

The man said nothing; his face remained a harsh cipher.

"You're fucking useless!" Carpenter complained. He swiveled his chair so he had a view out his office's one window. It was a bright, sunny day. It had to be warm outside. When he had arrived at his office in the cool of the early morning, the day had had the feel of heating up before long. If he had his druthers, he'd now be on a hike with Maxine, following her lead as they meandered along some forest trail.

Carpenter noticed his gym bag wedged in a corner of his office. He had two gym bags in use, one at his Arlington condo and one at his office. Why not, he thought. The place Philly used to go spinning was a short walk away. If exercise was the way to keep Fred at his current distance, then by God he was going to exercise.

"How's that for a plan?" he directed at the photograph. He took the man's silence for consent.

When he returned to the office two hours later, Carpenter opened the bottom drawer of his desk that served as a catchall and rooted out the hammer he hadn't used in ages. Walking to the wall across from his desk, he selected a position that was as far as possible from the photograph of the black man. It took several tries, but he was pretty sure the latest solid sounding hammer thump had struck a stud. He positioned the picture hook and gave it a smack. The wall remained intact which emboldened him to deliver further blows and soon the picture hook was firmly flush with the wall. He wasn't handy but stepping back to observe his efforts, Carpenter thought he had acquitted himself well. He retrieved the photograph he had just purchased and mounted it on the hook. Again, stepping back, he was pleased with the result. The photograph was centered properly and at the right eye level to be viewed easily from his desk chair. When he got tired of looking at the black man, he could swivel his chair a modest turn and take in a very different photograph.

He remained surprised that he had made the purchase. Finishing the spinning class, he had showered and wandered into the art gallery that explained the name of Pedal Pusher Galleries. He'd been immediately drawn to the photographic exhibit, black and white shots of natural settings. He kept returning to one photograph which showed a woman hiker from the rear making her way along a rising path that was surrounded on both sides by trees losing their leaves. There was something about the woman's purposeful stride that reminded him of Maxine. Light suffused the foreground of the photograph but the pathway ahead of the hiker stretched into darkness. The shift from light to dark made Carpenter wonder what was ahead for the woman and he realized that his curiosity would not have been piqued had the woman been emerging from darkness and advancing forward on a well-lit portion of the path. He heard fallen leaves crunching under her tread. Her head was up, and he wondered whether she had a better view of where the path led than he did.

When he had given the gallery attendant his credit card, Carpenter remembered feeling that he was in some kind of trance, a slightly spaced out sensation that might have been produced by the spinning and subsequent shower. Watching his order being rung up, he couldn't recall whether he had ever before purchased a work of art. Ordinarily he would have been nonplussed by forking over two hundred dollars for something he didn't need, but on this occasion the expenditure left him untroubled.

Behind his desk, Carpenter gave his seat the requisite quarter turn and studied his new purchase. When he focused on the photograph, the black man was lost to view. Which was one of the reasons he had acquired the new photograph. The man's intensity and non-relenting, accusatory gaze sometimes became wearing. The new photograph was calming. True, there was an element of tension in the darkness shrouding the end of the path. But there was something about the woman's carriage as she moved forward that suggested she would be up to facing whatever was ahead of her.

Carpenter closed his eyes, pictured overtaking the woman on the path. Soon the darkness enveloped the path and he had to slow his pace for fear of bumping into something unseen. He was reminded of the relaxation counting exercises he used to employ regularly but lately had lost patience with. The new photograph might provide a substitute relaxation technique. Each day he resolved to advance a little further on the path. Something would eventually reveal itself. Or was that a pipe dream?

Carpenter opened his eyes and centered himself behind his desk. The man gave him a derisive look but, on this occasion, he didn't mind. "You can be replaced," he said.

39

Rachel sounded frantic. "I can't bring myself to open it," she said over the phone.

Philly fought down her own anxiety. Judge Sturdy had ruled in the Storm case so there was every reason to become hysterical. "For Christ's sake, open the damn thing!"

Philly heard the sound of an envelope being slit and papers rustling. It was all she could do to keep silent while Rachel did the necessary reading.

"Thank God!" Rachel let loose. "We're okay."

"What's okay?"

"Marilyn is going back to her mother with conditions. James Farrell is not to be involved in Marilyn's life and Marilyn needs to be enrolled in a different school."

Philly took her time digesting this information. On balance, Heather Storm should be pleased. James Farrell would be out of her life, but she had chosen her daughter over her lover. Marilyn might be disappointed but then again might feel relief. Farrell's reaction was impossible to predict.

"Put the decision in PDF and send it to me," Philly directed. "I'll call you after I finish reading it. And give a copy to Carpenter."

"Yes, ma'am."

"Nice job," Philly said. "I hope you're feeling proud of yourself."

"All I'm feeling is relief that I didn't blow it," Rachel replied.

"I want you to be the one to call Heather Storm," Philly said. "Then you need to call the Department attorney and work out getting Marilyn back to her mother."

"I can do that." Rachel paused. "What do you think Stephen Minor's reaction will be?"

Philly remembered the way Rachel had looked at James Farrell's attorney. "Why don't you call him and hear it from the horse's mouth."

"I can do that too."

Philly set down her phone and considered her next call. Amy Huff was not going to be pleased with what she had to report about the insurance company's $50,000 offer. As Philly had expected, Ruth Foster had laughed, described in graphic terms what Maple Leaf Assisted Living Center could do with itself, and slammed down her phone. The upside of that client call was that Philly didn't have to try to sell Carpenter's advice.

"Do you have a counteroffer?" Huff asked after Philly had reached her and rejected her client's offer.

"No," Philly said.

"Will you be getting back to me with a demand figure?"

"No."

"Why not?" Huff said, her irritation unmistakable.

"My client's current intention is to have the case tried."

"That makes no sense," Huff said. "If you presented a demand figure and my client met it, you'd avoid the expense and delay of litigation."

Philly had never liked coming across as unreasonable. Huff's reaction had common sense behind it, but practicing law meant that common sense wouldn't necessarily carry the day.

"True. And I'm sorry," Philly said, not feeling at all contrite. "I'm sure you've run up against this before, but there are some cases it just makes sense to try. This is one of those cases."

"Any judge hearing this case is going to inquire about settlement," Huff retorted.

Huff was right about that too. The trial judge would press her for a demand figure, and she would refuse to provide one. Which might land them with an unsympathetic judge. "We'll deal with the trial judge when the time comes," Philly said.

"Better you than me," Huff answered.

"I don't know what Farrell is going to do," Stephen Minor said. "I doubt he'll appeal. My guess is the case is over for him."

Which meant, Rachel thought as she cradled her phone against her ear, that there would be no more work connection between her and Minor. If she were someone different, someone more assertive, someone who didn't give a damn about conventions, she'd ask Minor out right now. But there wasn't a daredevil bone in her body.

"Now that the judge has ruled do you think Marilyn lied about your client?" Rachel asked.

Minor didn't answer right away. Rachel wished that he were sitting across from her. When they'd had coffee together, he had been easy to talk to. They had interests in common like art, the theater, classical music. Minor had admitted to being an exercise freak and a bit of a sports nut, but nobody was perfect.

"Yes, I think Marilyn lied," Minor said. "Before the trial, I wouldn't have said that. But after listening to Farrell testify, I don't think he did what Marilyn said he did." Another long pause. "But what the hell do I know?"

Rachel had run out of things to say. Small talk had never come easy for her. "Okay then," she said, thinking that she was now coming across as uninteresting. "I enjoyed working with you," she added, hoping that she wasn't sounding desperate to prolong the conversation.

"Same here," Minor said. "Look, I've got to run. I'll let you know if Farrell decides to do something crazy like appeal."

Rachel set her phone down. On a one to ten scale of pathetic, she had to be a ten. She was smart and good looking, but it was as if she exuded some off-putting pheromone that kept men at bay.

40

Philly was spending this morning in her Boston office. As she left the Brighton house, she turned to give Daisy a wave, but her daughter hadn't noticed. Daisy had pulled herself up against the chair where Sarah Ferguson sat and was reaching for a book in the babysitter's lap. Soon Daisy was settled in Sarah's lap and Sarah began to read. Philly had paused before walking out the door, taking in the scene, feeling for the moment superfluous. It wouldn't be long now before Daisy turned one. That would mean a birthday party. Christ! Daisy had no toddler friends. Her daughter lived in a world of grownups.

Now, Philly was seated in the visitor chair of her office while Rachel occupied the chair behind the desk—an odd rearrangement of positions, but then Rachel actually used the office more than Philly did. Each was reading a copy of the letter sent to Michael Waters from James Madison High School. There was not much to consider. In one short paragraph, principal Suzanne Lacey had informed Waters that the school had concluded its investigation, was taking no further action in connection with Caroline Fine's complaint, and was treating the matter as closed. Philly and Rachel looked up simultaneously.

"So that's it?" Rachel said. "It seems so anticlimactic."

Philly nodded her assent. There was something of a letdown when a complicated case was brought to an end out of the blue. "Are you surprised at this?" she asked.

"A little," Rachel said. "That vice-principal, Frye, seemed like a bulldog who wouldn't let go of a bone."

"I think his principal overruled him on this," Philly said. "My guess is that Lacey didn't want to subject Caroline Fine to anything further."

"Are you saying that Fine overdosing made this case go away?"

"I guess I am," Philly said, after considering the stark way Rachel had put it.

Rachel's look turned solemn. Philly was struck by how transparent Rachel was. "What?"

"I just wish I knew for sure," Rachel said.

"We're never going to know," Philly replied. "But for what it's worth, I think our client was telling the truth."

Rachel's expression darkened. "Stephen Minor thinks that James Farrell was telling the truth."

"He might be right. That's another question we'll never know the answer to."

"I never thought practicing law would be like this," Rachel said.

"Get used to it. By the way, anything going on with you and Minor?"

Rachel flushed, didn't say anything.

"I don't mean to be nosy, but I saw the way you were looking at the guy."

"Shit," Rachel said. "Was I that obvious?"

"Nothing he would have picked up on. Ask the guy out. It's better than spinning your wheels trying to find answers to questions that have no answers."

Rachel looked deflated. "I don't think I can ask him out."

"Yes, you can," Philly said. "You've just won your second case in a row. First the Storm case, now this. You're on a roll."

Philly waited until Rachel had gone to lunch before calling Michael Waters' cell phone number.

"Have you seen Lacey's letter?" Philly asked when Waters picked up.

"Yes. She left a copy in my mail slot."

"Congratulations."

"It's a big relief not to have this hanging over me."

"Does Wayne Gordon get a copy of the letter?" Philly asked. The union rep would want to publicize Waters' vindication and she thought that a bad idea.

"I'm not sure now that you mention it. I think I should give him a copy. He may have an attitude, but he was supportive throughout."

"You're probably right," Philly said. "But my advice is to tell him to shut up about the matter. Nobody has to know about this."

Waters laughed. "That's not exactly Wayne's way."

"That's what I'm worried about. My instincts are to keep this under your hat and keep going about your business as usual."

Waters didn't reply for a long moment. "What are you worried about?" he finally asked.

"Nothing specific. I think you can't go wrong by flying under everyone's radar. Keeping this quiet just makes sense."

"I'm not sure I can control Gordon. Regardless of Gordon, this is bound to get out among the faculty."

Philly was worried about the students, but she kept that concern to herself. "All right," she said. "I've said what I needed to say."

"I want to thank you and Ms. Boyle for everything. I hope you both know how grateful I am for everything you've done."

"Don't mention it," Philly said, employing Carpenter's standard line to deflect praise.

Philly had debated whether to go to the AA meeting. Isabella had gone into labor. Philly had offered to stay home, but Raul had insisted she attend the meeting. "This is our first child, and I am told that the labor is likely to be a long one," he'd said.

There was a small turnout in the basement of Saint Sebastian. Philly wondered whether the attendance had to do with the weather. Late May could be magical in Boston. When the days were warm and sunny and evenings were filled with the scent of flowering trees, the idea of the church's dimly lit basement had to be a turnoff.

As she took a seat to Melanie's right, Philly thought her sponsor's smile was forced.

"You haven't been keeping up your attendance," Melanie said, her tone accusatory.

"You're right," Philly said, deciding that owning up to her shortcomings might short-circuit Melanie's dwelling on them.

"You need to treat these meetings seriously," Melanie said, and Philly felt her irritation rising. It had been over a year since she'd had a drink. True, she still longed for a beer, a craving that would never go away. But Melanie seemed determined to dwell on negatives, had not even acknowledged her one-year sobriety milestone.

"Again, you're right," Philly said. "But you know how it is. Sometimes my kid and work get in the way."

"Showing up here is your priority," Melanie said. "I've also got a kid and a job as you know. Don't get to thinking that because you made it for a year you've got this beat. It doesn't work that way."

Philly *had* been thinking that with a year of sobriety under her belt she had gotten on top of her drinking. She remembered the time after she had first started going to meetings when Melanie had called her out, said she probably thought she was better than everyone else who attended meetings and didn't need to be at the church. At the time, Melanie had been right. And she still was. Philly felt that she didn't need to go to two or three weekly meetings. And Melanie hadn't even gone to college. It was hard accepting gospel truths from a woman who lacked her education.

"I'm trying," Philly said, stifling the urge to lash out at Melanie. She knew her sponsor cared for her.

"Let's come to order," Charlie announced. "Welcome everyone."

Philly was glad the meeting had begun. She didn't want to say anything that would alienate Melanie.

"Tonight I thought we'd talk about priorities," Charlie began, and Melanie nodded knowingly at Charlie's use of the word she had just employed. "If you had to name the first priority in your life, what would it be?"

"Family," said a young woman dressed in black jeans, a black leather jacket, low cut black boots.

"Same for me," said a bald, middle-aged man whose ponytail was more impressive than Charlie's and was secured in place by a red bandana.

Philly agreed with the two assessments. She realized that when she thought of family, she focused not only on Daisy but Raul and Isabella, Paul, and even Sarah Ferguson.

"I understand that response," Charlie said, shaking his head slowly. "I do. We have loved ones who we care for and who we worry about and who rely on us. Family seems like it has to be the most important thing in our lives. But I don't think it is or should be our top priority. I think our top priority is something different."

Charlie paused. Philly appreciated the group leader's timing. His pauses made you think of what alternative he had in mind.

"I think that for each of us, our top priority needs to be our self. I know that sounds selfish. But that's what I've come up with. We need to make sure we're doing okay because if we're not, any other priority, whether it's family or work or something else, is going to come undone. What do you think?" Charlie challenged. "Am I all wet?"

"I don't think you're all wet but I'm not sure I totally agree with you," Melanie said. "I think that if I ever took another drink, I'd lose everything I've got, especially my daughter. I know they'd take my daughter away from me. That's why I come here."

Philly didn't think she was in Melanie's boat. If she slipped, relapsed, she couldn't imagine that Daisy would be taken away from her. But then Carpenter preached that thinking something bad can't possibly happen, was a sure sign that it would.

"Anybody else have an opinion?" Charlie asked.

"I understand what you're saying," Philly spoke out. "But when I come here, I'm doing it for my family, my daughter really. I'm not really thinking about myself."

Charlie nodded, his ponytail bobbing.

"I'm here out of fear," the woman in black said. "I've also got a daughter. When I come here, I don't ever think it's because I want to be here."

Charlie again nodded, waited patiently to see if any other comment would be forthcoming. "I appreciate these last comments. I really do. But I've got this theory. The theory goes that until you want to be here for yourself, you're still at risk. Maybe that doesn't make any sense to some of you. But until you're here for yourself, you won't have the mindset to put behind you this disease we're battling that landed you here in the first place."

Philly had no comeback to Charlie's assertion. "Are you saying we all need therapy?" she asked.

"Maybe we do, maybe we don't," Charlie said. "The fact is that for most of us therapy isn't an option because of money or time or whatever. So that's why it's important to come here and talk because maybe through talk you'll get an insight as to what brought about this disease. We're all each of us has."

Melanie was looking at her expectantly and Philly was grateful that her pale, thin sponsor didn't have an I-told-you-so look on her face. "Okay, you made your point," she whispered to her sponsor. "But I still think my attendance is going to suck."

Later, Philly sat with Melanie over coffee, making the time to do so as a fence-mending gesture. Then she hurried to her car anxious to get home. Her cell phone chirped, and she stopped to view the message. Raul had sent a text: "A girl. All are well." So much for the myth of a long first labor.

41

Frank Stevens was over six feet tall and a solid slab of muscle. The three-sport letterman was dark-complexioned with widespread brown eyes and a rugged jaw. He had a determined, calm air. Simon figured Brittany Stern had used sexual favors to get Stevens to help Alison Lind. An unworthy thought, but possible.

"Frank is willing to testify for Ms. Lind," Stern declared. "He's the only guy who will as far as I can tell."

They were standing in the high school parking lot besides Brittany's car, a powder blue, four-door Chevy that looked like it had seen better days. It was a warm, sunny day and both students had a free period. Stevens closed his eyes and raised his face to the sun. His dark features glowed.

"You're a football, basketball and baseball star," Simon said, assessing that Stevens would likely excel in any sport he chose.

"I wouldn't say a star," Stevens replied, opening his eyes and facing Simon.

"Frank's being modest," Brittany said. "He's been a starter since his sophomore year. He'll be a three-sport letterman, three years running. Even in a small school like Middlemarch High, that's impressive."

Stevens responded with a self-deprecating shrug. "It's no big deal."

"So how can you help Ms. Lind?" Simon asked.

"Brittany's told me about the case. I can tell you that every coach I've ever had has cursed up a storm. Also, to a man, the coaches have gone with punishment drills."

Simon began jotting down key words on a pocket-sized notepad.

"I understand the boys' teams don't do all that well," Simon said.

"We don't totally suck," Stevens responded. "It's just that we're a small school even for the small school division, and the bigger schools have more manpower to stock their teams. It's no fun losing regularly but the guys who go out for the teams like to play."

"What are you going to do when you graduate?' Simon changed the subject.

"I've been accepted at Wesleyan," Stevens said. "I'm looking forward to college."

"What do you think of the guys who have coached the teams you've been on?"

"They're okay. I don't think any of them is a great coach. But they try. I've got no complaints about them."

"Do they play favorites?"

"I've never thought about that," Stevens said. "I don't think so. The team rosters are small, so I don't think playing favorites enters into who plays."

"Do you have any impression of Ms. Lind?"

Stern eyed Stevens with interest.

"Not really. She's got a reputation for being strict. And loud."

"Are any of the guys who coach the boys' teams strict?"

"Not the way I hear Lind is. The guys who coach the teams I've been on don't really bust balls if you know what I mean. Like I said, they curse and yell and give us punishment drills. But I wouldn't call them strict. That may sound inconsistent. It's hard to explain. It's like they don't really tax us physically. I've heard that's not the case with coach Lind."

Simon had never played any sport. He found it difficult to follow Stevens' last comments. "So how come you're the only guy who's willing to help Ms. Lind?" he asked.

Stevens took a deep breath and let the air out slowly. "Brittany explained coach Lind's lawsuit to me. I want to help. I'm gay."

The girl's shocked look couldn't have been faked, Simon thought. "Jesus!" she said softly. "Aren't you taking Jessica to the prom?"

"Yeah. That's probably not the best move I've ever made."

"Jesus!" she repeated. "Well, your secret's safe with me."

"No," Stevens said. "Now that I've told you, it's no longer a secret. I don't care what you say."

Brittany Stern leaned up against her car plainly floored by Stevens' revelation. "This is incredible!"

Simon found himself thinking like a lawyer. Would it be better or worse for Lind's case if it were known Stevens was gay?

"Are you going to tell Jessica?" Stern asked.

"I haven't gotten that far," Stevens said. "I'm sort of playing this by ear. I wasn't sure if I was going to get into this right now."

"Jesus! I don't fucking believe this!"

Simon decided that it would be better for Lind's case if Stevens testified and was straight. But there was no way he was going to tell the athlete to keep his sexual orientation under wraps. He remembered when he had told Rachel that he was gay. There was that moment of disappointment in her eyes that told him he had been right in thinking that Rachel was interested in a relationship between them. He pictured Stevens revealing his sexual orientation to this girl, Jessica, and disappointing a girl who had been hoping for romance the night of her prom.

"Thanks for coming forward to help Ms. Lind," Simon said, figuring it was time for this meeting to come to a close.

"Don't mention it," Stevens said.

Stern moved to Stevens and gave him a kiss on the cheek. "I never would have guessed," she said. "And for the record, I'm keeping my mouth shut."

Raul would have to be hit with a tranquilizer dart prepared for an elephant if he were ever to calm down. In Isabella's hospital room, he had administered extravagant hugs and kisses to Philly, Daisy, Paul, and Sarah Ferguson surprising Paul and causing Sarah to blush.

"Isabella was wonderful," Raul gushed. "She was so brave, so determined. And look, please, at Rosalind. Have you ever seen such a beautiful baby?"

Philly was holding Daisy and her daughter was struggling to be put down. But when Raul pointed to his new daughter, Daisy quieted, stretched to get a better look.

"See the baby," Philly whispered, pointing. Rosalind's eyes were closed. Thick black hair spilled out of the hood of a dark blue one piece. The baby had Raul's dark coloring. Philly was willing to bet that when the baby opened her eyes, Isabella's luminous dark eyes would be revealed. Philly moved closer to Isabella as the newborn snuggled against her mother.

"That was one short labor," Philly said to Isabella.

"I suppose I'm lucky," Isabella replied. "As soon as you left the house contractions came on quickly. I was fully dilated when I was wheeled into the delivery room. I was told this is not usually the way it goes with a first pregnancy."

"She's beautiful," Philly said, echoing Raul's comment. "Congratulations."

Philly became conscious of Paul at her side. "I want one of those," he whispered. "With you."

Philly gave his hand a squeeze.

"Say something," Paul continued in a whisper.

"The thought has entered my mind," Philly whispered back.

"That's a good thing, right?"

Philly nodded. "Right," she said softly.

Philly maneuvered Daisy closer to the newborn. "You can touch her if you're gentle," she said, and she drew Daisy's hand to the sleeping Rosalind. Daisy touched Rosalind's arm as the room fell silent. "Be gentle," she reminded her daughter.

Daisy continued to make contact with Rosalind's swaddled arm and the baby responded with a full body spasm that caused Daisy to withdraw her hand.

"She's going to be your new best buddy," Philly whispered to Daisy. "It'll be like you have a little sister."

Daisy began to squirm, and Philly handed her off to Paul. "Since we're all assembled," Philly announced, "here's a house update. Two down and one to go. We just need a buyer for Sarah's house."

"It would be me holding everybody up," Sarah groused.

"We're in this together," Philly reminded her babysitter. "I have a feeling it's all going to come together."

"I'm going to throw you all out soon," Isabella declared. "I'm exhausted and it'll soon be time for a feeding."

"Feedings are my favorite time," Raul enthused. "Look at them. The two women in my life."

"You're forgetting me and Sarah," Philly responded, and that brought Raul up short. "When we all move in together, it's going to be a zoo."

June

Philly's Attitude Playlist

Hollaback Girl

Gwen Stefani

42

Carpenter had told her more than once that if the client wanted to see you after you won a case, it meant bad news. Philly figured Heather Storm's unhappy look presaged another instance in which a Carpenter dictum proved to be correct. Storm had refused to discuss the meeting's purpose on the phone.

So sitting in the Boston office conference room with Rachel present and Heather Storm seemingly at a loss as to how to begin, Philly braced herself. "How's Marilyn doing?" she prompted, certain that whatever was troubling Storm likely had to do with her daughter.

Storm sighed. She was still painfully thin and the washed out jeans, white T-shirt, and a pale blue sweater vest she wore hung loose on her body. The woman's bony arms made for the rare occasion when Philly appreciated having some meat on her bones.

"The new school's working out well for Marilyn. She's made some new friends. I talked with one of her teachers who says she's getting on well."

With the good news out of the way, Philly waited for the bad news. Rachel also seemed to be steeling herself for an unhappy update; her brow was furrowed, and she hadn't smiled since they sat down.

Storm took in a deep breath and let the air out slowly. "A few nights ago, Marilyn told me that she had made up what she'd said about James."

Rachel's mouth dropped open. Philly fought to keep a neutral expression. "Who else knows about this?" she asked.

"Just James. I felt I had to call him."

Philly wished that she had been consulted before that call had been made. Still she couldn't fault Storm—the woman was in love with James Farrell and it was a natural reaction to let Farrell know what Marilyn had said. "What was his reaction?"

"I thought he'd be angry," Storm said. "I actually thought he'd want to hurt Marilyn for what she put him through. At first he didn't say anything. But then when he thanked me for believing him, he didn't sound angry, more like he was resigned."

"Is that it?" Philly probed.

Storm shook her head. "He said that didn't change things as far as he and Marilyn were concerned. He didn't want anything to do with her. I told him we could go back to court and get that order changed. He said he didn't want to."

"I could mention all this to Mr. Farrell's lawyer," Rachel spoke for the first time.

"I don't think that's going to change James' mind," Storm replied.

"What about Marilyn?" Philly asked. "Did you ask her whether she'd be okay with Mr. Farrell moving back in with the two of you?"

"I brought that up and she said she liked it with just the two of us."

"How did Marilyn come to bring the subject up?" Rachel asked. Philly observed that Rachel had thrown off her shock at Marilyn's admission and was back to thinking about potential legal steps.

"I asked her whether she missed James, and that's when she blurted out that she'd lied about him. I don't know. Maybe she was feeling guilty about what she'd done."

"What do you want us to do?" Philly asked Storm.

"I want the three of us back together," Storm said with feeling.

"Two of the three of you don't seem to want that to happen," Philly opted for bluntness. "We can't make Mr. Farrell want to rejoin you and Marilyn any more than we can make Marilyn want to welcome Mr. Farrell back into her life."

Storm slumped in her seat. Her bony arms wrapped around her as if she were cold and wanted to ward off shivering.

"What about Ms. Boyle's suggestion?" Philly said. "She can contact Mr. Farrell's lawyer with this news. Maybe after the lawyer talks with him, Mr. Farrell will have a change of heart."

Storm lowered her eyes, continued to hug herself tightly. "Sure, why not. I've got nothing to lose."

It occurred to Philly that Storm could have made up Marilyn's revelation. In any event, what if Marilyn ultimately denied making a confession to her mother when the matter returned to court?

"Ms. Boyle will call Mr. Farrell's lawyer," Philly said. "We'll get back to you when we hear back from the lawyer."

Storm nodded without enthusiasm.

"There's nothing to stop you from going back to court and trying to get the court order changed so that Mr. Farrell is able to contact you and Marilyn."

"If James wants nothing to do with Marilyn, I don't see the point."

"Then we contact his lawyer and wait to see what happens."

"Okay," Storm said. "That's sort of a plan."

43

Swan boats leisurely circumnavigated the pond in the center of the Boston Public Garden. Rachel had wanted to sit down with Stephen Minor over lunch, but James Farrell's lawyer said he wanted to stretch his legs. Rachel had to admit it was nice to be outside in the sun with a cool breeze stirring the flowers. They had strolled across the Boston Common to the Public Garden in silence and Rachel was relieved when Minor finally pointed to the vacant bench near the swan boat loading area. "Did you talk to your client?" she led off.

Minor nodded. He gazed out over the water and lifted his face toward the sun.

"And?" Rachel prompted.

"It's pretty much what I thought would be the case. Farrell isn't going to do anything. He has no interest in maintaining a relationship with Marilyn. I can't say I blame him after what she put him through."

Rachel accepted that Marilyn had probably done the most vicious thing a child could do to a parent. Still, even when that happened, did a parent permanently sever all relations with the child? Marilyn had to have been troubled to have done what she did. Did the demons haunting her warrant Farrell giving his daughter another chance?

"Doesn't he want to clear his name?"

"It's not a high priority. He doesn't want to go back to court."

"Is Farrell going to help support his daughter?" Rachel asked.

Minor shrugged. "I think so but I'm not sure. If I had to guess, I'd say he'll help your client out in a pinch but won't be happy doing it."

"What about him and my client?"

"I'd say that's over. Farrell said that he was going to move on."

What did moving on mean? Rachel considered. Did anyone ever truly distance himself from a past misery?

"Heather Storm is going to be disappointed," Rachel said.

"The whole thing is sad."

Rachel realized that the business part of this get together was over. The Storms were on their own. She tried to think of a small talk subject and failed. She had willed herself to think on her feet in the course of litigation yet now, in what should have been a less stressful situation, she was tongue-tied. Minor cast a quick glance at his watch, a sure sign that he was already planning his escape.

"Enough shop talk," Rachel said to her own surprise. "Would you be interested in having dinner with me sometime?"

Minor looked startled, but Rachel observed that her direct question had swept away his non-communicative air. For the first time this afternoon he was regarding her with interest.

"Not particularly," Minor said, and Rachel felt crushed because Minor was smiling as he dismissed her suggestion. "But I would be interested in taking you to a Red Sox game next week."

Rachel decided not to feign an interest in sports that she didn't have. "Okay," she said. "But I'm not a sports fan. I'll probably be lousy company. I don't know anything about baseball."

"This is the Red Sox we're talking about. The seats I have are great."

"The seats will probably be wasted on me."

"Why don't you stop telling it like it is?" Minor urged.

"Okay," Rachel said. She didn't know whether to feel annoyed that Minor seemed to be enjoying her discomfort.

But then Minor's look turned serious. "I'm seeing another woman," he said. "I wanted to be clear about that up front."

"Just so you won't be seeing her at this game you're taking me to," Rachel said, amazed that she had come up with a pretty fair comeback.

"No, I won't."

"Did you ask this woman to go to the game?"

Minor nodded; *he* now looked uncomfortable which Rachel thought was a case of turnabout is fair play.

"I guess I'm your second choice."

"You could put it that way."

Rachel didn't see any other way to put it. She debated whether pride should get in the way of something she wanted to do. "Go Red Sox," she said, making what she hoped was the right decision and drawing a laugh from Minor that sounded somewhat forced.

44

Carpenter still couldn't get a handle on the woman who had been assigned by the Massachusetts Commission Against Discrimination to hear Alison Lind's case against Middlemarch High School. Anne Forrester had denied the high school's motion to dismiss Lind's case but that was no guaranty she would rule in Lind's favor at trial. The fortyish hearing officer's expression was hard to read. Carpenter continued to suspect that the short, stocky, stoop-shouldered woman hadn't played sports. Carpenter attributed his unaccustomed nervousness to the fact that Lind's case was the first of many where getting paid depended on winning.

The MCAD hearing room was crowded. Lind and her companion, Beth Finegold, were both in attendance. Again, Lind appeared nervous, Finegold calm. Norman Joyce, the high school principal, had been subpoenaed and he looked thoroughly uncomfortable. Richard Morgan and his daughter were present and so were Brittany Stern and Frank Stevens, the student witnesses that Simon had produced. A number of other young people were probably there to be witnesses for the high school, many of whom, Lind had confirmed, were the disgruntled seniors she had stripped of starter positions. Other adults in the room were probably parents of the complaining students. Darren Grayson, the school attorney, tall and slim, sported the same confident air he had displayed during the previous agency hearing.

"Let's come to order," Forrester directed. "We have a lot of witnesses and I'd like to try to complete testimony today if possible. I won't require opening statements from counsel. I would ask Ms. Lind to call her first witness."

Carpenter rose. "Norman Joyce," he announced, and was pleased to see the principal blanch as he made his way to the witness chair.

Carpenter quickly established that Joyce had been principal at Middlemarch High School for three years and had held assistant principal and principal positions at other high schools for another seventeen years.

"Were you the official who fired Ms. Lind?" Carpenter asked.

"Yes."

"Why did you fire her?"

Joyce stared at his hands as if he wished they held a note card prop. "There had been complaints from students on the team and parents. The complaints had to do with Ms. Lind's style of coaching, use of profanity, punishing girls on the team. That kind of thing."

"Does that complete your answer?"

"Pretty much," Joyce said after directing a nervous glance in Grayson's direction.

"Did you interview Ms. Lind in connection with these complaints before you fired her?"

"Yes."

"What was her response to the complaints?"

Joyce again stared at his hands. "She admitted that she swore and yelled at players." Joyce paused and looked upward. "She said the girls complaining about her had been demoted from starters because they weren't playing well."

"Did Ms. Lind say anything else in her defense?"

"That was generally what she said."

"Isn't it true that the complaining students and their complaining parents objected to the starter demotions?"

"I would say so."

"As principal of the high school, do you believe that starter positions on school teams should be based on merit?"

Joyce shot another nervous look in Grayson's direction. Carpenter did his best to confront Joyce with his hard stare in the hope of rattling the witness. He really didn't care how Joyce answered his last question.

"I'm sure merit is important."

"Is merit more important than seniority?"

"It could be. I'm sure seniority and experience are also important."

"In your view should a coach be fired for basing starting positions on merit over seniority?"

"It would depend on the circumstances."

Carpenter knew a lawyer directed fallback position when he heard one from a witness. "What circumstances would those be?" he pressed.

Joyce sighed. "I'd want to hear what else was going on."

"Really?" Carpenter said. "Was one reason you fired Ms. Lind her decision to start certain girls over others?"

"That was a factor that entered into my decision given the dissension that resulted."

"The complainers against Ms. Lind were demoted starter seniors, correct?"

"I believe so."

"Before you fired Ms. Lind, did you determine whether her starter decisions were based upon merit?"

"I don't understand your question."

"Really?" Carpenter repeated, this time raising his voice. "Were the girls Ms. Lind chose to start better players than the complaining seniors who were demoted from starting positions?"

Joyce shifted position in the witness chair. "I really couldn't say."

"So, when you made the decision to fire Ms. Lind, is it correct that you didn't know whether the starters selected by Ms. Lind for the girls' soccer team were better players than the demoted seniors who complained about Ms. Lind?"

Joyce slumped in his chair. "I guess so."

"Do male coaches of boys' high school sports teams at Middlemarch swear and yell at their players?"

"I suspect they do on occasion."

"Before you fired Ms. Lind, did you make any effort to find out whether male coaches yelled and swore at the boys on their teams?"

"Nothing specific."

"When you fired Ms. Lind, is it true that for all you knew, her swearing and yelling was no different or perhaps less intense than the swearing and yelling of male coaches?"

Joyce blinked rapidly for a moment. "I guess that's right."

Forrester was writing, her expression unreadable. At least she's writing, Carpenter thought.

"What was the girls' soccer team's record in the just concluded spring season?"

Joyce colored. "The team didn't win any games."

"This team that didn't win a game—were the starters on the team the seniors who complained about Ms. Lind?"

"I believe so."

"With Ms. Lind not around, who coached that winless team?"

"That would have been Mr. Klinger."

"Are you talking about Mr. Howard Klinger, a math teacher, who coached the girls' soccer team before Ms. Lind took over?"

"That's right."

"This would be the same Mr. Klinger who never had a winning season before coach Lind took over, correct?"

"Yes."

"In your opinion is Mr. Klinger an effective coach?"

"I haven't heard any complaints about him."

"That's not my question. Is Mr. Klinger, the man who never had a winning season before Ms. Lind took over the team, and who led the team to a winless season this year, an effective coach?"

"In terms of won-lost record, probably not. In terms of players and parents not complaining about his coaching I would say yes."

"Are you saying, Mr. Joyce, that a coach's won-lost record plays no role in assessing whether a coach is effective?"

"I'm not saying that."

"Are you saying that a coach is effective if no one complains about him or her?"

"I'm not saying that."

"Why hasn't Mr. Klinger been fired since his won-lost record is abysmal?"

"As I said, wins and losses don't necessarily determine whether a coach is effective."

"Tell us one thing that Mr. Klinger has done as a coach that indicates he's effective?"

Joyce lowered his head and studied his hands. "I couldn't say really. I haven't really looked into his coaching technique."

"Why not? The man just led his coached team to a winless season."

"I just haven't done anything to review the situation."

"How did Ms. Lind do as a coach when it came to wins and losses?"

"Her teams had winning records."

"What about the boys' teams coached by male coaches? In the last three years has any boys' team had a winning record?"

"I don't believe so."

"Do you attribute the winning records of Ms. Lind's team to her coaching?"

"I'm sure her coaching had something to do with it."

"When it comes to wins and losses, she was the best coach at the high school in recent years, wasn't she?"

"I think that's correct."

"Why haven't you fired all the male coaches who can't seem to coach any team to a winning season?"

"As I said, winning and losing is only a part of whether a coach is retained."

"Does the other part have to do with complaints from players and their parents when the players are demoted from starter positions because they are not better players than other team members?"

"We treat complaints from students and parents seriously as I said."

Carpenter noticed that Forrester had stopped writing. She was regarding Joyce skeptically which was a positive sign. Time to sum up, he thought, putting aside that Joyce hadn't really answered his last question.

"In your experience as a principal, do high school students and teachers and school administrators take pride in a winning sports team?"

Joyce glanced in Grayson's direction. "I would say so."

"Let's try to summarize what you've testified to today," Carpenter said. "Ms. Lind's teams had better won-lost records than the teams coached by males, correct?"

"Yes."

"You fired Ms. Lind without making any effort to determine whether any male coach yelled and swore, correct?"

"Yes."

"Seniors were demoted from starter positions and you have no idea whether the demotions were based on merit, correct?"

"I never evaluated any of the players if that's what you mean."

"No," Carpenter said, again raising his voice. "That's not what I mean. Did you make any attempt to find out whether the demoted seniors were better players than the players who took their places or inferior players to the players who took their places?"

"I never got into that level of detail."

"You fired Ms. Lind because seniors who were demoted from starter positions and their parents complained about the seniors' demotions, correct?"

"That was one reason. We had never had students and parents complaining so intensely about a coach before the complaints came in about Ms. Lind."

"Were the complaints the principal reason for firing Ms. Lind?"

Joyce paused. "I'd say so," he finally said.

"Would a girls' soccer team member who was not starting but was better than starting players have a legitimate complaint in your opinion?"

"That's possible," Joyce said after another long pause.

Carpenter leaned down to consult with Simon. "I'm inclined to stop here," he whispered.

Simon nodded. "I don't think the hearing officer is impressed with Mr. Joyce," he replied in a whisper.

"No further questions," Carpenter announced. He glanced toward Grayson. The school lawyer now had a tactical decision to make. He could cross-examine Joyce now, or call Joyce as a witness when it was time to present the school's case.

"Just a few questions," Grayson said, and Carpenter agreed with his opponent's decision. In Grayson's shoes, he'd want to finish with Joyce immediately and not see hide nor hair of the man for the rest of the case.

"Why did the complaints by students and teachers as to Ms. Lind play a role in your decision to fire her?"

"As I said, we never had such an outpouring of complaints about a coach before. There seemed to be a lot of dissention as to Ms. Lind's coaching style and the way she related to the girls on her team. I viewed that dissention as a negative."

"You were asked about looking into male coaches swearing, yelling, and ordering punishment drills. Why didn't you perform an investigation into male coaches?"

"I didn't think it was necessary. Even if male coaches were doing all those things, nobody had ever complained about the male coaches. For whatever reason, students and parents found Ms. Lind's swearing and yelling offensive and complained about *her* conduct."

Grayson nodded having gotten the response from Joyce he was looking for. "I'd like to direct your attention to the subject of high school teams' won-lost records. Mr. Carpenter asked you a number of questions on that subject. For a school such as Middlemarch High School, is a team's won-lost record a major consideration in evaluating a coach?"

"I'd say it's a consideration, but I wouldn't call it a major consideration. Our high school is small, and the larger high schools have an advantage over us when it comes to team sports. As an educator, I'm particularly interested in whether the team has good spirit and players are enjoying their athletic experience. That didn't seem to be the case with Ms. Lind's team given the serious outcry by students and parents as to her manner and conduct."

"I have nothing further," Grayson said before taking his seat.

Carpenter stood. "How is it," he said, "that Ms. Lind's teams are successful against the larger high schools you mentioned, and no male-coached team is successful?"

"I really couldn't say," Joyce replied.

"Might the answer be that Ms. Lind is a far superior coach to the male coaches at Middlemarch High School?"

"That's possible. But as I said, I don't view won-lost records as what determines whether a coach is successful."

"What are high school athletics supposed to teach students?' Carpenter changed his approach.

"Oh, teamwork and cooperation. Work ethic. Trying to do your best in competition and testing yourself. Things like that."

"Is the idea that if you work hard and do your best you will be rewarded for those efforts?"

Joyce glanced at Grayson and Carpenter sensed the principal wasn't sure of the direction of these questions. "I would agree with that."

"Is one of the purposes of high school athletics for a student to learn that it doesn't matter how good you are—what determines whether you get to play is whether you're a complainer and have seniority?"

"No, I . . ."

"Is one of the purposes of high school athletics for a student to learn that merit is of no moment because what really counts is to complain loudly so you'll get your way?"

"No, I . . ."

"Those seniors who complained? Tell me this Mr. Joyce. If the seniors who complained were inferior to juniors and sophomores but got their starting roles restored from complaining and from their parents complaining, what valuable lesson were those seniors taught?"

Joyce reddened. "The new coach made the decision on who the starters were."

"You didn't answer my question. What lesson did those seniors learn if they were inferior to juniors and sophomores and got their starting roles back because they complained and their parents complained?"

"I can't speak for them. You'll have to ask them."

"I'm asking *you*, Mr. Joyce, and it's clear *you* don't have an answer. Nothing further."

"Anything else, Mr. Grayson?" Forrester inquired.

"No, Your Honor."

Forrester turned to the Middlemarch principal. "I have a question for you," Mr. Joyce. "Does your administration evaluate teachers and coaches?"

"Of course."

"Before she was fired, how did Ms. Lind's evaluations stack up against the evaluations of male coaches?"

Joyce averted Forrester's gaze. "I'd say her evaluations were on a par with the evaluations of the male coaches."

"On a par," Forrester repeated, and she wrote in her notebook. "If the complaints you told us about hadn't come forth, would Ms. Lind have been fired?"

Joyce shifted in his seat. "Probably not."

"We'll take a short break," Forrester announced.

Carpenter didn't think Darren Grayson had scored any points in his cross-examination of Richard Morgan after the break, and so far, in his opinion, Grayson was faring no better in taking on Morgan's daughter, Fran. Under Simon's direct examination, the elder Morgan testified that Alison Lind was the best coach he had observed at Middlemarch High School, even better than the man who had coached the baseball teams on which his son had been a star pitcher. Morgan had marveled at how Lind had the girls' soccer team in phenomenal physical condition so that at the end of a game, the Middlemarch team often got its win by wearing down its opponents, being fitter and faster. Morgan couldn't recall any game he attended in which a Lind-coached team had been outworked or outhustled. His daughter Fran, a natural athlete, had never truly gotten in shape until Lind began coaching her. According to Morgan, Lind had the courage to start Fran as a freshman. Some gutless coaches would have let Fran sit on the bench in deference to inferior upperclassmen. Yes, Morgan had heard Lind swear. But Lind's swearing was no worse than the swearing exhibited by the male coaches his son had played for. Besides, Morgan went on—wasn't swearing up a storm what coaches did?

Grayson had tried to get the elder Morgan to acknowledge that a school administration didn't have to tolerate a coach's profanity. Morgan had laughed at Grayson and refused to be pigeonholed. If a school system wanted to hire namby-pamby coaches who never uttered a four-letter word, then Morgan was of the view the school system should put that in its job description. "The school would get no takers if that happened," Morgan had predicted. "And besides," Morgan had added, "kids today swear worse than any coach I've been around."

In response to questions from Simon, Fran Morgan had testified that Lind was able to transfer her competitive drive and intensity to the girls on her team. If it hadn't been for Lind's superior coaching, she wouldn't have become an immediate starter when she went to college. Lind's swearing was no big deal. "It's part of her competitive fire," Fran had testified on direct examination. "For me and the girls I played with, Coach's language just rolled off our backs.

And when it came to punishment drills, I can't think of a time when we didn't deserve what Coach had us do."

Carpenter wouldn't have tried Grayson's approach in cross-examining Fran Morgan. The high school's lawyer tried to downplay the success of Lind-coached teams.

"Would you agree that a favorable won-lost record doesn't necessarily make for a good coach?" Grayson had just asked.

"No," Fran fired back. "Why would I agree with such an asinine statement?"

"Do you agree that a coach needs to be a positive role model?" Grayson asked.

"Not really. May I explain?"

"No," Grayson cut Fran Morgan off.

"I want to hear the witness' answer," Forrester took charge. "What did you want to say?"

Fran Morgan turned in her seat and faced Forrester. "Any kid who goes out for a high school team wants to win. That's just the way it is. If you don't want to win, you shouldn't be playing, in my opinion. Coach Lind wanted our teams to win. She came up with strategies to help us win. She scouted other teams and had a game plan for us. Not all of us liked her all of the time. But I respected her. I think all the girls I played with respected her. She didn't mince words. She yelled at you if you screwed up. But so what? When I played for Coach Lind, I wasn't looking for her to be my friend. I was looking for her to be my coach. And she was. She made me a better player. When we think of role models, we mistakenly think of people with no warts or blemishes. Coach wasn't like that, but she was a great coach."

Forrester nodded to Grayson to continue.

"Was Coach Lind a bully?" Grayson asked.

"Not in my opinion."

"Since you have a lot of opinions," Grayson pursued, "is it your opinion that the only way a coach can be a good coach is to come on strong to her players?"

Fran Morgan took her time before answering. "Not necessarily. But I think it's important to high school players that the coach be herself. A team takes on the personality of its coach. The girls' soccer teams I was on had a certain swagger and I think it came from Coach Lind. We didn't give an inch on the field. When we were in a group, we could stare down the guys on the boys' teams because we were winners and they weren't. I can't tell you how big a deal that was. Maybe a soft-spoken coach could have gotten similar results for us, but I don't think so."

Carpenter wondered when Grayson would decide to quit while he was behind, and he soon had his answer. "Nothing further," Grayson said.

It struck Carpenter that Brittany Stern had the same tenacity as Fran Morgan. Under Simon's carefully sequenced questions, Stern had testified that the recently concluded winless soccer season was hard to take. "We had a nucleus of sophomores and juniors who were committed to winning and willing to work our butts off," Stern had explained. "When Coach Klinger took over, he benched a lot of the girls in that core group and played the seniors. There are a bunch of those seniors here today, so I'll say this to their face. They were lazy and didn't give a damn. That's why we lost. And then there was the fact that Coach Klinger really didn't know very much about the game of soccer."

Carpenter had glanced to the rear of the hearing room at that point in Stern's testimony and had observed Lind sitting erect but without emotion, while her partner, Beth Finegold, was wiping tears from her eyes.

"It was a shitty year," Stern had concluded her direct testimony without showing any concern that she had uttered a tepid oath. Apparently the team did take on the personality of its coach. "There were times when I considered quitting the team."

Now Grayson rose to cross-examine. The Morgans had been a handful and Grayson had to be thinking that he was in for more of the same with Stern.

"There was nothing to prevent you from quitting the team if you were unhappy, was there?" Grayson began, and Carpenter began to wonder whether Grayson was one of those guys who exuded confidence but lacked judgment; he would never have brought up quitting the team had he had to cross-examine Stern.

"Actually, there were two things that prevented me from quitting the team," Stern rounded on Grayson. "First, I love the game and I was damned if I was going to give it up because the school saddled us with a useless, spineless coach. Second, I'm not a quitter."

For a moment it appeared to Carpenter that Grayson was incapable of asking another question.

"Are you saying that the school can't hire a coach with a coaching philosophy you disagree with?"

"No. But I am saying a team is entitled to a coach that *has* a coaching philosophy. Coach Klinger probably doesn't know how to lace up soccer shoes."

"Do you play any other sport?"

"I play basketball in the winter."

"Who coaches the basketball team?"

"Mr. Spire."

"Are you a starter on the team?"

"I became a starter mid-season."

"How did the team do last season?"

"We won one game."

"Did you regard Mr. Spire as a good coach?"

"I would say so."

"Does Mr. Spire yell and curse?"

"No."

"Then it's possible for a good coach to perform coaching duties without yelling and swearing, isn't it?"

"That's Mr. Spire's personality."

"That's not what I asked you," Grayson persisted. "Would you agree that Mr. Spire is able to be a good coach without yelling and swearing?"

Stern glared at Grayson. Carpenter said a silent prayer that Stern's competitive nature would take a back seat and that she not fight Grayson on the point.

"I'd agree with that."

"Nothing further," Grayson said, and Carpenter had to acknowledge that his opponent had managed to end on a high note.

Whispering increased when Simon called Frank Stevens to the stand. Carpenter turned in his seat and observed a number of the girls who were likely to testify for the school huddled together in an animated discussion. Several girls not in the huddle were staring at Stevens with what could only be described as lust.

As Stevens answered Simon's background questions, Carpenter understood that he was probably looking at the boy who was the consensus leader of the senior class. Stevens was an imposing physical specimen. He responded to Simon's questions in a low, well-modulated voice and seemed totally self-possessed.

"As a three-year, three-sport letterman, did you have an opportunity to observe the male coaches who coached the teams you were on?" Simon asked.

"I did."

"Did any of the coaches conduct themselves with yelling or swearing?"

"That would be all of them."

"With respect to the swearing, what were some of the epithets you heard?"

Stevens met Simon's gaze as he gathered his thoughts. "I would say f-bombs were the most common epithet. *Lazy bastards* was another frequently used term that sticks in my mind." Stevens paused and his serious expression gave way to a smile. "This is a sex discrimination and sexual orientation discrimination case, isn't it?"

"Yes," Simon answered.

"Then you might be interested in some of the other things the male coaches said to try to get us to play harder."

"I would indeed," Simon responded.

"At some point, I would say that every male coach I ever played for compared us to sissified girls. I remember my football coach in junior year screaming at the team during practice saying we were playing like a bunch of limp-wristed girls. He said we reminded him of pansies and that we should all be wearing dresses."

Carpenter guessed that Stevens had departed from their scripted direct testimony and Simon was trying to decide how best to traverse the road Stevens had opened up.

Simon paused very briefly, and then continued. "Were you personally offended by any of the epithets or other comments you've mentioned to us today?"

"Yes and no," Stevens responded. "Truthfully, I didn't mind the f-bombs or being called a lazy bastard. These days, f-bombs are so common it's like they're nothing special. However, I did mind being called a pansy and I did mind being compared to a girl."

"Is there any reason you took offense to the remarks you just mentioned?"

Stevens took a deep breath. "Yes. As a gay man, I regarded those snide comments related to gender and sexual orientation as offensive."

Carpenter resisted turning around when gasps of surprise came from the rear of the hearing room. Forrester called for quiet. Stevens sent an odd smile in Simon's direction.

"As a student athlete, did you form any impression of the girls' teams at Middlemarch High School?" Simon asked when Forrester had restored order.

"I did."

"What were those impressions?"

Grayson started to rise to object but quickly took his seat. Carpenter thought that was the right call, Forrester was going to let in all evidence, so objections were pointless.

"The girls' soccer team was the class act of the school when it came to teams. They were the only consistent winners. Fran Morgan said they had a swagger and she was right. All of our teams played against teams from bigger high schools. But that never affected the girls' soccer teams when they were coached by Ms. Lind. She got those girls to play. I don't mean to be sexist. I mean this as a compliment. Ms. Lind's teams played the way good boys' teams play. I don't know. Maybe I shouldn't have said that. Maybe I'm being hypocritical."

Carpenter was pleased that Forrester regarded Stevens with interest. If Forrester had participated in athletics as a girl, she might identify with Stevens' last statement.

"Nothing further," Simon said, taking his seat.

It seemed to Carpenter that Grayson again rose cautiously. Stevens' sexual orientation had to be a surprise to the school's lawyer.

"Did you ever complain to anyone about a coach's swearing?" Grayson led off.

"No."

"Did you ever complain to anyone about a coach's yelling?"

"No."

"Did you ever complain to anyone about any remark made by a coach that you found offensive?"

"No."

"Did you ever complain to anyone about the coaching techniques of any coach you played for?"

"No."

"Did you ever complain to anyone about a coach's decision as to starting players?"

"No."

"Did you ever observe a coach you played for playing favorites?"

"No."

"Did you ever observe a coach you played for discriminating against any student?"

"No."

Grayson paused and Carpenter suspected that the school's lawyer would not ask another question. If Grayson had scored any points with his questions, Forrester hadn't recorded any.

"No further questions."

"We'll break for lunch," Forrester said. "Be ready to resume in one hour sharp."

During lunch, Carpenter dealt with Lind's entourage while Simon and Lind and Beth Finegold sat at a separate table to prepare for Lind's afternoon testimony. Fran Morgan and Brittany Stern were particularly upbeat as they inhaled their sandwiches. Richard Morgan and Frank Stevens were more reserved.

"I think you and Mr. Jeffries kicked ass," Stern said. "Joyce came across as the loser he is."

"I think Coach Lind is going to get her job back," Fran Morgan enthused. "That is going to be so great."

Carpenter exchanged a look with the elder Morgan. "This is far from over," he cautioned the young women.

"I suppose they'll put some parents on and a bunch of the sorry-ass seniors who shouldn't be playing," Stern said. "What else can they do?"

Carpenter and Simon had put themselves in Grayson's position. Were they representing the school, they would call a member of the school committee to testify that Lind was a poor role model. They'd stay away from seniors and their parents.

"I know it's tempting to make snap judgments as to which side had the better of it while a case is going on," Carpenter said. "But I've learned from experience that a case is never over until it's really over."

The young women were looking at him like he was crazy, but Carpenter didn't mind. Lind had yet to testify and who knew how she'd come across. Also, maybe Grayson had a surprise or two up his sleeve.

Before the afternoon session resumed, Beth Finegold had taken Alison Lind aside and had had at her companion in a forceful tone that was accompanied by impressive hand waving and finger pointing on Finegold's part. Carpenter knew a pep talk when he saw one. He couldn't make out what Finegold was saying but the woman's emotion came through loud and clear. It was odd, he thought. Lind had been described as a motivator, a passionate coach dedicated to her players. Yet for some reason, Finegold felt a need to kick start her partner's motor.

Whatever Finegold had said to Lind seemed to have gotten through. Simon's direct testimony questions so far had been answered by Lind in a confident tone without any evidence of nerves. Forrester had been writing, another good sign.

"Your complaint claims that the high school engaged in discrimination against you based on your sex and sexual orientation," Simon prefaced his next question. "What do you base that claim on?"

Lind glanced in Finegold's direction and squared her shoulders. "Mr. Joyce told me I was fired for swearing and yelling and having players go through punishment drills. Except for Mr. Spires, every single male, heterosexual coach did the exact same thing I did and none of them got fired." Lind paused, genuinely angry, and Carpenter caught a glimpse of how she might by a holy terror patrolling the sideline of a soccer field as she screamed directions and encouragement at her players. "Mr. Joyce also told me about complaints that my partner accompanied me to an away tournament that had an overnight stay. But that was fine for one of the male coaches when he took his girlfriend to an away meet with a nighttime stopover. There's a double standard going on here."

"What do you say to Mr. Joyce's comment that senior players on your team and their parents complained about you to him?"

"I don't mind that they complained. They have a right to do that. I do mind that what was motivating the complainers was the fact that I demoted some of the seniors from being starters. The girls I demoted deserved to be demoted. Nobody has a right to a starter position. You have to earn that role. The girls I demoted weren't good enough to start. It was that simple. When I coach a team, I put my best players out there because they've earned the right to play. Nobody ever handed anything to me when I was a student-athlete. I had to earn everything I achieved. It wouldn't have been fair to the girls who had earned starter roles if I didn't play them."

Lind's answer hung in the air as Forrester wrote in her notebook. When the hearing officer looked up, Simon refocused on his witness.

"Were you present when Mr. Joyce talked about whether you were an appropriate role model?"

"Yes."

"Do you see yourself as an appropriate role model when you coached?"

"To be honest, until this case, I never thought too much about being a role model. Of course, coaches and teachers set an example for students. But I went about coaching and teaching by trying to be myself. The last thing I am is perfect. I do yell and swear on occasion. I'm the first to admit that and maybe there were times when I should have toned it down. But I tried to be fair to my players and students. I think I was. So, yes, I do think I was an appropriate role model."

"Nothing further," Simon said.

As Grayson rose to cross-examine, Carpenter studied Lind. Their client looked composed. There was a determined set to her jaw and there was an intensity in her gaze as she regarded Grayson.

"Do you ever let your emotions get the better of you?" Grayson began.

Simon started to rise to object but Carpenter restrained him. "Forrester's going to overrule any objection you make," he whispered.

"I'm sure that's happened."

"Last year, in the game against Worcester Central, did you call a referee an asshole?"

Lind colored and her fingers closed into fists. "Yeah, I did."

"Was that one of the occasions when your emotions got the better of you?"

"Yes and no," Lind said after a long pause.

"Are you saying that it's acceptable for a coach to call a referee an asshole in the course of a game?"

"Yes and no," Lind repeated.

"Answer my question," Grayson demanded. "My question calls for a yes or no answer."

"I can't answer you yes or no," Lind persisted.

"Your Honor," Grayson addressed Forrester. "I would ask you to direct the witness to answer my question yes or no."

Forrester regarded Lind for a long moment. "Why can't you respond to Mr. Grayson's question with a yes or no answer?"

"Because it's not that simple," Lind said with some heat.

"Okay," Forrester said. "Why don't you explain yourself and then we'll come back to Mr. Grayson's point."

"I remember the Worcester Central game," Lind said. "The score was tied one apiece late in the second half. Brittany Stern had worked the ball into the Worcester Central penalty area when she was kicked from behind in the calf by a Worcester Central defender who made no effort to play the ball. Brittany went down. She was hurt and had to come out of the game. The referee was right there. He saw the play, but he didn't call a penalty. I shouted to him, 'Where's the penalty?' He told me to shut the hell up or he'd throw me out of the game. So I called him an asshole." Lind paused. "Let me correct that. I called him a fucking asshole, and he did throw me out of the game which is what I was hoping he'd do."

"Let me understand," Forrester said. "You wanted to be thrown out of the game?"

"I was trying to stand up for my players. The player who hurt Brittany had committed a blatant foul and I wanted to support Brittany. I also wanted to get the team energized. I was afraid they'd let down because Brittany was out of the game and she was our best player. Before I left the game, I called the team over and told them they owed it to Brittany to win the game. And that's what happened. The rest of the team got charged up and went after it. Our center forward scored a goal just before the second half ended. I wish I'd been around to see that."

Forrester was regarding Lind inscrutably. "Do you think it was appropriate to call this referee a . . . fucking asshole?"

Lind nodded. "On that occasion yes. I realize that can be hard to understand. I'm not condoning the language I used. But I was angry, and I was determined to stand up for my players. Now that I'm thinking about this again, I wouldn't have done anything differently. My only regret is not seeing the winning goal. You have no idea what it meant to the team to beat Worcester Central without our best player."

Forrester spent some time writing in her notebook. When she looked up, she motioned to Grayson to continue his cross-examination.

Grayson had marshaled a number of other incidents in which Lind had sworn at referees, opposing coaches, and her own players. Lind recalled each incident and explained her actions. For the most part she was unrepentant. Carpenter wondered whether Forrester could truly identify with a fanatical coach with rough edges. For someone who had no interest in competitive sports, it was easy to assess Lind as a domineering autocrat who let her emotions run out of control. Carpenter saw it differently; Lind wanted to win and her actions made sense if you accepted that all-consuming desire as a reasonable objective.

"We're running late," Forrester said at the conclusion of Lind's testimony. "Let's start fresh tomorrow and begin the respondent's case."

That evening in Brighton, Philly sat in an easy chair in the living room holding Rosalind while Isabella used the second-floor bathroom. Raul was also upstairs, tapping away at his home computer, trying to solve a problem that Connie had left him with. Unlike Daisy, their baby was awake, her expression solemn. Daisy at this age seemed a lifetime ago.

Philly eased to a standing position and began to walk about the living room, humming to the baby. Philly knew that she should be feeling guilty for soaking up good baby vibes while Carpenter and Simon were gearing up for a second day of trial. Carpenter had given her a brief recap of the day's proceedings in the

Lind case. On balance, he thought that Lind had come out marginally ahead. Tomorrow, he reminded her, was another day.

Philly eased Lady Gaga's first CD into her boom box and turned down the volume. She fast forwarded to the song that gave the CD its name and began to dance across the living room floor. She had loved doing this with Daisy—still did—and Rosalind seemed okay with the motion. "Fame," she whispered to the baby and Rosalind blinked.

"Fame," Philly whispered again, bringing her face close to Rosalind's and then pulling back, the baby unfazed by a large head looming close and then receding. Philly couldn't remember what a baby's vision was like during the first weeks of life.

At times when she had twirled Daisy as she was now twirling Rosalind, she had thought about how glorious it would be to be a full-time mom. But even if she and Paul had a kid, she now realized that Daisy, Rosalind, and another baby wouldn't provide a sufficient world for her. She wanted to continue to practice law. Even if it meant throwing gobs of money at Sarah, she didn't want to give up the law.

Rosalind performed a full body shudder and settled back down. Lady Gaga began singing about money. A door closed on the second floor. Philly fast forwarded the CD until she came to *Brown Eyes*. "Brown eyes," she whispered to Rosalind.

Isabella came down the stairs and collapsed on the living room couch. "Long day?" Philly asked.

Isabella nodded. "I'm trying to imagine what it's going to be like when Rosalind doesn't sleep most of the day."

"Then naps for you are going to be out."

"I'm beginning to wonder whether I'm going to make it back to work."

"Stop thinking about that right now. Tomorrow night I want you to take Raul out to dinner. I'll take the little ones. I'll try to get Paul to come over to help."

"I don't know."

"I do. Do it for me. I kind of like this kid of yours. I need more bonding time."

"We'll see."

"We'll see doesn't cut it. It's a done deal. You'll probably only be gone for a little over an hour. Besides I want to see what it's like dealing with two little ones."

"Are you suggesting what I think you're suggesting?"

Philly laughed. "No comment. Is it a deal?"

Isabella sighed. "Deal," she said without conviction.

45

Grayson's first witness the next morning was Jessica Cree, one of the girls sitting in a bloc at the back of the hearing room. During her direct testimony, Cree described Alison Lind as "lewd and crude," an autocrat who made snap judgments about a player's ability that she wouldn't change. "It's my way or the highway," was the way Cree described Lind's coaching philosophy. Cree claimed that she was as good a player as Cynthia Harvey, the junior who had replaced her in the starting lineup. During Cree's direct testimony Brittany Stern had passed Simon a note that Carpenter had yet to see.

Simon rose and consulted his cross-examination outline. Cree appeared unruffled by Simon's taking his time. She was a tall, lithe girl with chestnut colored hair that was wavy, wet-looking, as if she had just emerged from a shower and had dried off incompletely.

"You mentioned Cynthia Harvey," Simon began. "Do you see her here in this room?"

Cree nodded and pointed. "She's next to Brittany."

"Would you please rise, Ms. Harvey," Simon requested.

The girl who stood was also tall and lithe, but when it came to upper body muscle mass, there was no comparison. If the two ever squared off, Carpenter would put his money on the younger girl.

"Thank you, Ms. Harvey. Please take your seat." Simon refocused on Cree. "Isn't it true that Ms. Harvey is a faster runner than you are?"

Cree hesitated. She had looked unperturbed a moment ago but was now disconcerted.

"Probably," Cree said.

"Probably?" Simon raised his voice. "Isn't it a fact that Coach Lind conducts time trials among the girls' soccer team with players racing each other in fifty-yard and hundred-yard dashes?"

"Yes."

"Isn't it also a fact that you were paired off with Ms. Harvey in several of those time trials?"

"Yes."

"When you were paired off, did you ever defeat her in a time trial?"

Cree colored. "I don't think so."

"Did Coach Lind also have the girls' soccer team do timed agility drills?"

"Yes."

"Did Coach Lind post the agility drill times of the girls on the bulletin board in her office?"

"Yes."

"Did you ever look at those times?"

"I'm sure I did."

"Did you ever post a faster time than Ms. Harvey in an agility drill?"

"I couldn't tell you off the top of my head."

Simon removed a sheaf of papers from a file folder. "May I have these documents marked as one exhibit and placed before the witness?"

"Yes," Forrester ruled, and she designated an exhibit number.

"Ms. Cree, I've handed you the results of the timed agility drills for the two months before Ms. Harvey replaced you as a starter and for the two months after she replaced you as a starter. Please review these documents and tell me if you ever beat Ms. Harvey's time on any agility drill during this four-month period."

Cree gave scant attention to the documents she was perusing. "I don't see any time where I beat her."

"When you were a starter, what position did you play?"

"Right forward."

"How many goals did you score in total for the girls' soccer team?"

"Two."

"Is that the total over three years?"

"Yes."

"In the months after she replaced you as a starter, how many goals did Ms. Harvey score?"

"I don't know."

"Does coach Lind post scoring statistics on her bulletin board?"

"Yes."

"I'm reading from a posting that coach Lind made at the end of the single year in which you were replaced by Ms. Harvey as a starter. Ms. Harvey scored, it says here, four goals. Does that seem to you to be a correct number?"

Cree had moved past discomfort to what bordered on physical pain.

"I suppose so."

"Do you believe that a starting position should be earned?"

Cree looked at Grayson pleadingly. The school's lawyer had nothing to offer his witness, not even an encouraging look.

"I suppose so."

"Isn't it a fact that Ms. Harvey earned the right to start over you by outperforming you in drills and on the field?"

"I wouldn't agree with that."

"I didn't ask you whether you agreed with what I said," Simon said mincingly. "I asked you whether Ms. Harvey had earned the right to start over you by outperforming you. What is your answer to *my* question?"

"All right, she did better than me. Is that what you want me to say?"

Simon glared at Cree. One of the things Carpenter liked about Simon was that he could be ferocious. He was so slight and frail that he didn't look like the kind of guy who could rip you to pieces verbally.

"I don't want you to say anything but the truth. I think we've finally got that out of you." Simon paused, consulted his cross-examination outline. "Is it true that you went to the senior prom with Mr. Stevens, who testified yesterday?"

Cree turned redder than she had been so far. "Yes."

"Would you agree that Mr. Stevens, your senior prom date, is honest and honorable?"

"Objection," Grayson interposed.

"I'll hear the answer," Forrester ruled.

Cree paused and Carpenter now had a good idea as to the contents of the note Brittany Stern had passed on to Simon. At the prom, Cree probably had had no idea Stevens was gay. Would she now trash her senior prom date? Carpenter didn't think so.

"Yes," Cree said without enthusiasm."

"Nothing further."

"Any redirect, Mr. Grayson?" Forrester asked.

"Nothing further."

"Five-minute recess," Forrester declared.

During the break, Carpenter held out a dollar bill to Simon and proposed a bet. Carpenter was prepared to wager that Grayson wouldn't call another demoted starter—or the parents of a demoted starter—to the stand. Why embarrass another senior or her parents? Which meant that Grayson might rest his case after calling the school committee member he had listed as a potential witness. Simon declined his wager, offering instead two to one odds if he could take Carpenter's position.

"The respondent calls Betsy Faulkner," Grayson announced after Forrester called the hearing back to order.

The school committee member was middle-aged with a pasty complexion. She sported thick, tortoiseshell framed glasses. Faulkner sat erect in the witness chair and seemed eager for Grayson to begin.

Grayson's initial questions established that Faulkner's tenure on the school committee had been seven years. She had a teaching certificate which she had kept active and had obtained a master's degree in education.

"Does the school committee support Mr. Joyce's termination of Ms. Lind's employment?"

"Oh, yes," Faulkner gushed. "We're unanimously behind the principal on this."

"Why is that?"

"The school committee viewed Ms. Lind as unprofessional what with her swearing and yelling. Since I've been on the school committee, I can't recall any coach subject to the tidal wave of criticism that was directed at Ms. Lind. This came from students on the team and their parents. In backing Mr. Joyce on his decision, the school committee viewed Ms. Lind as totally insensitive. By that I mean we regarded her as insensitive to others' feelings, and insensitive to any approach other than her own." Faulkner paused. "May I add something?" she asked Grayson.

"Please," Grayson took the hint.

"Nothing I've heard at this hearing changes my opinion as a school committee member. I know the thinking and mindset of the other members of the committee and I'm sure they would second my view."

"Objection," Carpenter said rising quickly. For a moment he felt lightheaded. Carefully, he reached out to touch the table and closed his eyes, picturing himself in the photograph in his office pursuing the hiker who was moving resolutely along a path toward woods. The exercise steadied him, and he opened his eyes. "Ms. Faulkner isn't a mind reader and her testimony as to what other school committee members might do should be stricken."

Forrester frowned. "You've made a valid point, Mr. Carpenter. But I've been liberal when it comes to letting testimony in. I'm inclined to let Ms. Faulkner's answer stand, but I assure you I will give it the weight it deserves."

Carpenter sat.

"Are you all right?" Simon whispered.

"Yes," Carpenter lied. The lightheadedness had returned as soon as he had resumed his seat.

"As a school committee member, how do you perceive Ms. Lind as a role model?"

"I perceive her as a very bad role model for the reasons I've stated. I'm referring to the yelling, swearing, and lack of sensitivity I just mentioned. These traits don't square with a positive role model in my opinion."

"Nothing further."

Carpenter wasn't sure if he could stand without teetering. He helped himself to water from the pitcher placed on the counsel table he shared with Simon.

"Mr. Carpenter?" Forrester prompted.

"A moment, please, Your Honor."

"We can take a recess," Simon whispered.

Carpenter shook his head although he didn't trust himself to close his eyes. With his eyes closed he was sure that his head would spin. An image of Camellia Kim unexpectedly popped into his head. She was next to him on a spinning bike pedaling like a madwoman and giving him a stern look, nodding at him to pick up his own pace. He took a deep breath and let the air out slowly. He repeated the deep breath and felt that his legs would sustain him once he got to his feet. "Thank you, Your Honor," he said, rising.

"Was Coach Lind fair to her players?" Carpenter started off.

"What do you mean by fair?" Faulkner came back.

"By fair I mean did she treat them like women by making coaching decisions based on players' performance as opposed to favoritism?"

"I really couldn't say. I don't think she was fair to a player if she hurt the player's feelings."

"What player's feelings did she hurt?"

"Well, Ms. Cree for one. That was my impression when Ms. Cree testified."

"Are you saying that Ms. Lind should have retained Ms. Cree as a starter over Ms. Harvey even though Ms. Harvey was the superior player?'

"No, that's not what I'm saying."

"Did you view Ms. Cree's feelings being hurt because she was demoted from her starting role?"

"That's the way it seemed to me."

"Isn't it a good thing that Ms. Cree's feelings were hurt in that she learned the valuable lesson that people advance through merit and ability as opposed to loud whining?"

"I wouldn't necessarily call that a good thing."

Carpenter paused and considered the possibility that Faulkner was an idiot. He felt his anger rising. Which was a good thing, he thought, since he no longer felt unsteady.

"Are you one of those people in education who believe learning should never involve competition because the losing person's feelings would be hurt?"

"I lean in that direction," Faulkner replied forthrightly.

"Have you ever experienced a setback in your professional life?"

"I'm sure I have."

"Name one," Carpenter challenged.

"I once applied for a teaching position I didn't get," Faulkner replied after some thought.

"Were you told why you didn't get the position?"

"Yes. I was told that the candidate chosen was more qualified."

"Were your feelings hurt on receiving that news?"

"I wasn't happy if that's what you mean so I suppose my feelings were hurt."

"Do you agree that because your feelings were hurt you should have been given the position over the candidate you were told was more qualified than you?"

"Not really."

"If coach Lind had chosen not to start Cynthia Harvey over Jessica Cree, do you think that would have hurt Ms. Harvey's feelings since she was a better player than Ms. Cree?'

Faulkner squinted at Carpenter. "I suppose that's possible," she said grudgingly.

"Would you agree that there are some situations where it is inevitable someone's feelings will be hurt?"

"I suppose that's also possible."

"What if any lesson did you learn from not getting the position you told us you applied for?"

"I'm not sure I learned anything in particular. I applied for another job and got it."

"Should a school prepare its students for disappointments such as not being given a position that is applied for?"

"That makes sense."

"As an educator, how do you think a school should prepare students for such disappointments?"

"By providing a nurturing, protective environment."

"How about by letting students experience disappointment and learning from the disappointment? Would that be an acceptable approach?"

"That would depend on how that is done. If done in a nurturing, protective, and sensitive way, that might prove helpful."

"You said that you sat through this hearing, is that correct?"

"Yes."

"Did you hear the testimony from Fran Miller and Brittany Stern that they admired Coach Lind as a role model?"

"I did."

"So, in fact, students who played for Ms. Lind regarded her as a positive role model, correct?"

"Yes, but that's not my view."

"When will the school committee begin to fire all the male coaches who yell and swear?"

"We have no plans on doing that."

"Are the male coaches who yell and swear good role models in your view?"

Faulkner didn't answer straightaway. "They could probably use some work," she finally said.

"What do you plan to do to ensure they get that work?" Carpenter said.

"I'll have to think about that. I'm sure the committee will take up the subject."

"What's there to take up? The male coaches yell and swear. Why aren't they being fired just as Ms. Lind was?"

"Nobody's complained about them for one thing."

"Is it your testimony that male coaches should remain on the job for doing the same yelling and swearing that got Ms. Lind fired as long as no one complains?'

"As I said, the complaints about Ms. Lind were numerous and they influenced the committee."

"Please answer Mr. Carpenter's question," Forrester intervened. "Are you saying that male coaches who yelled and swore are being kept on the job because no one complained about that conduct?"

"That's certainly an important reason, yes."

Carpenter huddled with Simon. "I think Forrester has had it with her not answering questions," Simon whispered.

Carpenter nodded; he had formed the same opinion. "Nothing further," he said.

"That concludes the respondent's case," Grayson announced.

"Any rebuttal witnesses?" Forrester asked.

Carpenter and Simon conferred briefly. "No, Your Honor," Simon declared.

Forrester consulted her calendar. "Each party can have two weeks to submit a legal memorandum. It would be helpful to me if you focused on the hearing testimony and what conclusions you wish me to draw from that testimony. Is that agreeable?"

Simon and Grayson replied that it was.

"Then we are adjourned," Forrester said.

After Forrester left, Lind and her supporters congregated in the rear of the hearing room. Grayson and those supporting the school's position had promptly exited the room. Carpenter stood next to Richard Morgan several steps back from Lind, Beth Finegold, Fran Morgan, Frank Stevens, Brittany Stern, and Cynthia Harvey. Simon was answering questions from the group and Carpenter liked his direct approach.

"Now that it's over, how do you think it went?" Beth Finegold asked.

Simon gave Carpenter a brief glance before responding. "For a lawyer," he said, "there's a simple way to look at a case once the evidence is all in. A lawyer will ask himself which side he would rather be on." Simon paused, drawing out the suspense. He turned his gaze to Lind. "I'd rather be arguing your position than the school's."

"You're damn right!" Finegold raised her voice.

"I want to thank you all for assisting Ms. Lind," Simon directed at the witnesses. "You all did an excellent job."

Carpenter turned to Richard Morgan. "Any impressions?"

"I thought you did a good job," the elder Morgan replied. "That young guy with you seems to know what he's doing."

Carpenter nodded. Simon had come up with key witnesses and had prepared them well. "Where did the Town of Kingsbury find that school committee woman? Is it my imagination, or is the woman a dolt?"

"It's not your imagination," the elder Morgan replied. "I think she ran unopposed last time around."

"Don't let that happen again."

"Shit," Morgan said. "If I wasn't so busy and didn't hate politics, I'd oppose her myself."

"Now you're talking."

"That's all I'm doing, talking. Running against her? It's not going to happen."

Carpenter didn't press the subject. There was an upside to incompetent people holding public office. It was good for the practice of law.

46

Carpenter hated what he was doing now, sitting on the edge of a doctor's examining table with his feet hanging nowhere close to the floor. With the air conditioning in Dr. Specter's examining room ramped up, he felt chilled. It was bad enough to sweat all night. Did he have to freeze on a warm June day as well? Weren't the other indignities of a medical exam enough? Specter had prodded him, palpated him, peered into his eyes, ears, and throat and pronounced him fit.

"Put your shirt on," she directed, and Carpenter was only too happy to oblige. He supposed it was good news that she had found nothing further wrong with him other than the big C. But the bad news was that there was no medical explanation for why he had been lightheaded during the Lind hearing.

"What should I do?" he asked. "Am I just supposed to ignore what happened yesterday? Nothing like that ever happened to me before."

"Try ignoring it," Specter said. "Let's see how that goes."

"Jesus!" Carpenter muttered.

"What?" Specter replied. "I've checked you out. Nothing's changed since your last examination. I could order a bunch of expensive tests that will turn up nothing. Would it make you feel better if I did that?"

Carpenter figured he was getting his comeuppance, saddled with a physician who was as crushingly blunt with her patients as he was with his clients. "I don't know what to think," he said discouragingly.

"Go exercise today," Specter said. "Do whatever routine your personal trainer has laid out for you. If you start feeling lightheaded, stop at once and call me. If you don't start feeling lightheaded, call me to report that."

"You want me to exercise?"

"That's what I just said. Should I write it down for you?"

Carpenter felt his irritation rising until he saw that his doctor was grinning broadly. "Are you joking about the exercise?" he asked.

"No, I'm serious about the exercise. I'm smiling because I can see I'm driving you nuts. You don't like taking direction, do you?" Specter's green eyes flashed amusement. "I'm thinking it's bugging you that I'm younger than you and in charge of your health."

Carpenter decided to follow advice he gave to clients—admit nothing. He kept his mouth shut. Why give Specter the satisfaction of knowing that she had pegged him correctly?

Specter placed a hand on his shoulder. "One thing I've learned is that it's important for patients in a situation like yours to be as active as possible. Listen to your body. If you're overdoing it, your body will let you know. As best as I can determine, the episode you had yesterday was an aberration."

Carpenter nodded. He was already thinking ahead. He'd give Camellia Kim a call and see if she could fit him in for a half hour. The image of the woman had steadied him yesterday. Maybe actually seeing her would square him away today. "Okay," he said.

Philly had gotten in a solid hour of work in her second-floor home office. She had prepared two notices of deposition, one for Warren Lord, the golfer who had struck Martin Hays, the second for his golfing companion that day, Alan Atkinson. Carpenter had recommended taking depositions quickly; before the end of the month, she'd depose Lord in the morning, and Rachel would depose Atkinson in the afternoon. Martin Hays' suit had named Lord and the Mayfair Country Club as defendants. Lord had filed an answer denying the allegations in Hays' complaint while the country club had moved to dismiss Hays' lawsuit. Carpenter had been surprised that Lord hadn't filed a motion to dismiss Hays' case, claiming that his errant golf shot was an accident. Philly had also wondered at Lord's strategy; perhaps Lord had gotten wind that Ryan Cannon and Jake Mobley were prepared to testify against him. Philly had finished a broad outline of her deposition questions for Lord when she heard Daisy and Rosalind crying in unison. Sarah and Isabella probably could use some relief.

Entering the living room, Philly found Daisy bored with being read to, struggling to move off Sarah's lap. Isabella had settled into a corner of the couch and was struggling to free a breast to nurse her wailing daughter. Philly scooped up Daisy and offered Sarah a look of sympathy. "What's with all the noise, pumpkin?"

"I think she wants to run around," Sarah observed. "I was hoping that reading to her would settle her down but as soon as Rosalind began to complain, she wouldn't sit still."

Isabella had settled into nursing Rosalind; her eyes closed, and Philly thought it was a tossup as to which of the nursing couple would drop off to sleep first.

"I'm going to take Daisy outside with the stroller," Philly decided.

"I don't think she's going to want to be belted in," Sarah said.

"I'm going to let her push it," Philly explained. "That'll knock her out."

"We won't be long," Sarah said to Isabella.

"Take your time," Isabella said without opening her eyes.

Outside the sun was up and the humidity had kicked in. Philly positioned Daisy behind the stroller. "Push," she urged.

Daisy's progression was unsteady. She'd push the stroller a few feet then plop down on her amply padded bottom and the stroller would roll away. But the moment Philly brought it back, Daisy would pull herself up and toddle on, smiling widely, drool pooling above her chin. Philly had brought a hat for her daughter, but the stroller was effectively blocking the sun.

"I'm a little worried about Isabella," Sarah said. "She seems to have no energy."

Philly couldn't remember her own energy level following pregnancy. "She's been through a lot," she responded to Sarah.

"I know, but still . . ."

Philly forced herself to focus while keeping an eye on Daisy. "I insisted she and Raul go out for dinner the other night. When they came back home, it looked to me like they both had had a good time."

"Maybe I'm a worrywart," Sarah said. "But since Raul has gone back to work, I've noticed a change."

"I'm glad you brought it up. I'll try to be more observant. I think one of the things worrying Isabella is returning to work."

"That worries me too. If you're both gone, I'm going to have my hands full. I thought it would be no problem. But now all I can think about is that expression how your eyes are too big for your stomach."

Philly didn't want to think about childcare problems. Sarah had been a godsend but maybe at her age caring for two babies might be too much. "Let me think about this," she said. Now was not the time to bring up having another baby. And Philly realized that as Daisy and Rosalind grew, their childcare demands would also grow. At the same time, Sarah's energy level would decrease. That was an unhappy combination of trends.

Camellia Kim added a five-pound weight to the shoulder strengthening machine. "Let's see what you've got, big boy."

Carpenter was amazed at how hard he had to work to compensate for the extra five pounds. He completed his first rep of twelve and wasn't sure he could get through two more. "What do you think of that lightheadedness I had?" he asked, as he tried to recover his wind. Kim had listened impassively to his account of what happened at the Lind hearing and had yet to offer an assessment.

"What did you say your doctor called it?"

"An aberration," Carpenter repeated.

"I'm really not qualified to offer an opinion," Kim said.

Carpenter wasn't willing to let her off the hook. Her expression was unreadable, but he was sure she had an opinion. "I don't care; I want to know what you think." Carpenter had left out the part where he had pictured Kim spinning next to him. Some innocent things could only be taken the wrong way.

"I don't like that word aberration. I'm sure there's another, more specific explanation. I don't believe it was nothing. It was definitely something if you were unable to stand up. I would be concerned if it happened again."

"My doctor wants me to keep exercising. I'm not sure that's such a good idea if there really is something going on with me."

"I agree with your doctor," Kim said. "I wouldn't stop exercising." She pointed to the shoulder machine. "Next rep."

Carpenter's shoulders quivered as he muscled his arms outstretched with the twelfth repetition. There was no way in hell he could complete a third series of twelve.

"Is your appetite still poor?" Kim asked.

"Yeah. It's pretty much the same."

"When we're finished, I've got something for you to try," Kim said. "After you called me for an appointment, I was explaining your situation to my grandmother. She knows a lot about herbal remedies. She gave me a powder to give to you. You're supposed to take a teaspoon and mix it with hot water and drink it down before you go to bed."

Great, Carpenter thought. Another piss stop in the night.

"You won't like the taste," Kim added.

Kim's last point wasn't necessarily a negative. A bad taste was probably better than no taste at all.

"If you get diarrhea or start feeling feverish, stop taking it."

Maybe, Carpenter thought, Kim would soon run out of selling points.

"Oh yeah. If you experience itching, you also need to stop."

"Shit," Carpenter muttered under his breath.

Kim gestured toward the shoulder machine. "Last one."

Carpenter couldn't extend his arms on the twelfth lift. He strained, his shoulders again quivering. Kim leaned forward, placed her hands over his and gave him just enough of a gentle assist so that his arms fully extended.

"Nice job," Kim said. "For a guy who gets lightheaded, that wasn't bad."

Carpenter grumbled, letting his frustration out. Still, Kim's compliment had been nice. To date, she hadn't handed out praise routinely.

"You have my card. Call my cell phone in a couple of days and let me know how you're doing."

"Did your grandmother tell you that this powder of hers worked before?"

"How could she tell me that? This is something she mixed up especially for you."

"Jesus!" Carpenter invoked again. He'd begun to itch already and he hadn't even taken the damn powder yet. With his luck diarrhea would hit before he made it out the door.

47

It was five thirty in the morning, and Philly sat at her desk trying to get in some work before Daisy awakened. She hadn't slept well and at five o'clock, had sat bolt upright in bed. Dropping off again was out of the question. She foresaw becoming one of those women who, faced with childrearing and work demands, decided to serve the two masters by doing without sleep. How did other women survive? She at least had Sarah Ferguson to fall back on in a pinch.

When she and Philip had exercised regularly, she'd needed less sleep, invigorated by biking and spinning workouts. She had gotten her bike tuned in late April, thinking of using the longer daylight hours of spring to do road workouts. But here it was almost the beginning of summer and she had yet to be out on the road. When Paul slept over, she could, at least in theory, get up early and get in a ride while he was on Daisy duty. But where was the fun in that? She wanted to wake up next to Paul and prolong the morning hours they spent together, not shorten them. The tradeoffs she was considering all felt wrong.

Philly forced herself to focus on the motion filed by the Salem Stampede to dismiss Martina Glass' case. The hockey team claimed that it could not be responsible for a fan falling on Glass. The team had followed its liquor policy and had stopped serving alcoholic beverages prior to the accident. The team had not been negligent in any way and had no way of knowing that Fred Dunn posed a risk as to anything let alone a risk of falling. If there was negligence, the negligence was on the part of Dunn.

Dunn, on the other hand, had not filed a motion to dismiss Martina Glass' complaint. Instead, Dunn's lawyer had filed an answer denying negligence on Dunn's part, and had presented a series of affirmative defenses. The only defense that worried Philly was Dunn's claim that he had not fallen but rather had been pushed. Was that scenario even possible? Dunn had gone to the hockey game with two friends. Was Dunn claiming that a friend had pushed him over a railing so that he landed on Glass? Or was Dunn claiming that another party had given him a shove? The friends were witnesses no matter what set of facts was behind Dunn's claim that he was pushed. Perhaps Dunn and his friends had concocted a defense and would stick to a made-up story in which an unknown third party was blamed. What had seemed to Philly to be a straightforward case of liability now looked like a contentious tractor pull.

The first task was to oppose the Salem Stampede's motion to dismiss. She'd argue that a motion to dismiss wasn't appropriate until discovery had taken place and facts in possession of the defendants were brought to light. How would she prove how many drinks Dunn and his buddies had been served? While the young men had sounded to Glass as if they had been drinking, would they admit to being drunk? Unlikely. She started to get a bad feeling about the case. Maybe Carpenter would have some suggestions. Ruminating about the Glass case had left Philly tense and edgy. So much for work having a calming effect. Maybe a case with a more favorable prospect would help her chill out.

Philly turned her attention to the Hays case and Warren Lord's upcoming deposition. She read over the accounts by Cannon and Mobley of how Lord had aimed his tee shot at Martin Hays. The sequence of her questions to Lord would be crucial. She needed to draw him out without revealing she had obtained information from Cannon and Mobley. That shouldn't be too difficult she reflected. When she needed to, she could play dumb.

Philly checked her watch. Daisy now rose like clockwork at six thirty. There was a half hour to flesh out her deposition outline before it was time to nurse.

"You're looking and acting more like your old self," Maxine said.

Carpenter nodded and continued to attack the cold cereal and fruit mix in front of him. For the first time in weeks he was hungry. Maxine had stocked his refrigerator and he envisioned making further inroads on her provisions once he finished his cereal. Maxine was standing next to the sink smiling at him, sipping coffee from a mug that though it had a chipped bottom, he couldn't bring himself to throw out. She was wearing men's pajama bottoms and a Boston College T-shirt.

"What?"

"It's just good to see you looking perky."

"I'm not perky!"

"Yes, you are. It's a welcome sight."

Carpenter wondered whether his restored appetite had to do with the ground up herbs Camellia Kim's grandmother had given him. He had put off trying the mix until he couldn't think of an answer to Maxine's question, "What do you have to lose?" He wondered what was in the mix and at the same time didn't want to know. What if he gave the mix to Dr. Specter to analyze and she reported back that the mix would only encourage Fred?

"I've given my official notice," Maxine said.

Carpenter knew that Maxine had meant it when she'd said she was going to retire. Nevertheless, her confirmation brought him up short. Maybe there had been a part of him that didn't believe she'd follow through on her pledge.

"I'll be a consultant for a short while to wind down some matters that I haven't been able to finish. But by the end of the year I'll be done."

Carpenter thought about waking up tomorrow without law to practice. He was certain that would drive him batshit in short order.

"Say something," Maxine urged.

"I knew you were going to do it," Carpenter said. "But I guess I wasn't totally sure you would. I'm trying to get used to the idea of you retired."

"You mean you're trying to get used to what it means for us," Maxine said. "I've told you what I want it to mean. I want us to move in together. What do you want it to mean?"

"You know I'm on board with moving in together. It's just going to be . . . I don't know . . . different what with me working and you not."

"I don't see a problem with that."

"I didn't say it was a problem," Carpenter replied. "I said it was different. It's going to take some getting used to."

"I'm looking forward to it. I don't think it's going to take much getting used to. I can't wait, to tell you the truth."

Carpenter wondered whether he was trying to come up with cold water to throw on Maxine's vision. It would be just like him to screw up the best thing in his life. "We need to find a house," he said.

"Or a condo," Maxine said.

"Or a condo. Let's start with a house. Christ, if Philly and her gang can buy another fucking house, I don't see why we can't."

"I'll start looking around."

Carpenter nodded. Here was another subject he could add to the list of things he didn't want to think about. Fred was at the top of that list followed by lack of billable hours in his law practice. Now he could add uprooting himself and having to adjust to a new environment.

"Change is good," Maxine reminded him.

"Change can be good or bad," Carpenter countered. "You're good. That's the given that's going to get me through this."

"You're not just perky, you're sweet."

Carpenter grumbled unintelligibly. "Don't push your luck," he cautioned.

48

With Rachel beside her in the conference room, Philly took a moment to size up Warren Lord and his attorney, Millicent Rudd. Lord looked to be in his fifties, a trim, dapper man who today was wearing a dark blue suit, a blue, long-sleeved dress shirt with a white collar, and a red patterned tie. Lord was tanned, with prominent cheek bones and brown eyes. His hair was long, startlingly white, slicked back on the sides, seemingly set in place with epoxy. Philly bet the guy didn't sweat, even in the summer.

Millicent Rudd was a seasoned trial lawyer, a senior lawyer in the law firm engaged by the insurance company that had issued Lord a sizable personal umbrella insurance policy to protect him against suits by third parties. She was younger than Lord, a tall, thin woman whose round face was framed by black hair touching her shoulders. Rudd had yet to smile.

Also present was Thomas Mast, the attorney for the Mayfair Country Club. Mast was in the litigation department of a mid-sized, firm that specialized in business matters and he looked like he wanted to be somewhere else. Which he would be if the motion to dismiss he had filed was allowed. Mast was short, overweight, and sported a moustache that was a shade lighter than his brown eyebrows and brown hair. Mast also hadn't produced a smile.

Jeannie Smith, Carpenter's stenographer of choice, completed the unsmiling group. Smith was old, closer to eighty than seventy. But in the five years since Philly had first met her, the stenographer's appearance hadn't changed. She had white hair, a dour look comparable to Carpenter's, and pendulous jowls that shook slightly as she recorded testimony.

Philly, Rudd, and Mast quickly agreed to the deposition ground rules. Philly's background questions established what she and Rachel already knew. Lord and Atkinson had invited Ryan Cannon and Jake Mobley to view a small, upscale shopping mall outside of Hingham. The owner of the mall was in a cash bind and was prepared to sell the mall at a loss. Lord and Atkinson had ideas about how to bring in two new anchor tenants that would increase business at the site.

"What brought you to the Mayfair Country Club?" Philly asked.

"We had done some research on Cannon and Mobley and knew they liked to golf. We promised them a golfing outing if they came up from Atlanta to view the property. We like to golf too, and it seemed like a good way for the four of us to get to know each other."

"Who paid for their trip?"

"We did."

"At some point did you drive a golf ball off the seventh tee that struck another golfer ahead of you on the course?"

"Yeah. That was really unfortunate."

"Is it correct that you now know the man you struck was Martin Hays?"

"Right."

"Had you ever seen Hays before the day he was struck by the ball you hit?"

"I'd seen him at the club. I now know that he's a member."

"Before the day of the incident did you associate a name with his face?"

"No."

"On the day of the incident, did you recognize Mr. Hays on the course?"

"No."

"At some point on the day of the incident, did you become aware of the players ahead of you on the course?"

Lord paused. "I was aware that there were golfers playing ahead of our group."

"How many were there in the party ahead of your group?"

Again Lord paused. "I'm hesitating," he said, "because I now know there was a foursome ahead of us. But on the day of the accident, I don't know whether I actually counted how many were in the group."

Philly consulted her deposition outline. Lord was being cautious; Rudd had probably coached him carefully. Or perhaps Lord was no stranger to litigation, had been deposed before, and knew how to handle himself.

"Before the seventh hole, did any words pass between anyone in your foursome and the players immediately ahead of you on the course?"

"I think Alan may have called out to them to speed up their play at one point. I don't really remember."

"Did you call out to them to speed up their play?"

"Not that I recall. As I said, I have a vague memory of Alan calling out to them."

"Was there a response to Alan's calling out?"

"I don't remember one way or the other."

"How many times did Alan or anyone else in your group call out to the players ahead of you?"

"Again, I have a vague memory of Alan calling out once. I don't recall anyone else calling out."

"Besides your vague memory of Alan calling out once, was there any other communication or contact between your foursome and the players ahead of you?"

"Not that I remember."

"At some point did you reach the seventh hole tee?"

"Right."

"Who in your group drove first?"

"I did."

"Before you hit your seventh hole tee shot, did you observe any players in the group ahead of you?"

Lord scratched his head but as far as Philly could tell, he failed to displace a hair.

"I remember seeing players off in the distance, well beyond where any of our drives would reach."

"How many players did you see?"

"I didn't count them so I can't answer you."

"Do you wear glasses?"

"No, contact lenses. But I have reading glasses."

"Did you have the lenses in on the day of the incident?"

"Yes."

"What do you need the lenses for?"

"Far vision."

"What club did you use off the seventh tee?"

A look of concern passed fleetingly over Lord's face.

"That would have been a driver."

"Are you sure?"

"Yes. The seventh hole is the longest on the course."

"Isn't it true that you used an iron off the seventh tee?"

"No."

"You say you used a driver off the seventh tee. Is that something that you would expect Mr. Atkinson, Mr. Cannon, and Mr. Mobley to back you up on?"

Lord again looked uncomfortable for a fleeting moment. Philly now believed that Rudd had not contacted Cannon or Mobley in advance of this deposition.

"I can't speak for them. But I would expect them to confirm my account if they were watching me and remembered what they saw."

"Was any person in the group immediately ahead of you wearing any article of clothing that could be easily seen such as a bright yellow day-glow shell?"

Lord glanced briefly in Rudd's direction and refocused on Philly.

"I now know that Mr. Hays was wearing something like that in bright yellow. But at the time I hit my drive, I'm not sure whether that had registered with me."

"When you were on the seventh tee and saw those golfers off in the distance, was any of them wearing something bright yellow or wearing something else easily visible?"

"I don't know. That's certainly possible. Again, if I noticed, I don't believe it registered with me."

Philly paused. Lord was qualifying his answers, leaving open possibilities. So far, she hadn't been able to pin him down.

"What happened when you hit your drive off the seventh tee?"

"I sliced the ball and hit an awful drive that struck Mr. Hays. I wasn't able to track the flight of the ball. I followed through on my swing and when I looked up and out over the fairway, I didn't pick up the ball."

"Did anyone in your foursome see the track of the ball?"

"I don't believe that Alan did. He's being deposed later today, and you can ask him. I can't speak for Mr. Cannon and Mr. Mobley."

Philly turned over a page in her deposition outline and read over a line of questions that Rachel had suggested. Rachel, God bless her, had learned a hell of a lot about golf.

"Do you have a handicap, Mr. Lord?"

"Yes, I have a seven handicap."

"Would I be correct that with a seven handicap you are a proficient golfer?"

Lord smiled, displayed teeth as dazzlingly white as his hair. "You're being very kind. Proficient might be overstating it. I'd say I'm a slightly better than average golfer for my age."

"How far do you typically hit a driver?"

"If I hit the ball cleanly, I'd estimate between two hundred thirty to two hundred fifty yards."

"How far from the seventh tee was Mr. Hays when he was struck by your golf shot?"

"I couldn't tell you exactly."

"Are you able to estimate the distance he was from where you drove the ball?"

Lord scratched his head and again his hair was impervious to the gesture.

"This is just a guess, but I'd say maybe a hundred eighty yards give or take."

"Is there a club that you carry in your golf bag that gives you a distance of about one hundred eighty yards?"

Lord again directed a glance Rudd's way. His lawyer was busy writing. Philly had yet to observe concern on Rudd's part with any of her client's answers to questions.

"I guess that would be a five iron in normal conditions."

"Were conditions normal on the day of the incident?"

"I would say so for the most part. It was rather cold for mid-October, a bit colder than any of us liked."

"Did you in fact use a five iron off the seventh tee?"

"The question has already been asked by you and answered by Mr. Lord," Rudd interjected.

"That is not accurate," Philly said. She had the question read back to Lord and waited for his answer.

"No. As I told you before, I used a driver."

"What's the best part of your golf game?"

"What do you mean?"

"I mean are you able to tell us what is the best part of your golf game? For example, is putting the best part of your game? Or driving off the tee? Or perhaps your short iron game?"

Lord took his time thinking about his answer. Despite Rachel's brief tutorial on golf terms, Philly found it awkward to use golfing references that she had no firsthand knowledge of.

"I would say it was my iron game."

"Did you in fact on the seventh tee hit an iron shot deliberately at Mr. Hays?"

There was a flash of anger in Lord's eyes. Rudd looked up from her writing, but her expression remained a cipher as she turned slowly in her seat to regard her client.

"No."

"Did you on the seventh tee hit a driver shot deliberately at Mr. Hays?"

"No."

"Did anyone in your group shout out 'fore' or any other warning to Mr. Hays?"

"I don't believe so."

Philly's remaining questions brought out information that she and Rachel had suspected Lord would testify to. Neither Lord not Atkinson had gone over the Mayfair Country Club golfing rules before the start of their round and had not briefed Cannon or Mobley about those rules. Lord had talked about the Hays incident with Alan Atkinson but not with Ryan Cannon or Jake Mobley. Lord denied that either he or Atkinson had suggested finishing the round of golf after Hays was taken away in an ambulance. The foursome had viewed the shopping mall outside of Hingham before Cannon and Mobley returned to Logan Airport to fly back to Atlanta. Cannon had called Lord the following day to thank him for the opportunity but informed Lord that his investment group declined to proceed further. No, Lord had not inquired as to Hays' condition after the incident but had been told subsequently that Hays had lost an eye.

Philly huddled briefly with Rachel. "Anything else you think I should ask?" she whispered.

Rachel took her time reviewing her notes. "I can't think of anything else," she whispered back. "But someone's lying."

"What else is new?"

Philly sat up straight and regarded Lord and Rudd. Lord hadn't lost any of his luster. He appeared confident and relaxed as if being questioned was a walk in the park. Rudd's expression revealed nothing. Mast looked bored and his attitude irked her.

"Did you ever receive a written copy of the Mayfair Country Club golf rules?" Philly asked. Mast straightened in his chair at the mention of his client.

"I may have received something like that twenty years ago when I first became a club member."

"What about more recently?"

"Not that I recall."

"Are the club's golf rules posted anywhere?"

"Yes, in the clubhouse."

"In the last ten years, do you recall any instance in which the club told or reminded club members to review the rules with invited guests?"

"No. But in the clubhouse, there's a sign next to the rules that says something like members and invited guests are responsible for reviewing the rules."

"Have you ever seen or heard a club member telling a guest to review the rules?"

Lord glanced at Mast. The club's attorney had been taking notes since the start of this line of questions.

"Not that I can recall," Lord said.

"Have you ever heard or observed a club member explaining the golf rules to a non-member?"

"Not that I can recall."

"No further questions," Philly said.

Rudd declined to cross-examine her client. Mast asked for a moment and Philly was now glad she had thought to question Lord about the country club's rules.

"Were you familiar with the club's rules on golf?" Mast asked.

"I would say so. I hadn't read them in a while, but I was aware of them."

"How long would it take to review the rules?" Mast followed up.

"I would guess five minutes give or take."

"Is there a rule reminding golfers to wait until the course is clear before hitting a shot?"

"I believe so."

"Did you follow that rule when you hit your drive from the seventh tee?"

"Yes. As I explained, the only golfers I saw were well ahead of us."

"I have nothing further," Mast said.

Philly read a note that Rachel had passed to her. "After the incident did you receive in the mail from the country club a copy of the golf rules?"

"Now that you mention it, I did. I should have remembered that when I answered one of your previous questions."

"Were the rules accompanied by a letter?"

Lord nodded. "It's coming back to me. The letter mentioned that a member had been struck by a ball while on the course. The letter recommended that golfers count the number of golfers in the party ahead of them and make sure all had cleared before hitting a shot."

"Is that specific instruction on counting the players ahead on the course in the rules posted in the club house?"

"I don't believe it is."

"Was the letter you just mentioned the first time that the club advised counting the number of golfers playing ahead of you?"

"I think it was."

"Do the rules posted in the clubhouse state that a player is to call out 'fore' when the player's golf shot goes off course?"

Lord again glanced in Rudd's direction. "I believe that's somewhere in the rules."

"No further questions," Philly said.

This time Mast stayed silent.

Lord, Rudd, and Mast had left the conference room and Jeannie Smith began checking the spelling of names that had been mentioned during Lord's testimony.

"Any comments?" Philly asked when the spell check had concluded. Carpenter valued Smith's take on a witness.

"The only time you got to him was when you asked him about the golf club he used. Mr. Lord didn't like those questions. He was a cool customer but, on that occasion, he appeared nervous."

Philly agreed. Smith wasn't aware of the affidavits of Cannon and Mobley, yet even she had noticed Lord's discomfort. "Any other impressions?"

Smith shrugged. "I don't know the first thing about golf. I never understood why people get worked up over hitting a small white ball all over the place. Maybe golfers need to wear helmets the way they do in football and hockey."

Rachel laughed. "That would take a lot of fun out of the game."

"I wasn't aware golf was fun," Smith rejoined. "Whenever people talk about playing the game, they say it drives them nuts."

"I'm actually going to take a lesson," Rachel said, surprising Philly.

"Why would you want to do that?" Smith inquired.

"This case has got me curious."

Smith rolled her eyes. "A golf lesson," she said sarcastically. "Now there's a waste of time."

Philly would have bet that Millicent Rudd would also represent Alan Atkinson at his deposition, but Atkinson showed up in the conference room with his own lawyer, Eugene Brownwood. Atkinson had none of Lord's confidence and poise. He appeared to be about Lord's age but any resemblance between the two men ended there. Atkinson looked rumpled; his dark gray suit was wrinkled, and his tie knot off center. He was portly, bald in the back, and when introductions were made, he delivered a weak, moist handshake. Lord hadn't broken a sweat during his questioning, but Atkinson looked like he would balance out Lord's ability to retain moisture.

Eugene Brownwood passed out a business card that announced he was a sole practitioner. Mast studied the card, but Rudd barely glanced at it. Philly wondered whether Rudd had produced Brownwood to represent Atkinson. She pegged Brownwood to be her age. He was thin, trim, with a long angular face. Philly wasn't much on fashion and style, but she doubted that his long, almost muttonchop sideburns were in vogue.

Once Atkinson was sworn in by Jeannie Smith, Rachel began with background questions. Atkinson viewed himself as the backroom guy in his business partnership while Lord was the face of the company, the man who pitched projects to prospective investors. Atkinson had an MBA and would work up the financials for the deals he and Lord presented to investors. Atkinson considered Lord a personal friend in addition to a business partner. When they saw each other socially, it was typically on a golf course. Atkinson had not met with Millicent Rudd but acknowledged that Rudd, through Lord, had recommended Eugene Brownwood. Atkinson had not been present at Lord's deposition and had not discussed that deposition with anyone.

"Did you at some time become aware of a party playing ahead of your foursome on the day Mr. Hays was struck by Mr. Lord's tee shot?" Rachel asked after turning the focus of her questions to the round of golf at the Mayfair Country Club.

"Yes."

"When was that?"

"I couldn't say exactly. Probably around the second or third hole."

"What made you aware of the group ahead of you?"

"They were taking forever to play a hole."

"Did you recognize anyone in the group ahead of you?"

"No."

"At some time before you reached the seventh tee did you become aware of how many golfers were in the group ahead of you?"

"I'm not sure. I think I was aware there was a foursome ahead of us, but I don't really remember counting the number in the group."

"Was any member of the group ahead of you wearing anything distinctive?"

Atkinson paused, stroked his sideburns. Philly noted the mannerism.

"The man I now know as Mr. Hays was wearing a yellow slicker but I'm not sure whether I was aware of that while on the course. I was aware of it after Mr. Hays was hit."

"Did you ever call out to the group ahead of you on the course?"

Atkinson's hand again went to his sideburns and Philly was now convinced that the gesture was his "tell" that he was bothered by a question.

"At some point before the seventh tee I shouted out to the group to speed up their play."

"Did you get a response to that shout out?"

"No."

"Did anyone else in your foursome comment on the slow play of the group ahead of you?"

Atkinson looked toward Rudd, not Brownwood. "I think Warren also commented on the group's slow play but I'm not really sure."

"Who played first off the seventh tee in your group?"

"Warren did."

"Did you see his shot off the tee?"

"Not really."

"What do you mean by not really?" Rachel pressed.

"I was aware of Warren driving, but I wasn't really watching him. I was next up, and I was taking practice swings."

"Did you see the club Mr. Lord was using to hit off the seventh tee?"

"No," Atkinson said after reaching again for his sideburns. "I would presume it was a driver. The seventh hole is the longest on the course. Warren and I played it before. I don't think either of us ever used anything but a driver."

"Where was the group playing ahead of you when Mr. Lord hit his shot from the seventh tee?"

"I believe they were well out of range. I don't recall seeing anyone on the course where our drives would likely go."

"Did you see Mr. Hays in his yellow slicker before Mr. Lord hit his shot off the seventh tee?"

"No. I first saw him when he was lying on the side of the fairway."

"Isn't it true that you saw Mr. Hays prior to the time he was struck and went down by the side of the fairway?"

Atkinson reached for his sideburns. "No."

"Before Mr. Lord hit his ball from the seventh tee, were you the one in your foursome to say of him something like, 'Look at that asshole, he probably stopped to take a shit?'"

Atkinson's hands started for his face and then stopped abruptly. His hands began to shake. Rachel had asked her question in the same tone she had asked her previous questions and was looking at Atkinson, all innocence, all sweetness and light, as if she had put forward an innocuous question about the weather. Philly knew that she'd made the right choice to have Rachel conduct this deposition. If she were questioning Atkinson, she'd now be glaring at the man, giving off a confrontational air. Rachel's calmness would likely draw forth more information from Atkinson then the aggressive approach she would use.

"That's not true," Atkinson said with a fair amount of desperation.

"Did Mr. Lord then say, 'Maybe this will give him a wakeup call,' or words to that effect?"

"Where are you getting this crap? Did those two ass . . ."

Rudd's nudge to Atkinson's ribs caused him to cough and sputter.

"Let the record show that Ms. Rudd just elbowed the witness preventing him from finishing his answer," Rachel said without inflection.

"Ask your next question," Rudd said mincingly.

"Shouldn't Mr. Brownwood be elbowing his own client?" Rachel directed at Rudd.

"Very funny," Rudd said. "Ask your next question," she repeated

"Were you about to refer to two assholes?" Rachel asked Atkinson, her smile again in place.

Atkinson fingered the spot where Rudd's elbow had jarred him. "I wasn't referring to anything."

"Before Ms. Rudd jabbed you, what were you about to say?"

Atkinson gave each of his sideburns a tug in rapid succession. "I wasn't about to say anything."

"Were you about to mention Mr. Cannon and Mr. Mobley, the other two men in your foursome?"

"I just told you I wasn't about to mention anything."

"You seem to be perspiring, Mr. Atkinson. Do you need a moment?"

Atkinson colored, his forehead beaded with perspiration.

"No," Atkinson grunted.

Rachel took her time reviewing her notes. Philly suspected that she was deliberately letting Atkinson sweat. It was unfortunate that this deposition wasn't being videotaped. Philly didn't necessarily believe that a picture was worth a thousand words, but Atkinson's recent facial expressions were priceless.

Philly turned her attention to Mast. The country club's lawyer was engrossed in note taking. At one point he looked up and regarded Atkinson with undisguised contempt. Then he resumed writing.

"Did Mr. Lord use an iron to drive from the seventh tee?"

"Not that I'm aware."

"Did Mr. Lord deliberately direct his drive from the seventh tee at Mr. Hays?"

"Not that I'm aware."

Rachel looked up from her deposition outline. "Isn't it true that you and Mr. Lord wished to complete the round of golf after Mr. Hays was taken away in an ambulance?"

"No," Atkinson said peevishly.

"Isn't it true that your foursome's round of golf ended when Mr. Cannon and Mr. Mobley turned down an invitation to complete the round?"

Atkinson slumped in his chair. Rudd, to her credit, showed no emotion with respect to Atkinson's recent testimony. Eugene Brownwood looked at sea. The way he shot glances at Rudd suggested to Philly that he wanted to consult with her. Mast was staring at Atkinson, poised to jot down his answer.

"No," Atkinson said.

Rachel took her time with further questions, but Philly knew that the fireworks had pretty much ended.

Rachel consulted Philly when she came to the end of her prepared outline. "Anything else?" she whispered.

Philly shook her head. "I'd leave it," she whispered back. "Nice job."

"No further questions," Rachel said.

Neither Rudd nor Brownwood had questions, but Mast did.

"I'm not totally sure what's going on here," Mast said, "but I'm sensing from some of Ms. Boyle's questions that Mr. Lord may have seen Mr. Hays and aimed a golf shot at him. Would there be any truth to that?"

Atkinson produced a handkerchief and wiped his brow. He then ran the handkerchief over his sideburns. "No," he said weakly.

"As a club member, would you agree that the club regards golfers' safety as important?"

"I guess so," Atkinson replied.

"Has the country club ever condoned a golfer's deliberately directing a golf ball in the direction of another golfer?"

"Not that I know of."

"Nothing further," Mast said.

Philly huddled with Rachel. "We could be losing the country club as a defendant if Lord deliberately tried to hit Hays," she whispered.

"I know," Rachel whispered in response. "We may be stuck with arguing that the country club didn't do a good enough job promoting safety."

"Try to get Atkinson to agree with that," Philly suggested.

"Mr. Atkinson," Rachel resumed. "You said that you guessed the country club regarded safety as important. Do you remember testifying to that?"

"Yes."

"Besides posting rules in the clubhouse, what did the country club do to promote golfers' safety?"

Atkinson became distracted for a moment. "Nothing specific that I can think of."

"Nothing further," Rachel said. "Does anybody have any further questions for the witness? No? Then this deposition is concluded."

Rudd, Brownwood, and Atkinson had left the room together before Jeannie Smith began to stow her equipment. Mast had lingered, asked Philly to call him, and then departed. Philly had a good idea what Mast wanted to chat about. She'd keep him waiting for a while. First, she needed to have a serious planning session with Carpenter.

"Now that's a cheery group," Smith commented as the last of the tools of her trade made it into their carrying case. "Those lawyers aren't going to want that witness to get in front of a jury."

Rachel beamed and rightly so, Philly thought. She had done a good job dismantling Atkinson. She wondered whether there was any legal theory that could be used to make Atkinson a defendant.

"Who was the guy referring to before the woman lawyer gave him a nudge?" Smith asked.

"Those would be the smoking guns," Philly said.

49

"My name is Josh and I'll be giving you your lesson today."

Rachel took in the name tag. Josh Horgan looked like a surfer. He had long light brown hair that curled up at the edges, an impressive tan, and a long, lanky body that looked like it didn't have an ounce of fat on it.

"You guys ever play golf before?"

Rachel and Stephen Minor shook their heads. Wanting to surprise Minor, Rachel hadn't told him their destination and was deflated when his first words on arriving were, "You're kidding, right?" The Red Sox game had gone well enough. Her first view of the brilliant green field under the tiers of lights at Fenway Park had been exhilarating, and she had mustered up interest when Minor had taught her how to keep score. She had figured another date was appropriate with her getting to choose what they would do.

"Well don't believe that line that you never forget your first time," Horgan said. "This is a lesson that you're probably not going to want to remember."

Horgan handed out two drivers and took them through stretching exercises. With the club behind her head, grasped near the ends, Rachel twisted this way and that and heard bones creak.

"People think golfers aren't real athletes," Horgan said. "That's not true. You need to limber up before playing. The last thing you want to do is hurt yourself."

Minor was able to easily replicate Horgan's movements. Rachel was embarrassed by her uncoordinated attempts to follow his lead. What had she been thinking? Impressing Minor was out. Before the hour was up, he would view her as the hapless klutz she was.

"What brought you out here for a lesson?" Horgan asked.

"I'm along for the ride," Minor said.

"I'm a lawyer and I have a case that involves golf," Rachel explained. "I wanted to see what it was like to try to hit a golf ball."

"You've come to the right place," Horgan said. "You a lawyer too?"

Minor nodded. Rachel wished he'd lose the put-upon attitude. The prospect of a third date was dimming by the minute.

When warmups were over, Horgan demonstrated a swing in slow motion, breaking down the parts. Rachel knew enough about golf clubs to know that he was holding an iron. When Horgan cut loose with a full swing in real time, she couldn't believe how fluid his motion was. He handed each of them an iron and reclaimed the drivers he had given them. "Let's take it in steps," he instructed.

Minor was able to replicate Horgan's demonstration immediately. His swing wasn't as fluid as Horgan's, but it wasn't too bad. "Good," Horgan told Minor. "It's all in the hips. You're getting it."

The word *good* wasn't going to apply to her efforts. Rachel felt awkward raising the club head and executing the downswing. Half the time she didn't remember to keep her head down.

"Stop for a minute." Horgan came up behind her and with his foot tapped the instep of her right foot so that it moved further away from her left. "Let's get you balanced and feeling centered. Relax," he instructed as he placed his hands over hers where she was gripping the club. "No resistance." He led her through a series of swings and Rachel did her best to let him control the movements. The swings continued to feel unnatural, but she felt less stiff and awkward. It was hard to concentrate with his arms on the outside of hers, his solid chest against her back. "Better," Horgan said. "Now you try."

Rachel tried to clear her mind. She closed her eyes and imagined Horgan controlling the club grip, his hands over her hands, his body enwrapping hers. She took her first practice swing with her eyes closed. Then she opened her eyes and tried several others.

"Much better," Horgan said. He came up behind her and put his hands on her hips. Golf, Rachel decided, might turn out to be a sexy game.

"You want to keep your hips centered but flexible. Relax and try a few more. Rotate your hips when you go into your swing."

When Horgan stepped away, Rachel went through several more practice swings. Glancing at her watch she realized that almost half of the hour lesson had passed and they had yet to hit a ball.

"Now for the real thing," Horgan said. He set a ball down on one of the driving area tees and executed what looked to Rachel a perfect swing. His iron shot soared in a majestic arc and landed off in the distance. Horgan hit a second shot that mirrored his first. "Now it's your turn."

They were on adjacent driving areas; they were each right-handed and the way they were positioned, Rachel had a view of Minor's back. She waited until he swung his club. Minor made contact with the ball and delivered a line drive that Rachel immediately lost sight of.

"Not bad for a first swing."

Rachel concentrated on the ball Horgan had set at her feet. She completed a few practice swings and brought the head of her iron up against the ball. Keep your head down, she reminded herself. She swung and missed.

"Again," Horgan directed. "The swing wasn't bad."

Watching Minor continue to make contact on his practice shots, Rachel tried to relax. She took several deep breaths before again going through practice swings. When she addressed the ball, she visualized hitting it. When she swung for real and made contact, she saw the ball rise in an arc that while less majestic than Horgan's trajectories, at least looked like an arc.

"All right!" Horgan exclaimed. "How did that feel?"

"Pretty good," Rachel replied, meaning it.

Minor didn't turn around at her exchange with Horgan. He placed another ball down by his feet and made ready to hit another shot.

"Again," Horgan said.

Rachel set a ball down in front of her. There had to be over fifty golf balls in the bucket Horgan had brought out for her. She went through her practice swings before again addressing the new ball. She tried the visualization routine she had used previously. This time she didn't hit the ball squarely. She caught the top of the ball and it trickled down from the driving area.

"Again," Horgan said. "Your swing is okay for the first time."

"I thought I was supposed to forget the first time," Rachel came back.

Horgan laughed. "Are we talking about the same thing?" he said with a big grin.

Minor completed another swing. Rachel wasn't sure whether he had heard her last back and forth with Horgan.

"I'll probably have to let you know," she said to Horgan as she placed another ball at her feet.

Minor had emptied out his bucket when the hour for the lesson came to a close. Horgan was in no rush. "Keep going," he said when Rachel pointed to her watch.

With Minor as well as Horgan watching her, Rachel felt self-conscious. She had made good contact on two additional shots and she had to admit that each time she struck the ball cleanly it had been surprisingly satisfying. She went through her ritual before each swing and managed two more clean hits from the last fifteen balls in her bucket. She had noticed Minor glancing at his watch as her bucket emptied but Horgan seemed uninterested in the time. The instructor carefully regarded each of her swings and offered hints when she failed to strike the ball cleanly.

When her bucket was empty, Minor offered to contribute to the cost of the lesson, but Rachel refused. "My treat," she insisted.

When she paid Horgan, he asked for her card. "You never know when I may need a lawyer," he said as he gathered up the clubs and buckets.

Rachel fished out a business card from her wallet and Horgan studied it.

"What about my card?" Minor said lightly. "I'm a lawyer too."

"No offense, but you're not as cute," Horgan said, giving them a curt wave as he headed off. "I'm late for my next lesson," he called out over his shoulder.

"Okay," Minor said. "I've got to admit that was fun."

"Yeah, it was," Rachel said. She was watching Horgan walk off, thinking again how good it had felt when he had moved up close behind her. Maybe the guy gave private lessons.

50

Simon couldn't remember an occasion when there was a festive mood in the conference room. Most meetings there focused on trial strategy in pending cases with either Carpenter or Philly giving out assignments that needed to be completed yesterday. But today celebratory laughter filled the room and with good reason. Anne Forrester's decision in Alison Lind's discrimination case was a complete victory for the soccer coach. Lind was more subdued than Simon thought she'd be. She probably had yet to come to terms with the fact that her old job was waiting for her. But her partner, Beth Finegold, was not restrained. She had brought two bottles of champagne to the conference room and Simon suspected that Finegold would have preferred shaking the bottles and sending spray flying rather than pour out small portions in the paper cups Carpenter had unearthed for the occasion. For the most part, Lind's supporters were in attendance: Brittany Stern, Cynthia Harvey, Frank Stevens, and Fran Morgan. Stern and Harvey were probably under the legal drinking age, but nobody seemed to care. Finegold had organized a victory lunch at a nearby restaurant. Carpenter had begged off from attending and looked like he wanted to speed up the hands on the clock so the luncheon crowd would head off and leave him alone.

"This has got to feel good," Frank Stevens said, coming up beside Simon with a cup of champagne.

"There's no feeling quite like it," Simon admitted.

"I read the decision," Stevens said. "It seems like the hearing officer bought into everything you argued."

Simon nodded. The hearing officer had endorsed each contention made by Lind, specifically finding that Lind was the most successful coach at the high school and had not acted differently than any male coach. Lind's basing starting positions on demonstrated merit couldn't be faulted. Forrester ordered Lind reinstated with back pay and would award her attorney fees once Carpenter had submitted an affidavit as to the time expended on Lind's behalf. To ice the cake, Forrester added one hundred thousand dollars to Lind's damage award for emotional distress.

"Does the school get to appeal?" Stevens asked.

"Yes," Simon replied. Carpenter didn't think the school would appeal, but Simon kept that intelligence to himself.

"School's over now, but I wonder how Ms. Lind will be treated when she returns in September." Stevens said.

"Maybe she'll opt to coach elsewhere," Simon said, repeating Carpenter's theory.

"Why would she do that after fighting to get her job back?"

"She's proven her point," Simon replied. "Sometimes, after a legal battle, it just makes sense to move on to a new environment, even if you win."

Stevens stared at his cup of champagne. "I don't really like this stuff," he said, nodding toward the paper cup.

Simon knocked back what was left in his cup. "I prefer wine frankly, but this will do in a pinch."

Stevens shifted beside him. "Do you have a business card?" he asked.

Simon extracted a card from his wallet. "You need a lawyer?" he said, handing the card over.

"Not really," Stevens owned up. "But I may want to get in touch. You never know what might come up."

Simon couldn't decide if he was being hit on and didn't mind if that were the case. "You now know where to find me."

51

This morning, Philly's Skype image was surprisingly clear as she directed Rachel to summarize the depositions in Martin Hays' case. To Rachel it was weird to direct her remarks to a computer screen positioned on the conference room table while the people needing to hear what she had to say were seated on either side of her.

"What do you think this guy Mast wants to talk to you about?" Simon asked when Rachel had concluded her summary.

"I think he's going to come in with a lowball settlement offer," Philly said. "So far, the only claim of negligence against Mayfair Country Club is that the club didn't remind golfers about its rules and about counting the golfers in the foursome up ahead. That sounds weak to me."

Carpenter drummed his fingers on the conference room table. "That may be enough to keep the country club in the case."

"But if Lord deliberately tried to hit Hays, how can the country club be responsible for that?" Simon questioned.

"It may be a reach," Carpenter conceded. "But a jury might buy the argument that if the country club had been more rigorous about enforcing its rules and safe practices, Lord wouldn't have acted as he did."

"I think I'd rather argue the country club's position on that," Rachel said.

Carpenter nodded his assent as he kept up a steady drumbeat of finger taps on the top of the conference room table. "We might want to get hold of that private detective you used," he directed at Philly's computer screen image.

"Why?" Philly asked.

"If Lord tried deliberately to hit Hays, that would be an intentional act on his part that might not be covered by his insurance. His personal umbrella policy probably covers negligent acts but not intentional acts such as assault and battery. I'd like to know Lord's personal net worth."

Rachel wondered when, if ever, she would be able to identify potential pitfalls in a case the way Carpenter did as a matter of course. Millicent Rudd was defending Lord, but she was really representing his insurance company. If she got a look at the affidavits of Cannon and Mobley, she might well advise the insurer to refuse to pay for any damages that Lord had caused Hays.

"Shit!" Philly muttered.

"Which is why that detective of yours needs to get us some financial information on Lord as soon as possible," Carpenter said to Philly's image.

"How will he do that?" Rachel asked, genuinely curious.

"You don't want to know," Carpenter answered.

"What do I say to Mast?" Philly asked.

"Hear the man out," Carpenter replied. "Talk is cheap."

Philly put off calling Thomas Mast until Daisy had gone down for a late morning nap. Sarah Ferguson had not been able to babysit today. Isabella was taking Rosalind for an outing in a stroller and Philly thought it was a good thing that Isabella had gotten outside. It wasn't that Isabella seemed overwhelmed by her newborn. But Sarah was right; Isabella just didn't seem to have any energy. Philly thought she had a simple solution, but it was expensive, and it might be presumptuous, too.

"We think that our pending motion to dismiss Martin Hays' case will be allowed," Mast said without fanfare once he took Philly's call. "But my client's insurer is prepared to offer twenty-five thousand dollars to settle your client's claims against Mayfair Country Club. The offer will remain open for a week. We're in court on the country club's motion to dismiss in two weeks."

Philly took no satisfaction in having correctly predicted that Mast would come in with a lowball offer. Mast had to think that the country club had some exposure or he wouldn't be putting any money on the table before the court hearing. But Mast's timing was also clever in a way. If Philly thought the motion to dismiss was likely to be granted, she would have an incentive to accept the lowball offer before that motion got heard.

"I'll get back to you." Philly said.

"Is this something you're willing to recommend?"

"I don't know."

"Okay, play it close to the vest," Mast said irritably.

"No, I really don't know," Philly replied.

Mast didn't say anything. Philly willed him to conclude the discussion; they had nothing more to say to each other.

"All right," Mast said. "I didn't mean to bite your head off. It's been one of those mornings."

"I can identify with that."

"You're looking and acting feistier," Maxine said to Carpenter, approvingly.

Carpenter didn't think her comment had to do with his taking charge of washing the dinner dishes. They were spending the night at her condo and when they were there, Maxine usually insisted on cooking *and* doing the dishes. But tonight he had directed her to sit and relax while he saw to the washing up.

"Yeah, I am," Carpenter replied. Maxine knew about the ground up herbs prepared for him by Camellia Kim's grandmother, but he kept silent about that development tonight. He had no idea whether the herb concoction was working on his condition but, in case it was, he didn't want to jinx anything by saying so out loud.

"Does this mean you're up for some action tonight?"

"That can be arranged."

"Good."

Carpenter's appetite had returned and night sweats had stopped. He wondered whether these and other symptoms would come and go without warning.

"There's a house in east Arlington that might be a possibility," Maxine said.

There was only one suitable response to Maxine's observation. "Maybe we should take a look," Carpenter said.

52

Sarah Ferguson was taking Daisy outside with the stroller, and Isabella had joined her, pushing Rosalind in a second stroller. June was a glorious month to be outside, with a caressing warmth that they would soon look back on as deliciously cool. But Isabella hadn't seemed eager for a walk; resigned was a better description.

Philly revisited her plan to draw Isabella out of whatever funk her housemate was in. The problem was that her plan cost money—$2,000 give or take—and money was now something she needed to pay attention to. Previously, she'd been able to pay her share of the mortgage, pay Sarah, make her monthly payment to her investment account, and cover her share of the Boston office, all on her own. But this month she'd had to dip into Philip's trust fund, money that his family had insisted she take. Had money come in from the Alison Lind case, she wouldn't have had to make an inroad in Philip's stash. But the hearing officer had yet to award attorney fees and there was always the chance that Middlemarch High School would appeal the hearing officer's decision.

Philly considered the next call she had to make. Thomas Mast had dangled twenty-five thousand dollars in front of Martin Hays. After a tortuous conference call, Hays had opted not to accept the $25,000 settlement offer, and to follow Carpenter's advice to counteroffer $75,000. Carpenter didn't believe the counteroffer would be accepted, but he seemed confident that Mast would come back with an offer higher than his first. Carpenter had recommended that Hays accept any offer that came close to $50,000 and Hays had agreed.

"That's never going to fly," Mast said once Philly delivered her counteroffer. "The country club is not willing to go through a negotiation process on this. I thought I had been clear about that. We'll just have to see what happens at the hearing on the motion to dismiss."

Philly let Mast's rejection hang in the air for a long moment. "I understand," she said. This wasn't the first time she'd had to reject a settlement proposal that would have resulted in quick, needed cash in her pocket. Hopefully her tone had stayed neutral without disappointment seeping in. "You *had* been clear before. But I'm simply telling you what is necessary from my client's perspective to resolve this case before we go to court. And you're right. We will have to see what happens at the hearing on the motion to dismiss."

"Okay then," Mast said. "Thanks for getting back to me."

It was odd, Philly thought. The just concluded phone call should have heightened her concerns about her cash flow. Instead, Philly saw clearly that the gift she wanted to get Isabella was the right move. So what if the Philip nest egg took another hit? Years ago, she had come to terms with the fact that she'd never be rich. But she could have a life that was good, and it was okay if Philip helped her do that.

Outside her second-floor home office window, the sun was bright. The sloped roof of the neighboring house shimmered with haze in the full afternoon sun. Philly was thinking about what her view would be like if they were ever to pull off the deal for the new house when her telephone rang. She recognized the exchange. Talk about serendipity. "Hi," she said.

"I have good news," their broker said. I've got a potential buyer for Ms. Ferguson's house. If the house passes a home inspection, I think we're good to go."

"Great," Philly said. If she was worried about cash flow before, now she could worry in earnest, but there was no looking back. Nor did she want to. "Let me know as soon as you hear."

July

Philly's Attitude Playlist

Born This Way

Lady Gaga

53

On this July Fourth barbecue, Daisy was mobile. The baby fat on her chunky legs jiggled as she stomped and staggered about. Philly had squeezed purple shorts over her rubber pants and diaper and, every once in a while, Daisy would lose her balance, plop down on her bum, right herself, and resume forward motion. She reminded Philly of a punch-drunk windup toy. She had lathered her daughter with sun block and had stuck a Boston Red Sox cap on her head. Daisy was making unintelligible noises as she lurched about. She seemed interested in being in motion and didn't stay still long enough for adults to fuss over her.

Paul and Raul manned the grill. Philly wondered whether they'd become close when their entourages moved to the new house. The home inspection on Sarah's house had come back favorable and now four house closings were being coordinated by the broker. Philly had followed the strategy she had employed when buying her current house. She turned the legal work over to Morton, one of Carpenter's Barrister friends, and stepped aside. Between the sale of the Brighton property, Sarah's house, Paul's condo, and the purchase of the new house in Brighton, Morton would have a lot of work and could afford to be fair with fees.

Almost everyone Philly cared about would put in an appearance today. Her parents had arrived early from Fall River and were chatting up Sarah Ferguson. Philip's parents would arrive later in the afternoon as would Carpenter and Maxine. Rachel and Simon had also told her that they would be there in the afternoon. Her AA sponsor, Melanie, had shown up with her daughter, Frances, and miraculously, Frances and Jenny, Paul's daughter, seemed to have hit it off. Gerald Hatch had shown up with a date, a dark-haired, dark complexioned girl who didn't seem self-conscious about being thrown into a mix of people she didn't know. Rainy, her long ago drinking buddy and former lover, had arrived with the same woman he had been seeing last summer. He and Monica seemed to be a serious couple. Connie had arrived with her new husband, Bernard, and Philly still wasn't sure whether the geezer knew that Connie was back in the states let alone married.

It was cramped in the back of the house mainly because the grill was in use and because Philly's recent purchase, two refurbished spinning bikes, claimed a corner of the blacktop. Isabella was on the bike that Philly had given her, sitting erect, her legs pedaling smoothly, with Rosalind settled in a baby sling secured around her mother's neck. For the past two mornings, Philly and Isabella had gotten up early, fed their kids, and gone for a forty-minute workout. Philly would bring her boom box outside, set the volume low, and settle into a brisk pace that Isabella matched. Rosalind slept in a bassinet while they pedaled, while Daisy stomped about the small backyard. Halfway through their first morning on the bikes, Isabella began to smile. When the ride was over, Isabella had given her a heartfelt hug and Philly knew she'd made the right decision in buying the bikes.

"Hamburgers and hot dogs are done!" Paul called out and people began drifting toward the grill.

Philly thought, with amusement, that her life had gone from happy to sappy. How else to explain her constant thinking about wanting to make a baby with Paul.

Daisy came waddling toward her grinning, spewing drool, her baseball cap awry. "Hey, pumpkin," Philly said scooping up her daughter. "Did you know that your mother's body has been taken over by aliens? I used to be a tough customer. Now I'm all goopy. What the hell happened? I'll tell you what happened. You happened."

When Carpenter arrived, his immediate reaction was that Philly had betrayed him by not letting him know. He tried to maintain a neutral expression but doubted that he had succeeded. Seeing Connie had given him a start and being introduced to her husband was an even bigger shock. Hadn't Connie insisted that she'd never marry again? While Maxine and Connie embraced, Carpenter and Bernard favored each other with forced smiles. Then the women began to chat, moved off, and left them alone. Connie looked good. She'd lost weight but had retained her full figure. Bernard proved to be the older brother of a man Carpenter had gotten to know when he had visited Connie in Rwanda. As he watched Connie and Maxine jabber away, his irritation eased. In similar circumstances, he would probably have kept his mouth shut as opposed to giving Philly a heads up.

"Connie has spoken very highly of you," Bernard said.

Carpenter suppressed the urge to make light of the comment. "You're a lucky man, Bernard. Connie's a terrific woman."

"I know this. I have been blessed with a miracle. I had resigned myself to living out my days as a lonely old man."

Connie and Maxine had met each other exactly once about two years ago. Yet they were carrying on as long-time friends catching up on their doings after an absence. Carpenter believed that he and Bernard had probably said all they were going to say to each other. He could ask Bernard about his younger brother with the wonderful first name of Bosco. Or he could keep silent. He cast a sideways glance at Bernard. The Rwandan seemed content to watch the women. He took a page from Bernard's book and kept his mouth shut.

Gerald Hatch's date was named Wendy. Daisy had conked out on Gerald's shoulder. Philly had handed Daisy off to Gerald when her daughter started to fuss, and Wendy looked surprised as Gerald soothed the toddler into sleep while showering her with soft kisses. Wendy had to be seeing a side of Gerald that she couldn't have imagined. Philly suspected that if Wendy wasn't hooked on Gerald, she soon would be.

"You promise to e-mail me when you get to college?" Philly asked.

"No," Gerald said seriously before breaking into a grin. "Let's say it's a definite maybe." He looked at Wendy and gestured at Daisy. "I should have told you this before but you're looking at my real girlfriend."

"A little young, don't you think?" Wendy came back.

"You may have a point. But in the interest of full disclosure, I've given my heart to this little one."

Gerald was totally at ease, relaxed, natural, joking. He had been awarded the Spanish excellence award at his high school graduation and Raul and Isabella had confirmed that he was fluent. At UMass-Amherst he was planning on a double major—Spanish and history.

"Okay, I will e-mail you. In return, I expect periodic Daisy photographs."

"That can be arranged," Philly said. "If you want you can set Daisy down in her crib."

"I don't think so. I want to take advantage of my Daisy contact time."

Carpenter did a double take when Simon showed up with Frank Stevens. Wasn't Stevens a little young? Simon looked his composed self. "You remember Frank Stevens," he had said matter-of-factly. "He was a witness for Alison Lind."

Rachel immediately joined their party and Carpenter couldn't pinpoint what was different about her. She, too, had a date, a tall, wiry guy with light brown hair whose name was Josh. There was a laid-back attitude about Josh that made Carpenter wonder if he had knocked off a joint or two before arriving.

"How's your golf game?" Simon asked Rachel.

Rachel colored. "You'll have to ask my teacher," she said, nodding in Josh's direction.

"Needs a lot of work," Josh opined. "I've recommended evening sessions to work on hip rotation. The swing is all in the hips."

Rachel was now crimson. Carpenter had seen her nonplussed before but nothing like this.

"I'm betting Rachel is one heck of a lawyer," Josh said. "Her focus is amazing. Her swing has really come along."

"Time to change the subject," Rachel said, dragging Josh toward the grill.

"I've told you about Rachel," Simon commented to Frank Stevens. "Smartest person in our law school class. It's nice to see her happy."

So that was what was different about Rachel, Carpenter thought.

"You keeping up with AA?" Rainy asked Philly. Monica was standing beside Rainy and gave him a nudge with her elbow.

"It's all right," Philly said. "Rainy got me to go to the program in the first place, so he gets to ask. I'm not keeping up the way my sponsor would like." She pointed to Melanie who was on the grass sitting beside Jenny and Frances. "But I'm going reasonably regularly."

"Don't stop," Rainy said, all business.

"I have to admit that I've thought about stopping. But I won't."

"Don't," Rainy repeated.

"How are you two doing?" Philly changed the subject. If looks told the story she knew the answer to her question. Rainy looked as fit and trim as ever. He'd kept his full close-cut beard. He was one of those guys who never aged so you'd notice. Monica was simply a knockout—tall, thin, prominent cheekbones, a model's body. They were holding hands, their fingers lightly linked.

"I'd say we're doing okay," Rainy said. "We've been living together for a while now and we haven't killed each other. I'll take the small victories."

"I've been happy," Monica said. "It's been good."

Sappiness was everywhere.

54

"Why shouldn't I allow the Salem Stampede's motion to dismiss?" Judge Clarence Ford challenged. "Where's the negligence on the defendant's part?"

Philly glanced at Simon as she rose, conscious of the small army of lawyers waiting behind her, soon to have their turn at addressing pointed questions from the bench. Usually Simon wouldn't pass up an opportunity for court time but, on this occasion, he had urged Philly to do the honors. "My mother knows Martina," he said. "If Martina's claim against the hockey club is thrown out, I don't want to have to explain to her what happened."

Philly took her time settling herself. Carpenter had drummed into her head that it was a bad omen when a judge started with questions for the party opposing a motion to dismiss. Judge Ford's leanings were not discernible from the stern look etched on his craggy face. But Philly decided to assume that the judge was inclined to rule against her client.

"Some acts that cause injury are inherently negligent and that is what we are dealing with in this case," Philly began. "If a ceiling tile had fallen and subjected Martina Glass to the severe injuries she suffered, would the team that sold her the ticket be able to claim that no negligence was involved? Hardly. True, in this case we do not have a ceiling tile falling on Ms. Glass. What fell on Ms. Glass was one Fred Dunn, an individual twice the size of Ms. Glass and a defendant in this case. When one purchases a ticket to a hockey game, the expectation of the purchaser, Ms. Glass in this case, is that no object of any kind will fall on the purchaser causing serious injury."

Philly paused. Judge Ford's features remained solemn and unreadable. He was perched on a high bench in an old, dimly lit courtroom in Essex Superior Court and he reminded Philly of a ruler surveying his realm. And for a judge, his courtroom was his realm.

"It may be," Philly continued, "that the Salem Stampede has rights against Mr. Dunn. But there can be no question that a paying customer was injured in an arena under the control of the hockey club and there can be no real dispute that the hockey club owed Ms. Glass a duty to keep her safe."

"Are you comparing Mr. Dunn to a ceiling tile?' the judge inquired.

"Yes," Philly said, deciding that there was no reason to qualify her position and that an unequivocal answer was called for.

"Was it foreseeable that Mr. Dunn would fall on the plaintiff?" the judge followed up.

"In the legal sense, yes," Philly responded. "The plaintiff also claims that the hockey club is strictly liable for the injuries she experienced as a result of Mr. Dunn falling on her. As Your Honor knows, a plaintiff doesn't have to prove negligence or an intent to harm if a defendant is strictly liable for her injuries. Under strict liability, a defendant may be held liable without being at fault."

"What should the Salem Stampede have done to prevent Mr. Dunn falling on the plaintiff?"

"Make sure that there was no possibility that a fan seated above any other fan could fall on the fan below."

"That's reasonable, isn't it?" the judge asked Wayne Martin, the hockey club's lawyer.

Martin rose smartly. He was young and rugged looking, and Philly pegged him for a former hockey player.

"No, respectfully, it is not reasonable," Martin said. "The Salem Stampede has provided a picture of the seating arrangement. There is a secure, low barrier in front of the row of seats occupied by Mr. Dunn. It is neither reasonable nor foreseeable to envision a fan falling over the barrier and onto a fan seated below."

"But that's what happened here," the judge said. "Who does your client say is to blame for the plaintiff's injuries?"

"Mr. Dunn."

"Mr. Dunn has filed an answer in this case. He claims that he was pushed. He also claims that the barrier wasn't high enough to prevent his fall. Shouldn't we let a jury sort all this out?'

"If Mr. Dunn was pushed," Martin replied, "that act cannot be the responsibility of the Salem Stampede. Also, the height of the barrier was approved by the City of Salem's building department. The barrier cannot be so high that a seated fan can't see the hockey game."

"Ms. Piper claims that your motion to dismiss should not be decided at this time," the judge continued. "She argues that the plaintiff is entitled to discovery before the hockey team's dismissal motion is heard. Do you quarrel with that?"

"I do, Your Honor," Martin said determinedly. "Besides saying that discovery is necessary, the plaintiff offers no indication why discovery is necessary. What does the plaintiff hope to learn in discovery that is not already before the court?"

"What do you hope to learn in discovery, Ms. Piper?" the judge turned his artillery on Philly.

"For starters, the plaintiff seeks to learn the amount of alcohol served to and consumed by Mr. Dunn and his party. Also, for starters, the plaintiff seeks information concerning the push Mr. Dunn claims he received. Were the aisles so narrow that it was reasonably foreseeable that one fan squeezing past another would cause the other to topple over the barrier that's been referred to? Has the Salem Stampede ever received complaints about the seating arrangements? Again, Your Honor, this is just for starters."

Philly sat down abruptly. Martin remained seated. Philly had experienced Judge Ford's style before; Ford had been seesawing back and forth in his questions for opposing counsel, perhaps hoping to surprise one of the litigators.

"What do you say to Ms. Piper's argument that the Salem Stampede is liable for the plaintiff's injuries simply because she paid money to an event and should have been kept safe."

"My client did everything in its power to keep her safe," Martin returned smartly. "This is not a case appropriate for strict liability. This is a negligence case and the Salem Stampede did not act negligently in anyway whatsoever."

The judge consulted the pleadings before him. "Ms. Piper has noted in her legal memorandum that the language on the back of the plaintiff's ticket warns of dangers involved in attending a hockey game such as a puck that is fired into the stands. As she points out, the ticket does not warn of bodies falling on anyone buying a ticket. Isn't that failure to warn of falling bodies a reason to deny your motion to dismiss?"

"No," Martin said, shaking his head emphatically. "The language on the back of the ticket stub simply points out commonly understood risks that accompany watching a hockey game. A fan falling over a barrier is not at all analogous to any of the risks of injury inherent in the game of hockey."

"Is the arena where this game was played owned by the Salem Stampede?" the judge asked Martin.

"No, Your Honor. The team leases the arena for games."

"If a ceiling tile fell on a fan as Ms. Piper mentioned earlier on, wouldn't your client be liable for any of the fan's resulting injuries?"

"No, Your Honor. The arena owner might be, however."

"But in that example your client would have sold the fan the ticket. If I were that fan, I would certainly sue the entity that I paid money to. While your client may have claims against the arena owner, I'm thinking that has no bearing on the fan's rights against your client."

"I would disagree," Martin responded but with far less force than in his previous answers to the judge's questions. Philly considered that her comparing Fred Dunn to a ceiling tile—an analogy that out of nowhere had popped into her head—had somehow struck a nerve with Judge Ford.

"The Salem Stampede had no ability or authority to deal with the arena's ceiling tiles. There would be no basis for a negligence claim against the hockey club if a tile fell and injured a fan."

"I think I've heard enough," Judge Ford said with an audible sigh. "I'm going to take the matter under advisement. Thank you, counsel."

On the drive back from court, Simon sat motionless in the passenger seat. "Any thoughts?" Philly asked.

"I think the judge is going to deny the motion to dismiss."

Philly agreed but was reluctant to voice her view for fear of jinxing the outcome. If cynicism was a disease, Carpenter was a carrier who plainly had infected her.

"What's with this guy Josh?" Philly asked, opting for gossip. Rachel's barbecue date hadn't struck her as a guy Rachel would have much to do with.

"I hadn't met him before your cookout," Simon said. "Rachel wanted to take a golf lesson because of the Martin Hays case and this guy gave her the lesson."

"He seemed like a free spirit," Philly threw out to get Simon talking.

"Turns out he teaches golf and tennis. He's also pretty serious about online poker."

Philly had never associated a laid-back attitude with poker success. "Sounds like he's into a little bit of everything."

Simon had shifted a half turn in his seat so that he was now facing her. Philly wondered if she had come across as prying. Which she was, of course. Rachel and Simon were close; Rachel would have confided in Simon before anyone else.

"I think Rachel likes the guy," Simon said. "She's always been serious, career driven. In law school, if I had to guess, I think she out-studied everyone else. This guy Josh seems to have loosened her up."

Philly nodded, not sure whether a loosened-up Rachel was a good thing. Then there was the guy who had accompanied Simon to the cookout. Turnabout was fair play—maybe Rachel had something to say about Frank Stevens.

55

"On behalf of the Mayflower Country Club, I'm authorized to offer Mr. Hays thirty-five thousand dollars," Thomas Mast said.

Philly bounced Daisy up and down on her knee. Just having been fed, her daughter was full of energy. Which wasn't always the case. Sometimes after a feeding Daisy conked out. Philly had long ago stopped worrying about Daisy letting out a sudden shriek while she was on a business call. She entertained a perverse notion that a shrill Daisy utterance might jolt Mast to raise his offer. She was in no hurry to respond to his proposal. She stared for a moment at the bright glare outside her second-story home office window. The sun was directly overhead. When she and Isabella had finished their spinning drill at eight this morning, the humidity had already kicked in.

"Any response?" Mast pressed.

"I'm authorized to counter-offer at sixty-five thousand dollars."

Mast said nothing. Daisy began to squirm, and Philly set her down on her office floor, arranging a giant piece of coloring paper and a box of crayons within easy reach. Daisy grabbed a blue crayon in a chubby fist and began to scribble on the paper.

"Are we playing a split the difference game that ends at fifty thousand?" Mast asked.

"No," Philly said. "We're playing a split the difference game that ends at fifty-five thousand."

"You need to make the game end at fifty."

"You need to make the game end above fifty."

"Fifty-one is above fifty."

"But it's not fifty-five."

"It's never going to be fifty-five."

"How about fifty-two five?"

"How about fifty-one?"

"Help me out here," Philly said.

"I just did. I went to fifty-one."

Divisible by three, Philly realized. Mast was dangling a $17,000 attorney fee in front of her nose. Martin Hays would walk away with $34,000.

"It wasn't clear to me that you had actually gone to fifty-one," Philly said. "Thanks for clarifying. We have a deal."

"I'll draw up the release forms and the agreement to be filed with the court," Mast replied.

"Nice doing business with you," Philly said. She set her phone down and it immediately rang. "Philomena Piper," she said, grateful that Daisy was still into violent artwork.

"I've got some good news," Carpenter said.

"I like the sound of that."

"Anne Forester awarded full attorney fees in the Alison Lind case. We're talking sixty K."

"No shit!"

"It gets better," Carpenter said. "Darren Grayson, the school attorney, gave me a call. He wanted to know if we would agree to take fifteen thou off the attorney fee award if Middlemarch High School didn't appeal. I told him no. He took a few more runs at me and I kept telling him no. Finally, he caved. His client will pay the award and not appeal. There's some insurance that kicks in, so the school isn't paying everything out of pocket."

Philly began doing math in her head. "How does this work?" she asked. "Our contingency arrangement with Lind calls for a third. Does the attorney fee award go into the pot with the damage award?"

"It works out better for Lind if we pocket the attorney fee award and she gets to keep her full damage award which is loaded with back pay and the emotional distress award," Carpenter said. "We've also got to back out the retainer she paid us."

"Right," Philly said. She had forgotten about the retainer that Lind had paid. They'd be splitting less than $60,000—$54,000, actually. "Have you told Lind?" she asked.

"I thought I'd tell you first."

"The Mayfair Country Club has agreed to settle for fifty-one thousand," Philly revealed.

"Nice," Carpenter said. "Divisible by three. This is turning out to be a decent day."

"How do you want to carve all this up?" Philly asked.

"I was thinking close to four equal shares," Carpenter replied. "Maybe we give ourselves a little bit more for having brought the cases in and having to deal with office overhead. Simon prepared the Lind case for trial. He brought in the witnesses who made a difference."

"Okay," Philly said. "Rachel's been working her butt off for Martin Hays. She's been doing good work."

"How about this," Carpenter said. "We give Rachel and Simon four thou each on the Hays case with you and me splitting the extra thou. On the Lind case we're talking about carving up fifty-four thou. How about we give each of them thirteen K and we each put an extra thou in our pocket."

"Done," Philly said.

Carpenter didn't say anything for a long moment. "We needed this," he finally observed.

"Tell me about it," Philly replied. "You know this little extra money we're directing our way?" she changed the subject. "I'd like to throw a little of it at those two private investigators. If the Salem Stampede's motion to dismiss is denied, I want them to do some digging in the Martina Glass case."

"What do you have in mind?"

"I want them to try to find witnesses to the accident. Somebody at the hockey game must have seen a big, muscular guy fall out of the stands. Someone must have noticed how much alcohol the guy who fell was putting away."

"Sure," Carpenter said. "But you need to clear it with the client. Technically she's on the hook for expenses."

"Okay, I'll do that."

"Let me ask you something," Carpenter said. "Would you be throwing money at these investigators if we hadn't made these modest scores?"

"Truthfully, no," Philly admitted. "That's a pretty sorry state of affairs, isn't it?"

"I suppose so," Carpenter acknowledged. "It's human nature. We get to feel flush for a fleeting moment so we think we can be generous. The moment will be up in thirty days and we'll have to do it all over again. In this business, there are no laurels to rest on. You have to keep doing it again and again. There's no fucking end."

When Philly hung up her phone, she realized that Daisy was asleep on the floor, lying on her stomach, her ass in the air. Blue crayon marks lined the cheek facing her. "That's what lawyer talk will do to you," she whispered. "Put you out like a light."

56

Ruth Foster had been pressing them to take the deposition of Richard Mason, the administrator of the Maple Leaf Assisted Living Center. "I want to make that rotten bastard squirm and I don't care what it costs," is the way she had put it. Philly had turned the task over to Simon.

The conference room was crowded, and the air conditioner struggled to wring some of the heat and humidity out of the air. The occupants' dispositions did nothing to cool the atmosphere. Ruth Foster was in attendance breathing fire. Mary Foster hadn't been the same since her injury. She had become frail and dependent, her spark gone. Her doctors presently disagreed whether a hip replacement would improve her ambulation. Jeannie Smith, the stenographer, was in sullen good form glaring at her recording device when it didn't start up promptly. Philly wasn't sure, but she thought she heard the word *shit* escape Smith's lips.

But Richard Mason looked cool and confident. Ruth Foster had called Richard Mason a sack of shit, but he certainly didn't look like one to Philly. He was a young man with sandy hair, blue eyes, and a self-possessed bearing. If Simon didn't take him down a notch, perhaps Ruth Foster's staring daggers at him would dent his armor.

A full complement of opposing lawyers was arranged around the table. They introduced themselves and Philly paired them up with their clients. Amy Huff, the dapper young woman with straight brown hair and no-nonsense attitude represented the Center; Robert Boyd, the rumpled man with the jaded air belonged to Harrison Blaine; and the heavy set, bored looking woman, Marcia Livingston, went with Harry Fried.

Simon's background questions established that Richard Mason was the son of the president of the company that owned Maple Leaf Assisted Living Center. Mason had pursued a liberal arts program in college, had then taken some time off to travel in Europe, and had made it through the first year of an MBA program before dropping out and abandoning that graduate degree path. Mason had been selling cars for several years before taking courses and obtaining practical experience that led to his qualifying for the position of executive director of an assisted living facility.

"Is it correct to say that your father got you your present job?" Simon asked once Mason had completed recounting his educational and work experience.

"He certainly helped," Mason said, not appearing offended by Simon's blunt question. "He definitely encouraged me to get the educational background and job experience for the job. I'm glad I listened to him."

"Did anyone else interview for the job you now hold?" Simon persisted.

"I don't think so. As far as my father was concerned, I think the job was mine if I wanted it, and I wanted it."

Simon asked Mason to identify an e-mail stream that started with an e-mail that Ruth Foster had sent to Mason.

"I recognize this," Mason said. "Ruth Foster sent me the e-mail that's on the bottom of the page and my reply follows just above her e-mail."

"Would you please read aloud Ms. Foster's e-mail to you?"

Mason cleared his throat. "'I want to make you aware of a dangerous situation. On a visit to my mother late this morning, I was passing by the entrance to the dining room and was almost knocked down by a wheelchair. A second wheelchair followed close behind. It was clear to me that the two men in the wheelchairs were racing. That is unacceptable. Someone is likely to get seriously hurt. What are you going to do about this dangerous situation?'"

"What was your reply?"

"I told Ms. Foster that I would look into the situation."

"Did you?"

"Yes."

"What did you do to look into the situation?'

Mason paused. "This was some time ago so I may not be recalling everything I did. I remember interviewing dining room staff and none of them were aware of any wheelchair racing. I got the same answer when I interviewed housekeeping staff."

"Did you do anything else?" Simon asked.

"At the moment, I can't recall anything else."

"Did you report back to Ms. Foster as to what you found out?"

Mason knitted his brows. "You know, I don't think so."

"Did you interview any residents of the assisted living facility?"

"I don't think so."

"Did you send out any notice warning against wheelchair racing?"

"No. I wasn't convinced that racing was going on."

"Did you doubt Ms. Foster's e-mail account to you?"

Mason paused. His eyes met Ruth Foster's and then he promptly looked away. "I wouldn't put it that I doubted what she said. I just didn't receive confirmation of what she said from facility staff. I thought it likely that a wheelchair had come too close to her, but it didn't seem to me from staff interviews that dangerous activity was going on."

"Was it your decision not to interview any resident of the facility who used a wheelchair?"

"I guess you could say that. I didn't see a need to interview any resident once facility staff reported back to me that they weren't aware of any racing."

"Did you learn that residents were racing wheelchairs after Mary Foster was injured?"

"Yes."

"How did you learn that wheelchair racing had been going on?"

"Residents told me that it had been going on."

"Does that mean you interviewed residents after Mary Foster was injured?"

"Yes."

"Did you interview staff after Mary Foster had been injured?"

"Yes."

"Did staff confirm wheelchair racing in the same way residents did?"

"No. Staff was not aware of wheelchair racing."

"What did Maple Leaf Assisted Living Center do about wheelchair racing once residents confirmed it had been going on?"

Mason glanced at Huff. "I instructed housekeeping staff to pay attention to the hallway near the dining room at mealtimes to make sure no racing occurred. Also, I sent out a memo to all the residents explaining that wheelchair racing would not be tolerated."

Simon introduced the memo as a deposition exhibit. "Before this memo was sent out, did the Center have a rule that banned wheelchair racing?"

"I believe it was understood that such an activity was prohibited."

"That's not what I asked you. Did the Center have a rule banning wheelchair racing?"

"Not a specific rule."

"Does the Center claim that the two men in wheelchairs, Harrison Blaine and Harry Fried, are responsible for Mary Foster's injuries?"

"Yes."

"What's the basis of that claim?"

Philly expected Simon's last question to rouse the wheelchair racers' counsel to something approaching consciousness, but Robert Boyd and Marcia Livingston continued to look bored.

"I believe that has to do with Mr. Blaine and Mr. Fried using their wheelchairs irresponsibly," Mason responded.

"In what manner were they using their wheelchairs irresponsibly?"

"It appears they were racing each other."

"What do you mean it appears?"

"That's what residents said they were doing."

Simon consulted his notes. "Are you aware that in this case Mr. Blaine and Mr. Fried have claimed that Maple Leaf Assisted Living Center is responsible for Mary Foster's injuries?"

"I'm aware of that."

"What is your understanding of why Mr. Blaine and Mr. Fried claim the Center is responsible for Ms. Foster's injuries?"

Mason again glanced at his lawyer, who regarded him without expression. "I believe they claim the Center didn't have adequate security and failed to monitor wheelchair locomotion."

"What security measures did the Center employ at the time Ms. Foster was injured?"

"We had a security guard on duty during the night."

"Is that it?" Simon asked.

"During the day, each member of the Center's staff was responsible for maintaining security."

"Did the Center monitor wheelchair activity at the time Mary Foster was injured?"

"Not specifically," Mason replied. "Residents who required a wheelchair were trained in the wheelchair's use. The Center is a home for all our residents including residents with wheelchairs. As the Center's name implies, the Center assists residents in daily living. The Center doesn't micromanage residents' lives."

"If you had interviewed residents at the time of Ruth Foster's e-mail message to you and been told by residents of wheelchair racing, would you have put in place the monitoring measures and warning memo you put into effect after Mary Foster's injury?"

At long last something moved Amy Huff to speak. "Objection," Huff said. "You may answer."

"I might have," Mason said.

"Did other residents besides Mr. Blaine and Mr. Fried race their wheelchairs?"

"I learned that a few other men raced their wheelchairs."

"Did you also learn that residents bet money on the outcome of wheelchair races?"

Like a school of fish, Huff, Boyd, and Livingston turned as one toward Mason. Philly had wondered what it would take to get a rise out of the three attorneys.

"Some residents reported that bets were being made."

"Were those reports accurate?"

"I can't answer for sure, but I suspect they were."

"Did the Center interview residents who witnessed Mary Foster being struck by a wheelchair?"

"Yes."

Simon introduced the residents' statements obtained by the Center into evidence. "Did the Center file a report of Mary Foster's injury with state regulators?"

"Yes."

"Is this the report?" Simon asked, handing Mason a document.

"Yes."

Simon introduced the report as a deposition exhibit. "What did the report conclude?"

Mason studied the document. "Basically, Mary Foster was struck by a wheelchair navigated by Mr. Blaine who at the time was in a race with a wheelchair operated by Mr. Fried."

Simon leaned toward her and Philly used her notepad to shield their whispered discussion.

"I can't think of anything else," Simon said.

Philly glanced at Ruth Foster. "Neither can I. But I'd check in with Ruth Foster before I rested."

Simon briefly conferred with Ruth Foster. "No further questions," he said when he resumed his seat.

Harrison Blaine's lawyer spoke next. "I have a few questions for you," Boyd announced. "Did you ever personally observe any wheelchair race?"

Mason shook his head. "No."

"Is it true then that your only knowledge of alleged wheelchair racing comes from what other people have told you?"

"That's right."

"Did Mr. Blaine or Mr. Fried ever admit to you that they raced their wheelchairs?"

"Not to me they didn't."

"Did they admit to wheelchair racing to anyone other than you?"

"I don't know one way or the other."

"Was the report to state regulators you testified about based solely on what other people said to you and other Center employees?"

Mason pondered the question. "I'd say that's right."

"Nothing further," Boyd said.

"No questions," Huff and Livingston said together.

"The deposition is concluded," Simon said.

Mason and the lawyers representing the defendants left en masse. Jeannie Smith consulted her notes and began to check the spelling of names with Simon. Ruth Foster took the seat vacated by Mason. "What's next?" she demanded.

Philly had expected the question. "We can take the depositions of Blaine and Fried," she replied. "We could also schedule depositions of residents who witnessed the accident and who witnessed racing."

"Is that what you're going to do?" Foster followed up.

"We're going to try to obtain sworn statements from residents who witnessed your mother being struck and who witnessed wheelchair racing and betting," Philly responded. "Residents are old and I want to make sure we preserve their testimony. The safest way to do that is to take their depositions but sworn statements may be easier on them. We're probably not going to take the depositions of Blaine and Fried. We don't want to give them a preview of what they will be asked at trial."

"They're old too," Foster said. "Why wouldn't we want to pin down their testimony?"

"That is a reason to take their depositions," Philly conceded. "But that takes time, and our preference is to push for a speedy trial. Which brings me to your mother. Will she be able to testify?"

"She's not doing well," Foster said. "We've been paying for home health aides to help her. That's not cheap."

"We could take your mother's deposition to preserve her testimony."

"I'd have to think about that," Foster replied. "I'm not sure I want to put her through that right now."

"When is a final decision going to be made on hip replacement surgery for your mother?"

"I don't know," Foster said glumly. "I goddamn hate this. Mason was a slippery bastard. I didn't think he had it in him."

"What do you think of his testimony that people on his staff weren't aware of wheelchair racing?"

"I think it's a crock!" Foster erupted. "The day I almost got hit it was very noisy. You'd have to be deaf not to hear the shouting."

"Did you see any staff member present?"

"Not that I remember."

"We're going to give some further consideration to next steps," Philly said. "I'll call you shortly."

Foster nodded and left the room. Jeannie Smith was stowing her stenographer gear.

"Any impressions?" Philly asked the stenographer.

Smith shrugged causing her impressive jowls to shake. Her crown of white curly hair had been matted down when she entered the room and hadn't perked up. The humidity had been stifling when Philly left her house.

"I'd say your strongest case is against the guy who hit your client," Smith said.

Philly had been thinking the same thing. Carpenter wanted a trial at which each defendant hurled accusations at all the other defendants. But maybe the way to go was to cut a deal with the center and leave the trial to deal with Blaine and Fried.

"This guy Mason seemed a bit too slick for his own good," Smith added. "I'd play up his daddy getting him his job. Jurors won't like that in this economy."

Simon nodded at Smith's last comment. Like Carpenter, Simon would likely prefer to try the case against all defendants.

57

"We close on September first," Philly whispered into Paul's ear. Two fans were going in her bedroom and the windows were open, yet she felt glued to Paul. She didn't want to think about the sound when they pried themselves apart. The sheets were so damp the blowing air gave her a sudden chill.

"It's really going to happen," Paul said in a tone that made Philly wonder whether he was having second thoughts.

"That's what the broker said," Philly informed him. "Our lawyer, Morton, is set to go. The other buyers are set to go. Our tenants are going to get a place together. So yeah, I'd say it's going to happen. You nervous?"

"I'd be lying if I said I wasn't. Communal living is going to take some getting used to. I've been by myself for a long time."

"Too long," Philly said. "Given what you do for a living, I can't believe you'd get nervous over this."

"I can't help it," Paul said.

Philly wondered whether she had pushed Paul into the new house purchase. Maybe he needed stability on his home front to counterbalance the risks that he took in his work. "If you want alone down time, we're going to have a pretty big bedroom to hide out in."

"Dealing with other people is work," Paul observed. "Sometimes hard work."

"You're right," Philly conceded. "When I moved in with Philip there was a part of me that was certain it was the wrong move. You may have noticed I'm not the easiest person to get along with."

"You could have fooled me."

"I'm too sticky to give you a poke. I was used to being alone and the idea of having another person around 24/7 seemed intolerable. But it turned out to be the right decision. This move is going to be even better."

Paul was silent. Philly felt his heart beating, a slow steady pulse that vibrated against her ribs.

"Have you given any more thought to us making a baby?" Paul asked.

"I have," Philly said, deciding to keep Paul in suspense.

"And?"

"I think it's a great idea. Since there will never be a good time, I vote for now."

"Are you thinking marriage?"

"I am."

"Which do you want to come first?"

"It doesn't make any difference to me. Your call."

"Let's work on both objectives at the same time. What the hell."

Philly became conscious of the uptick in Paul's heartbeat. "We need to get unstuck," she whispered.

"On three," Paul said, and he began to count down.

"Can't sleep?"

Carpenter startled, thinking that until this moment he had regarded the expression jumping out of your skin as hyperbole. "Christ! You scared me to death!"

"Sorry," Maxine said. She slid onto one of the vacant chairs at the kitchen table in her condo. Carpenter glanced at the stove clock—four thirty in the morning. He had been awake for a half hour.

"What's going on?" Maxine asked.

"I'm not sure," Carpenter said. "I got up at four and knew I wasn't going to be able to go back to sleep."

"What are you thinking about?"

Carpenter reached out and took Maxine's hand. She was wearing a white terry cloth robe that made her disappear. She had set the condo air conditioning to kick in at seventy-four degrees and he couldn't understand why she wasn't roasting. He was warm in just boxers and a T-shirt. "Work," he said, finally responding to Maxine's question.

"Now there's a subject that's not exactly calming for you."

"Tell me about it," Carpenter groused. "Recently we were all able to take a paycheck. But the next payday is nowhere in sight. "It's starting to wear on me. It was bad enough when there was just me and Philly and I only had her to worry about. But now with Simon and Rachel in the mix. . ."

Maxine took her free hand and stroked the backs of his fingers. Her feathery touch sent a chill down his back. "You're lucky to have Simon and Rachel," she said. "They've been very quick learners. You should be grateful they're around and stop worrying about paying them. You've been more than fair to them when fees have come in. They know what they've signed on for."

Maxine was right, but that knowledge wasn't enough. "I can't help it. It bothers me."

Maxine slid onto his lap and Carpenter held her close. "I used to be able to do these relaxation exercises," he said. "These days they don't do the trick."

"I know a relaxation exercise that will knock you out."

"I know you do," Carpenter said, keeping hold of Maxine. "I'll take a rain check."

Maxine didn't say anything and for that Carpenter was grateful. She knew when to stay silent, when to wait him out. "How's the house hunt going?" he finally asked.

"I'm going to be looking at two condos this week. Hopefully they'll be better than the houses we've looked at."

Carpenter realized his ambivalence about a new place had vanished. He was ready for the move. "Maybe I'll come with you," he said.

"Now I'm really worried. Are you feeling all right?"

58

Earlier in the day the heat in Philly's upstairs office had been oppressive, but a summer storm had cleared the air a bit and a pleasant breeze was blowing through the open window when the phone rang.

"It's Herb McCauley," a voice said, and for a moment she couldn't place the name. "Barney Freedman's partner."

"Right," Philly said, embarrassed.

"People remember Barney but for some reason they don't remember me."

"I remember you," Philly said. "You're the more laid-back guy."

McCauley laughed. "I wouldn't go that far. I've got the information you wanted on Warren Lord."

Philly arranged a notepad in front of her. "Shoot."

"The bottom line is a net worth of approximately four point three million. I can break it down for you if you want."

Philly circled the sum on her notepad. Not for the first time she wondered how a person managed to acquire such immense wealth. Lord's net worth was so astronomical that she and Lord had to be living in two parallel universes that never intersected. "Shoot," she said again.

"He's got equity in two homes that total over a million, and he's got a retirement account that's over two million. The rest is pretty much cash and stocks."

"This is helpful. You know where to send the bill."

"I do," McCauley replied.

"Should I ask how you got this information?"

"You can ask. But it's the old story. If I tell you, we'd probably have to kill you."

"Ignorance is bliss it is," Philly responded cheerfully.

"I don't have anything on that hockey game accident you wanted us to look into. Sorry. Realistically, we may have to wait until the fall when the new season starts."

"What about the list of season ticket holders we got from the hockey club in discovery?" Philly asked.

"The problem is that there are no assigned seats for season ticket holders. Plus, your client doesn't know any of the other season ticket holders. To be honest, we haven't called any of them. Is that something you want us to do?"

Philly wasn't sure how to respond. Now that Judge Ford had denied the motion to dismiss Martina Glass' case, she wanted to turn McCauley loose, but she didn't want to pay McCauley and Freedman a lot of money to dig up information. "I don't know," she said. "I'll have to think about it."

"My advice is to hold off until the season starts in the fall. We think it's the most cost-effective way to go."

"All right," Philly said. "Let's leave it to the fall unless I tell you something to the contrary."

"Have a nice day," McCauley said and, when the line went dead, Philly thought that Freedman would never have offered such a pleasantry.

Philly hadn't expected a call from Michael Waters. She couldn't imagine him calling with anything but bad news. Daisy and Isabella and Rosalind were at Sarah Ferguson's house and Philly was glad to be alone for what promised to be an unpleasant conversation. "How have you been?" she inquired.

"Good," Waters replied. "I'm enjoying one of the major perks of teaching: a more than two-month hiatus."

"That sounds inviting."

"I thought you'd be interested in some news about Caroline Fine."

Carpenter often griped that lawyers finished a case and never learned about the aftershocks that inevitably followed the case's closure. Philly realized that she shared Carpenter's curiosity even if it involved hearing bad news. "I'm interested," she said.

"Caroline won't be returning to James Madison for her senior year. She's taking her senior year at a private school and she's going to defer applying to college for a while."

"I thought she was obsessed about getting into Princeton," Philly responded. "Or was that the main character in her story?" she added.

"Apparently the real-life Caroline is not obsessed about any college."

"How did you find this out?"

"She told me."

Philly's knee-jerk response was that nothing good could come from a client talking to an opponent after a case had been closed. "How did that happen?" she asked.

"With all the snow days this year, school ended late June. I didn't get around to cleaning out my classroom until a few days ago, and she walked in on me while I was boxing things up."

Talk about awkward, Philly thought. In Waters' place she would have wanted three witnesses present.

"I was at my desk and she entered my classroom and closed the door behind her. I told her to open the door for obvious reasons. She ignored me, and just started talking. She stayed next to the closed door, and I didn't move from my desk. It was like she had prepared what she wanted to say in advance. She said she didn't want to become the character in her story and was going to finish high school at a private school. Then, she said, she was going to take a year off—maybe two—and worry about college later."

"Is that it? I didn't hear an apology."

"She didn't give one," Waters said. "She said that she thought I'd be interested in what she'd decided to do. I debated whether to say anything to her. I'm sure if you were around, you would have advised me to shut my mouth. But I began to think about what it had taken for Caroline to come and talk to me. So I said I was very pleased that she let me know her plans."

"Is that it?" Philly repeated.

"Yes. She opened the door and left without another word."

Philly replayed Waters' account. The encounter couldn't have lasted more than a few minutes. "What do you make of that?" she asked.

"I can't be sure, but I think she's going to be all right. I think she wanted to get off the track she was on: excelling in high school, aiming for a prestigious college, living up to everyone's expectations when she wasn't clear on what she wanted."

"She picked a hell of a way to derail the course she was headed on. She tried to ruin you. I'm not sure you're right about her. I might feel differently if she had offered an apology."

"I think her coming to see me was her apology. I don't think she was able to bring herself to do anything more."

"You're pretty forgiving considering what she put you through," Philly said. In Waters' place she doubted she would have been as understanding and low key.

"Her story was a cry for help," Waters repeated what he had said to school officials. "Her cry just got out of hand. What I don't understand is why she made up her sexual harassment claim. I think I took her story the way she wanted me to when I reported her. I'm not sure why she felt she had to take it further. Maybe she hadn't thought through what it would be like if I *did* report her and she panicked and made something up when Lacey confronted her with my report. But whatever her motivations, I'm okay with forgiving her. She sought me out to be the one to get her out of her rut. If I can't forgive her, I'll never be the teacher she thought I was."

Jesus, Philly thought. She had forgiven Colin Feeney, the teenager who had run down Philip while driving drunk. Maybe she would have been able to muster forgiveness for Fine in Waters' position. "I appreciate your letting me know what happened. You deserve a lot of credit for the way you handled this situation. Enjoy your hiatus and get recharged. Come September you're going to have to do it all over again."

"I'm looking forward to it," Waters said.

59

Philly's Skype image was clear. Carpenter thought she looked good: thinner, fitter. It was the middle of the summer and her pale white skin didn't show any red or tan. Perhaps she had cut her hair; her cap of black curls didn't seem as impressive as when he last saw her. "You're looking good," he said. "I take it everything is okay with you."

"Yeah," Philly said, and she sat up straighter. "I feel guilty I'm not spending as much time on the law as I would like. But that's largely to do with the lack of business. I don't know. I'm enjoying my time with my daughter. I'm trying to psych myself up for moving into a new house. I'm hanging in there. I can't complain." She paused, looked him in the eye. "And I'm still going to AA meetings in case you were wondering."

"Glad to hear it," Carpenter said. "Maxine and I are looking for a place to move in together. I may have told you that Maxine's retiring; she gave her notice."

"Where are you looking?"

"Arlington."

Philly nodded and Carpenter wondered what she would do if he too retired and joined Maxine. Philly would probably keep practicing. But she might end up drifting apart from Simon and Rachel.

"How are *you* doing?" Philly asked.

Carpenter knew she was referring to his cancer. "Recently, pretty well. There was a spell when I wasn't eating much and waking up drenched in sweat. None of that's happened for a while."

"We're going to have to make a big score in one of our tort cases to make this year worthwhile," Philly said.

Carpenter had been thinking the same thing. "I'm betting on that golfer," he said. "We need to get that case tried this year."

"Same with the wheelchair case," Philly said. "We need a trial this year."

Carpenter thought about Mary Foster. "The Foster woman's old and not doing so well, right?"

Philly nodded.

"Make a motion to expedite the trial and cite those facts in the motion."

"Okay. "

"Throw in a motion for a speedy trial in the golfer case. We've got nothing to lose doing that."

"Okay," Philly repeated. "At least we've got a few things going."

"We need more," Carpenter replied. For the moment, he was enjoying himself. With Philly not putting in a lot of time in the Boston office, he almost forgot how much he liked having her around.

"We're just going to keep grinding, aren't we?" Philly said.

"That's my plan," Carpenter said. "I hope it's yours."

"Count me in," Philly said. "I've got nothing else."

"There's that," Carpenter replied.

60

Carpenter had left the office early for a session with his personal trainer, so Simon appropriated his office chair. This gave Simon a clear view of a photograph of an unsmiling black man with a flinty stare. Why would Carpenter want to make eye contact with such an unforgiving expression? If he pivoted the chair, he was confronted with a photograph of a woman hiking on a path that sloped upward toward trees; she was leaning forward, perhaps to counterbalance the weight of her backpack. Again, Simon was befuddled. It wasn't just that Carpenter didn't seem like a nature-loving type. It was more that the photograph was divorced from the practical realism that seemed to define him.

Simon was in the office because he wanted some time alone without distraction, and his thoughts turned to Frank Stevens. There was roughly a nine-year difference in their ages. With that much of a gap, he would never have sought out Frank. But Frank had approached him, his forwardness premeditated, and Simon couldn't figure out why. Was it because he was the antithesis of the muscular jocks that Frank had spent much of his high school years hanging out with? Simon suspected that their relationship was a summer thing and that once Frank left for college, space and time would put an end to it. Simon wasn't naturally drawn to an athletic physical specimen, but once Frank had initiated sex, Simon found that his attitude was, well, very different. Still, nine years!

"Hey!" Rachel said, stepping into the office.

"Hey yourself," Simon came back. "Is it just me or do you feel like you're trespassing when Carpenter and Philly aren't around?"

"It's just you," Rachel said, grinning broadly. "No, I know what you mean," she quickly backtracked.

"What were you working on?" Simon asked.

"Nothing. I can't seem to concentrate. Otherwise, I wouldn't have wandered in here to bother you."

"What's bugging you?" Simon asked.

Rachel virtually collapsed onto Carpenter's visitor's chair. "This stays between us, right?"

"Sure."

"It's Josh," Rachel said. "I can't stop thinking about him. He's caring, funny, and the sex is great. I feel like I've been reborn."

With one difference, the adjectives Rachel had listed applied to his involvement with Frank. Unlike Rachel, Simon didn't feel reborn. Maybe that had to do with the nine-year age difference that troubled him. But the rest was spot on.

"It's driving me nuts," Rachel said.

"Good," Simon said.

"Good?"

"Yes, good. You're letting loose for the first time since I've known you. That's got to be good."

"My golf game's improving," Rachel said smiling. "Tennis may be next. Josh is giving me a lesson this weekend. He's got all this free time on his hands. I think I told you that he was into online poker, but the Justice Department has shut down the sites."

"You look happy, Rachel. Go with it."

"I am happy. I feel guilty I'm so happy. What's wrong with me?"

"Very little. Josh is a lucky guy."

As Rachel became lost in thought. Simon realized that she might be his closest friend. Last year, when he had turned down a job offer from another firm, one of the reasons that he'd never mentioned to anyone was that he would lose contact with Rachel.

"What's got *you* down?" Rachel asked.

This was a moment of truth of sorts, Simon reflected. If he couldn't confide in Rachel, who could he confide in? She had opened up to him. Why couldn't he reciprocate?

"Forget I asked," Rachel said, sounding peeved.

"I'm sorry," Simon said. "I prefer to keep some things private."

"That's one approach," Rachel came back. "I doubt it's a fulfilling approach, but to each his own."

"Don't be annoyed with me."

"Well I am!" Rachel exclaimed. "We're friends. I'm here for you."

Simon had rarely seen Rachel irritated. She had such a calm demeanor and innocent look that it was hard to imagine her pissed off. But here she was put out with him.

"This stays between us, right?" Simon returned the phrase Rachel had used.

"Of course."

"I don't know what to make of Frank Stevens. We've been seeing each other but there's nine years separating us. There's a part of me that can't shake the idea I'm taking advantage of him. I know that's not correct because he was the one who initiated things. And I know he's not a child."

Rachel was looking at him with the same calm deliberate expression she wore when she assessed legal problems. Her thoughtfulness and evident concern made Simon wonder why he hadn't confided in her before today.

"Do you feel anything for him?" Rachel asked.

"Yes," Simon admitted. "But I was thinking about what you said about Josh. I don't feel reborn by any means."

"We're different," Rachel said. "I've led a very tame social life not to mention sex life. Maybe going from zero to sixty miles an hour in a few seconds is why I'm feeling reborn. If you're happy being with him, why not give it a chance? Weren't you the one who just told me to go with it?"

Simon didn't like his own words coming back to haunt him, but perhaps he had it coming. "What about the age difference?"

"What about it? Age is just a number. Isn't that the smart remark that you hear all the time these days? You haven't been seeing Frank long. If you like being with him let things play out a little while longer. But remember that this sage advice is coming from someone whose dating experience is virtually nil."

Rachel had been right to throw back at him his suggestion that she go with the flow. Simon couldn't figure out why it was so hard to follow his own advice. "Thanks," he said.

"You're welcome. Aren't you glad we talked?"

August

Philly's Spinning Playlist

The Way You Make Me Feel

Michael Jackson

61

Carpenter had finished a third set of twelve reps on a shoulder strengthening machine. Camellia Kim had added five pounds for that final rep and although it had required straining and a fair amount of grunting, Carpenter had gotten through it.

"Nice job," Kim said. "Looking good."

Carpenter silently relished the compliment. He was feeling stronger, fitter. The damn spinning also seemed to be working. When he mounted stairs, he was seldom winded and on walks with Maxine he was able to keep pace.

"You mind if I ask you something?" Carpenter said as he followed Kim to a machine that would work his legs.

"Of course not."

"I've been feeling better since I started taking that mixture your grandmother made up for me. Do you mind if I give it to my doctor so she can have it analyzed? Maybe it can help someone else."

Kim colored as she guided him onto his back and positioned his bent legs so that his feet were flush against the metal resistance plate he'd be pushing against to straighten his knees. He wasn't expecting Kim's reaction. The personal trainer had never been fazed by anything he said to her.

"My grandmother would not like that," Kim said. "She made up the mixture for you and she doesn't like doctors much. I can tell you that she would say no."

Carpenter suspected that he wasn't the first person to request that a western doctor look at one of the grandmother's concoctions. Did he really need the grandmother's permission? "Could you ask your grandmother just the same?" Carpenter requested. "Even if it could help just one other person, it would be a big deal to that person. It's been a big deal for me."

Kim remained flushed. She gave him the signal to start his first rep. Carpenter was certain that she wanted to change the subject. "Will you ask?" he said once he recovered.

"Okay, I will ask. No more interruptions. You have work to do."

Carpenter thought his request had been reasonable, but Kim was putting him off. But perhaps he shouldn't push her. Perhaps he should count his blessings for feeling better and keep his mouth shut. "Do you have time for a spin when we're done?" he asked.

"I'm sorry. Today is not possible. But you should take a class. I think the aerobic exercise is making a difference for you."

"I guess I will," Carpenter said before starting his next rep. Kim was right about one thing—his new exercise regime was making a difference in an area he would not have predicted. Since embarking on weight training and taking a spinning class when he had the chance, he had stopped talking to Fred. In recent days when he looked at the photograph of the woman heading up a forest path, all he saw was a woman heading up a forest path.

"I'm going to add five pounds for your last rep."

Carpenter nodded. He could get used to this physical fitness nonsense. And why not? It wasn't as if he had work to do.

62

Discovery had concluded in Martin Hays' suit against Warren Lord, and Philly wanted Rachel on the line when she returned a call to Millicent Rudd, Lord's attorney. Hays had been deposed and Rudd now knew the testimony that Ryan Cannon and Jake Mobley would present on Hays' behalf. Carpenter, whose instincts never seemed to be wrong in these situations, predicted that Rudd would make a low six-figure offer to settle the case.

Philly dialed her Boston office to bring Rachel into the call. The second-floor office in Brighton was becoming cramped. Earlier this week she had made her first attempt to box up the contents for the movers. Boxes now occupied most of her floor space and a section of the hall corridor outside her office door. The downstairs was also becoming overrun with boxes. Philip's possessions were disappearing. A lot of what he had owned had been disposed of during the move from their shared apartment to this house. Before the next move, some of his furniture that had made it to the living room would be given away. Before too long, she suspected that Philip would only be alive for her when she looked into Daisy's blue eyes.

Philly centered her notepad on her desk and took a deep breath. When she reached Rachel, she placed her on hold, and then added Millicent Rudd to the conference call. "It's your dime," Philly said when they were all connected.

"My client is interested in settling the case," Rudd said straightaway. "Do you have a demand figure?"

"No," Philly said, repeating Carpenter's directive on how to answer that question.

"Would you be able to get back to me with a demand figure?"

"No," Philly repeated. "My client wishes to have the case tried."

"I'm authorized to make a substantial settlement offer," Rudd said. Carpenter had predicted a six-figure offer that started with a one.

"My client is prepared to settle this case for one hundred fifty thousand dollars," Rudd announced.

Philly stayed silent. Rudd had been engaged by Lord's insurance company. Lord may have committed an intentional assault and battery which likely would not be covered by his insurance policy. Had the company decided to continue to provide Lord with a defense anyway? Or was the $150,000 coming out of Lord's pocket? Did that even make a difference?

"Any reaction?" Rudd prompted.

"Rachel and I will pass the offer on to our client. If you don't hear back from us within a week, consider the offer rejected."

"I don't think it's reasonable of you not to present a demand figure," Rudd complained.

"I'm sure you don't," Philly replied. "But our client's instructions have been clear. He wants the case tried."

That intelligence reduced Rudd to silence. Philly suspected that in playing out scenarios as to how this call would progress, Rudd had not considered being stonewalled.

"Okay," Rudd said. "However, I'd appreciate a return call one way or the other on your client's response to my client's offer."

Philly decided to throw Rudd a bone. "I'll get back to you," she said.

When Rudd dropped off the call, Philly asked Rachel for her impressions.

"This is embarrassing," Rachel replied. "For a moment there, all I could think about was the fifty-thousand-dollar fee we could take in. Divisible by three, and all that."

"I had the same thought," Philly confessed. "We do have to report Rudd's offer to Hays. We're going to recommend that he reject it."

"Is there an offer you would recommend he accept?" Rachel asked.

"Carpenter and I were talking about that. Carpenter would recommend accepting a seven hundred fifty-thousand-dollar offer. He thinks a jury could come in with a seven-figure award."

"Seven hundred fifty is divisible by three," Rachel pointed out.

"But the quotient's a lot better," Philly replied.

63

Sitting in his office, Carpenter thought about Delaney's prediction that the Red Sox would make the playoffs. The Barristers' rules required Delaney to make his prediction before September first. This year, Delaney said that he could have made his selection in July. "The Sox are a lock," he had said, which made Carpenter think Delaney had put a jinx on the home team.

There was a knock on his door. Rachel entered and sat in his visitor chair. "Alison Lind called Simon," she said. "She's accepted a position at a school in western Massachusetts. She'll be teaching physical education and coaching soccer."

"Did she say why she's making a move?" Carpenter asked.

"She told Simon it was just something she needed to do."

Carpenter nodded. He agreed with Lind that in her situation, getting out of Dodge was the right move.

"Lind's calling the girls on the team who supported her to tell them that she's leaving."

"Good for her," Carpenter said. "That the classy thing to do."

Philly knew Paul wasn't asleep. He was lying on his back and his breathing was quick and shallow. Paul usually slept on his stomach. When he dropped off, his breathing was slow and deep.

"I thought I tired you out," Philly whispered.

"You did. The thing is I keep thinking about the move. It's got me more than a little nervous."

"I'll give you something to be nervous about. What if we just made a baby?"

"I'd be elated, not nervous. I think my nerves have to do with all the people I'll have to get used to."

"You know them," Philly pointed out. "You like them."

"Maybe that's because I haven't had to live with them 24/7."

"Then I hope we just did make a baby," Philly said. "A baby will take your mind off what makes you nervous."

"Very funny."

"We could talk about names?" Philly suggested.

"Our last names when we get married or kids' first and last names?"

"Your choice," Philly said.

"Our married names."

"You could become a Piper."

"Paul Piper?"

"Okay, that wouldn't work. I could become a Sullivan."

"Do you want to become a Sullivan?"

Philly had more or less assumed that she would keep her last name and their kids would be named Sullivan. She hadn't really given the matter much thought. For the first time she considered the potential awkwardness of Daisy being a Piper and a baby she made with Paul being a Sullivan. Would Paul want to formally adopt Daisy? And then there was Paul's daughter Jenny to think about. These were all fair questions, but she realized that she didn't much care how the questions were answered.

"If you want me to, then I want to become a Sullivan. If you're indifferent, maybe I'll flip a coin."

"I want you to."

"Done. Still nervous?"

Paul moved against her. "Do you really think we just made a baby?"

64

Carpenter had been certain that Warren Lord's attorney would promptly make another six-figure offer to settle Martin Hays' case once Philly had formally rejected the previous offer. Even if Lord's insurer was refusing to represent him because Lord had deliberately struck Hays, surely Lord would throw at least $200,000 at Hays to protect the lion's share of Lord's more than $4,000,000 net worth.

Philly now had Rudd on the line and had set about hooking Rachel up to the call. From her second-floor vantage point, harsh sunlight bore down on her neighbor's rooftop. The sky was a cloudless pale blue. This morning when she and Isabella had gone through their spinning ritual, there had been a chill in the air. Isabella had wondered aloud whether they would keep up the exercise routine when the mornings became cold.

"Okay," Philly said, when Rachel joined the call. "We're all on the line."

"I need to ask whether you've reconsidered about presenting a demand figure," Rudd started off.

"No," Philly replied. Carpenter had told her to hang tough on this issue in part because he really wanted the case tried, and in part because any legitimate demand figure presented would be rejected as too high. True, Martin Hays might have a different idea about settling his case. But until Hays had weighed in with explicit instructions, Carpenter didn't want to present Rudd with a settlement demand.

"That's unfortunate," Rudd said. "I'm authorized to increase Mr. Lord's previous settlement proposal. Mr. Lord has authorized me to propose a settlement of two hundred twenty-five thousand dollars."

Another divisible by three proposal, Philly thought. "I'll pass your client's offer along," she said.

"Will you recommend the offer?" Rudd inquired.

"No," Philly said, again following Carpenter's script.

"May I ask why?" Rudd pursued.

"We've gone over this," Philly said, letting her tone sound mildly annoyed. Perhaps Rudd would be convinced not to make further lowball offers. "Mr. Hays believes that a jury trial is the best chance he has to be fully compensated for the loss of his eye. He wants Mr. Lord to pay for his assault and battery."

"In the absence of a demand figure, I've just made a substantial proposal that would fully compensate Mr. Hays and put this matter behind the parties," Rudd came back, her own irritation evident.

Philly consulted her notes from her last discussion with Carpenter before replying to Rudd. "Sometimes," she said, "parties have such widely differing views on what a case is worth that settlement discussions are meaningless. For example, a plaintiff may think she's entitled to a seven-figure judgment while a defendant may think a modest six-figure settlement is stretching things."

"Are you telling me that Hays won't settle this case for less than a million?" Rudd exclaimed.

"I wasn't saying anything about Mr. Hays," Philly replied quickly. "I was just giving you an example." Carpenter wanted there to be a reference to a seven-figure number in this discussion and Philly had thought she'd been clever to refer to a hypothetical plaintiff as a she.

All right," Rudd said, totally exasperated. "Get back to me on the offer I made."

"Okay," Philly said, and Rudd disconnected.

"How does Carpenter predict where these discussions end up?" Rachel asked.

"He's a legal Yoda with plenty of Jedi mind tricks up his sleeve."

"It's scary," Rachel said. "Would you be handling it this way if Carpenter weren't around?"

Philly gave Rachel's question serious thought. "Probably not," she said. "I'd probably pin Hays down and try to get a sense as to what he would take. But I think I'd have to tell Hays that going to trial might be his best chance for a big recovery. It's complicated."

"Too complicated," Rachel said. "Who's going to try this case?"

"I'm thinking you and me," Philly responded.

"Not Simon or Carpenter?"

"The case came to me and you've done all the work on it. It should be the two of us."

"Who's going to do the opening and closing arguments to the jury?"

"Do you want to?" Philly asked.

"Not really. The idea of standing in front of a jury paralyzes me."

Philly remembered the first time she addressed a jury. She'd been nervous thinking about the event but once she settled in front of the jury with Daisy inside her, she became totally calm.

"I'll do the closing," Philly said. "You might be best for the opening argument."

"Oh God!"

"That's the spirit."

Back at Philly's desk, Rachel tried to banish all thoughts of standing in front of a jury. The idea made her heart race and her vision blurry. Was there a recorded case of a lawyer passing out during her first opening argument before a jury? Rachel could be a trailblazer. How could one brief phone conversation with Philly sap the mellowness she had absorbed from Josh? Or thought she had.

Rachel didn't doubt that she could question a witness in front of a jury. But delivering an argument while looking twelve people in the eye was another thing altogether. Maybe she needed to tell Philly no. Philly wouldn't like that response and neither would Carpenter. But at the moment, she preferred their disappointment and disapproval to being a nervous wreck for months to come.

65

A Visiting Lecturer

Carpenter wouldn't have predicted ending a work week with Connie coming to his office, but this Friday she appeared as scheduled. She had called first thing in the morning to make an appointment, saying that his legal services might be required. Carpenter could have begged off for any number of reasons. They had been in a relationship that might affect any legal representation he provided, being paid money by an ex had to be a bad idea on general principles, and each of them had moved on to a new and improved relationship that neither wanted to screw up. At least he didn't want to mess things up with Maxine. And as far as he could tell, Connie was devoted to Bernard. Maybe if he had been up to his ears in work, he would have said no. But it was too late now. He had said he'd meet with her. Curiosity and stupidity had carried the day.

Connie seemed oblivious to the awkwardness of the moment as she smiled at him across the conference room table. It struck Carpenter that in the years they'd been seeing each other, Connie had never come to his office. And, with the exception of a forgettable holiday party, he had never visited Connie's place of business. While they were a couple, they had tacitly but plainly decided not to mix their personal and professional lives.

Connie's white dress emphasized how black her skin was. He was struck again by how much thinner she was than when they had been a couple and how the loss of a few pounds suited her. "You're looking good," Carpenter said, opting to break the silence.

"You're not looking so bad yourself," Connie said.

Carpenter realized that he might never tell Connie he had leukemia. Only Maxine and the three lawyers he practiced with knew of his condition. Christ! Even his Barrister buddies were in the dark about his diagnosis.

"What's this about you needing a lawyer?" Carpenter asked.

"I didn't say *I* needed a lawyer," Connie clarified. "I said your legal services might be required."

Carpenter was relieved; perhaps he wouldn't need to represent Connie after all.

"Bernard may need a lawyer."

Great, Carpenter thought. He'd be representing the guy who replaced him with Connie. If he screwed up, he'd have two people he knew pissed off at him.

"I'm hoping it's all a misunderstanding."

"Why don't you tell me what happened?" Carpenter said, trying to move into lawyer mode and to ignore the distraction that was Connie.

"I told you that Bernard is lecturing at Brandeis," Connie said. "His lectures have been very well received. Bernard agreed to teach a seminar over the summer. There are fifteen students in the class. Bernard has held some of the teaching sessions at our apartment. A female student is claiming that Bernard made a pass at her at one of those sessions."

Carpenter tried not to show emotion. The nature of Bernard's problem might just as well have been a flashing sign blinking *STAY AWAY.* "Why don't we put Bernard in touch with Philly?" he suggested.

"I know Philly, but I don't really know her," Connie said. "I know you. I want you to hear me out."

Carpenter nodded, curiosity continuing to trump common sense.

"The female student claims that she was a late arrival and was in our bedroom where students had put their coats. She was leaving the bedroom when she claims that Bernard entered and pressed against her, trying to kiss her. The student claims that she jerked free and left the apartment. A few of the students in the living room heard her say, 'Get away from me.' When Bernard went back to the living room to start the seminar, one of the students asked what had just happened. Bernard said there seems to have been a misunderstanding."

Carpenter digested this thumbnail account. Philly had already run into two he-said she-said situations this year. In each case the she-said had turned out to be false. "What does Bernard say happened?"

"He said that he did approach the bedroom to check on the room. He had previously told the students that they could deposit their things on the bed.

He said he bumped into the student as she was leaving and that it was awkward because she did press against him. He denies trying to kiss the student. He agrees that she did say, 'Get away from me.' He pretty much confirmed what he said to the other students, that it seemed there had been a misunderstanding."

Carpenter studied Connie. It had to be difficult for her to approach him on this loaded subject. "Was the student white or black or other?" he asked.

"Why is that important?"

Carpenter didn't respond. The student's skin color might not be important but might end up being a crucial aspect of the case.

"Black," Connie supplied. "I still don't see why that's important."

"What's the college doing?"

"They're conducting an investigation. Bernard is scheduled to be interviewed after Labor Day. I don't want him to be interviewed without a lawyer."

"What does Bernard have to say about that?"

"He says he doesn't need a lawyer. He says he has nothing to hide."

Carpenter let Bernard's foolishness slide. "Is Bernard continuing with his seminar?"

"Yes, but sessions in our apartment are out."

"I want Philly to be out front on this," Carpenter said. "I'll help her, but I don't want to be the point person for obvious reasons."

"The reasons aren't obvious to me," Connie declared.

"There's our past relationship," Carpenter said, holding up one finger. "There's our past relationship," he continued, holding up another finger. "And, last but not least, there's our past relationship," he said with three fingers now aloft. "That's three strikes. I'm out."

"Very funny. I don't want Philly, I want you. This is very important to me."

Carpenter silently fretted. If he gave in to Connie, it wouldn't be the first time he did the wrong thing for the wrong reason.

"Bernard can pay your fees if that's what you're worried about. I've made Bernard a very rich man."

Carpenter waved Connie's statement away with a sweep of his hand. "That's not what I'm concerned about and you know it."

"Please," Connie said, and it was the way she said it that Carpenter knew he would relent.

"Does Bernard have any theory as to why the student is saying what she's saying?"

"No. The student who's making the allegation had been going with a white student for a number of months. The white student broke things off about a month before the first seminar at our apartment."

"How do you know that?"

"A student in the seminar told Bernard that. Bernard doesn't think it's relevant but I'm not so sure."

"Why do you think it might be relevant?"

"I don't know. I need some sharp lawyer to tell me."

"Then you've come to the right place."

It was Friday evening and Josh's roommates had gotten a start on the weekend by clearing out early, so they had the apartment to themselves. Rachel tried to summon up an upbeat mood and failed. She sat at the small kitchen table sipping wine while Josh saw to fixing dinner. With no wasted motion, he was throwing together a vegetarian meal consisting of salad and varieties of beans she had never heard of. He was wearing khaki cargo shorts and a tie-dyed T-shirt featuring an enormous purple eye on the back. His arms and legs were bronzed. There were times when Rachel thought that Josh was born too late; he would have loved being a 1960's hippie. Watching him move while he performed any task typically mesmerized her but not this evening.

"Okay, what's bugging you?" Josh said without turning around as he chopped up a purple onion.

"Nothing."

"I don't believe you."

It wasn't as if they hadn't confided in each other. Each knew about the other's family and they were getting a handle on each other's likes and dislikes. But to date, neither had shared a serious worry with the other. Rachel was probably unfairly judging Josh as not very deep what with his tennis and golf and yoga and martial arts and vegetarian passions. Most of her time when she was with him all she could think about was sex which left little time for assessing any of his other qualities. When she was with him, it was as if she turned off her brain and decided to enjoy the moment and not think too far ahead.

"Maybe I can help," Josh said as he shelled peas.

"We have this jury trial coming up and Philly wants me to do the opening argument," Rachel blurted out. "It's that golfer case." If Josh had been facing her, she didn't think she could have gotten the words out."

"So?"

"So it terrifies me. I don't think I can stand in front of a jury and make an opening argument."

Josh began to open a can of lentils. He still hadn't turned around. The tendons of his forearms flexed as he worked the can opener.

"You've done hearings, right?"

"Right. But arguing before a jury is different."

"I'm sure it is," Josh said as he spooned lentils onto their plates. "Maybe you could do that exercise where you imagine all the jurors naked. Isn't that what they tell people who are afraid of public speaking?"

"You're not helping," Rachel replied, but without conviction, smiling in spite of herself at the thought of a motley group of twelve naked people.

Josh brought their plates to the kitchen table and sat across from her. "Simon told me you're the smartest person he knows."

"Standing in front of a jury isn't about smarts."

"Then what's it about?"

"It's about being an actor. It's about putting on a performance."

"That doesn't sound right," Josh said.

"Well, it is right," Rachel dug in her heels.

Josh offered her salad dressing but took none for himself. He was eating methodically and watching her intently and after a time she couldn't meet his gaze.

"I know why Philly wants you to do the opening argument," Josh said.

"Why is that?"

"It's because you're down to earth. You believe in your golfer's case. If you didn't, we'd have never met. If you tell your golfer's story as if you mean it, I think a jury would eat it up."

"Simon should do the opening," Rachel said. "He'd put on a show."

"Maybe Philly doesn't want a show," Josh countered. "I don't think Philly would ask you to do something if she didn't think you could do it. True, I don't know the woman."

"I don't want to live in fear during the rest of the year thinking about this," Rachel said. "I'm going to tell Philly I don't want to do the argument."

Josh ate for a time in silence, then sipped at a beer. Beer seemed to be the only non-health food indulgence he permitted himself.

"Before you tell Philly no, why don't you write out your argument and let me hear it."

"That's not going to change anything."

"You may be right. But humor me. I'm going to videotape it."

"Why?"

"Humor me," Josh repeated.

"I don't see the point."

Josh leveled his fork in her direction and there was nothing mellow about the hard look in his eyes.

"So far, I haven't asked you to do anything for me," Josh said. "I'm asking you to do this for me. For *me*."

Rachel swallowed the mixture of nervousness and stubbornness that had settled in her gut. "Well, when you put it that way . . ."

66

Rosalind was asleep in an infant seat and Daisy was lurching about the hardtop holding a bright red toy shovel and pointing it this way and that while Philly and Isabella pedaled furiously on their spinning bikes.

Philly had put a Prince CD in her boom box and *Alphabet Street* at medium volume charged the cool Saturday morning air. A difficult song to spin to, but Philly loved its high energy. Philly cast a glance at Isabella. "Are you packed?" she asked, raising her voice to be heard over the music.

Isabella nodded. "But Raul is not. His procrastination is driving me crazy."

"You nervous?"

Isabella shrugged. "A little. I want the move to be over."

Philly agreed. Counting down the days had become a drag.

"How's Paul doing with the move?" Isabella asked.

"He's nervous," Philly admitted. "He's never had a living arrangement like the one we're about to have."

"We're really counting on Sarah," Isabella said. "I wonder if it's going to be too much for her. After Labor Day, I'll be returning to work half time."

Philly had been entertaining the same worry. "We've got to make it clear to her that she shouldn't overdo it."

"What are your plans today?" Isabella asked.

"I'm driving up to North Andover," Philly replied. "I'm taking Daisy to see Philip's parents."

"Nice," Isabella said. Philly hoped that pronouncement proved correct.

"This is a pleasant surprise," Pamela said when they were settled for lunch at the dining room table in the cool, air-conditioned house of Philip's parents. Philip's sister seemed delighted to see them and had positioned Daisy at the head of the table, perched in a highchair. Pamela's daughter, Geneva or Genie, was to Daisy's right, Philly to her daughter's left. Philip's parents couldn't take their eyes off their granddaughter, made silly faces at her, and Philly reflected anew on the bittersweet nature of each reunion they had with Daisy. It seemed to Philly that Daisy's grandparents had stopped aging. She had noted the lack of change at the barbecue last month. Philip's mother, tall and stout, had been a matron for some time now. Philip's father, short and balding, looked like an absentminded professor. It was still a mystery how they had produced their lanky blond son.

"Is this a special occasion?" Pamela asked, after the grownups and Genie had made inroads on their sandwiches. "Is there any reason you wanted to see us?"

Philly had forgotten how direct Pamela was. "There's a lot going on that I wanted to fill you in on," Philly eased into the topics she had resolved to cover. "For one thing, you know we're moving very soon."

"I don't know how you put up with communal living," Pamela said. "It's got to be a zoo. Especially with another little baby in the mix."

"What little baby?" Genie piped up.

Philly kept silent. Let Pamela deal with her daughter's question. Genie was definitely Pamela's daughter. They were dressed identically in dark jeans and white tennis shirts. They shared Philip's fair coloring.

"Philly and Daisy are moving to a new house," Pamela explained, "and there will be another family living with them. That family has a little baby girl."

"I want a little baby," Genie declared.

"Don't hold your breath!" Pamela exclaimed.

Philip's parents lowered their heads and Philly decided to shift the focus where it needed to be. "I need to tell you a couple of other things," she said, and that got the Sizemore clan to sit up and take notice. Even Genie favored her with a solemn look. "You remember Paul Sullivan, don't you?"

"The police officer you brought to Thanksgiving," Philip's mother said.

"The dreamboat," Pamela added.

Philly nodded. "Paul's asked me to marry him and I said yes."

"Wow!" Pamela said. "Congratulations."

Philip's parents were silent.

"I wanted to tell you face-to-face," Philly continued. "This isn't going to change anything with you and Daisy," she directed at Philip's parents who had colored. "You will always be Daisy's grandparents and you need to be in her life. I want you in her life."

There were tears in Philip's mother's eyes. Philip's father was blushing pink.

"Paul and I are also planning to have more kids," Philly addressed the last item on her checklist while she had gotten up a head of steam. "If we're lucky, Daisy's going to have a brother or sister. I'm hoping you play a role in the next baby's life as well. I'd like you to be grandparents and aunt for all our family."

Philip's mother was now openly crying, and Pamela got up and put an arm around her. Genie had retained her solemn expression; Philly wondered how much the girl understood. Genie now had to be somewhere near four and half.

"Come on," Pamela said softly to her mother. "We all know Philip would have wanted Philly to move on. This is all happy news."

Philip's mother dabbed at her eyes with a napkin and offered a faint nod. "It brings everything back," she whispered. "It's times like these I can't believe he's gone."

Nobody said anything. Daisy moved cheerios around on her highchair tray, occasionally popping one in her mouth. She had shaken her head when a half sandwich had been placed before her. Philly eyed the half-eaten sandwiches on the plates about the table and wondered if she should have waited before delivering her news.

"I'm very happy for you, dear," Philip's mother said to Philly, at last. "Don't mind me."

"Of course I'm going to mind you," Philly said.

"Why is grandma crying?" Genie asked.

Philly turned to Pamela. This was another question she was not about to answer.

"It's a long story," Pamela said to her daughter. "You know my brother Philip died. I've spoken to you about that before. We were talking about Philip and it's sad to think about him dying."

"I don't want anyone else to die," Genie said with feeling.

Philly wondered whether, if pushed by a four and half year-old Daisy, she would have the nerve to say what she was thinking—that everyone died. She remained silent, again waiting for Pamela to take charge, wondering whether Pamela would be brutally honest with her daughter on the subject of death.

"Okay," Pamela said to Genie. "I think that's something we're all agreed on."

67

A Father and Mother

Robert Finn hadn't referred a case to Carpenter in a long while. When Carpenter thanked him for recommending Keith and Jane Spring, Finn had surprised him. "You won't be thanking me," Finn had said with feeling. "This is one sorry, miserable mess." Coming from Finn, a reserved and prim lawyer with a general practice, this blunt assessment gave Carpenter pause. When Finn provided a brief outline of what had happened, he quickly concluded that sorry, miserable mess didn't do justice to what had befallen the Springs.

The couple was now seated across from Carpenter and Simon in the conference room. They looked to be in their mid-forties. There was a deadness in their eyes which Carpenter attributed to the shock of their younger son having been killed. He wondered when, if ever, signs of life would surface in the couple's gaze. Probably never, for after all, the gun shot that had killed their youngest son had been fired by his older brother.

Keith Spring was a large man with thick black hair, a craggy face, and broad shoulders. Next to him, Jane Spring seemed a slip of a thing, small, almost painfully thin, her thinning hair an indeterminate color. Carpenter saw no way around proceeding directly.

"Mr. Finn filled me in generally about what happened," Carpenter began. "We're sorry for your loss. We understand that you wish to explore your legal rights against the therapist who was treating your eldest son. Is that correct?"

Jane Spring stared at him blankly. Keith Spring made an effort to focus. "I'd rather strangle the bastard," he said, "but I suppose suing the asshole is the best we can do."

"What are your boys' names?" Simon asked. Carpenter noted the present tense.

"Darren was the one who was shot," Keith Spring replied. "Ryan pulled the trigger."

"How old are they?" Simon continued.

"Ryan's twenty-two. Darren was sixteen."

Jane Spring closed her eyes as if she were blotting out the explosive incident that had irrevocably shattered her world.

"This happened at your house?" Carpenter prompted.

Keith Spring nodded. "I need to give you some background first." He glanced at his wife, took in her closed eyes, and shook his head in a gesture that Carpenter found both angry and resigned.

"Ryan was diagnosed with a personality disorder when he was nine. He had been having problems at school and at home before the diagnosis. Things got worse as he got older. Private schools didn't help. Tutors didn't help. He didn't graduate from high school. The longest he's held a part-time job was about two months. There was a period a couple of years back when we lost track of him. It turned out he was living on the streets of Boston and had gotten himself into drugs. He was involuntarily committed on two occasions. For the last year or so he'd been living at home and seeing a psychologist twice a week."

Carpenter studied his notes from his discussion with Robert Finn. "That would be Dr. Roland Butler?"

"Right." Keith Spring again glanced at his wife. Jane Spring's eyes remained closed. Her expression was distant, but Carpenter believed that she had been paying attention to the discussion for some time.

"We actually began to hope. Butler seemed to be reaching Ryan. Don't ask me how. But after a session with Butler, it was sometimes possible to have a calm discussion with Ryan."

"How would you describe your relationship with Ryan?" Simon asked.

Jane Spring's eyes shot open and she stared at her husband.

"Ryan and I don't get along," Keith Spring said. "I don't have much patience in dealing with him. We find it hard to be civil to each other. Jane does better with Ryan."

Jane Spring again closed her eyes.

"How was your relationship with Darren?" Simon continued.

"I'd say a lot better," Keith Spring responded. "Darren was a good student, liked sports. He had a good sense of humor. He was just a regular kid."

"Did your sons get along?" Carpenter asked.

"For the most part," Keith Spring said. "Darren was patient with Ryan; he'd carve out time to spend with him. They'd play outside together when they were younger. I think it was tough on Darren having a brother who was so troubled."

Simon looked toward Carpenter, who gave the young lawyer a nod to proceed.

"Has anyone explained to you what suing a mental health professional involves in a case like this?" Simon asked.

"Mr. Finn talked with us about that," Keith Spring responded. "He said it would be challenging to make a case."

"There's a statute that spells out what someone has to prove," Simon explained. "You'd be claiming that Dr. Butler negligently failed to warn you about Ryan being a danger to commit a violent act. What the statute says is that a therapist doesn't have a duty to warn unless . . ." Simon paused and looked at his notes. "The patient has a history of physical violence that is known to the mental health professional and the professional has a reasonable basis to believe that there is a clear and present danger that the patient would attempt to kill or inflict serious bodily injury against a reasonably identified victim. If those conditions are met, the professional has to use reasonable precautions to protect the potential victim."

"Well that should be easy to show," Keith Spring let loose. "For Christ's sake! Ryan showed Dr. Butler a gun and said he felt like killing me. What else do you need?"

Carpenter ignored the question. "I understand that you confronted Dr. Butler," he said. "Go over the details of what you said to each other."

"I called the asshole after the shooting. Ryan had come home from seeing him. Butler said that during the session Ryan had been angry with me, said I was too controlling, and he couldn't take it anymore."

Jane Spring opened her eyes and stared at her husband.

"He told Butler he felt like killing me and he pulled a gun out of his backpack and began waving it around."

Courtesy of Robert Finn, Carpenter knew the answer to his next question but asked it anyway. "What did Butler say happened to the gun?"

Keith Spring seemed to withdraw into himself for a long moment. "Butler said that he asked Ryan for the gun and that Ryan gave it to him. Butler said that Ryan then told him that he didn't mean what he had said about wanting to kill me."

"Had Ryan ever been violent with you or anyone else?" Simon asked.

Spring took his time with the question. "No," he finally said.

"What was Dr. Butler's reaction when you told him about the shooting?" Simon pursued.

"He didn't say anything for a while. Then he said the shooting was shocking, something he never would have imagined. He said he was sorry and extended his sympathy to us." Here Spring nodded toward his wife who continued to stare at her husband. "Then we got into what happened at the therapy session."

"Have you been a controlling father when it comes to Ryan?" Simon next asked.

Carpenter was reminded again why he valued Simon. The young lawyer didn't give a damn whose feelings got hurt when a question needed to be asked and answered.

Spring glanced at his wife who showed interest in what her husband would say.

"I've been trying to get him to fly right," Spring said. "If that makes me controlling, so be it."

Carpenter decided that he'd heard enough. "Before you came in, Mr. Jeffries and I made an assessment about your case. What we've heard at this meeting doesn't change our view. We think that your case is iffy and that there is a likelihood your case might be dismissed and never go to trial."

Carpenter met Spring's sullen glare and continued. "Ryan had never been violent before, had no history of violence which is what the statute specifies must be present. Also, he handed over his gun to Butler, and he took back what he said about feeling like he wanted to kill you. There was no reasonable basis for Butler to believe that Ryan had another weapon in his backpack. The bottom line is that we think it could prove difficult for you to satisfy the statutory requirements that Mr. Jeffries just laid out for you."

Spring smoldered in silence. "I don't give a shit," he finally erupted. "I want to sue that bastard. I don't care about the money. We've got plenty of that. The son we had hopes for is gone because of Butler and I want the bastard to pay. He should have let me know Ryan brought a gun to the session. I might have grabbed his backpack when he came home and searched it. I might not have let him into the house. Instead, we got into an argument—I can't even remember what got us going—and Ryan pulled out a gun and started waving it around. I tried to take the gun from him and that's when it went off. The shot went through the ceiling and killed Darren instantly. It was a thousand to one chance that would happen, but I should have been given a heads up. Fuck Butler. I want him to pay."

Carpenter wondered whether if he took the case, he had just heard part of the closing argument he would make to a jury. That is, if the case ever made it to a jury.

"I don't want to sue," Jane Spring said. "It won't bring Darren back. We're just going to wallow in the misery if we sue."

"Great!" Spring exclaimed. "Another fucking country heard from. It figures. Well I want to sue and I'm going to whether you go along or not. And if you two won't take my case I'll find a lawyer who will."

Carpenter strove for a neutral expression. "Mr. Jeffries and I will confer. We'll get back to you right after the long holiday weekend."

"Can I stop my husband from suing?" Jane Spring said.

"We'll get back to you on that as well," Carpenter replied.

September

Philly's Spinning Playlist

Bulletproof

La Roux

68

Philly was still in a Prince mood and had *7* sounding from her boom box, the volume up higher than necessary, a sure way to piss off new neighbors, but she didn't care. They were largely moved in. Frick and Frack Movers had employed several moving vans, had carted the large pieces of furniture where they needed to go, and had settled the boxes in the rooms the contents would be placed. Unpacking would probably take a month, maybe two, and Philly was resigned to living in clutter for a while. So what? They had moved in.

On the spinning bike next to hers, Isabella sported a loopy grin. Philly smiled in response. Last night at two in the morning she had awakened unexpectedly, felt a need to roam about the first floor, and had come upon Isabella pacing in the living room. Isabella had given her a long, hard hug and then told her to wait while she went off to the kitchen. Philly heard a hollow pop that sounded like a champagne bottle opening and then Isabella had returned with two fluted plastic glasses, one with champagne and the second with sparkling cider. "I've been saving this for when we had a minute alone," Isabella whispered. Then she said, "To us," before they touched glasses and drank. When she had returned to her bedroom, Philly had briefly toyed with the idea of waking Paul and inaugurating their new queen-sized bed. But Paul was so dead to the world that she'd decided to show mercy.

Rosalind stirred in her infant seat and opened her eyes. Isabella waved at her daughter and was favored with a lengthy yawn in return. Daisy was exploring the backyard which was larger than the backyard at their old house. She was dressed in a sweatshirt and jeans with an elastic waist band. Daisy still had the heavy legged walk of a toddler, more of a tromp than a walk. She was babbling to herself, the high-pitched sounds reminding Philly of a bird chirping with joy. Philly wanted to preserve this moment. If this was as good as it got, that was fine with her.

"I'm happy," Isabella said. "Already I like this house better than the old one."

"That makes two of us," Philly said.

The screen door to the back porch opened and Sarah Ferguson emerged in a white terry cloth bathrobe. "You two are nuts," she pronounced.

"You've got that right," Philly replied.

"I'm taking breakfast orders," Sarah said.

Philly followed Isabella's lead. She increased her bike's resistance and stood up on the pedals, running in place. "Surprise us," she said.

With two desks, Philly's second floor new home office was cramped. Paul needed a workspace, so they had agreed to share. Philly felt vaguely guilty about not letting Paul know his desk had been Philip's. Her view out the new office's window was of an oak tree, fully leafed out, and through the open window she heard Daisy's shrieks from the backyard where she was playing with Paul.

Raul had gotten her computer equipment set up and her Inbox contained a message to call Carpenter. Philly considered dealing with the call tomorrow. She wanted this day to be consumed by domestic chores, even those that involved drudgery. But although Carpenter had provided no hint of an emergency, she figured that a calamity couldn't be ruled out since Carpenter knew that she had moving in tasks on this day. What the hell, she thought, as she dialed Carpenter's cell phone number.

"Carpenter."

"I got your message to call," Philly said.

"I thought you'd be tied up today."

"That didn't stop you from leaving me a message to call you."

"I figured you wouldn't pick it up today."

"I was making sure Raul had hooked up my computer okay and saw your message."

"How the hell is Raul?"

"We're all good. What did you want to talk about?"

"It can wait."

"I know you, remember? What's up?"

Carpenter filled her in on the story of Mr. and Mrs. Spring and their sons, and then started rehashing the case involving Connie's husband. Philly saw this call for what it was. Carpenter needed a sounding board. It helped him sort out his thinking when someone was listening. His questions were specific. He wanted to know whether he should stay away from a case involving a suit against a therapist that had all the earmarks of a loser, and whether he should reverse direction and turn down the case he had agreed to take involving Connie's husband.

"You'd be telling me to stay away from a case like Bernard's if I was in your position," Philly pointed out.

"I know that. I tried to steer the case your way, but Connie wanted me. What can I say?"

"You could say no."

"You're right, I could have. But I didn't. Now I need to hear you tell me it was okay to say yes."

"In that case, as long as Simon stays with you on the case, I think it was okay to say yes."

"Thanks for telling me what I wanted to hear."

"Seriously, I think with Simon involved it *is* okay. Simon will tell you if he thinks you're doing something you shouldn't be doing."

"Granted, Simon is refreshingly blunt. What about the suit against the therapist?"

"From the way you described it, I'd agree the case sounds like a loser. The older son had no history of violence."

"Here's the pathetic part," Carpenter said. "If we were busy, I would have told the father to take a hike."

"You haven't accepted the case. You can still tell the father to take a hike."

"If we take this case on it will probably be on a contingency fee basis with a modest nonrefundable retainer. I can't believe I'm thinking about the retainer money. Maybe it's influencing me. Maybe I took Bernard's case because of the billable hours."

Did Carpenter feel like he was selling out, somehow? Well, maybe he was. But so what? Philly thought. The father was right; if Carpenter didn't take the man's case, some other lawyer would. Some other lawyer might tell the father that the case was a slam dunk. Philly did know that Carpenter had a conscience, although it often surprised her when it popped to the surface. "Tell him you'll take the case but put it in writing that you think it may be difficult to win."

"I'd already thought about giving the guy a written assessment. I just hate taking on a case that I think is going to lose. I fucking hate it."

"I'm okay with you turning it down," Philly said.

"Screw it," Carpenter exclaimed. "I'll sign on and spell out in the engagement letter that we've advised him the case is a long shot. I'll figure out a nice way to say it, something like your case sucks but I'm a money-grubbing lawyer who will take it anyway."

"That should get things off to a good start," Philly said, laughing. "By the way, we have a November trial date for the golf case, and a December trial date for the wheelchair case."

"That's good to hear. You want me to help with either of those? I'm sort of feeling left out here."

"We'll be running things by you. Rachel and I will do the golf case, and Simon and I will do the wheelchair case. Each of them has worked with the witnesses. I think we'll be all right. By the way, I want Rachel to do the opening argument in the golf case."

"Did she agree?"

"She's not happy about it. But she hasn't told me no."

"Give her time," Carpenter said. "She probably needs to work up to saying no."

69

Bernard Mucowahandi had a charming manner, a lilting way of speaking, and made eye contact when addressing you. These were all pluses, but Simon knew that he was not in a proper state of mind to make any reasoned judgment on whether he liked the Rwandan. Frank Stevens had left for college. Simon could honestly say that he had felt nothing as Frank's departure day loomed but, now that the day had come and gone, he felt unsettled. He hadn't expected to miss Frank, but that was what had happened. There was an unmistakable void in his life and, for reasons he couldn't explain, Simon couldn't bring himself to fill the void with e-mail messages or telephone calls. He had yet to contact Frank.

"We thought it was important to meet with you without Connie present," Carpenter said. "You know about my relationship with Connie and if my representing you makes you uncomfortable in any way, now is the time to speak up."

Simon made a conscious effort to put Frank out of his mind. In his view, Bernard Mucowahandi didn't look uncomfortable. Rather, he seemed irritated as if this meeting was a necessary ordeal he needed to get past so he could turn his attention to something worthwhile.

"Please, call me Bernard. There is no need for formality." Bernard paused, placed his hands on the conference room table, and flashed a brief conspiratorial smile. "If I may be frank with you, I am glad that Connie is not at this meeting. She is insisting that I need a lawyer, but I do not understand why. The college is investigating the student's charges. I will tell my story and the student will tell hers. Then the college will decide. I believe I will be completely exonerated."

Carpenter appeared poised to deliver his you-can't-trust-anyone speech but seemed to think better of it. In this case, though, Simon believed that Carpenter's trust-no-one message needed to be delivered. Their prospective client sounded dangerously naïve.

"Connie is simply looking out for you," Carpenter said. "In this country, the kind of charges directed at you have to be taken seriously. There will be lawyers advising college officials, the student who has complained about you may retain a lawyer, and, in my opinion, you should have counsel as well. What we first need to get out of the way is whether, given my past relationship with Connie, I should be representing you."

"Is your past relationship with Connie a problem for you in representing me?"

"At the moment no," Carpenter responded. "But it's hard to predict what twists and turns may happen in your case. It would be perfectly reasonable for you to make sure that my previous relationship with Connie never becomes a problem by having someone else represent you from the beginning. You won't be hurting my feelings if that's the route you decide to take. Just so you know, when I suggested that your case be handled by another lawyer Simon and I work with, Connie said no, that she wanted me personally involved. However, this is not Connie's decision to make. It's yours."

"Connie trusts you," Bernard said. "Therefore, I trust you. Let us consider your previous relationship with Connie a closed matter. For the moment," he added with a weak smile, borrowing Carpenter's previous qualifier.

"Tell us about the woman who has complained against you?" Carpenter requested.

"That would be Crystal Queen," Bernard said, his irritation plainly visible.

Simon wrote down the name thinking it sounded like the stage name of a porn star.

"What do you know about her?" Carpenter followed up.

"Not very much. She is one of fifteen students in my seminar. The subject of the seminar is to explore whether there are any parallels between Rwanda's attempt at reconciliation after the massacre of Tutsis and moderate Hutus, and this country's period of reconstruction after the Civil War. It has been an enjoyable class. The students are engaged and discussions are lively. But Miss Queen is not as vocal as other students. She rarely argues a point during discussions."

"Why do you think she's making the accusations against you?" Simon asked.

"I have no explanation."

"Why don't you tell us about what happened the night in question?" Carpenter asked.

"I was holding a seminar session at our apartment. I believe it was the third seminar session held there. Connie was working late at the office. That was the arrangement we adopted. She did not want to be around while students were in the apartment. I had been in the kitchen making sure that the coffee maker was on and Styrofoam cups were set out. And there were cookies and doughnuts to be arranged. Everything was in order and when I walked to the bedroom to make sure the students had deposited their coats and jackets and belongings on the bed, I bumped into Miss Queen."

Here Bernard paused as if trying to picture the encounter anew. He nodded his head slightly and closed his eyes for a moment.

Simon interrupted. "Do you mean you physically bumped into her?"

"Yes. Exactly. Crystal Queen is strikingly attractive," Bernard resumed. "You would find this out eventually so there is no need for me to avoid the fact. We literally collided in the doorway to the bedroom. It was a very awkward moment. Our upper bodies were pressed against each other and I nearly lost my balance. I reached for her shoulders to steady myself, but she pushed me away and I staggered backward out of the doorway into the hall. She said, 'Get away from me,' and her voice was raised. I attempted to apologize but she hurried by me and left the apartment."

"Did you touch her breasts or any other area of her body?" Simon asked.

Bernard shook his head. "When we collided, I felt her breasts against my chest. But I did not touch her there or anyplace else." Bernard paused. "Except for her shoulders as I just mentioned."

"Is that it?" Simon questioned.

"Yes," Bernard said. "That was pretty much it. It all happened very quickly."

"I have a question for you," Carpenter said. "What did you do with the article of clothing Ms. Queen left on the bed?"

Simon shared Bernard's confusion. "I do not understand," Bernard said.

"Ms. Queen was leaving the bedroom where students had deposited their coats and jackets and other belongings. You said that after the two of you collided, she brushed past you and left the apartment. You didn't say she went back to the bed and retrieved an article of clothing."

Bernard frowned in concentration. "No, she did not go back for any clothing or anything else such as a purse. And there was no extra article of clothing or anything else on the bed after all the students left. I am sure of that. Where are you going with this?"

"If Ms. Queen hadn't gone into your bedroom to drop an item of clothing on your bed, then what the hell was she doing there?"

"I don't know," Bernard said, puzzled.

"Here's your first assignment," Carpenter said to Simon. "You need to find out what Ms. Queen was doing in the bedroom."

For the moment, Simon had no idea how to do that. "Do you have a list of the students in your seminar?" he asked Bernard.

Bernard extracted a piece of paper from a tan, leather messenger bag. "Here is a copy of the class list with names, telephone numbers, addresses, and e-mail addresses."

"This is useful," Simon said. "Do the other fourteen students know about the allegations Ms. Queen has made against you?"

"I do not know. Perhaps, perhaps not."

"After Ms. Queen left your apartment, did the seminar proceed normally?" Carpenter queried.

"I would say so. When I joined the other students in the living room, some were laughing and looking at me in an amused way. But once the seminar started, I thought it went well."

"You now have your second assignment," Carpenter directed at Simon. "Something was funny to some of the students. We need to get the joke."

70

An Alleged Killer

Philly knew that it was a bad idea to have her first meeting with a client at the new Brighton house. There were half emptied boxes everywhere and the upstairs office would never be suitable for meeting with clients. Sarah had taken the kids to the playroom next to her third floor living quarters, but Daisy's high-pitched laugher reached the ground floor. Fay Richardson's call had suggested an urgency that wouldn't allow for trying to get downtown to meet in a more professional setting, so Philly had done her best to clear the decks, invited Richardson to Brighton, and summoned Rachel and Simon to join them.

"Excuse the clutter," Philly apologized to Richardson. "You said this was an emergency, so we'll have to make do. I was simply unable to get to my Boston office this afternoon."

"No problem," Richardson said, as she looked about the living room distractedly. She was seated in a chair facing Rachel and Simon on the couch, and Philly had her younger colleagues move over so that she could join them. Richardson had been referred by a woman Philly had helped several years back.

"How do you know Muriel Parker?" Philly asked.

"I work for a small publishing company and Muriel's ad agency does some work for us. We've become friends. She was at my office, saw I was upset, and when I told her what was wrong, she gave me your name. She said you had helped her during a difficult time in her life."

Philly made a mental note to thank Muriel Parker and find out how her agency was doing. Richardson appeared to be in her early thirties. She was wearing a short-sleeved white silk blouse and black slacks and fiddled nervously with a pendant that hung from a thin gold chain about her neck. Philly couldn't think of a thing to say to lighten the mood of this meeting. There was a pinched, tense look to Richardson's dark features which was to be expected given what the woman was going through.

"When we talked on the phone you gave me a general description of what's been happening," Philly said. "I'd like you to go through it again for Rachel and Simon."

Richardson sighed, squared her shoulders and met the young lawyers' inquiring looks. "I had been dating a man named Al Townsend for about a year. We had moved in together about six months ago, but things started to sour in the relationship and I moved out. Less than a month after I left, I found out I was pregnant. I had an abortion. Somehow Al found out about it."

Her colleagues' looks were nonjudgmental, so far. Philly waited for the punch line.

"Al telephoned me. He was furious that I hadn't told him about the pregnancy or given him a chance to talk before I had the abortion. His ranting and raving only convinced me that I was lucky to be rid of him and had made the right decision. Having the baby would have meant he would be in my life."

Simon seemed ready to interject a question but fortunately kept his peace. Philly didn't want Richardson sidetracked.

"A few days ago, someone at work told me that I was mentioned on a billboard outside of the main road heading from the north into Mercer where I live. Mercer's east of Worcester; it's a small town. The person who told me about the billboard wouldn't tell me what it was about but said that I needed to see it. The location isn't on the route I usually take to and from work, so took the long way back from work to Mercer so I could approach the town from the north. I almost went off the road when I saw what Al had done."

Richardson paused and Philly hoped that she was able to continue.

"The billboard didn't have my name on it, but it did have a picture of Al holding a newborn. The message on the billboard said, 'My child will never live to be one month old because her mother decided to kill my baby.'"

Richardson broke into tears and Philly hustled to the kitchen opting for napkins when she couldn't find tissues. When she returned to the living room Rachel was squatting beside Richardson's chair, her arm around the potential client.

Richardson wiped her eyes and blew her nose. "I want the billboard taken down. That creep has no right to publicly humiliate me. Abortion is legal. I'm not a killer."

Philly envisioned right to life zealots having a field day with the case, invoking the right to free speech. She had done some quick Internet research and had a general idea of each side's legal arguments.

"I assume your ex-boyfriend rented the billboard space," Simon said.

"I don't know," Richardson said in a frustrated tone. "What difference does that make?"

"Maybe none," Simon said. "I'm just thinking about whether any lawsuit has to involve the owner of the billboard."

"I don't give a damn who you have to sue. I want that billboard taken down."

"We're interested in taking your case," Philly said, turning to business arrangements in the hope of calming Richardson down. She reviewed their hourly rates and explained the terms of the engagement letter she would be sending to Richardson.

"If I win the case, will I be able to recover the legal fees I have to pay you?" Richardson asked.

"It's possible," Philly said, "but I wouldn't count on that at this time. We'll need to do more research. The first order of business is to get a complaint filed and to request a court to order the billboard taken down."

Richardson stared at her hands, her shoulders shaking. She twisted several of the napkins Philly had fetched into a tightly wound, thick strand. "How much is this going to cost?" she asked.

Philly did some rough estimating. "I would guess somewhere between five and seven thousand dollars through the injunction stage."

"Shit!" Richardson muttered.

"Are you able to pay for our services?" Philly asked, dreading the no answer that she suspected would be forthcoming.

"Not really," Richardson said. "But my parents can. I just hate asking them for the money."

"Do they know about this situation?" Rachel asked.

"Yeah, they do."

"Are they behind you on this?" Rachel followed up.

Richardson shrugged. "They say they are. But I think the truth is that they're conflicted because they wanted a grandchild in the worst way. Also, my father and Al seemed to get along."

Carpenter would probably turn down Richardson's case because payment for legal fees appeared problematic. During the first year she associated with Carpenter, Philly had ignored his warnings and taken on cases where she took a financial beating, because the clients had no one to turn to and she couldn't say no to them. But standing up for someone's rights was a lot easier when she was practicing alone. Now she had Carpenter and Rachel and Simon to factor in. Maybe Rachel and Simon would be in Carpenter's camp and not want to undertake a case where the chances of being paid were dubious.

"I want you to do something for me," Philly said. "I want you to ask your parents to help pay for your legal fees. That said, if you sign the engagement letter I'll be sending you, I will take your case, and I'll try to get into court as soon as possible."

Philly was pleased to see Rachel and Simon nod approval of her decision. That left Carpenter. He would be rip-shit.

"Okay," Richardson said. She stood up uncertainly and offered her hand to Philly. "It's a deal."

"I'll draft the engagement letter and call Carpenter," Philly said when she returned to the living room after showing Richardson out. "I'm thinking Rachel takes first shot at a court complaint and Simon takes the first cut of an affidavit from Richardson. I'll work on the legal memorandum."

Rachel looked up after writing on her notepad. "What are the legal theories besides right to privacy?" she asked.

"From a quick Internet search, I'd say right to privacy is the main legal claim that helps with getting an injunction," Philly responded. "We can throw in a libel count. Also, the Massachusetts right to privacy statute provides for damages but doesn't make allowance for recovering attorney fees."

"We need a photograph of the billboard," Simon said. "If I can borrow Rachel's car, I'll handle that. We need to make sure we're quoting the message exactly."

Philly nodded. "See if you can find out who owns the billboard space."

"Are you hoping that the billboard owner will take the billboard down if sued?" Rachel asked.

"That's my hope," Philly said.

"Are we just supposed to drop everything else?" Simon wanted to know.

Philly thought about their few pending cases. "For the moment the answer is yes," she said, knowing that Carpenter might have other ideas.

Philly had filled Carpenter in on Fay Richardson's case and now braced herself for his explosion. As the silence on the other end of the phone lengthened, she found Carpenter's restraint more ominous than a nasty chewing out.

"I wish you had gone over this with me before taking this woman on," Carpenter said, and Philly was surprised by his neutral tone.

"She needed an answer right away. The woman's a wreck. I couldn't have lived with myself if I put her off and told her I'd have to think about it and then get back to her."

"I suppose this is the price to pay because we're not officially a firm," Carpenter said.

Philly knew what Carpenter was getting at. If they had formed a firm, each of them would have a say on taking on a new case. Maybe that explained why they'd declined to officially tie the firm knot.

"I suppose," Philly said neutrally.

"Remember years ago, when I kept on telling you not to get sucked into cases where you wouldn't get paid? You wouldn't listen to me then, so I suppose you're not going to listen to me now."

"You should have seen this woman," Philly replied. "She was at the end of her rope."

"Everyone's at the end of his or her rope in one way or another," Carpenter said. "I'm not going to give you a hard time over this. You're good-hearted—it's one of the things I admire in you."

"Thanks."

"But just so we're clear, I wouldn't have taken the case."

"We're clear."

"This ex-boyfriend has got to be a first-class creep," Paul delivered his verdict after Philly had filled him in on Fay Richardson's case.

Philly didn't say anything for a while. They were in their bedroom, lying close together, facing each other. Her hand was resting on Paul's chest and she matched her breathing to the beat of his heart.

"Before Philip died, I thought about getting an abortion," Philly said softly. "I didn't think I could handle being a mother."

"What made you change your mind?"

The time when she learned she was pregnant seemed buried in a distant past. "It was a combination of things," she said. "Philip really wanted the child. He was devastated when he realized what I was thinking. Carpenter told me that Philip really cared about me which wasn't easy for him to say. And Maxine basically told me I'd come to regret it if I didn't go through with the pregnancy."

"You made the right decision," Paul said.

"I know. I can't imagine my life without Daisy in it. But I'm trying to understand the mindset of the woman I told you about. Even when the father's an asshole, it's got to be gut-wrenching to terminate a pregnancy."

"There's being an asshole and there's being an asshole. This billboard thing crosses a line. I think this woman was right not to want the guy in her life."

"I know," Philly said. "But still . . . I don't know. I keep thinking about the fetus."

"Maybe just focus on your client," Paul said. "She's being unfairly attacked here."

Paul was right. Philly thought of some of the jerks she had dated when she was younger. If she'd gotten pregnant from one of those assholes, she'd have no qualms about terminating the pregnancy. "Let's change the subject," she said.

"Okay," Paul agreed. "I've picked up a copy of the papers we need to file for a marriage license."

"Wow! That's definitely a subject change."

"Maybe I'm old fashioned, but I want to be married before this baby we've been trying to make gets born."

"Then I'm old fashioned too," Philly said. "Let's do it."

71

Simon was sitting in a student snack bar on the Brandeis campus when his cell phone sounded. His heartbeat speeded up when he saw the calling number. "Hi."

"Hi yourself," Frank Stevens said. "Do you miss me?"

"What do you think?"

"I think you do, and it's come as a surprise to you."

Simon decided to own up. Frank being at Wesleyan College in Connecticut and not likely to return to the Boston area in the immediate future made it easier to be honest. "You're right," he said.

"Well I miss you too if you must know. Although I'm probably not as surprised as you to have this feeling."

"How are you?" Simon asked.

"Good. I've got a decent roommate, I like most of my professors, and football practice is in full swing."

Simon found himself at a loss for words, an occurrence so rare that he was taken aback.

"I was thinking," Frank said. "Why don't you come down for a visit?"

Simon spotted the two students he was scheduled to meet. He caught their eye and waved them over. "I'll have to get back to you on that."

"You're blowing me off!" Frank complained. "You're a coward!"

"No, I'll have to get back to you. I'm working right now. I've got two potential witnesses I've got to interview. They just showed up. Bye."

"Can I get you anything?" Simon requested once Dwayne Morrison and Monica Little had taken seats at his table.

"Coffee," the students said in unison and then shared a laugh.

Simon signaled a waitress and placed the order. Dwayne Morrison was a tall, thin, African American with sharp features and narrow streaks of hair that traced each side of his jaw line. Monica Little was also tall. The co-ed had long dark hair, a gap-toothed smile, and lively blue eyes. They were probably a couple what with the way they sat close together and touched each other's arms with unselfconscious directness as they chatted.

The first student Simon had called politely but firmly declined to talk. Morrison had been the second. Bernard had approved an opening gambit in which Simon explained that the college was looking into Crystal Queen's leaving the seminar before it began, and that Bernard wanted to do his own investigation of the incident. The approach was lame, but it was the best they could come up with.

Morrison hadn't had any reservations about meeting with Simon; he offered to bring another seminar student to the meeting and seemed eager to cooperate.

"Is Mr. Mucowahandi in trouble?" Monica Little asked once her coffee was served.

"I wouldn't say that," Simon answered evasively. "A college official contacted him as a matter of routine, and he asked my office to talk to the students who attended the seminar."

"Sounds to me like he's in deep shit," Morrison said. "You're a lawyer, right? People don't get themselves a lawyer unless they're looking at a shit storm."

"That's not necessarily true," Simon countered. "Most times people wait until they're knee deep in a problem before calling a lawyer. But sometimes people show some smarts and contact a lawyer before trouble starts."

Morrison wasn't buying Simon's attempt to downplay Mucowahandi's difficulties. "Sounds like the shit has already hit the fan for your man," he said, shaking his head.

"What's your take on what happened before the seminar started?" Simon directed to both students.

"Here's what I remember," Morrison said. "Most of us taking the seminar were in the living room talking and joking around. It was great of Mr. Mucowahandi to have us over to his place for some of the sessions. It was a relief not to be in a seminar room on campus. It was relaxing in a way that loosened us up, you know what I mean? We were all talking to each other while he was setting up refreshments in the kitchen. Crystal was a late arrival." Morrison looked toward Little as if for confirmation and his fellow student nodded. "She saw us all talking and she headed in the direction of the bedroom. Next thing I hear her calling out, 'Stay away from me,' and when I looked up, she was moving fast back to the front door of the apartment. I heard the door open and close. Then Mr. Mucowahandi came to the living room and said something like there seems to be a misunderstanding. I think he went to check on the kitchen. Then he came back to the living room and took the chair he usually took and started the seminar."

Simon's note taking finally caught up with Morrison's account. "What do you remember?" he asked Little.

"It's pretty much what Dwayne said."

Simon consulted the outline he had prepared for this meeting. "How much time passed between the time Ms. Queen arrived and left?"

"I really couldn't tell you," Morrison said. "I wasn't really paying attention to her."

"I'd guess five minutes," Little said.

"That seems like a long time to drop something on a bed," Simon prodded.

"I agree," Little said.

"Maybe she used the bathroom," Morrison offered.

"No, she didn't," Little said with certainty. "You can't help but hear when the toilet flushes even over us talking. I didn't hear the toilet."

"Were you keeping track of her?" Morrison asked his companion.

"Sort of," Little admitted sheepishly. "She was wearing a necklace I liked and wanted to get a look at."

"What else was Ms. Queen wearing?" Simon asked.

"I couldn't tell you," Morrison said. "Who cares?"

"She was wearing dark blue hip-hugger jeans and a white T-shirt," Little said. "She had on medium heeled pumps and a maroon blazer over the T-shirt."

Morrison looked at Little with incredulity. "Chicks remember that kind of shit," he directed at Simon as if seeking male support in the face of female peculiarities.

"What was she wearing when she left the apartment?" Simon continued.

"The same things she was wearing when she arrived," Little responded.

"You *were* checking her out," Morrison said.

"So what?" Little replied. "She could be a goddamn model."

"You're right about that," Morrison confirmed.

Simon checked his outline. "When Mr. Mucowahandi returned to the living room after Ms. Queen left the apartment, how did he seem to you?"

"Surprised," Morrison said.

"Somewhat embarrassed," Little added.

"When Mr. Mucowahandi returned to the living room were you guys laughing at something?"

Morrison and Little exchanged a glance and Morrison nodded to his companion.

"We were," Little said. "You have to understand that we'd had a number of seminar meetings previously. Mr. Mucowahandi is a very lively and dynamic instructor. He tries to get everyone to participate in the discussions we have, and he was pretty successful doing that except for Crystal. She wouldn't join in on her own. He'd have to call on her to draw her out. He'd say something like, 'We haven't heard from you in a while, Miss Queen.' But even when he asked her to contribute, she rarely said much of anything."

"What does this have to do with what you guys were laughing at?" Simon asked.

"A lot of us thought Crystal had a crush on Mr. Mucowahandi," Little said. "Christ, I have a crush on him."

"What am I, chopped liver?' Morrison said, grinning.

"You're a poor substitute for the real thing. Mr. Mucowahandi is the real thing."

"Whoa! That's harsh. I'm the real thing and you know it."

Little playfully punched Morrison's arm. "I guess you'll just have to do. For the moment."

After the couple left, Simon called Carpenter to report, and Carpenter instructed him to hold off on further interviews. The snack bar was filling up and Simon went outside. The day was overcast but muggy. He found a bench alongside a walkway between school buildings and sat down. The thought of the legal and investigative work he had to do in Fay Richardson's case made him question the decision he had reached to visit Frank. Had work made him so compulsive that he couldn't make a spontaneous gesture? What the hell, he thought, no guts no glory. He tried Frank's cell phone and was directed to voicemail. He sent a text message: *How about this weekend?*

Josh had borrowed a video camera from a friend and set it up in his bedroom. Last week Rachel had attended opening arguments in a superior court tort suit. With that experience fresh in mind, she had outlined an opening jury argument for Martin Hays' case on three five by eight note cards. She now shuffled the cards nervously as Josh positioned the camera. If she was petrified with only Josh as an audience, how was she going to survive confronting twelve blank stares?

"I'm almost all set," Josh said.

I can't do this, Rachel thought. Maybe if Josh left the room?

"Move next to my dresser," Josh directed. "Good. Right there. Once I get the camera going, do you want me to leave?"

Yes, she thought. "No," is what she said.

"We're rolling," Josh announced.

Rachel made a false start and had to regroup—she had forgotten to introduce herself and Philly.

"Start again," Josh said. "It's no big deal."

Rachel closed her eyes and remembered Josh holding her hips during her first golf lesson. She thought back to standing with Martin Hays looking out over the fairway from the seventh tee. She opened her eyes and looked at the camera.

"My name is Rachel Boyle and with me today is Philomena Piper. We represent the plaintiff in this case, Martin Hays. Mr. Hays lost an eye. Mr. Hays was struck by a golf ball hit off the seventh tee by the defendant in this case, Warren Lord. This was not an errant golf shot hit by Mr. Lord. As you will hear from two impartial witnesses to this tragedy, Mr. Lord deliberately tried to hit Mr. Hays with his golf shot from the seventh tee. Unfortunately, Mr. Lord was successful in striking Mr. Hays in the face with his deliberately aimed shot."

Rachel realized that she hadn't looked at her note cards and didn't need to. Josh was smiling at her. Rachel refocused her attention on the camera.

Rachel snuggled close to Josh on his bed as he pressed PLAY and her trial run of the oral argument was repeated. She knew she was going to cringe at the sound of her own voice and the awkwardness of her movements. But instead, Rachel was struck by how natural she appeared. Her voice was steady, her posture was relaxed and professional. The Rachel talking at her seemed sincere and knowledgeable, was easy to understand. The Rachel talking at her was matter of fact and displayed no histrionics. The Rachel talking at her was believable.

"What's your verdict?" Josh asked when the video came to an end.

"I'm horny," Rachel said turning and spinning quickly so that she was on top of Josh.

"Good, but that's not what I meant."

"You made your point," Rachel said.

"Good. Now what was that about horny?"

72

When her phone rang, Philly was noticing that the leaves on the oak tree outside her home office window had yet to turn, although the nearby maples were showing brilliant patches of red and orange. During this morning's backyard spin with Isabella, there had been an autumn chill in the air so she had dressed Daisy in layers—a sweater and jacket over a long-sleeved pullover. Before settling her daughter in a baby seat, Isabella had stuffed Rosalind into a winter snow suit, pulling the hood up and tying it under the baby's chin. It wasn't even October yet and cold had returned. As they started peddling, Philly had wondered whether their morning spin days were numbered. There was no good place to set up the bikes indoors. The music would wake whoever was still in bed.

"Philomena Piper."

"Herb McCauley," came over the line and it again took Philly a moment to place the name. Ah—the private detective. "Great," she said. "Does this mean you have something to report?"

"It does," McCauley said. "The Salem Stampede held a pre-season scrimmage and fan appreciation afternoon. I showed up and sat in the stands where your client, Martina Glass, sat. There were other fans seated nearby and because I'm such a friendly, sociable guy, I struck up several conversations. I ran into a couple who were there the night of the accident. They're willing to meet with you."

"Do they have anything helpful to say?" Philly asked.

"I believe they do."

"When can I meet them?"

"Is this afternoon soon enough?"

"This afternoon's good. Boston or Brighton?"

"Brighton," McCauley said. "I've got your new address. I'll pick them up and drive them back to Salem where they live."

"That's going beyond the call of duty."

"All part of the service. Besides, I'm bored, and this is a diversion."

By lunchtime, Sarah Ferguson looked like she needed a break and a nap, so Philly took over. Isabella was due back from her morning half day of work in an hour. Philly first fed Rosalind using a bottle of breast milk previously expressed by Isabella, all the while keeping an eye on Daisy who lying on her belly on the living room floor, scribbled with crayons on broad sheets of drawing paper. Watching Rosalind drink, Philly realized that while Daisy might be ready to give up the breast, she wasn't. Was this the first of many instances when she would put her own desires before Daisy's?

Rosalind's eyes closed and she stopped sucking. Philly wiped her face with a diaper, positioned the baby over her shoulder, and gently rubbed her back. An impressive burp erupted from Rosalind causing the baby to wriggle suddenly and dramatically before again becoming still. Philly paced about the living room for another few minutes before settling Rosalind in a basinet on the living room floor. Time for Daisy to have some real food and juice from a sippy cup which Daisy had quickly mastered.

Daisy held up one of her scribbled drawings. "Nice job," Philly complimented before her daughter began to tear the paper. "Speaking of jobs," Philly continued addressing her daughter, "I've got to get you fed and clean and this room tidied up. We're having company for legal work. If you help out, maybe I'll introduce you."

Daisy scattered her crayons across the living room floor.

"That's not helping."

Isabella had returned from work and, after changing into knock around clothes, had taken Daisy and Rosalind out for a walk. Sarah, revitalized after her nap, was now helping Philly make the living room presentable.

"How are you doing with the little ones?" Philly asked.

"They're exhausting," Sarah replied. "I'm not complaining, mind you. It's just a fact."

"Complaining is fine. It's not only allowed, it's encouraged."

"I'm okay," Sarah said in a tone that caused Philly to doubt Sarah's claim.

"How's life on the third floor?"

"I've settled in," Sarah said. "It's taken some getting used to people moving around on the lower floors. I've been living alone for quite a while."

Sarah had bent over to retrieve Daisy's scattered crayons and Philly noticed how she straightened up slowly.

"I know you're concerned about me," Sarah said, catching Philly's glance. "I know you're worried I might have bitten off more than I can chew. So I just want to say to you that I'm getting what I wanted. Daisy and Rosalind are great.

I enjoy them. And I'm no longer lonely. I like the constant activity. I'm grateful to be a part of this adventure."

"You're a key person in making this work," Philly said. "But remember the deal. Speak up when you need a break."

"I remember the deal all right."

Jeremy and Mary Rhodes were around Carpenter's age. Jeremy had a large frame, long arms and legs. Philly guessed he had played hockey in his younger days. His wife was short and stocky with gray hair cut short and a determined set to her jaw. The couple was dressed identically in jeans and flannel shirts. They had shed Boston Bruins jackets before taking seats on the couch. Jeremy sat up straight, a resigned, stoical look on his face. Mary leaned forward expectantly; she seemed wound up and anxious to get started.

"This is the couple I was telling you about," Herb McCauley got the ball rolling. "They saw the guy fall on Martina Glass."

Mary Rhodes nodded earnestly in response to McCauley's pronouncement while her husband's expression never changed.

"Why don't you tell Ms. Piper what you saw," McCauley prompted.

"You probably remember it a lot better than I do," Jeremy Rhodes said to his wife. "Besides I can see you're itching to go."

"We're season ticket holders," Mary Rhodes began. "We're big hockey fans. Bruins tickets cost too much, so we have to watch them on TV. But we like live action and the Stampede games are usually entertaining. And the price is right. We don't splurge on a lot of things, but Stampede tickets are one of the indulgences we allow ourselves."

Mary Rhodes hadn't struck Philly as a talker but now she wondered when the woman would stop rambling and provide a helpful fact.

"A lot of fans like to sit close up to be near the action on the ice, but Jeremy and I like to be high up. That way you get to see the whole ice surface and you don't miss much."

Jeremy nudged his wife.

"Right," Mary Rhodes said. "So we were sitting behind and to the left of where the woman who got hurt was sitting. Our seats were right about center ice. Jeremy and I had seen her around. I wouldn't be surprised if she was a season ticket holder like us."

Jeremy delivered another elbow nudge.

"Right. So there were three, big, young guys sitting above and behind the woman who got hurt. They'd been knocking back beers at a pretty good pace. Jeremy and I don't go in for beers. Jeremy would be running to the bathroom half the night and I hate that bloated feeling."

"These people don't have all day," Jeremy interceded.

His wife smiled genially. "Right. So one of the three guys leaves his seat. I don't know why I noticed it, but I did. I've never understood why people leave their seats in the middle of a period. If you have to go to the bathroom it shouldn't be that hard to hold it until the period comes to an end."

"Christ, Mary!" Jeremy sputtered.

"Right. So the guy who left his seat comes back. Only he doesn't go directly back to his seat. He must have gone out to get peanuts because he was holding three bags of peanuts. Speaking for myself, I don't like the peanuts they sell at Stampede games. They're too salty if you ask me and those damn shells make a mess. Pieces of shell get all over you. Whenever I get peanuts, I find I'm picking pieces of shell off clothes a week later."

"Nobody asked you," Jeremy said, not bothering to hide his irritation.

"Right. Anyway, there are about five people between where the guy with the peanuts was standing in the aisle and the guy's seat. To get to his seat, he was going to have to squeeze by five people. Only he doesn't return to his seat. Instead, what he does is call out to one of his friends. He gets the friend's attention and then he says the friend's name which I can't remember, and he says something like, 'It's third and ten, the quarterback drops back to pass.' Then the guy tossed one of the peanut bags to the friend he's talking to. Only the guy's aim was off and when the friend tried to catch the bag of peanuts he leaned forward and fell over the rail onto the woman who got hurt."

It took Philly a long moment to realize that she was staring at Mary Rhodes open-mouthed. There was no way the woman could have made that story up.

"Did anyone interview you to ask what you saw?" Philly found her voice.

"No," Mary said, shaking her head in a way that made Philly think the woman had wanted to be interviewed.

"Were you contacted by anyone to ask if you saw the accident?"

"No," Mary said. "If anybody had asked, I would have told them exactly what I told you."

"Do you have any idea how much the three guys had to drink?" McCauley chimed in.

"I really wasn't keeping count," Mary Rhodes said.

"At least four beers each," Jeremy Rhodes said.

"Were *you* keeping count?" Philly asked.

"Yeah," Jeremy said. "I really wanted a beer and I was envious of these guys knocking back beers without having to think about it. There was a time when I could knock off a six pack and not feel any the worse for wear. But Mary's right. These days one beer has me peeing all night."

"What happened after the guy fell on the woman?" Philly resumed her questions.

"I couldn't really see her," Mary said. "She must have been lying on the surface below her chair. I saw the guy who fell on her get to his feet. He was a huge guy."

Philly made a few notes. "What happened after the guy who fell on her got up?"

"He brushed himself off and stood there staring. He had to be looking at where the woman was lying. An attendant came over to see what was going on and must have called for help, because about ten minutes later an EMT team arrived. They worked a stretcher in to where the woman was lying and got her on it. Then they lifted the stretcher, got it out of the seating area, and went down some stairs to where there was an exit."

"Did you see or hear the injured woman?" McCauley asked.

"They had strapped her onto the stretcher so she wasn't moving," Mary said. "I didn't hear her say anything if that's what you were asking."

"Did you recognize any other people in attendance?" McCauley followed up.

"I don't remember," Mary said.

"In what period did this happen?" McCauley directed at Jeremy.

"Near the middle of the third period."

McCauley had run out of questions, and Philly decided to take charge. She explained the pending lawsuit to the couple. Mary's eyes lit up and Philly wondered whether the woman was picturing herself as a star witness in the case. Jeremy looked like he'd rather be elsewhere. "Would you be agreeable to providing affidavits as to what you observed?" Philly concluded her presentation.

"I'd love to," Mary gushed.

"We're going to have to think about it," Jeremy responded.

"What's to think about?" Mary fired back. "We were witnesses to a terrible tragedy. We have a duty to help that poor woman."

Jeremy stood up. "We're going to run this by our lawyer," he said. "Before we get involved in this case, we're going to get some advice as to what we're getting ourselves into."

"But . . ."

"But nothing," Jeremy cut Mary off. "We need to get back home," he said to McCauley.

"Your husband's right," Philly said to Mary. "You should consult an attorney so you know what you're getting yourself into. I'd simply point out that you're both witnesses in this case and can be subpoenaed to a trial. Also, any party to the case can take your depositions."

"I've got one more question," McCauley said. "How many beers can a person be served at these Stampede games?"

"There's a sign at each beer concession stand that says there's an overall limit of three to a customer," Jeremy replied.

"That wasn't my question," McCauley said. "I asked you how many beers a customer can be served."

"How many beers can you drink before the five-minute mark of the third period when they stop serving beer?" Jeremy came back. "Does that answer your question?"

"I believe it does," McCauley said, grinning broadly.

McCauley had given Jeremy Rhodes the key to his car and told him he'd join him in few minutes. "What's your verdict?" he asked Philly once the Rhodes had departed.

"I guess the good news is that the couple can establish that two of the three guys were negligent—the guy who fell on Martina and the guy who threw the bag of peanuts. The problem is that these guys may have no money."

"That sounds like the bad news." McCauley said.

"No. The bad news is that this couple's testimony may clear the Salem Stampede, the defendant with deep pockets."

"I've got a thought about that," McCauley said, grinning mischievously. "I think Barney and I need to take in a Stampede game. I always wanted to see how many beers I could knock back in two periods and five minutes of hockey. And by the way, I always keep my receipts when I buy beer."

Philly found herself smiling. "Does that make Mr. Freedman the designated driver?"

McCauley's upbeat mood vanished. "Christ!" he said. "Knowing Barney, we'll probably have to flip for it. With my luck, I'll end up sober behind the wheel."

73

Simon settled into his bus seat and opened his laptop. He tried to put out of his mind the scene when Frank would pick him up at the station. If he let it, the image of that encounter would distract him for the entire journey, and he needed to focus on Fay Richardson's case.

It had taken the better part of yesterday to unearth the identity of the billboard owner and take a photograph of the billboard. Billboards required a permit and mercifully, a helpful Mercer town clerk searched town records to get him what he needed. If he'd had to rely on online searches, he would have come up empty. BillboardBits, LLC owned the billboard in question. The company was managed by Rita Stout. Simon had googled Stout and had discovered that she was a vice-president of an organization called Massachusetts Citizens to Preserve Life. That organization was a vigorous pro-life advocacy group opposed to abortion in any circumstance including rape and incest.

Simon had sent Rachel an e-mail with his discoveries since she was working on Fay Richardson's court complaint. He now turned his attention to drafting an affidavit for Richardson to sign. Setting forth the background facts in the case proceeded smoothly. But Simon's efforts bogged down when he tried to craft the paragraphs of the affidavit that claimed Richardson was irreparably harmed. To obtain injunctive relief, Richardson would have to show harm that was now irreparable and couldn't be cured after a trial.

Simon closed his eyes but that strategy backfired when an image of a smiling Frank came to mind. Simon stared at his laptop. Richardson, he decided, was harmed each day that the billboard wrongfully accused her of being a killer. Each day that the vicious charge remained on public display was a day of public humiliation for Richardson that could never be reclaimed. Simon took a deep breath and began to type.

Carpenter had been advised by two psychiatrists who came highly recommended that the claims of Keith and Jane Spring against Roland Butler appeared weak. This advice briefly caused him to consider refunding the Springs' modest retainer and telling the couple to find another lawyer. But he held off severing ties with the Springs until he had talked with Rudolf Nelson who, by his own count, had testified in approximately one hundred cases on behalf of plaintiffs suing physicians. Nelson had practiced internal medicine and had a degree in psychology. Carpenter could recall only two other occasions when he had resorted to an expert witness who aggressively advertised himself as such.

The two psychiatrists he had reached out to believed that Roland Butler had not acted unprofessionally by failing to warn anyone about Ryan Spring being dangerous. Ryan had no history of physical violence, and the statute required such a history. Butler had defused the situation by taking possession of the gun Ryan had produced, and Ryan had retracted his previous statement that he wanted to kill his father. One psychiatrist viewed the situation as a classic case of Ryan wanting to orchestrate a scene whereby he would be prevented from doing something he had no intention of doing in the first place.

"Of course I can help your client," Nelson declared assertively after Carpenter had recounted what he knew of the shooting that had claimed the life of Darren Spring. "You said that the older brother—let's see, that would be Ryan—brought a gun to the psychologist's office. Do I have that right?"

"That's correct. But then he surrendered the gun."

"And Ryan said that he felt like killing his father?"

"Again correct, although he later retracted the statement."

"Those are very compelling and dramatic facts," Nelson stated, again in an assertive manner. "I'd say that at a minimum the psychologist should have contacted the father, the person threatened. Was the gun that Ryan left with the psychologist loaded?"

Carpenter didn't know whether he felt more chagrined by the fact that he didn't know the answer to Nelson's question, or by the fact that he hadn't thought to ask it. "I don't know."

"You might want to find that out," Nelson said, and Carpenter made a note that he was certain he would never need to refer to.

"What do you make of the facts that Ryan had no history of physical violence and he retracted his wish to kill his father?"

"Those facts are helpful to the psychologist but, on balance, Ryan's producing a gun should have set off warning alarms prompting the psychologist to call the family. The lack of a violent history may be a problem, but the boy producing a gun was something new in his behavior that was beyond troubling. Suppose Ryan had fired the gun in the psychologist's office before turning it over. Wouldn't that negate the lack of a violent history?"

Carpenter believed that Nelson had made fair points, points that Keith Spring had made.

"I've had to work with facts a lot less compelling than those you've presented," Nelson said. "I'm very interested in your clients' case."

"When's the last time you treated a patient?" Carpenter asked.

"That would be roughly eight years ago," Nelson said, seemingly unperturbed by the pointed question.

"Your website states that you've testified in approximately a hundred cases. What's your batting average?"

"A little under five hundred," Nelson responded promptly, again not sounding put out by another probing question.

Carpenter remembered when his practice largely involved plaintiff tort cases. He thought he had batted well over five hundred but, in fairness to Nelson, Nelson probably was brought into cases that were long shots.

"Doesn't the fact that Ryan surrendered the gun to his psychologist mean the psychologist is off the hook?" Carpenter asked.

"You seem to think it's not an unusual occurrence for a patient to pull out a gun during a therapy hour," Nelson retorted. "Let me tell you that has never happened to me, and I doubt it has ever happened to the overwhelming majority of therapists. So what if Ryan handed over the gun. As I just said, the fact that he had the gun and showed the gun during the session should have sounded a warning alarm that even this psychologist couldn't ignore. The psychologist should have contacted the father. End of story."

Carpenter was forced to acknowledge that Nelson had broken the case down to a simplistic level that jurors would have no trouble understanding. The man exuded confidence and was not likely to be ruffled by a grueling cross-examination. "I'm aware of your rates. I need to talk with my client and get back to you."

"I'll be expecting your call."

74

Carpenter was determined to confront as many unpleasant tasks as he could stomach. Keith and Jane Spring's case against Roland Butler was not a case he was looking forward to, yet the couple needed to hear what Rudolph Nelson had to say. Once Keith Spring heard Nelson's views, he would be pressing to get a lawsuit filed.

When Carpenter telephoned the Springs, he reached Keith who wanted to proceed with the call even though his wife was out. "I'll fill Jane in on what we discuss and I'm sure she'll agree with me on what to do," Spring said in a tone that made clear who was calling the shots on the suit against Butler. Jane Spring's previously stated reluctance to pursue a lawsuit apparently had been pushed to the side by her husband.

"I'd say that's pretty damn encouraging," Spring said after Carpenter recounted his discussion with Nelson. "I'd say hire the guy on the spot."

Carpenter knew that his lowering expectations speech would fall on deaf ears, but he delivered it anyway. Spring needed to be mindful of two psychiatrists taking a position contrary to Nelson's, of Nelson being a hired gun subject to impeachment, and of Ryan's history of nonviolence.

"So what," Spring had declared. "As far as I'm concerned, this guy Nelson you came up with is the only guy talking sense. I want you to hire him."

Spoken like a man who has been told what he wants to hear, Carpenter thought. "Consider it done," is what he said.

Carpenter next retrieved his file on Bernard Mucowahandi, a case that always would give him misgivings since Bernard was married to Connie. He took a deep breath and studied Simon's report of his interview with two of the seminar students. Simon had done well. But if Crystal Queen did in fact have a crush on Bernard, how the hell did you prove that? And even if you could prove a crush, would that proof be helpful? Simon had reported that the female student he had interviewed, Monica Little, had a crush on Bernard.

Carpenter felt he was missing something. He studied the photographs in his office for inspiration but found none. The unsmiling black man favored him with a condescending sneer. The woman hiker marching on an upslope seemed as lost as he was.

Carpenter focused on the question he had previously asked but that Simon had been unable to answer. What the hell was Crystal Queen doing in Bernard's bedroom? She hadn't entered the room to deposit clothing or anything else on the bed Bernard and Connie shared. But if Queen really had a crush on Bernard, there was at least one plausible answer to her presence in the bedroom.

Carpenter composed a short e-mail memo to Bernard: *Please let me know at once if anything is missing from your bedroom.*

Carpenter next printed out the pleadings that Philly had prepared for Fay Richardson. It was doubtful the woman would be able to pay for the legal services she needed but what the hell; he'd told Philly he wasn't going to question her decision to take the case. As he began to read the complaint Rachel had drafted, he began to understand Philly's desire to help Richardson. Richardson's ex-boyfriend had to be an asshole. No other word fit.

Carpenter completed his edits to Rachel's draft complaint, Simon's draft affidavit, and Philly's legal memorandum and sent the documents to Philly. He checked his watch. It was lunch time. He thought about the afternoon. A session with Camellia Kim sounded better than anything he had going in his office. Why the hell not? he thought.

75

The Worcester County Superior Court building was an old, dark, tired, gray edifice that Philly suspected would be kept on life support rather than have taxpayers foot the bill for a new courthouse. It was probably overkill to have three lawyers appear for the initial hearing in Fay Richardson's case, but Philly wanted both Simon and Rachel present since they had made valuable contributions to getting the case ready for court. Fay Richardson was wearing a white blouse and black skirt and in Philly's view was making a conscious effort to keep herself together.

Carpenter didn't know the judge assigned to the case—Terrence Murray. The judge's official photograph showed an unsmiling, gray-haired man in his fifties. Murray had practiced law with one of the larger firms in the Worchester area and had specialized in commercial litigation. While the judge's photograph suggested a stoic, hard-nosed individual, Philly was buoyed by one action taken by the jurist. Richardson's case was the only afternoon case on the judge's calendar; Philly took that as a sign that the judge recognized Richardson's desire for privacy.

When their entourage entered the second-floor courtroom, Richardson emitted an audible gasp and pointed to two men sitting in the first row of the gallery. Philly recognized Al Townsend from his billboard photograph: a bespectacled man with brown hair, a round face and a slight stoop. Next to him was a tall, trim man wearing a dark blue suit and red tie. Philly wondered whether there would ever come a day when she was taller than the lawyer opposing her.

Philly motioned for Rachel to take charge of Richardson and approached the two men and introduced herself.

"Patrick Lassiter," the tall man said, offering his hand. "This is my client, Al Townsend." Townsend nodded but made no offer to shake hands.

"Here's our legal memorandum," Philly said, and she waited while Lassiter unloaded copies of the various papers he intended to file with the court.

Lassiter would be filing an affidavit from Townsend, an affidavit from Rita Stout, the president of the billboard company, and a legal memorandum opposing Richardson's request for a preliminary injunction. Philly rejoined Rachel and Simon and parceled out the legal memorandum to Rachel and Stout's affidavit to Simon. She sat down on a gallery bench, took a deep breath, and began to read through Townsend's affidavit.

Richardson's former boyfriend stated that he had been given no information about Richardson's pregnancy, and had learned by chance that she had been pregnant and had aborted his baby. Townsend claimed a right to know about Richardson's pregnancy and a right to be consulted prior to Richardson's aborting his baby. As far as Philly's research disclosed, neither of these rights were recognized under the law. Townsend characterized his billboard display as a first amendment protest about having his fatherhood rights violated and extinguished. Philly made a few notes and exchanged documents with Simon.

Rita Stout's affidavit focused on claimed first amendment protections. She stated that she had approved Townsend's message because it expressed views similar to her own: life was sacrosanct, and Richardson had taken the life of Townsend's child.

Rachel handed her Lassiter's legal memorandum. Lassiter had amassed numerous first amendment cases that he claimed protected Townsend's right to protest Richardson's actions. Philly recognized some of the cases but had not read the majority of them. Lassiter claimed that Richardson's privacy rights were not violated because she was not mentioned by name on the billboard, but Philly believed that she had dealt with that claim. Simon had obtained three affidavits from friends of Richardson who stated that on viewing the billboard, they knew that it referred to Richardson and could not have referred to any other person.

When they had each finished reading Lassiter's court submissions, Philly asked Rachel and Simon for feedback.

"Overall," Simon said, "there's nothing unexpected here."

"I agree," Rachel said. "Calling our client a killer should sink the defendants."

Philly took a moment to review her argument outline. She had a comeback for each of Lassiter's points. It had been a while since she had argued a case before a judge, and she welcomed the opportunity. Let the games begin, she thought.

"All rise!" the court clerk directed as Judge Murray took the bench promptly at two o'clock. "I've read the papers," he announced. Philly tried not to read anything into Murray's dour expression.

"Tell me, Ms. Piper, what do you say about the defendants' first amendment arguments?" the judge inquired after counsel had introduced themselves.

Philly set her argument outline on the counsel table. During this morning's spin, she had silently rehearsed her answer to the judge's question while *Walk Away* sounded from her boom box.

"No first amendment protections apply to a libelous accusation that a woman is a killer," Philly began, opting for a no-nonsense opening sentence. "The billboard is a vicious personal attack that is entitled to no protection whatsoever."

"Isn't abortion a public issue about which public comment is permitted?" Murray followed up.

"The billboard message does not involve public comment. What it does is single out a specific individual, Ms. Richardson, and falsely accuses her of being a killer."

"If protesters can protest homosexuality at military funerals as the Supreme Court has ruled, why can't the defendants protest against what the plaintiff did?"

"Ms. Richardson is not a public figure and had a constitutional right to follow through with an abortion decision. It is not legitimate protest to falsely label an innocent, private citizen a killer. To reiterate, the billboard message is not a protest on any public issue; it is a personal, libelous attack on an individual exercising a constitutional right."

Philly couldn't tell whether her responses were registering with Murray. The judge's expression gave nothing away.

"Didn't abortion foes label anyone having or performing an abortion a baby killer?" Murray asked. "Protests using that language were permitted, weren't they?"

"Whether or not abortion foes used the term baby killer does not mean that label was or is permissible when directed at a specific individual who is not a public figure. Abortion is a constitutional right under both the federal and Massachusetts constitutions."

"You keep focusing on the word kill in the billboard message," Murray said. "Why don't I simply order the deletion of that word and leave the rest of the billboard message intact?"

"Because even with that word deleted, the billboard and its message violate the plaintiff's right to privacy by unfairly singling Ms. Richardson out for public condemnation," Philly replied promptly.

"Since when does a right to privacy trump a first amendment right?" the judge fired back.

"At a basic level," Philly replied, trying to keep her irritation under control, "when the alleged speech is a scurrilous, false, personal attack."

"Would Mr. Townsend be violating the plaintiff's right to privacy if he protested her abortion decision outside her house by holding up a protest sign?"

"Yes," Philly said forcefully, vowing not to concede a damn thing to this judge. "Here again, Ms. Richardson would be singled out for a personal attack solely because as a non-public figure she exercised a right protected by the federal and state constitutions. Her right to privacy is both a constitutional right and a right protected by statute in Massachusetts."

Judge Murray addressed Lassiter. "What am I to make of the word kill on the billboard?"

"The word accurately reflects Mr. Townsend's view of what transpired," Lassiter replied.

"Is Ms. Richardson a killer?" Murray continued.

"In Mr. Townsend's view she is."

"In his view," the judge repeated. "What about in fact? Is Ms. Richardson a killer in fact? Could she be charged with murder?"

"I don't believe she could be charged with murder," Lassiter conceded. "But Mr. Townsend is entitled to express his view as to what her conduct amounted to."

"Is he? Really?" Murray said, and Philly noticed that the judge's gaze had momentarily wandered, drifted toward the rear of the courtroom, and she wondered whether Murray was trying to search out Richardson who sat alone in the rear of the gallery. Philly began to second-guess her decision not to introduce Richardson.

"Do counsel have anything to add to what is in their submissions?" the judge inquired. Philly felt a stab of worry since the judge's questioning of her had been far more rigorous than his questioning of Lassiter. "No?" the judge continued. "Then I'm prepared to rule on the plaintiff's request for a preliminary injunction. Is the plaintiff present in the courtroom?"

"Yes, Your Honor." Philly turned and motioned for Richardson to stand. Her client did so reluctantly, appearing visibly shaken.

Murray regarded Richardson for a long moment, his expression blank. "You may be seated," he announced, and Richardson needed no urging to resume her seat.

Murray consulted a sheet of notepaper and Philly wondered whether he had prepared a draft ruling prior to hearing oral argument.

"Individuals have read the billboard in question and have identified the target of the billboard as Ms. Richardson," Murray began. "Mr. Townsend's view that the plaintiff is a killer doesn't make her one. The plaintiff is harmed every moment the billboard remains in place. The harm to the plaintiff is irreparable. In contrast, neither defendant suffers any harm if the billboard is taken down. I find and rule that the plaintiff has a substantial likelihood of success on the merits of her right to privacy and libel claims. The plaintiff's motion for a preliminary injunction is granted without requirement of a bond being posted. Are the defendants in the courtroom, Mr. Lassiter?"

"Mr. Townsend is, Your Honor."

"Please rise, Mr. Townsend," the judge directed.

Townsend stood, not meeting the judge's gaze.

"If the billboard isn't removed by six thirty tomorrow morning, I am going to hold you in contempt of court. Do you understand me, Mr. Townsend?"

Townsend nodded, his head lowered.

"I need a verbal response from you for the record."

"Yes, Your Honor."

"Mr. Lassiter. I want a letter from you on my desk by ten o'clock tomorrow morning informing me as to the status of the billboard."

"Yes, Your Honor," Lassiter said weakly.

"And you can inform Ms. Stout that contempt awaits her if the billboard is not removed as I have ordered."

"Yes, Your Honor," Lassiter repeated.

"The court will be in recess."

"Jesus," Rachel whispered as Murray left the bench.

"I thought he was going to deny the injunction," Simon said.

Philly couldn't process what had just happened. Did the judge have a daughter who had had to make a painful abortion decision? The judge had come down hard on the defendants and she couldn't figure out why. "I'm guessing here," she said. "I think the word kill got to him. Townsend went too far."

"Are you saying that the judge would have ruled the other way if the word kill hadn't been used?" Rachel asked.

"The thought occurred to me," Philly said.

"Thank you," a tearful Richardson said when she drew near the counsel table. "I'm not sure what happened. I thought the judge was giving you a hard time and that I was in trouble."

"We're not entirely sure what the judge was up to," Philly responded. "But when you get what you want, it's sometimes best not to agonize over how you got it."

As soon as Carpenter put his phone down after hearing from Philly on how the court hearing had gone in Fay Richardson's case, his phone sounded again.

"Carpenter."

"How did you know?" Bernard Mucowahandi asked, and Carpenter felt the rush of elation he always got when one of his hunches paid off. It was a feeling that never grew old. "Lucky guess," he replied to Bernard.

"I am certain that luck had nothing to do with it," Bernard responded.

"Then you'd be wrong," Carpenter said. "I *was* guessing. There had to be a reason Ms. Queen was in your bedroom. You're very fortunate that she took something."

"Fortunate!" Bernard snorted. "You will have to explain to me why I am fortunate because one of my students took a small, framed, black and white photograph of Connie and me from my bedside table."

"Is Connie prepared to back you up that the photograph is missing?" Carpenter avoided Bernard's request.

"Of course. She noticed its absence right away. I have to confess that I didn't notice the photograph was gone. But I still do not understand why the missing photograph is a fortunate occurrence."

"This helps you, Bernard. It bolsters one of your defenses. You can use the missing photograph to prove that Ms. Queen had a crush on you, was determined to take something that belonged to you as a memento of sorts, and acted aggressively and in a panic when she unexpectedly ran into you as she was leaving your bedroom with the photograph."

"I am still confused," Bernard complained. "If Miss Queen has a crush on me, why would she take a photograph that had Connie in it?"

"You don't get it, Bernard. Connie is no longer in the photograph. By this time, Queen has effectively cropped Connie out of the photograph. Now she'll be able to look only at you."

Bernard stayed silent; Carpenter wondered whether he was thinking there was a stalker in his life.

"Look at it this way," Carpenter said. "There are other things she could have done in your bedroom that wouldn't be helpful to your case. For example, suppose she simply lay down on your side of the bed to get close to you in some sick way so that she could fantasize about you? If she had done that, you would have a hell of a time proving she had done it, and it wouldn't be as helpful to you as her having walked off with your photograph."

Bernard again fell silent and this time Carpenter decided to wait him out.

"Where do you come up with these ideas?" Bernard finally asked.

"I don't know. Just lucky I guess."

"Do you really think she is fantasizing about me?" Bernard asked with what sounded to Carpenter like interest.

"That would be my guess."

"You have not seen Miss Queen in person, have you?" Bernard asked.

"That's correct."

"She is strikingly beautiful. The idea that she would be fantasizing about me must mean I have . . . how do you say it in this country . . . something going for me."

"You do have something going for you, Bernard. Her name is Connie."

"Yes, of course."

Jenny was sleeping over, sharing Daisy's room. Philly was grateful that Jenny wasn't complaining about not having a room of her own as she did at her mother's place. She sensed that Jenny didn't really know what to make of the menagerie assembled in their three family house. The young girl's bemused expression as Raul, Isabella, and Sarah went about their business in common areas would likely remain in place for some time. And God only knew what Jenny made of the fact that Isabella, upon learning that Jenny had been introduced to Spanish in the second grade, now only spoke to her in that language. Jenny probably thought that a trip to Brighton was on a par with Alice's descent down the rabbit hole.

Paul tiptoed into their bedroom after checking on the girls. "Both down for the count," he announced.

"Do you think Jenny's happy coming over here?" Philly asked as Paul settled into bed beside her.

"The verdict's out on that," Paul said. "I think she's a little overwhelmed by the number of people wandering around. Hell! I'm overwhelmed by that."

"You look like you're coping."

"Looks can be deceiving," Paul said. "You'll like this. Isabella was changing Rosalind's diaper and got Jenny to help. She went through the process in Spanish and made Jenny repeat each word. I think it's a safe bet that Jenny now knows the parts of the female body in Spanish."

"That's a good thing, right?"

"A very good thing. Jenny's horizons need some expanding in my opinion."

"Tomorrow's the big day," Philly said, changing the subject. "I don't want it to feel anticlimactic."

"It won't be for me," Paul replied. "That's because I'm the romantic one in this relationship."

Philly thought about Paul's observation and realized he was correct. "That's one of the reasons I'm marrying you."

"What are the others?"

"Here's one of the others."

"Okay, you've got my attention."

76

Philly adjusted the settings on her spinning bike so that they worked for Jenny. The young girl got on the bike and cast an uneasy glance at Isabella, who gave her a broad grin and a thumb's up signal. "Get those legs moving," Isabella exhorted. *All Summer Long* was blasting from her boom box and Philly suspected that Jenny was feeling sensory overload.

"Get yourself on a flat road," Philly directed. "That means you need some resistance but not very much. You don't want your legs moving without *any* resistance."

Jenny looked dubious about this morning's exercise, but apparently had resolved to give it a go. The temperature had dropped below forty last evening and there was a definite chill in the air. The sun hadn't risen but an orange glow had surfaced to the bikers' left. Philly was wearing a heavy sweatshirt with a hoodie and she jogged in place to get warm.

"Time for stretching," Philly announced, and Jenny and Isabella followed her lead as she did shoulder shrugs and arm loosening stretches. Jenny was looking at her intently, caught up in the adventure, for the moment not focused on being perched on a stationary bike on a cold morning when she could see her breath.

"Do you think we're nuts?" Philly asked Jenny.

Jenny smiled sheepishly. "A little," she said.

Paul opened the back door holding Rosalind; with Raul needing to be at work early, Paul often took Rosalind in tow during the mornings. He stepped aside and Daisy rushed forward onto the paved area where the spinning bikes sat.

"Look at me, dad!"

"Very impressive," Paul told his daughter.

Daisy made a beeline for the grassy area of the backyard and began to move in slow circles with her arms outstretched as if she were imitating an airplane.

This Love now sounded from her boom box and Philly helped Jenny stand on her pedals, first giving the girl's resistance knob a half turn to the right, increasing the resistance. "This is harder," Jenny said.

"You're doing fine," Philly told her.

Philly responded to the tug on her sweatpants. Daisy offered her a brown leaf tinged with red. "Thank you, pumpkin."

Daisy moved back to the grass. Philly glanced at Paul. He was holding Rosalind close, whispering in the baby's ear. Then he held Rosalind up so that she could take in the commotion raging in the back of the house. Well, the big day had gotten off to a wonderful start.

Philly and Paul sat at a corner table in a trendy, Boston Italian restaurant that Paul had read about. Paul was doing everything he could to make their low-key marriage day her day, Philly reflected. He had gone along with her wish to keep families at a remove which she knew was a sacrifice. His mother especially might be hurt by not being included. Moments ago, when their waiter asked for drink orders, he had followed her lead and requested a Virgin Mary.

"Happy?" Paul asked.

"Happy," Philly confirmed.

"I still think you should have let me spring for an engagement ring. I feel I'm shortchanging you."

Philly had kept her reasons for not wanting an engagement ring to herself. She debated whether to air them. She didn't want Paul to get the wrong idea.

"What are you thinking about?" Paul asked. "You've got this serious look."

Philly generally subscribed to Carpenter's mantra that if you didn't have to say anything, shut your mouth because what you didn't voice couldn't hurt you. A husband and wife might be better off not sharing everything. On this first day of her marriage Philly decided what the hell and opted not to follow her instincts.

"I'll tell you why I didn't want an engagement ring, but I don't want you to get upset."

"I'm hearing warning signals," Paul responded.

"You've gotten me to open up to you. The fact I'm willing to talk to you about the engagement ring is a big deal for me. It would be a lot easier for me to avoid the matter."

"I won't get upset," Paul said. "You've piqued my curiosity."

"This is hard to explain. Philip never gave me an engagement ring. He gave me a seashell with a hole that fit my ring finger as a temporary ring substitute. He was always going to buy me a real ring. Then he died."

Paul nodded at her uncertainly.

"I've gotten it in my head that the only engagement ring I will ever have will be that stupid shell. It's my way of remembering Philip. It's like I'm keeping what he gave me, exclusively his to give me. Already I don't think of him for days on end. Five years from now I'll probably forget what he looked like. I don't even want to think about telling Daisy about Philip."

Paul took her hand. "It's all right," he said. "I actually understand what you're saying."

"But here's another thing," Philly said, holding out her left hand. "This wedding ring is the only one I'll ever wear. It's all about you."

"That works for me."

"Have you decided on your orders?" the waiter interrupted.

Paul had a meeting in Cambridge and Philly gave in to an urge to visit Carpenter while she was in Boston. She made a bet with herself that the geezer wouldn't notice her wedding ring. Rachel and Simon were out of the office and she knocked on Carpenter's door.

"It's open."

Carpenter didn't look up when she entered. He was typing at his computer and Philly was greeted by his profile. He looked like he had regained some weight; he didn't have the gaunt look she'd noticed when his cancer symptoms had flared a while back.

Carpenter looked up and did a double take. "Oh, it's you. I didn't expect to see you today."

Philly appropriated the visitor chair and for a moment was nonplussed that she didn't have to clear away papers before sitting down. She glanced around the office. There wasn't as much clutter as she remembered. Maybe that was due to their lack of business.

"What are you working on?"

Carpenter frowned. "Today I'm going to file the complaint on behalf of Keith and Jane Spring if it kills me. I can't stop fiddling with it. It's like a turkey carcass after Thanksgiving that I feel a need to pick at."

"They're suing their son's psychologist, right?"

"Right," Carpenter confirmed. "I didn't think they had much of a case but this expert I've engaged who is a first class, opinionated son of a bitch has given me hope. I now actually think the case might make it to a jury."

"That's good to hear."

"Yeah," Carpenter said without conviction. "We've got contingency cases everywhere we look. I wish we had something meaty with billable hours."

"We've got what we've got," Philly said. She was tired of agonizing over the lack of billable hours. "Pretty soon those contingency cases will be coming up for trial. They're going to make or break our year."

"Don't remind me."

"I want to revisit whether to get you involved in the golf case and the wheelchair case," Philly broached. She had been fretting about her decision to assign major roles in the cases to Rachel and Simon. She wasn't going to entertain the thought that Carpenter's presence might mean the difference between winning and losing; they simply needed to win the cases, so she put the possibility of losing out of her mind. But Carpenter's experience might make the difference between just winning and winning big.

"I go back and forth on that," Carpenter said. "Where I end up is that you should go forward the way you planned. I think Rachel and Simon will deliver for you. But if it's okay with you, I want to be in the courtroom for both trials."

Philly nodded. "Great. I feel better already."

"Are those businessmen coming up from Georgia for the golf case?"

"They are."

"I'd like to hear Rachel's opening argument to the jury in that case," Carpenter said. "And I'd like to hear Simon's closing argument in the wheelchair case."

"We'll listen together," Philly decided. "How are you going to play the missing photograph in Connie's husband's case?" she changed the subject.

"I haven't decided. What I'd like to do is have someone break into wherever the hell the student lives and take a picture of the photograph sitting on the student's bedside table. She's going to deny she lifted the picture."

"She wouldn't be stupid enough to have the photograph in plain sight, would she?" Philly asked.

"Don't underestimate stupidity."

"Let me ask those two ex-cops whether they have any ideas on what to do," she said. "I'll get back to you."

"It's good to see you," Carpenter said. "I liked it better when you were around. Even though you took off whenever the hell you felt like it to do that spinning nonsense."

"Didn't you tell me that you had tried spinning?"

"I take the fifth."

"I need to get back home and rescue my babysitter. Daisy can be a handful."

"I'm glad you came by."

Philly paused at the door. "Next month is trial preparation. Then the real action begins."

Carpenter nodded. "By the way," he said. "Are congratulations in order?"

"I thought you wouldn't notice."

"A lot you know. I may look oblivious, but I don't miss a fucking thing."

October

Philly's Spinning Playlist

Controversy

Prince

77

Maxine returned to the living room after her second tour of the two-bedroom condo in Arlington with a grin on her face. The broker was in the kitchen on her cell phone and this was their first moment alone. Carpenter had to admit the place was nice, had a modern feel to it. He would have liked one more room, but the three-bedroom model was over the high end of the price range they had agreed on.

"I don't think we're going to do better than this," Maxine whispered after glancing toward the kitchen to make sure the broker was out of earshot. "Both bedrooms are good sized. It's got two full baths. What do you think?"

Carpenter stalled. Maxine would kill him on the spot if he owned up to not giving his full attention to the condo. But his thoughts, not for the first time, had unexpectedly gravitated to the September collapse of the Red Sox. The home team's failure to make the playoffs had left the Barristers in a funk, especially Delaney, who couldn't believe that his prediction the Sox would be playing baseball in October had gone down the drain. He tried to muster a rapt expression. Focus, he reminded himself.

Carpenter frequently pronounced that he could live in a cave. That curmudgeonly position was an exaggeration. He wanted someplace nice. He imagined the condo filled with their possessions and pictured a tight fit. "Do you really think it's big enough?" he asked.

Maxine studied the living room and the adjoining dining room. "A little more room would be nice," she admitted. "I figure the second bedroom would be a joint office and a guest bedroom."

Carpenter nodded. That was the logical plan.

"You don't really have a lot of furniture," Maxine pointed out. "Plus, I'm not particularly attached to everything I have. I'll just have to get rid of stuff."

If one of the tort cases produced a big score, Carpenter would opt for a three-bedroom unit. But that kind of thinking was playing with money you didn't have. Plus, even if a big jury verdict came in, the other side could appeal the verdict which meant that collecting actual cash could take years.

"What do you think?" Maxine prodded.

Carpenter thought about his cancer. If it finished him off in the next ten years, he wouldn't have to worry about outliving his money even if they went with the three-bedroom option. He realized that for his entire life he had never made a financial decision that left him exposed; he'd always taken the safe choice that made financial sense. But if they went with a three-bedroom unit and he died, Maxine would be left with a condo she couldn't afford. Then again, she could always downsize if he kicked the bucket.

"Do you need more time to think it over?" Maxine asked.

Carpenter responded with a shrug. It made sense for them not to overextend themselves financially particularly with Maxine retiring. He knew that it was his cancer making him think of taking a walk on the financial wild side. Fucking Fred was influencing an important life decision he needed to make!

"Do you have any questions?" the broker said emerging from the kitchen.

"Give us a few more minutes alone," Carpenter requested in a curt tone that sent the broker scurrying back to the kitchen.

"What are you thinking about?" Maxine asked.

"Going for the three-bedroom unit."

"That's outside our budget," Maxine pointed out.

Carpenter nodded. "I'm thinking what the hell."

"You're surprising me here."

"I'm surprising myself."

"We don't need the extra room."

"You're right. But it would be nice to have it."

"What's going on?" Maxine questioned.

"It's my cancer," he blurted out. "I'm thinking that if I don't have a lot of time left, I ought to enjoy the time I have left. I like the idea of more room. Maybe we could get some exercise equipment. Something like that."

Carpenter had to work at meeting Maxine's appraising look. He couldn't tell what she was thinking. Where did the idea of exercise equipment come from?

"When it comes to money," Carpenter said, "I've always made decisions that consider tomorrow. The fucking cancer changes that."

"If I didn't retire, the three-bedroom option makes more sense," Maxine said.

"No," Carpenter said adamantly. "I don't want you changing your mind on that. You're ready to pack it in, so end of story."

Maxine didn't say anything. She began to pace. Then she came to an abrupt stop and called out to the broker.

"Have you made a decision?" the broker asked.

"We want to see the three-bedroom unit," Maxine said.

78

Carpenter had Rachel stand at one of the short ends of the rectangular conference room table. He and Simon took seats at the opposite end of the table. Simon's laptop was plugged in and positioned on the table so that Philly could use Skype to watch. Carpenter had spent the better part of a day getting his head into the golf case. He had reviewed the affidavits of the Georgia businessmen, the deposition of the defendant, Warren Lord, and the deposition of Alan Atkinson, Lord's playing partner on the day that Martin Hays was struck by a golf ball. He had concluded his review by reading Hays' deposition. Now, Rachel would deliver a trial run of her opening argument.

"Whenever you're ready," Carpenter said to Rachel.

Rachel took a deep breath and briefly closed her eyes. She was holding several five by eight note cards. She opened her blue eyes and smiled shyly. There was something about her presence that Carpenter liked. He thought that she looked . . . well, sweet wasn't quite the word he wanted although that word fit . . . more like down to earth, without pretense.

"By the time this case is over, ladies and gentlemen, you're going to know more about the game of golf than you knew before. That's the way it's been for me. Before this case came my way, I had never held a golf club and I couldn't have told you the rules of the game or the technical terms that apply to the game. But I've come to learn about the game and so will you. You see, ladies and gentleman, the tragic injury to my client, Martin Hayes, who is the plaintiff in this case, occurred on a golf course. Mr. Hays was struck by a golf ball hit by the defendant in this case, Warren Lord. This was no accident. Mr. Lord deliberately aimed his shot at Mr. Hays as two witnesses with no axe to grind will tell you. Have you ever felt a golf ball? If you have, then you know how hard an object it is. Unfortunately, Mr. Lord's aim was on the mark. Mr. Hays was struck in the face by the golf ball that Mr. Lord fired at him, and witnesses will tell you that he went down as if shot. The first people on the scene couldn't tell whether Mr. Hays was alive or dead. He wasn't moving. Blood was on the ground by his head. I'm happy to tell you that Mr. Hays didn't die from his serious injuries. However, it is my unhappy duty to tell you that Mr. Hays permanently lost the use of his left eye after being hit by the golf shot Mr. Lord deliberately aimed at him."

Rachel paused and glanced at one of her note cards. Carpenter now understood why Philly wanted Rachel to deliver the opening argument in Hays' case.

She came across as sincere and believable. Her girl-next-door look added to these pluses. Carpenter jotted down a note. He thought it would be helpful if Rachel smacked a fist into her open hand after the word shot. But he didn't want to interrupt her to make the point.

Rachel detailed what brought Hays' foursome and Lord's foursome to the Mayfair Country Club in Needham. Then she recounted in a clear, calm voice what transpired on the seventh hole.

"How do we know Mr. Lord deliberately aimed his tee shot at Mr. Hays?" Rachel paused and Carpenter counted three beats. He liked the timing. Two beats would be too short a delay, four beats too long.

"We know that the shot was deliberately aimed at Mr. Hays because, as the Georgia businessmen I told you about will testify, Mr. Lord and Mr. Atkinson wanted to punish Mr. Hays and his playing partners for slow play. I've recounted for you what the two Georgia businessmen heard Mr. Lord and Mr. Atkinson say about that.

"We also know that Mr. Lord deliberately tried to hit Mr. Hays—which he succeeded in doing—because of the club he used to hit his golf ball off the seventh tee.

"As I studied up on golf, I learned that each kind of club is designed to hit a ball a certain distance with a certain amount of accuracy. That's why golfers carry around that whole bag of clubs: because each one is highly specialized. You choose the club that's right for the exact shot you have in mind. Over the years, golfers get better and better at picking just the right club.

"Now a golfer would usually use a club called a driver off the seventh tee at the Mayfair Country Club because the seventh hole was the longest on the course and a driver is the club of choice when you want to drive a golf ball far. Mr. Lord didn't use a driver. Mr. Lord used a golf club known as an iron and the iron he selected was one he used to achieve a distance that was the distance Mr. Hays was from the seventh tee. The Georgia businessmen will tell you that he used an iron as part of his assault and battery upon Mr. Hays."

Rachel had explained golfing terms in a way that was easy to follow. Carpenter vividly pictured the events giving rise to Hays' injury.

"We take our sight for granted. That's a mistake that you learn when you end up in Mr. Hays' position, the victim of an attack that results in the loss of an eye. You'll hear from Mr. and Mrs. Hays about how his life was been limited as a result of the terrible injury he incurred. Your job, ladies and gentlemen, will be to award him damages to compensate him for his loss of an eye due to Mr. Lord's unprovoked, cowardly attack."

Carpenter checked his watch. Thirteen minutes. "I wouldn't change much," he announced to Rachel. "Good job. I'll be making some suggestions to you about Hays' damages. Anybody else?"

"I liked it," Philly's disembodied voice sounded. "You're a natural."

"Simon?" Carpenter asked.

"Sounded good to me."

"Okay," Carpenter said, glancing at his notes. "Let's take it from the top and see how we can make it better."

Simon and Rachel had switched places. Simon had no note cards in front of him.

"Ladies and gentlemen. The evidence has been presented to you, and shortly you will be given instructions on the law. Then it will be time for you to deliberate and reach a verdict. Given the evidence you have heard there is only one verdict that you can return. A verdict in favor of Mary Foster against each of the defendants.

"At the time she was run down by Harrison Blaine's wheelchair, Mary Foster was seventy-nine years of age, in good health, a vigorous and active woman who enjoyed life and lived life to the fullest. Maple Leaf Assisted Living Center was her home. She paid the Center nearly five thousand dollars a month for a safe and nurturing environment which is what any of us would have expected to receive for payments of nearly five thousand dollars a month. Instead, Mary Foster's home was turned into a demolition derby arena that nearly cost her her life, and did cost her the joys and benefits of her senior years, her mobility, and her confidence."

Simon paused and Carpenter, not for the first time, was struck by the young lawyer's confidence and presence. Simon was slight of build, but he came across as being fierce and determined, a tough competitor.

"Who's at fault for Mary Foster's devastating injuries? Every single defendant is at fault. Since we have to start somewhere, let's start with the Maple Leaf Assisted Living Center which totally failed to provide a safe environment which it promised to do in its promotional materials. Do you remember those promotional materials? You will have them with you when you deliberate. I'm sure we each have our favorite quote from those materials. But here's my favorite. Quote. 'Our residents enjoy a safe and secure homelike environment so that their minds are at ease and their loved ones are secure in the knowledge that they are safe and sound.' Unquote. There was nothing safe or secure or even homelike about this facility. In a real sense, it was a house of horrors."

Carpenter jotted down the word horrors. He wanted to make sure that word remained in Simon's closing argument. Generally, he liked the use of a word that provided a jolt and had shock value.

"Maple Leaf Assisted Living Center staff knew about the wheelchair races that were going on weeks before Mary Foster was struck down. Did they do anything to stop this dangerous demolition derby?"

Carpenter counted off three beats.

"No, they didn't. They didn't do a damn thing even after Ruth Foster, Mary Foster's daughter, had complained about the wheelchair races in a written e-mail.

"I have a favor to ask each of you, ladies and gentlemen. When you retire to the jury room to deliberate, I want you to think of an elderly person you love. Perhaps that would be a mother or father. Perhaps that person would be a dear, close friend. I want you to picture this person finishing a meal at the Maple Leaf Assisted Living Center and leaving the dining room. I want you to picture your friend or parent being run down, trampled by a wheelchair driven by Harrison Blaine. I want you to see the person you love lying in a hallway in excruciating pain. And I want you to ask yourself what kind of outrage you would feel if that specific someone close to you was seriously injured in an environment that you were promised would keep your loved one safe and secure. I know my anger would be off the charts if what happened to Mary Foster happened to someone I loved. I know that I would want justice and compensation from the place that was paid nearly five thousand dollars a month to keep its residents safe. I know that I wouldn't rest until everyone responsible for my loved one's serious injuries was made to pay."

Simon paused. By an objective assessment, Carpenter knew that what Simon had just said could be considered over the top. But somehow, when Simon was making his pitch, the words struck just the right tone.

"The negligence of Maple Leaf Assisted Living Center couldn't be more clear. The Center largely did nothing and permitted a dangerous drag race to take place in a facility that catered to elderly people and that promised to keep residents safe.

"What about Harrison Blaine and his pal, Harry Fried? Here are two other individuals who didn't merely act negligently. They acted recklessly with no regard to the safety of others. They knew their behavior could harm someone else, and they went right ahead. Let's review together their outrageous conduct."

Carpenter realized that if he were making the closing argument in Mary Foster's case, his approach would be more low key than Simon's, his tone less biting. Perhaps it was Simon's slight build that permitted him to be constantly on the attack without appearing overbearing or over the top. Rachel would not be able to deliver the kind of closing argument Simon had presented. The wheelchair case required a forceful, no-holds-barred closing and Rachel likely wouldn't convey forcefully the outrage that Mary Foster's lawyer needed to present.

Now Simon was laying into the wheelchair racers, describing them as overage hot-rodders, who cared nothing for the safety of others as they created a menace by racing their wheelchairs. Listening to Simon, Carpenter believed that the jury would not be swayed to show Blaine and Fried leniency because of their age. Simon was painting the two men as elderly members of *The Wild Bunch.*

"How should Mary Foster be compensated for the injuries she received by the callous, indifferent, and egregious conduct of the defendants? We all know that she's entitled to compensation, but the real question is how much. Here are some things to consider. You've heard testimony that has given you a before and after look at Mary Foster. I'm talking about before and after she was run down by Harrison Blaine. Before she was viciously rammed, she was a vigorous woman who led an active life. She routinely visited with family and friends. She traveled. She doted on her grandchildren. All of those wonderful activities that she had earned the right to enjoy came to an end with the wheelchair assault on her. Now she is depressed, timid, unable to take care of herself. You've seen a film clip of her current life made by her daughter. Traveling and visiting friends and relatives are now out of the question. You saw for yourselves that Mary Foster can barely walk without assistance. You've also heard the costs of the medical care she will require as a result of the serious injuries caused her by the defendants.

"Each of these defendants needs to be taught a lesson and you are in a position to be the teacher. You are in a position to make them pay for what they did and pay a lot. Drag racing their wheelchairs was a big joke to Harrison Blaine and Harry Fried. Well, there's nothing funny about what happened to Mary Foster. Mr. Blaine and Mr. Fried should pay dearly for what they did to her. Maple Leaf Assisted Living Center should pay dearly for taking her money and doing nothing to keep her safe and ignoring the dangerous activities that were going on under the Center's roof in plain view of anyone with a pair of eyes. Each and every one of these defendants should pay for their role in injuring Mary Foster. The joys of her senior years have been taken from Mary Foster. What happened to her shouldn't happen to anybody. Make sure each of these defendants learns that lesson."

Carpenter found himself nodding in approval. There were times when he had appeared before a jury and felt somewhat the firebrand. But he doubted that he had ever conveyed Simon's intensity and passion. "Good," he said. When there was no dissenting opinion he added, "Let's do a recap and go over the closing argument from the beginning."

79

"Crystal Queen," Barney Freedman repeated to Philly over the phone. "That's a hell of a name. Where does she live?"

Philly provided the address furnished by Carpenter.

"Let me talk it over with Herb," Freedman said. "I'll have to get back to you."

Philly couldn't imagine the retired Cambridgeport cops actually breaking into Queen's apartment. But short of forced entry, she couldn't envision a way to learn whether Queen possessed a picture of Bernard Mucowahandi. "What are you thinking of doing?" she asked.

"You don't want to know."

"That seems to be a stock answer from you and your partner."

"What you don't know can't hurt you," Freedman retorted. Philly suspected that Freedman and Herb McCauley had loaded up on stock answers and trite sayings to deflect clients' questions.

"I'll take your word for that," Philly responded. "Thanks for agreeing to babysit the Georgia businessmen for the golf case coming up next month."

"My pleasure. I came to like those guys. Do you want us to do another asset check on Warren Lord?

"Let's wait until the trial starts."

"Fair enough."

"You guys do good work."

"We have our moments."

The Hays case continued to worry Rachel. Philly had assigned her the role of presenting the direct testimony, reserving for herself the role of cross-examining the defendants' witnesses. So in addition to presenting the opening argument, Rachel would present direct testimony from the Georgia businessmen, Hays, and Hays' wife who could speak to the damages her husband had suffered. Hays' treating physician was also her responsibility, and Philly had left her with the task of introducing into evidence Hays' medical records. Philly would take on the cross-examination of Warren Lord, the direct examination of Alan Atkinson, the cross-examination of any country club witness, and Philly would deliver Hays' closing argument.

Rachel eyed her trial notebook in the Hays' case. The three-ring binder was nearly full. While Philly was lead counsel and could be called upon to answer her questions, Rachel had come to learn that Philly's trial experience was not extensive. Compared to the years of litigation experience of Lord's counsel, Millicent Rudd, she and Philly were novices.

Josh had taken an interest in Hays' case. When he stayed at her place, she often found him studying her trial notebook. He'd scribble notes on yellow post-its and insert them on the margins of pages, his notes often augmented by arrows pointing out where his comments applied. So far most of his notes related to potential golf questions to ask the Georgia businessmen. But recently he had proposed questions to ask Hays about the loss of his eye. What had happened to Hays' depth perception? Was Hays able to drive at night with the same confidence as before his injury? Was Hays able to appreciate art at his pre-injury level? Did Hays now act more cautiously out of fear of losing his remaining eye?

Josh's interest in her work touched her. His videotaping of her opening argument was primarily responsible for her no longer living in fear of that moment. True, she remained nervous at the thought of standing in front of a jury. But when the moment came to speak to the jurors, she now knew that she'd deliver. She thought of the few guys she had dated before Josh. She'd never sensed that any of them were in her corner when truly needed. But she had no doubts about Josh in that regard. He would be there for her.

Rachel realized that she had begun to accept the fact that Josh might be one of those guys who would never have a settled career. She pictured him content to make money by giving golf and tennis lessons and playing on-line poker if that ever again became legal. If they became a permanent couple, he wouldn't care if he brought less money to their relationship than she did. She still hadn't come to terms with embracing a laid-back Josh with no white-collar professional career intentions, but she realized that she was inching toward accepting it.

First things first, Rachel thought. Her next task was editing the testimony outlines she had prepared for Hays and his wife. Then she needed to begin drafting requests for jury instructions. There was no shortage to the unpleasant tasks that Philly had dumped on her plate.

80

Simon sat at what he and Rachel still considered Philly's desk in her Boston office and put aside the discovery requests that had been filed on behalf of Roland Butler, the psychologist being sued by Keith and Jane Spring. Carpenter had assigned him the task of dealing with the discovery requests and for the moment, he couldn't summon up the energy to begin grinding out draft responses. Instead, for a diversion, he went on the Internet to find out whatever he could about The Honorable Terrence Murray, the judge who had granted Fay Richardson an injunction in the abortion billboard case. The judge had come down hard on the defendants and while Philly and Rachel wondered why, he doubted they'd do anything proactive to satisfy their curiosity. Simon figured he'd absorbed, by some kind of osmosis, Carpenter's desire to understand what motivated people to do what they did.

Simon discovered more Terence Murrays than he wanted to think about. It took some winnowing, but he located a newspaper announcement of Murray's appointment to the bench. There was a brief account of Murray's legal career and a concluding paragraph that identified his wife and children, two daughters and a son, one daughter married. The judge was a resident of the Town of Holden.

Simon launched searches of the judge's wife and children, sensing that he might better find the answer to his question from something in the judge's life as opposed to a case the judge had presided over. Fairly rapidly, his search efforts turned up a potentially useful news article. A Leeann Murray—the name of the judge's unmarried daughter—living with her parents in Holden, had obtained a restraining order against a former boyfriend who had been pressuring her to have an abortion. Simon printed a copy of the article and studied it. Leeann Murray's former boyfriend had confronted her in a supermarket. There had been shouting and pushing and the judge's daughter—assuming he had the right woman—had ended up on the floor. Police had been called to the scene and had placed the ex-boyfriend in custody, but Ms. Murray had declined to press criminal charges. She had, however, sought a restraining order after the ex-boyfriend next accosted her outside a Starbucks. The ex-boyfriend was ordered not to come within one thousand feet of Ms. Murray, and ordered not to contact her by telephone, e-mail, or any other means.

Simon thought of doing further research but decided against it. The Town of Holden connection convinced him that he had tracked down the cause of Judge Murray's adamant reaction in the Richardson case. It wasn't, perhaps, about abortion as much as about bullying. The judge must have come away from his daughter's experience determined to protect any woman being bullied in a relationship.

Simon scanned the news article and sent it to Philly and Rachel. Then he turned his attention back to the discovery requests in the Spring case. For some reason, they didn't appear as daunting now. Suck it up, he told himself, and set to work.

It was dark outside. Philly stared out the living room window thinking that when Halloween arrived, they had better get an early start so Daisy would be sure to see other kids in costume while there was still light. Then again, maybe the holiday would better register with Daisy if they began to trick or treat in darkness when flashlight beams danced through the darkness. Whenever they departed, would Daisy make any sense of the craziness of the holiday?

Raul was sitting on an easy chair in the living room standing Rosalind on his thighs. He gripped her under her shoulders, yet the baby wobbled as if on unsure footing. Raul was singing to his daughter softly in Spanish and the baby sported a wet, sloppy grin. Watching this tableau, Philly thought that Raul seemed more like the man she had dated years ago when around his daughter. For the moment, they had the living room to themselves.

"How's it going?" Philly asked.

Raul kept his eyes on his daughter. "I would say reasonably well."

Philly reflected that she was now closer to Isabella than Raul. She partly attributed the bond to motherhood but knew that their friendship went deeper than that common link. "How's your business going?"

"It is progressing slowly but in the right direction. We are cautious. We can afford to be very patient."

Philly thought of the mutual fund investment program that Raul had started her on. On balance, she was doing better than if she had put the money in a bank to earn negligible interest. "Maybe I should transfer my modest mutual fund to you guys."

Raul had resumed singing to Rosalind and stopped abruptly. This time he glanced in her direction. "That would not be wise. We have the house together. I would not like Connie and I to be responsible for any funds you may have."

Philly decided not to push the subject; Raul was probably right. "How about the four grownups going out to dinner together?" she broached. "I'm heading for a busy stretch but now would be a good time. Besides, we have a built-in babysitter."

Raul continued to grip Rosalind under her shoulders and raised her in the air, oblivious to the strands of drool descending on him. "Sure," he said without enthusiasm. "You and Isabella should decide on a date."

"Okay," Philly said.

Rosalind squealed with delight as Raul moved her about and Philly decided she'd had it with trying to draw Raul out with small talk.

"Philly," Raul said, as she was about to rise from her chair. "I want to say thank you."

"What for?"

Raul settled Rosalind in his lap and made a sweeping gesture that took in the living room. "This house," Raul said. "You were right. It is better for us all."

81

Philly was working from home. She had Barney Freedman on the phone and once he imparted his news, she made the call a conference call with Carpenter.

"Tell Mr. Carpenter what you just told me," Philly requested.

"I was doing some reconnoitering of the apartment building where Crystal Queen lives," Freedman said. "I saw your client walking out of the building."

Carpenter didn't say anything. Philly imagined him taken aback by Freedman's news. "Reconnoitering?" he finally said.

"It's the blandest word I could come up with," Freedman retorted.

"How do you know it was my client?"

"I looked him up on the Brandeis website. If I was going to look for a picture of him in Queen's apartment, I thought it might be helpful to know what he looked like."

Carpenter again fell silent. "Any luck with the picture?" he finally asked.

"No. You might want to forego that approach."

"All right," Carpenter said. "Bill us for your time."

"It's on the house," Freedman said. "I was bored and had nothing to do so I decided to check things out. I'll let you know if Herb and I come up with anything else."

When Freedman rang off, Carpenter stayed on the line. "I hope this is simply a case of a client behaving stupidly," he said.

"Are you thinking there's something going on with Bernard and this student?" Philly asked.

"I'm trying not to think about that."

"You need to confront Bernard."

"I'm not worried about that. That's a given. It's Connie I'm worried about. What am I going to tell her if her husband can't keep his dick in his pants?"

Philly had no answer to that question.

"I want to make one last effort to try to settle this case," Millicent Rudd said.

Philly put her phone down on her desk and pressed the SPEAKER button so that she could write more easily. "I'm listening."

"Even though you continue to refuse to present a demand damage figure on behalf of Mr. Hays, I'm authorized to settle this matter for five hundred thousand dollars."

Philly jotted the figure down on her notepad and underlined it twice. The number wasn't evenly divisible by three but she quickly did a one-third division just the same and divided that quotient by four. "I'll present that to my client," Philly said. "Your efforts to try to settle the case are appreciated," she added. There was no reason not to be cordial to Rudd.

"Will you recommend the offer?"

Martin Hays might decide to accept Rudd's offer. Carpenter was inclined to roll the dice before a jury; he envisioned a seven-figure jury award if they lucked out. Philly was ambivalent. She recalled Rachel's trial run of Hays' opening argument to the jury and found herself leaning toward Carpenter's view.

"I don't know," she opted for honesty. "It's a substantial offer and, as I said, it's appreciated. I need to think about it."

"How soon will you be able to get back to me?"

"Quickly unless my client wishes a face-to-face meeting."

"Fair enough."

Philly turned off her speaker feature and contemplated next steps. She would e-mail Hays the terms of the proposed settlement and suggest a conference call with Carpenter. Baby steps, she thought. There was no point in getting ahead of herself.

"What were you doing at Crystal Queen's apartment building?" Carpenter confronted Bernard as soon as his client got on the line.

Bernard didn't respond straightaway. "What are you talking about?" he said after a long pause.

"You know goddamn well what I'm talking about."

"Why are you asking me such a question?"

"Because someone saw you leaving her apartment building and let me know about it."

"Who is this person?"

"That's none of your business. I asked you a question. What the hell were you doing there?"

Bernard didn't say anything, and Carpenter decided to wait him out, keeping the Connie threat card in reserve.

"I was trying to convince her to drop her complaint," Bernard said grudgingly.

"Shit!" Carpenter muttered. "That was beyond dumb, Bernard. You should have stayed clear of her. She's going to use your visit against you."

"I can always deny that I visited her."

"Christ! What are you trying to do, make things worse? Did you mention the photograph to her?"

There was a long pause before Bernard said, "Yes," in a small voice.

"I guess we can eliminate the element of surprise," Carpenter said. "I wanted to spring that on her when she wasn't expecting it. Now she'll be prepared for the question and the photograph will have disappeared."

Bernard remained silent and Carpenter thought through options. "What did she say to your request to drop her complaint?"

"She said no."

Great, Carpenter thought. "What else happened when you met with her?"

"Nothing," Bernard said. "It was a very short meeting, maybe five minutes at the most."

"If you want me to continue to represent you, don't ever pull a stunt like this again. Are we clear?"

"Yes. What are you going to do?"

"Damage control," Carpenter said. "I'm going to think about damage control."

82

"It's a lot of money," Martin Hays said dispiritedly.

"Yeah, it is," Carpenter said on their three-way call. "It's certainly your prerogative to accept the offer. But I'm going to recommend that you reject it and that we go to trial."

"But you said once I could lose at trial."

"I did say that," Carpenter affirmed. "I said it because any time you go to trial, losing is a possibility. But in your case, I don't believe it's a realistic possibility."

"Still . . ." Hays left his thought unfinished.

"If a jury finds in your favor," Carpenter said, "I think your award is going to be over a million dollars. Lord tried to harm you. I think a jury is going to make him pay."

Hays didn't respond. Philly thought about the $500,000 offer on the table. Carpenter was convinced that Lord was paying the lion's share because the insurance company could deny coverage since Lord had committed an intentional assault and battery. If settlement failed, Carpenter also believed that Millicent Rudd would try the case, but that Lord's insurer was only paying for part of the defense costs.

"I'm not trying to make life difficult for you," Carpenter said. "If you were in tough financial straits and needed immediate cash, that would be a reason to accept the offer and move on. It's my opinion that if you accept the offer, you'd be leaving money on the table. Ultimately it's your decision."

"I hate this," Hays said despondently. "You'd think I should be happy about having to decide whether to accept over three hundred thousand dollars, but I'm not."

"Maybe you should take some time and think it over," Philly said.

"What does Ms. Boyle think?" Hays asked.

"Frankly we haven't discussed the settlement offer with her," Carpenter said. "She's a junior lawyer and Ms. Piper and I typically deal with settlement offers."

"I'd be interested in what she has to say," Hays persisted.

Carpenter didn't say anything. Philly imagined him fuming; he wouldn't take kindly to anyone but the two of them counseling a client on a settlement proposal. But then Carpenter surprised her.

"Let's find out what she has to say. She's in the office. I'll get her and put you on a speaker phone over here on my end."

There was a long pause before Carpenter rejoined the call. "Ms. Boyle is now with me," he announced.

Carpenter went over Lord's settlement offer and his advice to Hays. Rachel didn't immediately respond when Carpenter told her that Hays wanted her opinion.

"Hi, Mr. Hays," Rachel began. "You need to know that I'm inexperienced when it comes to evaluating settlement offers in a case of this kind. But that said, if the money isn't crucial to you at this time, I would hold out and go for trial. I think what Lord did to you is outrageous. Every time I think about what you've been through, I get very angry. I could be wrong, but I think a jury is going to be angry as well."

Philly wondered whether Carpenter had tried to influence Rachel's input. She didn't think so.

"Okay," Hays said. "Tell them no."

83

It was a cool night and the goblins and witches and ballerinas and skeletons were out in force. Daisy was giddy as if the energy of costumed kids in motion had rubbed off on her. She was carrying a small paper bag with handles that she was constantly dropping. Philly had spent more time than she wanted to think about on Daisy's costume. Daisy was a pint-sized biker chick wearing a small black leather jacket and black leather pants, a soft felt blue cap mounted at an angle over her flyaway hair, a fake lightning bolt tattoo on each cheek. Philly had found baby black boots at a thrift store to round out the ensemble.

The bottoms of the boots were smooth in places and Daisy had already slipped and fallen several times.

Philly was grateful the holiday was going on as scheduled. An unexpected heavy wet snow had descended on New England, weighting down leafed tree limbs and causing them to snap. In some towns, Halloween had been postponed until debris was removed and downed power lines restrung. In Brighton, their lights flickered twice during the worst of the storm but, unlike many communities in New England, they had never lost power. Philly couldn't remember a Halloween when winter had intruded with snow.

The neighborhood they had chosen to trick or treat in had a lot of foot traffic. Paul had enlisted Jenny to help with Daisy and the older girl, dressed as a witch, didn't seem to mind the responsibility, sometimes carrying Daisy up the front steps of neighborhood houses. Jenny's presence permitted Philly and Paul to watch from the street whenever the witch and biker chick approached a house.

"I'm loving this," Philly said.

"You were a biker chick, right?" Paul asked.

"More or less. I was into black and a Goth look and spiky hair. I never turned down a motorcycle ride. Maybe that qualifies me as a biker chick."

"I'd say so. I don't remember any costume I wore as a kid. I just remember there coming a time when I realized I was too old to go out on Halloween."

"My folks used to say that back when they were kids, they went out alone. Parents weren't around."

"Those days are over," Paul said. "Being on duty tonight is hell. You wouldn't believe the weird calls a police department gets tonight."

Jenny helped Daisy open her bag and a middle-aged woman dropped something inside. Daisy peered into the open bag, but Philly couldn't tell whether she saw anything she liked.

"How come Jenny came over here tonight? I figured she'd want to be with her friends."

Paul shrugged. "I probably had something to do with her coming over. I made a few comments about how Daisy needed someone to show her the ropes. I didn't have to put on a hard sell."

"Your daughter's sweet," Philly said as she nodded her okay when Jenny gestured to the next house on the street.

"You were saying the next two months are going to be tough for you. What's going on?"

Philly realized that for a brief moment she had put her upcoming trials out of sight, out of mind. "I've got two trials coming up in the next two months. There's a lot of pressure to win. They're contingency cases and how we do is going to make or break our year financially. In terms of cash, it's been a slow year."

"If you ever need any money . . ."

"No, it's not that," Philly said. "I've got a lot of Philip's money left. It's just that it's been a struggle to generate billable hour work."

"Just let me know what I can do to help."

Daisy again peered inside her bag of treats. Philly thought back to the case that had gone to trial when she was early on in her pregnancy with Daisy. Even while pregnant she had been able to devote unlimited hours to the court case. Family responsibilities and drains on her time first started when Daisy was born. For her upcoming trial, she realized that she *was* going to need help.

"Since you asked, I'm going to look to you for a lot of help with Daisy," Philly said.

"That will be a pleasure."

"Plus, you may need to give me a wide berth when I get cranky."

"You? Cranky?"

"And I expect to be serviced immediately if the mood suddenly strikes me."

"As you know, service is my middle name."

"Then we're all set," Philly declared.

November

Philly's Untitled Playlist

Rolling in the Deep

Adele

84

Beatrice Gold was young and displayed the energy that accompanied youth. The Brandeis lawyer assigned to conduct an investigation of Crystal Queen's complaint against Bernard Mucowahandi had offered a vigorous handshake to each person in attendance, and then had taken the seat at the head of a long rectangular table. Six inches of file folders were stacked on the table in front of her chair and Carpenter couldn't imagine their contents. His file on Bernard's case was at best half an inch thick. What the hell had Gold dug up? Gold had long, straight black hair, a strong chin and full lips. She might qualify as beautiful. There was no doubt that Crystal Queen met any objective standard of beauty. Carpenter had studied pictures of Connie in her younger days; back then Connie was a knockout. But Queen had something intangible working for her, a kind of hidden, sensual sultriness that seemed ready to explode. Carpenter tried to stop staring at the tall, stately, young woman. He wondered whether Bernard's defense was off base. Why would Queen have a crush on someone like Bernard?

"Good morning, everyone," Gold began. "I've been assigned to do a preliminary investigation of Ms. Queen's complaint against Mr. Mucowahandi. My approach in cases of this nature is to bring together everyone with information and to ask questions with all present. I will not permit anyone else to ask questions. However, anyone may request me to ask a question of anyone else."

Carpenter disliked any process that didn't include the right to cross-examine, but he held his peace. Gold was going to run the proceedings as she saw fit.

"Mr. Mucowahandi is represented by Mr. Carpenter and Mr. Jeffries. Ms. Queen is present without counsel. Two students are present, Dwayne Morrison and Monica Little. Ms. Queen, you may make an opening statement if you desire and the same applies to Mr. Mucowahandi's counsel."

Crystal Queen shook her head and Carpenter did the same.

"I propose to start with Mr. Morrison and Ms. Little. I understand they are here at Mr. Mucowahandi's request. What would you like me to ask them, Mr. Carpenter?"

"I'll be addressing the students' testimony," Simon said. "Please ask them what they observed on the evening in question. I'm interested in their recounting the timing of events as well as what Ms. Queen was wearing."

Gold made a note on her notepad. "Why don't you start, Mr. Morrison?"

Morrison and Little recounted the stories they had related to Simon.

"What do you want me to focus on, Mr. Jeffries?" Gold inquired.

"Ms. Queen spent five minutes in the bedroom before her encounter with Mr. Mucowahandi. She did not use the bathroom. She was alone. Her attire was identical when she walked past the living room to the bedroom, and when she headed for the door after leaving the bedroom. This means that she didn't use the bedroom for its purpose, namely a place to deposit outerwear. The question becomes, what was Ms. Queen doing in the bedroom all that time?"

Gold wrote for a while and when she looked up, she focused on Queen. "Do you wish to answer that question, Ms. Queen?"

"I don't believe I was in the bedroom for five minutes. I doubt I was even there a minute. I considered placing a blazer I was wearing on the bed, but I decided not to. I didn't want to feel chilly."

"Ask her whether she handled any item in the bedroom?" Simon requested.

"Why don't you answer that question?" Gold said.

"I don't believe so," Queen replied. "I might have touched something, but I don't think so."

"Please ask Ms. Queen whether she removed any object from the bedroom."

"What do you say to that, Ms. Queen?"

"No."

"Do you wish me to ask Mr. Morrison or Ms. Little any questions?" Gold directed at Queen.

"Where do they get off to say I had a crush on him?" Queen said with some heat as she pointed at Bernard.

"Do either of you wish to respond?" Gold asked the students.

"You just had to look at her," Little said. "The only time she made eye contact during the seminars she attended was when she was making goo-goo eyes at Mr. Mucowahandi. If you ask me, she was ready to jump his bones in front of everyone."

"Goo-goo eyes," Gold repeated. "I haven't heard that expression in a while."

"We're not the only ones that felt that way," Morrison offered. "You can ask anyone else in the class. It was so obvious, we used to joke about it. She was coming on to him."

"Get serious," Queen responded. "Look at him. He's old."

Bernard didn't seem fazed by Queen's reference to his age. At that moment, the door to the conference room opened and Connie entered. Queen turned around, stared at Connie briefly, then pivoted so that she was again looking forward. Bernard had stated that on those nights when seminars took place in their apartment, Connie left the apartment early so as not to be around when the session started. But Carpenter was certain that Queen had recognized Connie. Unless there was a picture of Connie in the apartment or unless Queen had removed a picture of Connie from the apartment, this morning should have been the first time Queen had laid eyes on her.

"Is there anything else anyone wishes me to ask Mr. Morrison and Ms. Little? No? Then I want to thank you both for attending and you are excused."

When the door to the conference room closed behind Morrison and Little, Gold consulted her notepad. "Why don't we hear from you, Mr. Mucowahandi? Is there anything you wish to say?"

"Thank you," Bernard said affably. "I would like to tell my side of the story if I may."

Gold nodded and Bernard in a matter-of-fact manner recounted the events of the night in question. Carpenter had prepared a list of the items he wanted Bernard to cover and he checked off each one.

"Did you think that Ms. Queen had a crush on you?" Gold asked when Bernard had concluded his account.

"I had no sense of that one way or the other."

"Why did you enter the bedroom?" Gold followed up.

"I do not recall exactly whether I actually made it inside the bedroom. I wanted to glance inside the bedroom to make sure the room was in order and that the students had used the bed for their garments. But when I bumped into Miss Queen, I cannot recall if I actually entered the room."

"Is there anything you wish me to ask Mr. Mucowahandi?" Gold turned to Queen.

"Ask him why he came to my apartment a few days ago," Queen demanded.

Connie was sitting in the rear of the conference room. Her startled expression immediately gave way to a hard stare directed at her husband.

"Please answer that question," Gold said.

"My lawyer has informed me that in this country it was not appropriate for me to try to meet with Miss Queen," Bernard said in a tone that struck Carpenter if not defiant, at least unrepentant. "In my homeland, it is different. We make an effort to talk things out. I sincerely wanted to know why Miss Queen was making her charges against me."

"Why don't you provide some more details as to how you came to visit her?" Gold requested.

"I looked up her address in student records and went to her apartment."

"Did you use a buzzer system to announce yourself?"

"No, I did not. Someone was leaving the building as I looked at the names and apartment numbers listed outside the front door. I simply went inside while the door was open. I located Miss Queen's apartment number on a list in the entryway and took the elevator to her floor. I rang her bell. She opened the door and looked surprised to see me. I asked if I could come in and she nodded and stepped aside. Then she moved further along the hallway. She did not ask me to sit down. I remained by the door and asked her why she was making up the charges against me."

Carpenter noticed that Queen was regarding Bernard with anything but goo-goo eyes.

"Miss Queen said that she was telling the truth. I told her that she knew that she was not telling the truth, but she refused to admit that. I asked her if she thought we could work out our differences if we talked further and she said no. So I left."

"How long were you in her apartment?" Gold asked.

"A few minutes or so."

"Is there anything else you wish me to ask?"

Queen shook her head.

"Very well, Ms. Queen, why don't you now give us your version of what happened the night of the seminar.

Carpenter took notes and observed that Simon was doing the same. Queen's account tracked her letter sent to college authorities.

"Are there any questions you wish me to address to Ms. Queen?" Gold asked.

Carpenter caught Connie's eye. "Ask her whether before today she has ever seen the woman seated at the rear of the room or a picture of the woman."

"The answer is no to both questions," Queen preempted.

"Then ask her why it was clear she recognized the woman when she entered this room."

"I didn't recognize her! What's he talking about?"

"You need to wait for me to ask you the questions," Gold interjected.

"What is he, some kind of mind reader?"

"Please, Ms. Queen. You need to calm down and let me decide what questions to ask you."

Carpenter thought Queen looked even more beautiful when irate. Her eyes flashed. She reminded him of a pissed off princess with her sharp, prominent cheekbones and her hair done up in intricately twirled braids.

"Anything else for Ms. Queen, Mr. Carpenter?"

"Ask her why she took Mr. Mucowahandi's seminar?"

"Why did you?" Gold asked.

"It sounded interesting."

"Was it interesting?" Gold followed up.

"Pretty much."

"When Mr. Mucowahandi responded to your complaint, he noted that you seldom participated in class discussions. Why was that?"

Queen shrugged. "I don't believe in talking unless I have something to say. Some students like to hear the sound of their own voice."

"Did you write any paper for the seminar?" Gold asked.

"I had a topic, but I never wrote the paper. I left the seminar because he came after me that night."

"What was the topic?"

Queen hesitated a few beats. "The topic was to contrast rape as a terror tactic in the Rwandan massacre and in the Unites States civil war."

"Did you choose that topic?"

Queen nodded. "It was on a list of suggested topics that was in the course description."

Carpenter couldn't figure out where Gold was going with her recent questions. Still he made notes and resolved to take up the topic with Bernard after the hearing.

"Does anybody have anything else to add?"

Carpenter gestured toward Connie. "Mr. Mucowahandi's wife joined us after we began. She has something to contribute to this matter."

"Very well," Gold said. "Why don't you take a chair closer to the rest of us."

Connie advanced to where the group was sitting, and Carpenter was not surprised when the seat she took was directly across from Queen. During their relationship, there were times when Carpenter found Connie's emotions difficult to read. At the moment, her anger was crystal clear.

"Please tell us your full name and what you wish to add," Gold instructed.

Connie introduced herself and, in a clipped tone, described her discovery that the bedside table photograph of her and Bernard turned up missing after the seminar when Queen claimed she had been assaulted.

"How do you know the photograph hadn't gone missing before the seminar?" Gold asked.

"I know it was there before the seminar. I like a clean apartment and I do the cleaning myself. I know I dusted the bedside tables the weekend before the seminar and I would have noticed if it was missing. We didn't have any visitors after that cleaning until the seminar."

Gold wrote on her notepad. She then looked up and studied the two parties to the case. Carpenter couldn't tell from her expression what, if any, tentative conclusions she had reached.

"I can't think of anything else to add," Gold said. "I want to thank all of you for coming and for your cooperation. I will write up a report that likely will contain recommendations as to further proceedings. Feel free to email me in the next two weeks if you think of anything else you wish me to consider. Be advised that I may share your email with the other party. We are adjourned."

Queen was out the door before Gold.

"You went to see her," Connie snapped at Bernard when their party was alone.

"I wanted to try to put an end to this. It is very unpleasant."

"What the hell were you thinking? You've engaged Carpenter to help you. He can't help you if you go off on your own without consulting him."

"You are right," Bernard said in a chastened tone. "Mr. Carpenter has pointed out the error of my ways. Perhaps I wasn't thinking correctly. In Rwanda, this kind of misunderstanding would not be carried to such lengths and would have been resolved by discussion."

"I don't want to know how this would be handled in Rwanda," Connie fired back. "You're not in Rwanda, for God's sake."

"What do you make of Gold's questions about the seminar?" Carpenter changed the subject.

Bernard gave an ambiguous shrug. "I do not know why she asked about the course."

"Maybe your accuser was the subject of a sexual assault," Simon offered. "Maybe that explains her choice of seminar topic."

"What does that have to do with anything?" Connie asked.

"I'm not sure," Simon admitted. "We still don't know why Queen is making false charges against your husband. Maybe something happened in her life that led her to accuse Mr. Mucowahandi in knee-jerk fashion when he encountered her unexpectedly at the door to the bedroom."

Simon was voicing a theory that had been raised earlier. Carpenter wasn't sure whether anything said today supported the theory. "Let's call it a day," he suggested.

85

Carpenter introduced himself to Barney Freedman, recognizing the retired cop from Philly's description. They were standing outside the Middlesex Superior Court courtroom where Martin Hays' trial would be held, waiting for the clerk to open the doors. Freedman was a huge guy who looked reasonably fit for someone hauling around a large frame with considerable meat on it. Carpenter figured the two guys with him were the Georgia witnesses, two young suits with athletic builds and no hair out of place. He motioned Freedman aside.

"I'd like you to find out when you can about that woman whose apartment you went to check out."

"Crystal Queen," Freedman said. "I'm not likely to forget that name. Is this urgent?"

"Yeah, it is. I need to get any information you come up with to a hearing officer ASAP."

Freedman produced a cell phone. "I'll get my partner on it. I've got to hang around here and babysit these guys from Georgia until they testify."

Carpenter nodded and Freedman moved out of earshot to place his call.

Judge Marcus Lofton surprised Carpenter. The African American jurist had a jury impaneled before the afternoon recess—seven men and seven women. Two of the group would be designated alternates while the remaining twelve deliberated. The panel consisted of a diverse group in terms of age, jobs, and ethnicity. Whether any of the fourteen played golf or knew anything about the game was anyone's guess since the judge declined to question jurors on the subject. The judge had decided to limit the afternoon's session to opening arguments. Testimony would start first thing tomorrow morning.

Rachel now stood before the jury. Carpenter experienced the same trepidation he had felt when Philly addressed a jury for the first time. He remembered relaxing immediately once Philly had squared her shoulders and gotten her name out, and he silently prayed for a similar release of tension now.

"Good afternoon, ladies and gentlemen. My name is Rachel Boyle and along with Philomena Piper I represent the plaintiff in this case, Martin Hays. I'm going to ask Mr. Hays to stand so that you can associate a face with his name. Mr. Hays!"

Hays stood, nodded in the jury's direction, and then resumed his seat. Carpenter's pulse slowed and in a matter of moments he was caught up in Rachel's account. Rachel's down-to-earth sincerity was registering with the jury. The panel regarded her intently throughout her opening argument. When she smacked a closed fist into an open hand after describing Hays going down as if shot when hit by Warren Lord's tee drive, several jurors winced.

Millicent Rudd was a veteran defense attorney who presented as more businesslike than Rachel. Carpenter had never tried against Rudd but knew she had a reputation as a tough litigator.

"There is no question that Mr. Hays' injury was serious and unfortunate," Rudd got down to business after opening pleasantries. "But there is also no question that the injury was an accident and had nothing to do with anyone's negligence. It is not uncommon for someone to be struck by a golf shot that has been mishit. It's not just golfers who have been struck by golf balls that have flown off course. Spectators have also been injured and this happens at professional tournaments where the golfers are more skilled and accurate than any golfer involved in this case."

Carpenter gave opposing counsel her due; the jury was following her account with the same intensity as it had listened to Rachel.

"You will hear from Mr. Lord. He will tell you that he has played the golf course at the Mayfair Country Club many times as a member of the club. He knows that course well and it is true that the seventh hole is the longest hole on the golf course. Which is why, Mr. Lord will tell you, he chose a driver to hit his tee shot from the seventh tee, not an iron as has been suggested to you by plaintiff's counsel.

"The plaintiff, Mr. Hays, flubbed his shot off the seventh tee. There is no dispute about that. Mr. Hays went off searching for his ball and was lost to view from the seventh tee. Mr. Lord and his playing partner, Mr. Alan Atkinson, will tell you that they didn't see Mr. Hays emerge from the concealed area he had been searching. They will also tell you that it appeared to them that Mr. Hays' group could be seen far off in the distance. You will hear from Mr. Lord and from Mr. Atkinson, that when a foursome is playing, the foursome stays together during play. You will hear that this is basic golf etiquette and basic golf practice. Neither Mr. Lord nor Mr. Atkinson if playing in a foursome would have moved off into the distance if one of their group hadn't completed his play. They will tell you that when they saw Mr. Hays' companions off in the distance, they assumed that Mr. Hays' entire foursome had moved on together."

Carpenter couldn't remember Rudd's point about golfing etiquette being discussed by Philly or Rachel. Did that mean they hadn't thought of it?

"What you will hear is that Mr. Hays' playing partners bear responsibility for Mr. Hays' injuries by not staying with him and instead moving on."

Carpenter remembered that Hays' playing partners had been listed as witnesses for Hays. But he couldn't remember whether the playing partners had even been interviewed. He glanced at Philly and Rachel. If Rudd had just made a telling point, you couldn't tell that fact from their expressions.

"You are going to hear conflicting testimony in this case," Rudd continued. "The plaintiff's counsel has described to you the testimony she hopes to elicit from the playing partners of Mr. Lord and Mr. Atkinson, two Georgia businessmen. Mr. Lord and Mr. Atkinson will dispute the testimony from these out-of-towners if they testify as plaintiff's counsel indicated. As you assess the credibility of these Georgia businessmen, you might want to ask yourselves a very basic question: if you saw someone intentionally direct a golf shot at another golfer injuring that other golfer, would you report what you had seen? Would you have alerted authorities to the fact that a golfer tried to intentionally injure another golfer and succeeded? Of course you would. But the Georgia businessmen never reported anything to anybody in connection with what happened on the golf course. That is because nothing untoward happened on the golf course expect an unfortunate accident. We can speculate on why two out-of-town businessmen would now come forward with a story for the first time. But let the testimony be your guide to avoid speculation. This may very well be a case of two southern businessmen feeling resentful that they had journeyed to Boston for a business proposition that never bore fruit."

Carpenter's attention wandered as Rudd hammered away at her central theme that accidents happen that are no one's legal fault. He wondered whether he had been too hasty in urging Martin Hays to proceed to trial. The case was likely to turn on whether the jury believed the two Georgians. Rudd had done her best to paint them as outsiders, constantly referring to them as foreign businessmen and out-of-towners. With their southern accents, they were going to fit the image Rudd had painted. But if they stuck to their story and came across as believable, Hays had a chance to score big.

Carpenter fretted. Here he was again involved in a case that might turn into a crapshoot. He had confidence in Philly and Rachel but couldn't shake the nagging thought that things might now be different if he had been involved in the case from day one.

After the judge had adjourned court for the day, Philly and Rachel stayed in the courtroom because Carpenter had slipped Rachel a note that he wanted a word. Philly was impatient to leave. She and Rachel had work to do this evening.

Carpenter approached all business. "As far as I can tell," he said, "Rudd made two points that you're going to have to deal with. The first had to do with foursomes staying together. The second had to do with the Georgia witnesses not previously reporting what had happened."

Philly didn't like the feeling that Carpenter was second-guessing their readiness. She took a deep breath and reminded herself that she had asked Carpenter to sit in during this trial because she wanted his experience in the courtroom.

"One of Hays' playing partners will confirm what Hays is going to say. Hays told the rest of his foursome to go on ahead while he searched for his ball. Hays was angry at himself for hitting a lousy shot. The playing partner will also testify that it is not uncommon for members of a foursome to move ahead while one of the group searches for his ball."

Carpenter's jaw muscles worked as he assessed her response to his question.

"It's true that the Georgia witnesses didn't report the incident," Rachel said. "They'll admit that. At the time they thought the matter would be investigated and they weren't needed. They were in a bit of shock over what happened. Plus, they were available to answer questions as to what happened. When they got to the country club they signed in and wrote down their contact information."

Carpenter again said nothing. Philly evaluated the responses to the points Rudd had made. The responses were not overwhelming, but they were the truth. Wasn't it the geezer who was repeatedly saying that you had to play the hand you were dealt?

"Okay," Carpenter finally said. "Make sure you prep these witnesses for what Rudd is going to ask them."

"We'll be having dinner with the guys from Georgia and we'll make sure they're ready for Rudd's questions," Philly said.

"Good," Carpenter said. "You leading off with them?"

"That's the plan," Philly said.

86

Ryan Cannon's direct testimony tracked his affidavit. Rachel had opted for largely open-ended questions and Cannon provided useful embellishments to his answers. Carpenter believed that the first witness from Georgia had come across as credible. Now Rudd stood facing Cannon, and Carpenter said a silent prayer that the Georgian's credibility would remain intact.

"Did you ever give an account of what you claimed happened on the golf course to any Massachusetts official?" Rudd commenced.

"No."

"Did you report what you claim you observed to any Massachusetts law enforcement official?"

"No."

"Did you leave your name and contact information with anyone who came on the scene after Mr. Hays was struck?"

"Not right then. There was a heck of a lot of commotion and people trying to get Mr. Hays onto a stretcher. But I had already left my name before he was struck. When I signed in as a guest of Mr. Lord and Mr. Atkinson, I wrote down my name and address on the signup sheet they had. I can't remember if I put my phone number down, but I'm sure I put my e-mail address down. The information I provided should be at the country club. I would have been pleased to talk to anyone who reached out to me, but no one did."

Carpenter suppressed a smile. No doubt Rudd had gotten more of an answer than she had wanted. Cannon had been well prepped. Good for Rachel

"So you saw no reason to reach out to authorities, correct?" Rudd asked.

"I didn't think about reaching out to authorities one way or the other," Cannon replied. "To be blunt about it, I couldn't wait to get off the course and go home. Like I said before, Jake and I told Lord and Atkinson that we wouldn't continue playing. We ended up going to look at the property they wanted to show us more as a courtesy than anything else. As I explained, after what Mr. Lord had done, Jake and I knew we'd never do business with them. When the property tour ended, Jake and I flew back to Atlanta."

"In Georgia, is it the custom for foursomes to stick together until all members of the foursome complete a hole?" Rudd changed the subject.

"Yes and no. Do you want me to explain?"

"Did you and Mr. Mobley and Mr. Lord and Mr. Atkinson stick together on the day in question until each of you had completed the hole you were playing?"

"Yes, I believe we did."

"Isn't it true that Mr. Lord used a driver off the seventh tee?"

"No, not based on what I saw. I was less than ten feet away from the man. He used an iron, a five iron."

"Did you question his choice of clubs before he hit his seventh hole tee shot?"

"No, I was too shocked to say anything."

"So, for example, did you call out to Mr. Lord to inquire why he wasn't using a driver on the longest hole on the course?"

"No."

"You knew the seventh hole was the longest hole on the course, didn't you?"

"I did. The yardage was on the scorecard."

"Thank you, Mr. Cannon. That's helpful. How come you didn't want to be helpful to your playing partner and advise him he was using the wrong club on the seventh tee?"

"I'll repeat what I said to you. I guess I was too shocked by Lord saying he was going to teach Mr. Hays a lesson. I froze. I'm not proud of that, but that's what happened."

"Does that mean that you didn't call out to Mr. Hays to warn him of anything?"

"That's what it means. I didn't call out. I wish I had. As I said before, I lost sight of the ball."

"Isn't it true that there was nothing to call out to Mr. Hays because Mr. Lord in fact used a driver off the seventh tee and his shot simply went awry?"

"I'd feel a lot better about not calling out if that were the case, but it was not the case. Lord took aim at Mr. Hays with an iron and struck him."

"No further questions," Rudd said as she took her seat.

"One question," Rachel said. "You answered 'yes and no' when Ms. Rudd asked you whether it was common practice in Georgia for all parties to a foursome to complete a hole before moving on. When you offered to explain your answer, Ms. Rudd didn't take you up on your offer. Would you please explain your answer now for the jury?"

"Certainly," Cannon said, and he turned in the witness chair to face the jury. "Ideally, in Georgia, foursomes try to move on as a group. But what sometimes happens is someone in the foursome hits a ball out of bounds. The golfer who hit the ball out of bounds will often tell his playing partners to move ahead and he'll catch up after he finds his ball. I've done that countless times. It's a common courtesy you extend to your playing partners."

"No further questions," Rachel said.

Millicent Rudd had been hammering away at Jake Mobley for about fifteen minutes. As far as Carpenter could tell, she had made little headway in undermining his direct testimony.

"You say you tracked Mr. Lord's seventh hole tee shot, saw it heading for Mr. Hays, and did nothing to alert Mr. Hays? Is that your testimony?" Rudd said with incredulity she didn't bother to conceal.

"That's my testimony," Mobley confirmed.

"Isn't it true that you didn't call out to Mr. Hays because you didn't in fact see him or a golf ball headed his way?"

"No, that's not true. It all happened so quickly that I froze and I'm not proud of that."

"Did you believe that the foursome preceding your foursome was off in the distance when Mr. Lord hit his ball from the seventh tee?"

Mobley paused. "I may have been under that impression for a time, but I'm not sure. I became aware of Mr. Hays when Mr. Lord and Mr. Atkinson began talking about him. Until that happened, I don't believe I was aware of any golfer near our group. Like I said, I tracked the ball and saw it heading for Mr. Hays. You couldn't miss him. He was wearing a yellow shell."

Rudd established that Mobley didn't report anything he observed at the seventh hole to any government official. It was time for Rudd to stop, Carpenter thought, and she did.

Martin Hays struck Carpenter as nervous as he answered Rachel's initial questions. But in no time, Rachel established a rhythm with her direct testimony questions, and Hays became at ease. Philly's tactical decision to have Rachel conduct Hays' direct examination had been correct. Hays had bonded with Rachel, felt comfortable with her.

When it came to Hays' account of how he was living with the loss of his eye, he paused often, plainly uncomfortable describing his limitations. Rachel let Hays' silences lengthen until he was ready to resume his testimony. Then she gently prompted Hays to talk about all the things that had changed, become harder to do, or less satisfying. To Carpenter, the jurors looked largely sympathetic.

"I'd say the loss of my eye has made me more tentative," Hays concluded his testimony on damages. "It's taken some getting used to."

Rudd went on the attack immediately. "Isn't it true, Mr. Hays, that when you wandered off to look for the ball you had hit off the seventh tee, you were no longer visible from the seventh tee?"

Hays pondered Rudd's initial question with a serious expression. "I think you're right that while I was looking around in the rough and trees, I don't think you could see me from the seventh tee. But . . ."

"You've answered the question," Rudd interceded.

"I'm going to allow the witness to finish his answer," Judge Lofton ruled even before Philly could nudge Rachel to object.

"I was going to say," Hays continued, "that until I emerged from the trees, I probably wasn't visible from the seventh tee. But I *could* be seen from the seventh tee at the spot where I was hit."

"When you went to look for your ball, did you leave your golf bag by the side of the fairway?"

"No. I carried it with me."

"If you'd left it by the side of the fairway, wouldn't that have alerted the foursome behind you that you hadn't moved on with your playing partners?"

"Possibly."

"Is it correct that you claim that the foursome behind you was urging your group to speed up its play?"

"Yes, that's what I said before."

"When you emerged from the trees, did you have occasion to look toward the seventh tee?"

"I don't think I looked at the seventh tee."

"You testified that you asked the other three players in your foursome to move on while you looked for your ball, correct?"

"Correct."

"You told us that the foursome playing behind you wanted your group to speed up play. Weren't you concerned that they would think you had moved on with your golfing partners and might elect to tee off?"

"I really didn't think about that, so I guess I wasn't concerned," Hays acknowledged.

"You really didn't think about that," Rudd repeated. "Did you ever call out to the players on the seventh tee to let them know you were still on the course?"

"No."

"Did you give any consideration to the fact that your search for your ball would further irritate the foursome behind you because it would further delay their play?"

"I guess I didn't think about that either," Hays said.

"You didn't think about that," Rudd repeated.

"Have you ever been frustrated playing behind slow players who wouldn't let you play through?"

"I can think of a few times that's happened," Hays allowed.

"It can be frustrating to be behind players who are moving at a snail's pace, would you agree?"

"I would agree."

"When you claim that the foursome behind you urged your foursome to speed up its play, did you or your playing partners ever respond to those requests to play more quickly?"

"No."

"Would it be correct to say that you and your playing partners ignored the requests to pick up your pace?"

"I wouldn't say ignored. We just didn't respond directly to them."

"Is that proper golf etiquette to not respond to a request to play faster?"

"I don't know."

"Are you saying that you don't know about proper golf etiquette?"

"No. I'm saying that I don't know what the etiquette is in terms of responding to a request to play faster."

"Putting aside what's proper golf etiquette, is it simply good manners and common courtesy to respond to a request that's made to you?"

"Usually it is," Hays admitted. "But there was a snide edge to their requests, and I didn't think it was necessary to answer them given their tone. Sometimes it's better to ignore an insult."

Rudd regrouped. "You say you walked out toward the fairway after finding your ball among the trees. Is that correct?"

"Yes."

"Was it your intent to put the ball down on the fairway and hit a golf shot?"

"Yes."

"Isn't it true that one course of action open to you was to stay off the fairway and walk forward until you linked up with your playing partners?"

"Yes, I suppose . . ."

"But you didn't do that, did you?"

Philly nudged Rachel who rose and said, "Objection."

"Overruled," the judge responded.

"No, I didn't do that."

"By staying off the fairway, isn't it true that you would have been in a safer position than being on the fairway?"

"I suppose so."

"You suppose so," Rudd repeated. "You knew that an impatient foursome was playing behind you, correct?"

"Yes."

"You just told us that you never even looked in that foursome's direction, correct?"

"Yes."

"You never even glanced at the seventh tee, did you?"

"No."

Rudd paused to consult her notes. "You used a driver on the seventh tee, correct?"

"Yes."

"Isn't it true that your ball was mishit and travelled less than two hundred yards?"

"Yes, I think less than two hundred yards is about right."

"So a ball hit by a driver may only travel one hundred eighty yards, correct?"

"Yes, if mishit."

"Nothing further," Rudd said.

Philly took over from Rachel and called Alan Atkinson to the stand. It was unusual for a friend of the defendant to be called as a witness for the plaintiff, but Carpenter immediately saw why Philly had put the bald, portly, perspiring man in front of the jury.

Philly asked a few preliminary questions before focusing on the golfing outing. "Isn't it a fact that you saw Mr. Hays walk onto the fairway before Mr. Lord struck his drive from the seventh tee?"

Atkinson colored, touched his sideburns, and answered no in a soft voice.

"Would you please speak up, Mr. Atkinson?" Philly requested. "I could barely hear your answer and I want to make sure the jury hears you."

"No," Atkinson declared, his voice cracking.

"Isn't it a fact that you remarked on Mr. Hays appearing on the fairway?"

"Not that I recall." Again, his hands went to his face.

"In fact, isn't it true that you saw Mr. Hays and announced to your foursome, 'Look at that asshole, he probably stopped to take a shit,' or words to that effect?"

Carpenter didn't think that Atkinson could turn a brighter shade of red. The businessman grasped his sideburns with such force that Carpenter wouldn't have been surprised to see tufts of hair come loose in his hands.

"No."

"But you did hear Mr. Lord say, 'Maybe this will give him a wakeup call,' didn't you?"

"Not that I recall," Atkinson said in a barely audible voice.

A few of the jurors were smirking at Atkinson. Atkinson had been asked these same questions at his deposition and had to have expected the questions today at trial. Still the businessman was unable to steel himself to answer the questions calmly.

"You remember having your deposition taken by my colleague, Ms. Boyle, don't you?"

Atkinson nodded. "Yes," he said weakly.

"During that deposition, is it correct that you started to call Mr. Cannon and Mr. Mobley assholes before Ms. Rudd elbowed you to cut off your testimony?"

"Objection!" Rudd nearly shouted.

"I'll see counsel at sidebar," Judge Lofton said, and Carpenter would have loved to have been a fly on the wall to hear their discussion out of earshot of the jury. When the judge directed Philly and Rudd to resume their seats at counsel table, Philly sported a tightlipped smile and Rudd a pained expression.

"Please read the last question back to the witness," the judge directed the stenographer.

"You may answer the question," the judge directed Atkinson.

"No," Atkinson said, blushing for all he was worth.

Philly then read back Atkinson's deposition testimony: "Where are you getting this crap? Did those two ass . . ." Philly paused. "Isn't it true that you stopped what you were saying when Ms. Rudd elbowed you?"

Carpenter was convinced that if there were an ejection button attached to the witness chair, Atkinson wouldn't have hesitated to push it.

"I don't remember," Atkinson said, his head lowered.

"What were you about to say before you stopped at the word ass?"

At least three jurors were grinning broadly.

"I don't remember?"

"Isn't it a fact that you were about to call Mr. Cannon and Mr. Mobley assholes?"

Atkinson gave his sideburns another workout. "No," he replied.

"What did you mean by the word ass?" Philly asked in a neutral tone.

"I don't remember."

"Is it that you don't remember or that you remember but won't tell the jury what you remember?"

"I don't remember," Atkinson said with a touch of stubbornness.

"Isn't it true that you and Mr. Lord wanted to resume playing golf after Mr. Hays was taken away in an ambulance?"

"Not that I remember," Atkinson said, and one female juror rolled her eyes.

"Isn't it true that your claimed lack of memory has to do with your not wanting to say anything that would hurt the case of your business partner, Mr. Lord?"

"No," Atkinson said, his eyes lowered, and Carpenter believed that no juror believed the witness' last answer. Carpenter thought ahead. If Hays was victorious, Atkinson's testimony would be viewed as the turning point in the trial.

"Isn't it true that you did see Mr. Lord use an iron to hit his seventh hole tee shot?" Philly asked next.

"No, I didn't see what club he was using to hit his drive."

"After Mr. Hays was struck by a golf ball, isn't it a fact that you did see an iron in Mr. Lord's hand?"

"No, not that I remember," Atkinson said, and with that, Philly put an end to his ordeal.

Next, one of Martin Hays' playing partners was questioned by Rachel. He confirmed Hays' request to his playing partners to go on ahead while he searched for his lost ball, and also confirmed that this was common practice. Rudd got the witness to admit that it might have been safer for Hays to remain off the fairway after finding his ball.

Testimony from Hays' treating physician and wife followed. Hays' surgery and post-op treatments were described in flat tones by Hays' surgeon, and Hays' wife gave way to tears as she described Hays' efforts to cope with his injury. Rachel kept her questions short and her tone even. Under Rudd's brief questioning, the surgeon acknowledged that the surgery had gone well, and Hays had made a full recovery from his injury. Hays' wife admitted that in recent days, Hays was more like his old self but there were times when without warning he became depressed and withdrawn. When Rudd concluded her cross-examination of Hays' wife, Philly rested Hays' case.

Judge Lofton glanced at his watch. The trial had reached a natural recess point, but the judge requested Rudd to call her first witness, apparently committed to using every minute of available trial time.

Warren Lord's demeanor couldn't have contrasted more with Alan Atkinson's. Lord's full head of white hair and gleaming white teeth reminded Carpenter of Ted Baxter, the newscaster on the Mary Tyler Moore show. Lord was self-assured to the point that he gave the impression that he was deigning to put up with the inconvenience of the trial in which he was the defendant. Rudd took her time during direct examination, and Carpenter wondered whether Rudd was thinking that the longer Lord was on the stand, the greater the likelihood jurors would forget Alan Atkinson. Lord's testimony was predictable. He denied using an iron off the seventh tee, denied seeing Hays when he struck his drive from the seventh tee, and denied suggesting that golf continue after Hays had been taken from the golf course in an ambulance.

Philly began her cross-examination. "What's the longest drive you've ever hit?"

Lord smiled amiably. "In my younger days I was able to drive a ball three hundred yards on occasion. I haven't seen those younger days in a long time."

"What about in the last five years—what would you estimate your longest drive was in the last five years?"

"I'm guessing here, but I would say maybe two hundred sixty, two hundred seventy yards."

"When did you first take up the game of golf?"

"As a teenager."

"That would be how many years ago?"

"You're trying to get me to admit my age," Lord said, with a smile that several jurors responded to. "We're talking about forty years ago."

"In the last five years have you routinely driven the ball over two hundred twenty yards?"

"I'm not sure what you mean by routinely, but generally my drives go further than two hundred twenty yards unless I mishit the ball which I do more frequently than I would like."

"Did you use an iron for your tee shot on the seventh hole?"

"No," Lord said with an air of controlled indignation. "Why would I do that?"

"Do you have any explanation for two of your playing partners testifying that you in fact used an iron?"

"My explanation is that they were mistaken."

"Did you or Mr. Atkinson call out to Mr. Hays' foursome to speed up their play?"

"I don't remember calling out, but slow play irritates me and most other golfers I know so, if Mr. Hays' foursome was playing exceptionally slowly, which it was, I might well have said something. I'm pretty sure Alan told them to pick up the pace."

"Did you track the flight of your drive from the seventh tee?"

"Only at the end. I kept my head down when I hit the ball which is what you're supposed to do. But I'm pretty sure I picked up the ball just before it struck Mr. Hays."

"Did you call out to him?"

"There wasn't sufficient time."

"So you didn't call out, correct."

"Yes, that's what I just said."

Philly took a moment and regarded Lord evenly.

"Does Mayfair Country Club post each club member's handicap?"

"Yes."

"What's a handicap?"

"It's a number. The lower your handicap, the better a player you are considered to be. I'm a seven handicap which is pretty good. It means that if I were allowed seven additional strokes, I'd probably be able to make par on the course."

"Does the country club provide descriptions of the golf games of the club members that it assigns a handicap to?"

"Yes."

Philly received permission from Judge Lofton to hand Lord a document. "Do you recognize this document?" she asked.

"Yes, it's the club description of my golf game."

"Please read it to the jury."

Lord put on black-framed reading glasses. "Good all-around game. A long driver. Has excellent control of iron shots. Putting not a strong suit."

"Do you agree with that assessment of your game?"

Lord slowly removed his reading glasses, looking cautious for the first time.

"I guess so."

"May a club member seek to change a posted description of his golf game?"

"Yes."

"Have you ever requested a change in the description of your game?"

"No."

"Three years ago, did you win the country club's award for driving distance for your age group?"

"Yes."

"That would be using a driver club, is that right?"

"Yes, that's right."

"So, with the driver, you hit the ball the farthest of anyone else in your age group in the whole country club. Is that right?"

"I suppose you could say I was the longest hitter for my age group."

"Two years ago, did you win the country club's award for most accurate iron play for your age group?"

"Yes."

"So, with your iron club, you were the most accurate of anyone at your country club in your age group, correct?"

"Yes, I was, two years ago."

"Do you consider yourself a fast or slow player, Mr. Lord?"

"Fast, I guess," Lord said after some thought.

"You guess," Philly said. "Has anyone at the club ever complained about you playing too slowly?"

"I don't believe so."

Philly changed the subject. "In response to Ms. Rudd's earlier questions you described the business deal you and Mr. Atkinson were pitching to Mr. Cannon and Mr. Mobley. Do you recall that testimony?"

"I do."

"Is it correct that if the business deal had gone forward, neither you nor Mr. Atkinson would have invested personal funds?"

"Objection," Rudd intervened.

"Overruled," Judge Lofton said. "You asked numerous questions about the business deal on your direct examination. The stenographer will read back the question."

Carpenter liked Philly's question. Let the jury conclude that Lord was a pitchman with no personal exposure if the venture landed in the crapper.

"That's right," Lord finally answered.

"Does that mean that if the project failed, neither you nor Mr. Atkinson would be out so much as a penny?"

"Yes."

"And just so it's clear to the jury, if the project failed, would the loss be borne entirely by the investors such as those in Mr. Cannon's and Mr. Mobley's company?"

"Yes."

"Is this how you and Mr. Atkinson have made your living over the years—arranging projects in which other people were at risk if the project failed?"

"Our projects have been largely successful."

"I move to strike the answer as non-responsive to the question."

"Allowed," Judge Lofton ruled. "The jury will disregard Mr. Lord's last answer. I'm going to ask the stenographer to read back Ms. Piper's last question."

"Yes," Lord stated when the question had been read back.

"Is it correct that over the years you and Mr. Atkinson have been involved in two projects that failed?"

"Objection," Rudd declared. "This is neither relevant nor material."

"Again, overruled."

Lord stared at Philly. Carpenter now realized that the report on Lord by the two retired Cambridge cops had been detailed.

"Yes."

"Is it true that in each of those failed projects neither you nor Mr. Atkinson lost as much as a penny?"

"Objection," Rudd said again. "This line of questioning is probative of nothing."

"Overruled," the judge promptly said. "You asked general questions about Mr. Lord's business on direct examination and you also asked about the business matter that prompted Mr. Lord and Mr. Atkinson to invite Mr. Cannon and Mr. Mobley to Massachusetts."

"Ms. Piper's line of questions has nothing to do with this case," Rudd persisted. "The subject matter is neither relevant nor material."

"My ruling stands," Lofton said. "The jury may decide what's relevant and material."

Carpenter was surprised at Lofton's ruling. Were he the judge, he probably would have sustained Rudd's objection.

"Thank you, Your Honor," Philly said. "May my last question be read back to the witness?"

"Yes," Lord answered sullenly after the question was read back.

"In the situations where projects you pitched failed, is it true that you and Mr. Atkinson were paid for getting the investors to invest in the projects?"

"Yes."

Philly consulted her notes. "No further questions," she said.

"The defendant rests," Rudd announced.

"We'll have oral arguments tomorrow morning and then I'll charge the jury," Lofton declared. "We're adjourned."

Carpenter joined Philly and Rachel outside the courthouse. Overall, he thought they had carried the day, but juries couldn't be trusted—they were as bad as judges—and his instincts had often proved to be off the mark. "Nice job," he said. "Both of you. And those cops you hired must have done a great job digging. I think you really surprised the other side with what you knew."

Philly nodded. "They really came through. "Any thoughts about the closing argument?"

"Rudd's going to say that Hays should never have walked back onto the fairway. I'd address that by saying he had every right to continue to play the hole and, since he was in fact seen by Lord, it didn't matter where the hell Hays had walked previously." Carpenter paused. There had been another point that Rudd had made. "Oh yeah. Rudd's going to say that Hays made a full recovery from the surgery. You need to tell the jury that a full recovery means that Hays will go through the rest of his life with one eye all because Lord was a petty, vindictive piece of shit."

Carpenter smiled at Rachel's wide-eyed look. "Of course, you don't want to use the word shit. Try excrement." Rachel looked shocked. "I'm joking," Carpenter clarified.

Philly nodded. "Thanks. That's helpful."

"That's what I'm here for," Carpenter said. "To be helpful. I'll see you both tomorrow. Call me at home if you need to," he said to Philly.

87

Next morning, it was Rudd's turn first. Rudd stood in front of the jury without notes. She centered herself about eight feet from the jury box and established eye contract with each juror, her expression serious and composed. Then she began her closing argument.

Rudd went through preliminary, obligatory opening remarks, first thanking the jurors for their attention throughout the trial, then reminding them that Martin Hays, as the plaintiff, had the burden of proving his case, a burden, she said, he had failed to meet.

"Martin Hays admits that he disappeared from the view afforded at the seventh tee. There is no dispute that after encouraging his playing partners to move on without him, he disappeared from sight among the trees. When Mr. Lord's foursome arrived at the seventh tee, they saw that the golfers who were ahead of them on the course, were far off in the distance. That is where Mr. Hays should have been—far off in the distance, safe from any golf ball hit off the seventh tee. Instead, Mr. Hays placed more value on recovering his lost golf ball and resuming play than on his personal safety. He made the deliberate choice to search out a lost golf ball and play another golf shot rather than safely proceed out of range of the seventh tee to rejoin his playing partners. And he also chose to take his golf bag with him instead of leaving it beside the fairway to alert the foursome behind him that he was still on the course."

A few jurors were taking notes.

"You heard the testimony that it would have been safer for Mr. Hays to proceed toward the next hole away from the fairway. That's just common sense. But common sense is something Mr. Hays didn't bring to the golf course on the day in question. Instead of keeping out of harm's way, he moved out onto the fairway where he was most exposed to a drive from the seventh tee.

"That's not all. Mr. Hays could have taken a further precaution that common sense tells us he should have pursued. He could have looked at the seventh tee to see whether any golfers were at that spot ready to tee off. Instead—you remember his testimony—he never gave so much as a glance at the seventh tee. Rather, he marched out onto the fairway to hit the golf ball he had recovered. So once again, Mr. Hays deliberately chose to pass up commonsense protections for his personal safety and instead chose to behave negligently and carelessly."

Rudd's strategy was now clear. If Hays prevailed in the case but was negligent himself, any damage award would be reduced by the percentage of his negligence. And, of course, if Hays' negligence topped fifty percent, he would be primarily at fault and would be awarded nothing.

Rudd continued. "It is true that you heard conflicting testimony. Mr. Lord was clear that he was familiar with the course, knew the seventh hole to be the longest hole on the course, and used a driver off the seventh tee precisely because the hole was the longest hole on the course. You have heard testimony from two out-of-towners, two men from Georgia who claimed Mr. Lord used an iron for his drive on the seventh tee. The two Georgians also claimed that Mr. Lord and Mr. Atkinson made remarks that each of them categorically denied making.

"As club members, Mr. Lord and Mr. Atkinson had played the Mayfair Country Club course countless times without incident or complaint. On the day in question, they played the course in the exact same way they had played it in the past. They had no reason whatsoever to change their routine.

"In contrast, the two Georgians had never before played the course. Their account reflects the bitterness and frustration of two out-of-towners who had made a business trip that didn't bear fruit. Their account is widely out of line with how a golfer familiar with the course would play the seventh hole. Put another way, the testimony of the two Georgians was simply unbelievable.

"And let's remember something else about the two foreigners who came to court with a made-up story. Neither visitor from Georgia reported anything to any Massachusetts official. They claim that Mr. Lord directed his golf shot at Mr. Hays. That is a very serious allegation. That's the kind of allegation that you would think a responsible citizen would bring to the attention of authorities. Instead, what did the Georgians do? Nothing. Absolutely nothing. They left town in a hurry and made no effort to follow up on what they allege they observed.

"Please remember the testimony about drivers and how easy it is to mishit a driver. Martin Hays claimed he used a driver on the seventh tea and his ball traveled less than two hundred yards. Mr. Lord also mishit his seventh tee drive and his mishit drive traveled only about one hundred eighty yards. Each party to this case has confirmed that a mishit driver travels far less distance than a well hit drive."

Rudd hammered away at Hays being guilty of contributory negligence, a term that the judge would soon define. She closed her argument by saying that Hays was solely responsible for placing himself in a dangerous situation that unfortunately caused him injury.

Philly waited until Rudd had taken her seat and let another moment pass before setting herself in front of the jury. After thanking the jury for their patience and attention, Philly focused on the facts.

"My opponent said one thing I have to agree with. She pointed out that you heard conflicting testimony. Which you did. You heard two very different accounts of what happened on the seventh tee late last year. Which account are you going to believe?

"Let's look at the gentlemen who told you what they saw. First, we have two businessmen from Georgia who were invited to Massachusetts by the defendant, Mr. Lord, and Mr. Lord's business partner, Mr. Atkinson. They had no motivation to tell you anything but the truth which is exactly what they related. Their testimony couldn't have been clearer. Mr. Hays, wearing a bright yellow shell, was visible from the seventh tee *before* Mr. Lord hit his drive. Mr. Lord not only saw Mr. Hays, he said that he was going to teach Mr. Hays a lesson. And, so, in a spirit of meanness and arrogance, he deliberately aimed an iron shot from the seventh tee at Mr. Hays. With his award-winning accuracy, Mr. Lord hit his intended target causing Mr. Hays to be knocked to the ground and to lose an eye. Mr. Lord never had the decency to shout 'fore' as required by his country club's rules. He didn't do it because he didn't *want* to warn Mr. Hays.

"My opponent consistently referred to Mr. Cannon and Mr. Mobley as out-of-towners. Maybe she wanted you to favor Mr. Lord over Mr. Cannon and Mr. Mobley because Mr. Lord is from Massachusetts. I don't know about you, but I'd prefer two men—no matter where they came from—who had the guts to put their money where their mouths were and invest their own money in a project, rather than guys who just got paid to peddle the deal and never had to put a cent on the line. What would they be willing to say to get investors to buy their story about a property?

"And what would they be willing to say to try to get you to believe their story today?

"Mr. Lord predictably denied what Mr. Cannon and Mr. Mobley told you they saw. But what do we make of Mr. Atkinson, the other member of Mr. Lord's foursome? As the judge will soon instruct you, one of your jobs is to assess the credibility of the witnesses who provided testimony in this case. You had a chance to observe Mr. Atkinson. I submit to you that not a word out of Mr. Atkinson's mouth should be credited as true. It's understandable that a witness providing testimony in a courtroom might feel nervous. But Mr. Atkinson wouldn't look me or any of you in the eye. He constantly said he didn't remember things that occurred close by to where he was standing. Any direct question caused him to sweat and fidget and to tug on his sideburns. I'm surprised Mr. Atkinson had any sideburns left when his testimony was over. That nervous gesture on his part reminded me of what poker players call a tell."

Carpenter noticed that two of the younger members of the panel—both men—regarded her with interest and broad smiles.

"A tell is a mannerism that a poker player displays when he's bluffing. It's a tip off to the other players, if they know how to recognize it. I submit to you that every time Mr. Atkinson tugged at his sideburns, he provided a tip off that what he said next was either not the truth or was a false claim that he couldn't recall what had happened.

"When Ms. Boyle, my colleague, made her opening argument in this case, she promised you that you would learn something about the game of golf before this case was over. She kept her word. I'm sure there were times when you wondered whether all those facts about drivers and irons and distances and accuracy were important. But, as you learned, those facts were very important indeed. If Mr. Lord had used a driver off the seventh tee as he claimed he did, his drive could have been expected to carry well beyond where Mr. Hays was struck by Mr. Lord's ball. But his iron would carry the ball just the right distance to hit Mr. Hays, and both Mr. Cannon and Mr. Mobley swore to you that Mr. Lord chose and used an iron. And remember, Mr. Lord had won an award at his country club for the accuracy of his iron shots. What he did was deliberate: he shot at and hit Mr. Hays."

Several jurors began taking notes.

"My opponent has tried to convince you that Mr. Hays was negligent by returning to the fairway after finding his lost ball. Nothing could be further from the truth. Because the fact is, Mr. Lord saw Mr. Hays *before* he hit his drive from the seventh tee. It was Mr. Lord who made the decision to deliberately try to injure Mr. Hays by aiming his drive directly at Mr. Hays. Even if Mr. Hays was negligent in some way—which he absolutely wasn't—the fact that Mr. Lord saw him, deliberately aimed an iron shot at him, and in fact struck Mr. Hays with the golf shot, negates any negligent conduct on Mr. Hays' part."

Philly approached her last point, the subject of damages. "Mr. Hays was assaulted by a dangerous weapon. You each had a chance to feel a golf ball. You each know how hard a golf ball is. You can each imagine the force of the impact of a golf ball that has been hit a long way. And you each know in your heart what an arrogant, cruel, despicable thing it was for Mr. Lord to deliberately try to injure Mr. Hays. He behaved like an angry little boy who kicked another child when he thought he could get away with it. But you can make sure that he doesn't get away with it. You can hold him liable for his assault and battery. Sadly, you cannot restore to Mr. Hays the loss of his eye. But you can make the person responsible for that loss pay dearly for the injury he caused."

Philly made eye contact with each juror before taking her seat and setting down the note cards she had never even glanced at.

"I want to thank counsel for their closing arguments," Judge Lofton said. "It is now my responsibility, ladies and gentlemen of the jury, to instruct you on the principles of the law that you need to apply to the facts of this case."

The jury had suspended deliberations to break for lunch and Carpenter joined Philly, Rachel, and Hays for a sit-down meal at a diner near the courthouse. Rachel looked so tightly wound that Carpenter thought she might shatter. He wanted to tell her to relax, but he didn't want to embarrass her in front of Hays.

"I want to thank you both," Hays directed at Philly and Rachel. "You fought like hell for me. I appreciate it."

Carpenter couldn't be sure, but he thought Rachel's eyes began to tear up after the client compliment. She'd be a wreck, he thought, if the jury ruled against Hays.

"If you had it to do over again, would you have accepted the settlement offer?" Hays asked.

"I'll answer that," Carpenter took charge. "My answer is no and I'm hoping that is your answer as well. Listening to the testimony, I think that Cannon and Mobley came across as believable while Atkinson came across as evasive and trying to skew the truth to help his friend. Lord was a cool customer but I'm hoping that the jury finds him to be too slick for his own good."

Philly nodded. "No regrets from me," she said.

Rachel stayed silent making Carpenter wonder whether she now had second thoughts about going to trial. Win or lose Hays' case, Carpenter was convinced that Rachel had what it took to be a trial lawyer.

"Let's change the subject," Carpenter said. He turned to Hays. "Have you been back on the golf course since your injury?"

Hays laughed. "I have," he said. "What's odd is that my putting has improved. When I line up a put with one eye, I seem to get a better read."

"It's a good thing that didn't come out at trial," Philly said. "The jury might have thought your injury improved your life."

Hays laughed and Carpenter was relieved to see Rachel offer up a weak smile.

They were sitting in a conference room located next to the courtroom when Philly's cell phone sounded. "Okay," she said, before pocketing her phone. "The jury has reached a verdict."

Judge Lofton took the bench immediately after the jury was seated. Carpenter had moved to a seat in the front of the gallery. Rachel's hands were clasped together so tightly that her knuckles showed white. Philly sat straight in her chair staring at the jurors as if trying to discover what they had decided by reading something into their blank expressions.

"Has the jury reached a verdict?" the court clerk inquired.

"We have," the jury forewoman said, rising.

The clerk received the jury's answers to special questions and handed the document to the judge. Judge Lofton took his time reviewing the document.

The clerk returned the jurors' answers to the forewoman and began to go through the questions asked of the jurors.

"Question number one asks whether Mr. Lord was negligent. What say the jury, madam Forewoman?

"Yes," the forewoman responded.

"Question two. Did Mr. Lord's negligence damage Mr. Hays?"

"Yes."

"Question three. Was Mr. Hays negligent?"

"Yes."

"Question four. What was the percentage of Mr. Hays' negligence?"

"One percent."

Carpenter breathed a sigh of relief.

"What was the amount of Mr. Hays' damages?" the clerk next asked.

"One million two hundred fifty thousand dollars."

"Question six. Is Mr. Hays entitled to any punitive damages?"

"Yes."

"Question seven asks what is the amount of the punitive damages that Mr. Hays is entitled to?"

"Three hundred thousand dollars."

Rachel leaned over and hugged Philly. Carpenter had to stifle the urge to leave his seat and hug both women.

The clerk next read through questions addressing whether Lord had committed an assault and battery on Hays. The jury answered yes—an assault and battery had occurred. The jurors' remaining answers on this subject paralleled their responses made to the questions concerning negligence.

Carpenter glanced to his right to observe Warren Lord. On the witness stand Lord had appeared fit, active, in shape for his age. He had come across bordering on cocky. Now he appeared to be a defeated old man who sat slumped over, his head in his hands. Carpenter felt no sympathy.

Judge Lofton had the jury polled and each juror confirmed the jury's answers to the special questions. Then he thanked them for their service and announced that they were discharged. "You have no obligation to talk to anyone about this case. However, it is my practice to invite jurors to remain outside the courtroom should the lawyers in the case have questions for you and you wish to answer them. Again, you are under no obligation to remain. As I said, you are free to go."

When the jurors had departed, Judge Lofton asked if there were any further business before the court adjourned.

"Yes, Your Honor," Rachel said rising. "The plaintiff has several motions to present." Rachel approached Rudd's counsel table and deposited a small stack of paper in front of her. Then she approached the court clerk with original papers to be handed to the judge.

Carpenter was familiar with the post-trial pleadings having drafted them himself. Philly had elected to have Rachel argue these motions, and Carpenter wasn't about to second-guess her.

"I see that the plaintiff essentially wishes to put an attachment on Mr. Lord's homes and to enjoin him from transferring assets except to pay for necessary living expenses and medical emergencies. I have to say that this is somewhat irregular. My understanding is that Mr. Lord is fully insured."

"That is also our understanding," Rachel acknowledged. "But the plaintiff is concerned that Mr. Lord is not insured for intentional torts such as assault and battery."

Lofton stared at Rachel and then turned his attention to Rudd. "Ms. Rudd, are you able to shed any light on the situation?"

Millicent Rudd rose, reluctantly in Carpenter's opinion. "Mr. Lord and his insurer have reached an agreement. In the event of a verdict in the plaintiff's favor on the assault and battery count of the complaint, the insurer's obligation to indemnify Mr. Lord is for twenty percent of the total verdict including the verdict on negligence."

Slightly less than $310,000, Carpenter quickly calculated. Which meant Lord was personally on the hook for almost $1,240,000.

"What do you say in response to these emergency motions by the plaintiff?" Lofton directed at Rudd.

"Mr. Lord opposes the motions. There is no indication that he is unable to pay a judgment against him and Your Honor was correct to note that the motions are irregular at this juncture. In addition, Mr. Lord fully intends to appeal the jury's verdict."

Judge Lofton began a second review of the motions Rachel had presented. The judge took his time. When he looked up, his expression was unreadable.

"I'm going to allow the motion for an attachment on the real estate in the amount of one million, three hundred thousand dollars. I'm going to allow the motion to enjoin Mr. Lord from transferring liquid assets except for usual and customary living expenses and medical emergencies but only in the amount of two hundred fifty thousand dollars. Ms. Rudd, I am aware that these motions were thrust upon you with little notice. You are free to file an emergency motion at any time that seeks to vacate or modify the orders I've just entered. Anything else, counsel? No? Then let me commend you on a well-tried case. Court is adjourned."

Seven jurors were standing in the corridor when Carpenter opened the door to the courtroom and stood aside, holding the door to let Philly, Rachel, Hays, Rudd, and Lord exit. Rudd glanced fleetingly at the assembled jurors and immediately steered Lord to the bank of elevators down the corridor. Carpenter commandeered Hays and took him to the lawyers' conference room that he and Philly and Rachel had used earlier. Then he went back to join Philly and Rachel.

"We didn't believe that Mr. Atkinson," the forewoman was saying to Rachel. "He was very shifty looking."

"You were right about his tell," a young man in his twenties said to Philly. "I used to play poker online before they shut it down so I'm playing more live games. That tug on his sideburns was a dead giveaway he wasn't telling the truth."

"Will Mr. Hays be all right?" a bespectacled elderly man asked Rachel.

"It's not always easy for him," she replied. "He has his ups and downs."

"That poor man," the forewoman said somberly.

Carpenter smiled. Hays was no longer poor. Even after taxes he'd be doing okay.

"I've just got to say this," the young man who played poker said, directing his remarks to Rachel. "You did a good job explaining about golf. But if you ask me, it's nothing like poker and has got to be the dumbest, most boring game in the world."

Rachel shook her head and smiled. "It grows on you."

"Y'all have a nice day," the poker player said in an exaggerated southern drawl.

Philly and Rachel stared at the juror. The young man grinned back. "My family on my mother's side comes from South Carolina," he said. "I've never considered them foreigners."

"Does this mean you're suddenly rich?" Paul asked Philly later than night.

Philly snuggled next to him, noting the singular pronoun. She had been too tired for sex, but her mind was racing, thoughts going at high speed bouncing off the walls of what was left of her brain. "We haven't won anything until we collect. Plus, the defendant could appeal. Besides you should be asking whether *we're* rich."

"Do you think he will appeal?"

"I wouldn't if I was in his position. I would try to get a concession on the verdict by agreeing not to appeal."

"Would you give him a discount if he didn't appeal and paid promptly?"

Philly took her time with the question. "If it was a modest discount, I'd think about accepting a deal. Carpenter might want to toe a hard line."

"Don't you have the final say? Isn't this your case?"

"Well, it's true I brought in the case, but I'd be reluctant to go against a recommendation Carpenter made. He's got pretty good instincts. We've always been able to work things out."

"Are you going to follow your practice and split the legal fee nearly equally, four ways?" Paul asked. "I still don't understand why you've been doing that."

Paul was rubbing her back and Philly closed her eyes. If she wasn't careful, she'd drop off. "From the beginning when Carpenter and I started working together, we'd pretty much split fees equally. It made a big difference to me, and I guess I'd like to pass that on. Rachel did an amazing job. And even though Simon didn't work on this case, he's been doing other work that permitted me and Rachel to devote whatever time we needed to Martin Hays' trial, which is what helped us get a big win. So far, Carpenter and I think the way we've divided up legal fees has been fair."

"You and Carpenter are a bunch of softies," Paul kidded.

Philly thought about the trial. It had been an adrenaline rush to get back into the courtroom. But there had been a price. Less time with Daisy, less time with Paul, missed morning spins with Isabella. Next month she'd be going through the process again with Simon in the wheelchair case. And once again, she was going to want Carpenter present in the courtroom. She wanted the homelife things she had just put on hold, but she also wanted her legal life. She wanted everything.

"Are you still awake?"

Philly didn't answer right away. Paul's touch on her back seemed far away. "No," she finally whispered.

"Again," Rachel said. She was straddling Josh, running her hands up and down his chest. She couldn't remember ever feeling so energized. Martin Hays' trial should have left her exhausted and even dazed and confused. But from the moment the forewoman had announced the damage award, Rachel was in overdrive.

"I need some time to reload," Josh said.

He was favoring her with a strange look and Rachel realized that this was the first time he had seen her charged up. By inclination she was low key. She tended to be deliberate about anything and everything. But the jury verdict had left her on a high that she didn't want to get off. Maybe she'd suddenly crash but, for the moment, coming down off her high didn't seem possible.

She rolled off Josh and moved close to him. "What happened to my stud muffin?"

"Your stud muffin needs to catch his breath."

"I thought you were the one who was in shape."

"I am. And because I'm in shape I'll be there for the long haul."

Rachel wondered whether Josh was talking about sex or their relationship. She needed to calm down and took several deep breaths. She put her head on Josh's chest and listened to the slow beat of his heart. She closed her eyes and thought about the concluded trial. She had made an opening argument in front of a jury and had conducted the direct examination of nearly all the witnesses

Martin Hays had called in his case. The fact that her efforts had contributed to a seven-figure damage award was hard to take in.

"What are you thinking about?" Josh asked.

"The trial. Hearing the jury come in with a favorable verdict has been such a rush."

"I couldn't help notice you're a little wound up."

"It's a good wound up."

"I'd agree with that. Can I ask you something?"

"Sure."

"Would it be a problem for you if I lived my life the way I've been living my life? I can see myself playing golf and tennis for the foreseeable future. If online poker was currently legal, I'd probably earn my living that way. I'm hoping we'll stay together, but would it be a problem for you to be involved with a golf and tennis bum who plays poker?"

Rachel hadn't foreseen coming down from her high, but Josh's question started her descent. This was not the time when she wanted a serious discussion. Why the hell hadn't Josh picked up on her ebullient mood?

"Say something."

"I wasn't planning on having a serious discussion tonight."

"Neither was I, but here we are."

Josh was entitled to an honest answer to his question. "I've thought about it," Rachel admitted. "Just when I think I'm prepared to accept your lifestyle, I hear a nagging voice that questions my doing so. The voice has me thinking I'd be making a mistake. It's hard to explain."

"You're very good with words. I thought you explained it pretty well."

"Are you angry?"

"Angry? No, I'm ready."

Josh flipped on top of her and Rachel met his wicked grin. "Give me a minute."

"Now look who's out of shape."

Rachel tried to get back into the mood. She reminded herself that one reason she had made it through the Hays' trial was Josh. He had been there for her.

Rachel grabbed Josh's shoulders, pivoted her hips, and ended up on top of him. "I'm ready too."

88

When the phone rang, Carpenter said a silent prayer for good news from Herb McCauley. He had obtained an extension from Beatrice Gold to file written comments in Bernard Mucowahandi's case. but that time was running out. "I hope you have something for me."

"I'll let you be the judge of that," McCauley said.

Carpenter waited. He heard papers rustling on McCauley's end of the line.

"Crystal Queen has a sister who's two years older than she is. The sister went to college in Illinois, outside of Chicago. The sister filed a sexual harassment suit against her college and a biology professor she was taking a course from. She claimed that the professor had come on to her and that the two of them had had sex. She claimed that the professor had taken advantage of his position and her naivety."

"Naivety?" Carpenter questioned. There was a word he hadn't heard in a while.

"Naivety," McCauley repeated. "The complaint was settled informally, and the sister transferred to a new college."

Carpenter couldn't figure out whether this new information hurt or helped Bernard's case or, for that matter, whether it was relevant at all. "What did the biology professor have to say?"

There again was the sound of rustling papers. "The professor admitted that they had kissed on one occasion and that he had been foolish to let the kiss happen. He claimed that the sister had pursued him and been rather persistent about it. In a moment of weakness, he had let the sister kiss him."

Had the two sisters come up with a scheme to extract money from academics who thought with their dicks? Carpenter never rejected a notion out of hand, but this idea had to be nuts. "I suppose you're going to tell me that the sister is a knockout."

"I'll let you be the judge of that," McCauley said for the second time. "I'm sending you a photograph of the sister as we speak."

Philly was sitting in her home office trying to figure out what next to turn her attention to when her phone rang. She had been expecting Millicent Rudd's call but not this soon. She and Carpenter had spent an hour on the phone with Martin Hays going through potential scenarios. Lord owed almost a million and a quarter in liability and another three hundred thousand in punitive damages. He also owed interest on that amount, which would be charged from the date Hays first filed his complaint and was over $100,000 already. Hays had asked numerous questions. In the end he had agreed to Carpenter's suggested approach. Which was no surprise to Philly. After Carpenter's advice to reject a $500,000 settlement offer had proved correct, Hays probably thought the geezer was infallible.

"I want to see whether it's possible to negotiate a reduced payment amount if Lord agrees to drop his appeal," Rudd said.

They were ready for this. "What did you have in mind?" Philly asked.

"Your client waives interest and agrees to reduce the liability by two hundred fifty thousand dollars."

Philly smiled to herself. "Your offer is rejected. I'm authorized to make a counteroffer. The counteroffer expires at the close of business one week from today. There will be no other counteroffer if this counteroffer is rejected."

Philly paused for effect. She had nothing against Millicent Rudd, but Carpenter had instructed her to come across as a hard-ass.

"Our offer is this. Mr. Hays will agree to waive the interest and accept a seventy-five thousand reduction on the damage award. Your client waives Mr. Hays' one-percent negligence. This counteroffer is conditioned on the counteroffer's acceptance one week from today, upon execution of settlement papers within one week of the counteroffer's acceptance, and the payment to Hays within two days after the settlement papers are signed."

Rudd was silent. They both knew that Lord would be under enormous pressure to accept any reduction in the damage award. Interest, already exceeding $100,000, was accruing daily, and no doubt Lord was responsible for paying some or all of Rudd's charges.

"We're very close," Rudd said. "Would you be willing to consider splitting the difference between our two proposals?"

"No," Philly replied.

Rudd again fell silent. Philly suspected that Rudd had already received authority to accept virtually any reduction in the damage award.

"We have a deal," Rudd said.

"Excellent," Philly replied, meaning it. It was a great deal. Hays would walk away with just under a million dollars, the legal team with just under half a million.

When she put down her phone Philly sent an e-mail reporting the deal to Carpenter, Rachel, and Simon. She requested that Carpenter advise Rachel as to the documents that needed to be drafted to bring Hays' case to conclusion. Then she added a postscript to her e-mail telling Rachel that she was the one who was to notify Hays.

When she turned off her computer, Philly breathed a sigh of relief. Today was going to be a mother-daughter day. Everything else could wait until tomorrow.

89

And when tomorrow came, the first item was the Foster wheelchair case. Ruth Foster, not unexpectedly, was in high dudgeon, breathing fire. Philly couldn't recall the woman other than angry or complaining about something. They were in the Boston office where Carpenter and Simon had joined them.

"My mother's not doing well at all," Foster said. "After the trial, she's going to have the hip replacement surgery. To be honest, I'm not sure it's going to make a difference. I don't think she's ever going to get back to the way she was before that asshole rammed into her."

Philly glanced at Carpenter. He was regarding Foster intently, perhaps thinking what she was thinking: what would happen if Mary Foster became incapacitated or died before the trial.

"What exactly is your mother's medical status?" Carpenter asked.

"She needs a walker to get around. We've hired caregivers to look in on her. She spends too much time in her room. She's listless. She's become a fragile, old woman."

"How's her mental acuity?" Carpenter followed up.

"So-so," Foster said with a dismissive shrug. "She can carry on a conversation, but it's as if her mind is off somewhere else. It's hard to describe. She talks to you but it's as if she's not totally involved in the conversation."

"What's the latest from her attending physician?" Carpenter directed at Simon.

"It's pretty much what Ms. Foster has been saying. Since the accident, Mary Foster has been in decline."

"From a medical point of view, what does the physician recommend?" Philly asked Simon and Foster.

Foster fielded the question. "Her doctor wants to do the hip replacement as soon as possible. His hope is that my mother's mobility will improve and that she'll begin to feel more like her old self."

Philly assessed whether they should put off the trial so that Mary Foster's operation could take place sooner. She turned to Simon. "How did it go the last time you went over her testimony?"

"She seemed tentative. She remembers leaving the dining room and being knocked down. But her recall was hazy."

"We have witnesses to the incident, right?" Carpenter threw out.

"Right," Simon confirmed. "We've got a woman lined up to testify at trial. So it may not be necessary to call Mrs. Foster as a witness."

"What if your mother had her hip replacement surgery immediately?" Carpenter said.

"She'd never recover in time to be able to go to court," Foster pointed out.

"So what?" Carpenter retorted. "The court can go to her wherever she is. The jury can be carted off to hear her testimony in a hospital or in the assisted living center."

"I don't know," Ruth Foster said.

"There's a risk that the trial might be delayed," Carpenter pointed out. "The defendants are going to oppose any trial testimony in a setting that would produce sympathy for your mother. But it seems that the sooner the surgery takes place the better off your mother will be."

"I don't want the trial postponed," Foster said adamantly.

"Just a thought," Carpenter replied. "Talk to your mother's physician. See what he has to say. If it's reasonably likely that your mother could be transported to the courtroom in a wheelchair, we need to know that."

"Now that would be ironic," Foster said with undisguised bitterness. "A goddamn wheelchair!"

Next in line for Carpenter was Bernard Mucowahandi. "I do not know what to say," the Rwandan said after Carpenter had called him to tell him of Herb McCauley's report. "This is very strange."

"I may have misread this situation," Carpenter said, giving voice to his latest thinking. "I'd been assuming that Ms. Queen had a crush on you. That may be true. But another way to look at this situation is that she was targeting you for a sexual harassment suit by appearing to be coming on to you."

"I see," Barnard said in a flat tone.

"No offense," Carpenter continued, "but I have never been able to figure out why Queen would be smitten with you." Queen had seemed sincere when she had exclaimed that Bernard was old. But then again, two students had been certain that Queen was infatuated with Bernard. "That's not to take away from the fact that you're a very handsome man."

Bernard laughed, a good sign in Carpenter's opinion.

"What do you want to do?" Bernard asked.

"The notion that Queen had a crush on you is not consistent with the idea that Queen was out to get you," Carpenter said. "But, of course, lawyers—at least in this country—have no shame. We don't think twice about arguing inconsistent positions. I'm leaning toward keeping in play the defense that Queen acted as she did because she had a crush on you and adding the defense that she targeted you and was following in her older sister's footsteps."

Bernard took his time digesting this strategy. "Okay," he finally said. "But I would like to read what you write before you send it to the Brandeis lawyer."

"Of course," Carpenter said.

Philly entered the basement of Saint Sebastian's and sat down next to her sponsor, offering what she hoped came across as a friendly smile.

"You missed the last session," Melanie said reprovingly.

"I was on trial," Philly explained, not expecting Melanie to either understand or cut her any slack.

"I keep telling you that there's nothing more important than this." Melanie made a sweeping gesture that took in the basement.

This evening's session was sparsely attended. Charlie had moved to his position in the front of the room and regarded those in attendance with equanimity. If Charlie was disappointed in the poor turnout, you couldn't tell from his expression.

"Let's begin," Charlie announced. "I'd like to start by sharing with you. We all know that Thanksgiving is coming up. This is a holiday that has always been special to me. Just the name gives me a good feeling. But this year I was depressed about the holiday because it looked like I was going to spend it alone. Usually one or more of my kids puts in an appearance, but this year that's not going to happen."

Philly didn't want to think about the frenetic pace of the upcoming holiday. She and Paul and Daisy would put in a morning appearance at her parents' house in Fall River, an early afternoon appearance with Paul's family in Cambridge, and finally a visit with Philip's family in North Andover in the evening. Last year she had refused to look at the odometer to learn how many miles they had covered.

"For the first time in a long time I started to feel sorry for myself and thought about taking a drink. There was something about being alone that tore me up inside and seemed overwhelmingly sad. So I called my sponsor."

Charlie paused, choked up.

"Do you know what my sponsor said?" Charlie scanned the basement, but no one responded to his question. "He said that I was invited to join him and his family for Thanksgiving. He tried to make a joke out of it saying that maybe I'd get along with his family better than he did. But it was his gesture that mattered. It was a true act of kindness."

"You can come to my ex's house for Thanksgiving," a heavyset man in a stocking cap spoke up. "Maybe that'll stop her from picking on me all day."

"That's very kind of you," Charlie replied. "But the thing is, I decided to return my sponsor's kindness. I did that by accepting his invitation. I won't know anyone there except him. But I thought it was important to accept his offer of help."

Melanie dabbed at her eyes with the sleeve of the flannel shirt she was wearing.

"I've said this before," Charlie continued. "Help is all around us. We need to put away our pride or the feeling that we're inconveniencing the person who's trying to reach out to us. We need to open ourselves to accept the help that is offered to us."

Philly thought back to the trial in Martin Hays' case and believed that she had embraced Charlie's lesson. She had delegated most of the trial work to Rachel and her trust in Rachel had paid off. She'd be relying on Simon to handle the lion's share of the trial work in the wheelchair case. Somehow, she had gotten past the mindset that she had to do everything herself.

Nobody had any new business or offered to share. Charlie was not one to drag out a meeting needlessly. He quickly adjourned for refreshments.

Melanie stood and Philly tugged at the sleeve of her shirt. When Melanie faced her, she gave her sponsor a hug. "Thanks for keeping me toeing the line. I'm trying, I really am."

Melanie stared at her and Philly resisted the urge to smile. Melanie was probably in shock over the physical display of affection.

"Okay, then," Philly said. "I've got to go. There's a little munchkin I want to kiss goodnight. Even if she's asleep."

90

Carpenter studied his calendar. Tomorrow he'd send Bernard's supplemental response to the charges against him to Beatrice Gold at the college. Bernard had approved the document and said he'd gone over its wording with Connie. Carpenter resisted the futile task of imagining Connie's take on his legal strategy for her husband.

Then there was the Springs' suit against their son's psychologist. The attorney representing Roland Butler was scheduled to depose Keith Spring before the start of the Thanksgiving holiday weekend. Carpenter needed to get Spring to sit down in his office for face-to-face preparation, but so far his client had been dragging his feet.

Carpenter moved his calendar to the side of his desk, knowing he should feel buoyed. The Mucowahandi case involved billable hours. The Martin Hays contingency fee would make their year financially, and he and Philly were savoring the moment when they would hand Simon and Rachel a six-figure check. Then there was the prospect of another big score in the wheelchair case. And if that wasn't enough uplifting news, he and Maxine had made an offer on the three-bedroom Arlington condo that had been accepted, and Fred had been on an extended sabbatical. Still, Carpenter felt vaguely out of sorts. Maxine would observe that he could find something to grouse about during any happy occasion, but something really was eating at him and he couldn't figure out what it was.

Carpenter stared at the photograph. In recent weeks he'd been making more eye contact with the photograph than in the preceding months. The man returned his gaze with a sardonic smirk.

"What?" Carpenter said, realizing, as he asked his question, that he understood what was bugging him. The man gave a barely perceptible nod at his recognition.

He and Philly should stop pussyfooting around and form a law firm that included Simon and Rachel. The two young lawyers had proven their worth and he and Philly had lucked out in landing them. With the Hays case payout, Rachel and Simon could probably ditch their part-time jobs. A firm would mean that he would no longer fully control every aspect of his practice of law. Philly would have to be dealt with. And if Rachel and Simon started out as associates and became partners after a short time, he'd have three people to accommodate when it came to decisions. Was he ready to abandon his current personal dictatorship for the democracy of a firm? Surprisingly, he realized that the answer was maybe.

Carpenter gave the black man the finger, mouthed the words "fuck you" in his direction, and opened the Spring file. If he had to depose Keith Spring, the list of questions appeared endless.

In Brighton, Philly had just concluded a Skype meeting with Simon. The young lawyer had been all business as they finalized their respective roles for the trial of the wheelchair case. Philly would deliver the opening argument to the jury. Simon would deliver the closing argument to the jury. Direct and cross examinations were divvied up.

Philly heard Sarah Ferguson talking to Daisy. Sarah had established a routine. After breakfast, she'd take the girls outside to get some fresh air, no matter what the weather. Rosalind would nap when they came inside while Daisy launched on the arts and crafts project of the day. Rosalind would wake and, after a snack, Daisy would nap. Then there was lunch.

Daisy was now responding to Sarah with high pitched baby talk, partly babble and partly real words. Listening to her daughter, Philly realized that Sarah would likely be the first person to hear Daisy speak intelligibly.

Philly suddenly felt tired. She had been awaiting a crash after the high of the Hays trial. Or maybe she was simply exhausted from resuming her morning spinning schedule with Isabella. Despite the cold mornings, the mothers had made a pact to get up a half hour earlier than usual and put in some spinning time. They dressed in sweats and in no time at all became heated. Philly had bought tarps to cover their spinning bikes.

Philly realized that she needed a vacation. But the reality was that a vacation was out of the question until the wheelchair case was tried.

Philly checked her watch. Daisy would soon have her snack and then lie down. She decided she wanted some Daisy time before her daughter napped. Here was another occasion when the wheelchair case could wait.

91

Keith Spring's put-upon attitude was hard to take. Spring acted as if he was doing Carpenter a favor by consenting to be prepared for his own deposition, a deposition that could make or break his case. When Carpenter posed questions likely to be asked at his deposition, Spring brushed most of them aside without answering them. "I know what to say," he would respond with a belligerent wave of his hand.

Carpenter was rapidly running out of patience. "Here's a question for you," he said after locking eyes with Spring across the office conference room table. "Is it true, Mr. Spring, that you know everything there is to know about your son, Ryan?"

"What the hell kind of question is that?" Spring exploded.

"You don't get to answer a question with a question," Carpenter came back. "So answer the fucking question. Is it true that you know everything there is to know about your son, Ryan?"

Spring was momentarily startled and then glared angrily but Carpenter was past caring. Maybe the shock value of an f-bomb would work on Spring.

"You can't talk to me like that," Spring said.

"I just did. Answer the question. If you don't start cooperating, you can get yourself another lawyer."

The threat didn't seem to be working on Spring, and Carpenter had been reluctant to make it. Spring may be a smug, arrogant jerk, but Carpenter had a gut feeling that with the help of the expert Rudolf Nelson, Spring's case could prove to be a winner. If, that is, Spring would get his act together.

"Why would you ask me a question like that?" Spring said in a tone marginally less hostile than previously.

"To goad you," Carpenter replied. "Do you want to win your case?"

"What do you think?"

"To be blunt, I'm not sure. You keep coming across as an arrogant know-it-all. The lawyer for Roland Butler is going to pick up on that in three seconds at your deposition. She's going to bait you into flying off the handle. A jury is going to dislike you in a matter of minutes after taking in your act. You need to lose the attitude and let me help you. You need to pause and think before you answer a question and not spit out the first asinine, angry thought that pops into your head."

Spring went into a sulk and Carpenter realized they were at a crucial point in their relationship. There was an even chance Spring would head for the door.

"Why did you ask me if I thought I knew everything about Ryan?"

Spring seemed sincere in asking his question. "Because I wanted to see whether you'd say yes. Yes, is not the right answer to that question. None of us can know everything about someone else. But you might be arrogant enough to think that you can."

Spring didn't say anything for a long moment. "Okay," he said. "The answer is no."

"Did you ever see Ryan with a weapon of any kind?"

Spring appeared poised to answer off the cuff, but reined himself in. "No."

"Isn't it true, Mr. Spring, that you favored Darren over Ryan?"

Spring turned red but then settled down.

"There were days when I'm sure that was the case. Ryan had problems and I'm sure there were days when I became frustrated with him and wished he were more like Darren."

"Isn't it true that before the incident at your house when Darren was shot, Ryan had never exhibited any kind of violent behavior whatsoever?"

Spring took his time before responding. "I'd agree with that."

"Better," Carpenter said. "I'm going to be direct with you. At first, I wasn't too impressed with your chances of winning this case. And the expert we've got, Rudolf Nelson, is a bit of a loose cannon. But Nelson makes a telling point. Ryan showed up at Roland Butler's office with a gun. That was unusual to say the least. According to Nelson, Butler should have heard alarm bells even though Ryan had no history of violence. That's the theme we're going to beat to death. It's okay to admit that Ryan never acted out violently before. We can spin that fact."

Spring had listened intently. Now he nodded.

"Let's take it from the top," Carpenter said. "There were a whole bunch of questions that you didn't answer before. Let's give it another go."

Mary Foster's assisted living unit had a small living room. The last weak light of a gray afternoon came through the windows. Simon sat across from Foster in an easy chair with Foster ensconced in its twin, her walker within reach and a robe across her lap. He had tried small talk, but Foster had not become engaged. When he had asked her how she was feeling, she had said okay perfunctorily. At this rate, Mary Foster would be a disaster on the witness stand.

Foster was staring straight-ahead, not looking at him, and Simon was having difficulty picturing her as a career woman who had successfully juggled a job and motherhood. Ruth Foster consistently used words like energetic and lively to describe her mother, but those traits were not in evidence today and might not emerge at trial. Simon saw a diminished old lady barely aware of where she was and uninterested in anything. Somehow, that needed to be changed.

"I need to review some things with you. How did you get hurt?" Simon asked, pointing to her walker.

It took Foster a few beats to focus. "I was coming out of the dining room when I got knocked down."

"Do you know who knocked you down?"

"I don't remember," Foster said after a pause.

"Harrison Blaine knocked you down."

Foster nodded. "Yes, you're right. Harrison Blaine knocked me down."

"So what the hell are you going to do about it?" Simon shouted.

Foster startled, looked frightened. The home health aide in attendance, a small, wiry, Haitian woman appeared suddenly from the kitchen. "Is everything all right?'

"No," Simon said, standing and keeping his voice raised. "Everything is not all right."

"What can I do?" the home health aide asked tentatively.

"Nothing," Simon said. "Not a goddamn thing. She's the one who has to do something," he added, pointing at Foster.

Foster sank further into her chair. Simon wondered whether he was laying it on too thick. He resumed his seat so that he wasn't towering over Foster. "Some jerk ran into her with a wheelchair and she won't do anything about it."

The home health aide looked about frantically as if searching for an escape route.

"If someone ran into you with a wheelchair would you sit around and take it? Would you?"

"No, I . . ."

"No!" Simon shouted. "Of course you wouldn't take it. You'd fight back, wouldn't you?"

"I don't know, I . . ."

"Of course you know," Simon thundered, watching Foster out of the corner of his eye.

Simon got up from his chair and advanced on the aide who seemed rooted to the spot where she was standing with a glazed, timorous look. He took the home health aide by the hand and positioned her so that she was standing in front of Foster. He thought the aide would put up some resistance, but the woman offered none. "Ask her why she's given up and won't fight back," he demanded of the aide while pointing to Foster.

"I don't think it's my place to . . ."

"Of course it's your place. It's your goddamn duty. You're supposed to be her aide. So aid her. Ask her why she's given up and won't fight back."

The aide glanced fearfully to where Simon still had hold of her wrist. "Why do you not fight back?" she asked in a formal manner.

"I don't care," Foster said wearily.

"Did you hear that?" Simon bellowed. "She doesn't care. Can you believe it?"

The aide shook her head.

"I'm with *you,*" Simon said, keeping a grip on the aide. "I can't believe it either. Did you know that this woman was a fighter her entire life?"

The aide again shook her head.

"Well, it's true. She had a wonderful, successful career. She raised a bunch of kids. She never gave an inch."

Foster now stared at Simon with more curiosity than fear.

"You remember being a fighter, don't you, Mary?" Simon said with his face close to Foster's.

"I suppose so."

"Listen to her. She supposes so. Let me tell you. This woman was a fighter her whole life. It's hard to imagine she's given up. Isn't it hard to imagine her giving up?"

"Yes," the aide replied in a barely audible whisper.

Simon released the aide. "Don't move," he directed her. He went to his briefcase, returned with a photograph, and stuck the photograph under Foster's nose. "Who's this? Do you recognize him?"

Foster squinted at the photograph and then nodded. "That's Blaine."

"It sure is. Don't you want to punch that smiling face of his?"

Foster stared at the photograph.

"I know *I* want to punch the bastard," Simon said as he delivered a blow to Blaine's mouth.

Foster recoiled and Simon had to again grab the aide by the wrist to keep her in place.

"You try it," Simon urged Foster. "Give him a punch."

Foster shook his head.

"Then you try it," Simon said to the aide.

"I really shouldn't . . ."

"Of course you should. One good punch. You'll feel better immediately."

"I'm not sick," the aide pointed out.

"Just punch the guy for Christ's sake!"

The aide crossed herself and delivered a reasonably heavy blow to Blaine's mouth. The photograph was a mass of crinkles where Blaine's face had been.

"Feels good, doesn't it?"

The aide nodded.

"Now tell her to do it."

"You should punch the picture," the aide said.

"I don't want to."

"Just punch the damn thing!" Simon shouted.

Foster gave Blaine's visage a weak tap.

"You call that a punch?" Simon exploded. "Harder, damn it!"

Foster took a bigger swing and this time her blow made a small tear between Blaine's eyes.

"Much better," Simon said. "Do you feel better?"

Foster didn't have to think about it. "Yes. Yes, I do."

"What did this jerk Blaine do to you?" Simon kept his voice raised.

"He hurt me. He shouldn't have hurt me. I have trouble walking now. It's not fair."

"You need to say that Ms. Foster," Simon said in an even voice. "Will you say that?"

Mary Foster nodded tentatively.

Simon glanced at the aide's nametag. "And you need to follow Melody's instructions to the letter. Melody is doing a wonderful job for you." He gave the aide what he hoped was an encouraging, secret wink.

"Okay. I like Melody."

"Good," Simon said. He pointed to the picture of Blaine. "Tell me again what this jerk did to you."

"He hurt me," Foster said in a firm voice. "He hit me with his wheelchair. He came out of nowhere."

"That's exactly what he did," Simon affirmed. "How did this man hurt you?"

"I can't walk without that thing," Foster said, pointing to her walker. "I'm stuck here," she continued with a sweeping gesture that took in the small living room. "I'm afraid to go down to the dining room for meals. What if that man hurts me again?"

"We're not going to let that happen, are we?"

"No," Foster and Melody said together.

92

Philly was exhausted. Daisy had napped between each Thanksgiving celebration, but Philly hadn't, and now she was nearly comatose. Paul parked the car, extracted a sleeping Daisy from her car seat, and advanced to the front door. Philly roused herself to hustle to get the door open for him. Once inside, Paul made a beeline for Daisy's room and quickly emerged without her.

"Kill me now," Philly whispered. "I have bloody well had it."

"Come on, you enjoyed every minute of it."

Was there a minute that she had fully enjoyed? At her parents' home in Fall River Philly had felt the same tenseness that always kicked in when she was with her parents. The baggage of her rebellious teenage years was always present. Paul had been the one to keep conversation going, and Daisy fulfilled her role as the adorable grandchild to be doted on by grandparents. At Paul's parents' home, it had been a chaotic mob scene which fortunately included a number of elementary school girls who delighted in paying attention to Daisy. Last came the North Andover celebration in Philip's parents' spacious house where once again Philly was overwhelmed by bittersweet memories as Philip's parents played with Daisy.

"I just want to crash," Philly said.

"I just want a hug," Paul countered.

They held each other in the quiet living room. Sarah had gone out with friends and Raul and Isabella had done the same, taking Rosalind with them. Either they all were still out or had come back and gone to bed.

"I kind of like this three-part holiday," Paul said. "I still feel awkward in front of Philip's parents, but it wasn't as bad this year as last."

"I kept thinking how infrequently his parents get to see Daisy. The last time was when I drove out to see them to tell them about us. There's just no time to spend lots of time with everybody."

"Don't start blaming yourself. They can always drive down here. They can also offer to take her for a weekend. I think you've been great to them."

In North Andover, Philly had tried to picture Philip were he alive. How would he have aged? Would they have still been crazy about each other? When his blue eyes lighted on her would she feel the same sudden excitement she had felt when he was alive?

"It's okay to miss Philip," Paul said, and Philly marveled yet again how Paul seemed to be able to read her mind.

"It's getting harder and harder to do," she said.

December

Philly's Untitled Playlist

Brighter Than Sunshine

Aqualung

93

As the stenographer set up for Keith Spring's deposition, Carpenter studied the lawyer hired by Roland Butler's insurance company to defend him. Hillary Reese struck Carpenter as a cool customer: young, confident, a veteran of numerous jury trials. She had short dark hair, blue eyes, and scattered freckles above each cheek bone. Carpenter was grateful that Reese had elected to depose Keith Spring first; had she opted to depose his wife first, he had doubts whether Jane Spring would have survived the deposition. He remembered the initial client meeting when she had largely opted for silence and her husband had dominated the discussion. Obviously, Jane Spring had relented on opposing her husband's desire to bring suit.

Reese quickly went through predictable background questions before abruptly focusing a question that went to the heart of the lawsuit. "Before the night your younger son, Darren, was shot, had your older son, Ryan, ever exhibited violence or violent tendencies?"

Carpenter was relieved to see Spring taking his time with the question. "Ryan could get angry, but I wouldn't say he'd been violent."

"Can you give me an example of Ryan getting angry?"

"There were times when he got upset when he was told to do chores."

"Are you able to provide any other example?"

"As a teenager, he got angry over curfews and homework assignments. Things like that."

"But you didn't consider him violent, correct?"

Spring nodded. "Right. That's what I said before."

"Before the night Darren was shot, did you ever see Ryan with a weapon of any kind?"

"No."

"When Ryan produced a weapon in your house the night Darren was shot, did that surprise you?"

Spring chewed at his lower lip. "Yes."

"Was Ryan's producing a weapon out of character for him?"

"I'd say so."

"What was the weapon that Ryan produced the night Darren was shot?"

"It was a pistol."

"What was your reaction when you first saw the pistol?"

"I was surprised."

"Did you think the pistol was loaded?"

Spring paused. "I don't remember asking myself that question."

"What did you do when Ryan produced the pistol?"

"I asked him to give it to me."

"What did Ryan do when you asked him to give you the pistol?"

"He shook his head and said something like, 'No way.' He began to wave the pistol around, and I told him to calm down?"

"Was he agitated?"

"I thought he was somewhat agitated."

"Did he calm down?"

"Not really. He kept waiving the pistol around."

"What happened next?"

"When he got close to me, I grabbed his wrist and tried to take the gun away from him. He resisted. At some point the pistol went off."

"Did you ever take the pistol away from Ryan?"

"After the shot, I knocked his hand against a wall and the pistol fell to the floor. My wife came into the room and I asked her to check on Darren. I was worried that Darren hadn't come downstairs to see what was going on. My wife left the room and went upstairs and then she screamed. I ran upstairs and saw Darren lying on the floor in his room. There was a lot of blood."

"What did you do next?"

Spring took a deep breath and let the air out slowly. "I knelt down to see if I could help Darren. I didn't see anything I could do. I told my wife to call an ambulance which she did. When the EMTs arrived, they took one look at Darren and shook their heads. One of them used a cell phone to call the police."

"When you were struggling with Ryan over the pistol, did you make any effort to try to point the pistol to the ground?"

Spring again didn't answer immediately. A troubled, haunted look flashed across his features.

"I was trying to get the gun away from Ryan," Spring said. "I wasn't thinking about the ground."

"Do you have any explanation as to how Dr. Butler was able to take possession of the pistol produced in his office while you were never able to gain possession of the pistol Ryan produced at your home until the pistol was fired?"

This time Spring's troubled look was more pronounced. "I don't have an explanation."

"Have you considered the fact that if you hadn't grabbed for the pistol Ryan was holding that Ryan would have ultimately put the pistol down?"

Spring blanched, lowered his head. "No," he said barely above a whisper.

"Why do you blame Dr. Butler for what happened to your son Darren?"

Spring glared at Reese. Carpenter said a silent prayer that Spring wouldn't lose his cool. Reese's matter-of-fact questioning style had to be grating on Spring given the emotional horror of his younger son's death.

"He should have called the police," Spring said. "Ryan had pulled out a pistol in the guy's office and he didn't call the police. What the hell was he thinking?"

"Are you aware that Dr. Butler took possession of your son's pistol?"

"I'm aware of it now. I'm aware that's what he's said."

"When Ryan pulled out his pistol in your home, why didn't you immediately call the police instead of grabbing Ryan's wrist?"

"I wanted to get the pistol away from him."

"If you got the pistol away from Ryan, did you intend to follow that up by calling the police?"

"I can't remember thinking that far ahead."

"Did you think that if you got possession of your son's pistol, the risk of anything violent occurring would be eliminated?"

Spring emitted an exasperated sigh. "I don't recall thinking along those specific lines. I was trying to get hold of the pistol. That's what I was focusing on."

"Did you consider calling Dr. Butler before trying to take the pistol away from Ryan?"

"No, I don't think I did."

For the first time, Reese glanced at her notes. "You fault Dr. Butler for not calling the police. Do you fault him for anything else?"

Spring glowered at Reese but didn't give in to his irritation. "He should have called me or my wife to let us know what had happened. The way I understand it, Ryan made a threat against me."

"What threat do you understand he made against you?'

"Something like he wanted to get me."

"Isn't it true that Dr. Butler removed any threat to you by taking possession of the pistol that Ryan had produced in Dr. Butler's office?"

Spring glared at Reese. "Apparently not, given what happened."

"Are you aware that Ryan took back his threat against you?"

"I've heard that's what Butler says."

"Besides not calling the police and not calling you or your wife, is there anything else that you fault Dr. Butler for?"

"He shouldn't have let Ryan out of his office," Spring said with feeling. "Ryan pulling a gun in his office was so out of character that Butler should have figured out that something was very wrong. He shouldn't have let Ryan leave."

Reese jotted a note on her notepad. "What else do you fault Dr. Butler for that you haven't already mentioned?"

Spring drummed his fingers on the conference room table. "That's all I can think of at the moment."

Reese regarded Spring evenly. Carpenter couldn't read anything from her expression. He was generally pleased with the way his client had replied to Reese's pointed questions.

"Was there a time when Ryan left your house on a permanent basis?" Reese changed the subject.

"Yes."

"When did that happen?"

Spring became lost in thought. Reese was thorough. Carpenter had to give her that. The next hours were going to drag up painful memories for Spring, but there was no way around it. Spring had been adamant about bringing suit. Now he was going to discover the emotional cost of opting for litigation.

94

Carpenter picked up his office phone. "Carpenter."

"Richard Jenner. I represent Crystal Queen."

Carpenter had been thinking about Philly's upcoming wheelchair trial, and he paused a beat to shift gears. "What can I do for you?"

"I'm calling on behalf of my client to explore the possibility of a monetary settlement between our clients which would include my client's withdrawing her complaint with Brandeis against your client."

Carpenter had to fight the urge to tell Jenner to fuck off. That approach was Bernard's decision to make. "I'm listening," Carpenter said.

"I would like to propose a fifty-thousand-dollar cash settlement with mutual releases and the withdrawal of my client's complaint against your client."

I'll bet you would, Carpenter thought. "I'll convey your proposal to my client," is what he said.

"Here's my address and phone number," Jenner said, rattling off the information in a staccato fashion. "Is this something you'd recommend to your client?"

"What do you think?" Carpenter retorted. "I'll get back to you. I now know how to reach you."

Carpenter set down his phone. The man in the photograph across from his desk was smiling sardonically, a rare expression. The man hardly ever smiled, sardonically or otherwise.

"I'm glad I did something right," Carpenter addressed the photograph.

Carpenter knocked on the door to what had been Philly's office and entered. Rachel was seated behind the desk.

Rachel's mouth opened in shock as Carpenter related his discussion with Jenner. "What a sleaze ball," she exclaimed.

"Are you saying we should advise Bernard to reject the proposal?"

"Yes. Why would we recommend he accept it?"

"What if we got the price down to twenty thousand or less?"

"It's still sleazy. I couldn't recommend settling at any price."

"What if Bernard instructs us to negotiate a lower price?"

Carpenter tried for a neutral expression in the face of Rachel's incredulous stare. "That would be awful," she said.

"Bernard's a rich man," Carpenter reminded her. "He might think twenty thousand a small price to pay for getting out from under a sexual harassment charge."

"But he's got to have some principles," Rachel retorted.

"What if Bernard could pay Queen off for an amount that was less than what he would pay in legal fees to deal with this situation?"

"That would be selling out his principles in my opinion," Rachel said with what Carpenter regarded as a little less certainty.

"If I understand you correctly, you think that the West Memphis 3 made a wrong decision."

Rachel looked at sea. "Who are the West Memphis 3?"

"Funny you should ask. They were in the news a few months ago. They were convicted of murdering three young boys. They claimed they were innocent. They spent eighteen years in jail. DNA evidence was examined some years ago and none of the DNA linked up to any of the convicted men. They moved for a new trial. In the end, they were offered a deal. They could plead guilty while maintaining their innocence and be set free. They took the deal and walked out of jail."

Rachel remained silent, looking troubled. "That's a hard one," she said. "What should we advise Bernard to do?"

Carpenter knew he had made his point. "I'm not going to advise him one way or the other without listening to him. Let's find out what he wants to do. Get him on the phone."

Rachel pressed her speaker button when Bernard picked up his phone. Carpenter summarized his discussion with Queen's attorney.

"Were you expecting something like this?" Bernard asked.

"I thought about something like this after we learned what Queen's sister had done," Carpenter acknowledged.

"What should I do?"

"What do you want to do?"

"I would like this matter to go away," Bernard admitted. "Fifty thousand dollars is a lot of money, but I could afford to pay that amount."

Carpenter remained silent. Rachel was visibly disappointed in Bernard's initial response.

"What if Brandeis continues to investigate me after the complaint is withdrawn and I have paid the money she wants?" Bernard asked.

"That could happen," Carpenter said.

"I could pay money to Miss Queen and remain in trouble with the university. That is not satisfactory."

"No, it isn't," Carpenter confirmed the obvious.

"If I knew that the payment of money would put an end to the university's inquiry, I would seriously consider making the payment. Perhaps you could negotiate a lower amount."

"I'm sure I could negotiate a lower amount," Carpenter said. He thought of dangling a $15,000 counteroffer in front of Jenner's greedy nose. Under the divisible by three rule, he'd be presenting Jenner with a $5,000 pay day for making a few calls. Jenner had to be representing Queen on a contingency fee basis; he couldn't imagine Queen paying any lawyer an hourly rate.

"Then perhaps you should call this lawyer back and negotiate a lower amount."

Rachel appeared on the verge of urging Bernard to stand on principle. Carpenter put a finger over his lips and shook his head.

"Here's another possibility," Carpenter said, and he outlined the plan that had popped unbidden into his head.

Bernard didn't respond immediately. "If we do what you are suggesting," he finally said, "my problems may remain."

"That is a risk," Carpenter acknowledged.

"I will talk with Connie and let you know," Bernard said.

Rachel hung up her phone. "I like your idea," she said.

Carpenter shrugged. "It may not solve anything. But I'm curious as to what Connie is going to say. In the meantime, call Barney Freedman. There's no reason why we can't tie down two loose ends."

95

It had taken Judge William Henderson all of the previous day to seat a jury in Mary Foster's lawsuit. There had been a moment when Philly doubted the jury selection process would ever end. Henderson was a huge man with a large head, massive shoulders, and enormous hands. Carpenter had shared the intelligence that Henderson had gone to Harvard as an undergraduate and had achieved some renown as an offensive lineman on the university's football team. That suggested that at least in his youth, Henderson had been quick on his feet despite his size. But his manner in dealing with potential jurors was so plodding, Philly felt they were living in slow motion.

Today, the morning had begun with opening arguments, and Philly was pleased. She had made the initial opening argument to the jury and, not for the first time, she was surprised at how calm she had felt when it had finally come time to make her presentation. Yesterday evening's dry run in front of Carpenter, Simon, and Rachel had been helpful.

The fun began when it came time for each defendant's lawyer to address the jury. Carpenter had been right. Each defendant pointed accusing fingers in the directions of the other defendants. Amy Huff, on behalf of Maple Leaf Assisted Living Center, blamed the wheelchair racers for Mary Foster's injuries. According to Huff, Harrison Blaine and Harry Fried intentionally broke Center rules and were solely responsible for any injuries that Mary Foster sustained. Robert Boyd, the attorney representing Harrison Blaine, blamed the Center, which knew perfectly well, he said, how residents used wheelchairs and condoned the use. Marcia Livingston claimed that her client, Harry Fried, hadn't injured anyone; she blamed Harrison Blaine and the Center. At this rate, Philly thought, the defense lawyers were making Mary Foster's case.

Philly had wondered whether Judge Henderson would conduct the trial at the same snail's pace he had conducted jury selection. She didn't have to wonder long. "Call your first witness," the judge instructed after opening arguments had concluded. Simon announced, "Ruth Foster."

"Let me get this straight," Robert Boyd said, favoring the jury with a quick glance that displayed incredulity before focusing on Ruth Foster. "Are you saying that before your mother was injured you sent Richard Mason, the administrator of the Maple Leaf Assisted Living Center, an e-mail informing him of the dangers of wheelchair use?"

Ruth Foster glared at Boyd and Harrison Blaine's attorney met her gaze with equanimity. "Yes, that's exactly what I told him. Weren't you listening? I read my e-mail to the jury."

Boyd didn't seem to be fazed by Foster's barb. "Of course, I was listening," Boyd said. "But I want the jury to be clear on this point. I also want to be clear that neither Mr. Mason nor the Center did anything in response to your warning about unsafe wheelchair use. Is that the case?"

"Yes, that's the case. They sat on their thumbs."

"Sat on their thumbs," Boyd repeated, emphasizing each word. "Thank you, Ms. Foster. That image is very helpful. No further cross-examination."

Marcia Livingston regarded Loretta Frank with interest. "Thank you so much for your testimony," Harry Fried's lawyer began her cross-examination. "You told us about witnessing wheelchair races. About how many did you witness?"

Loretta Frank frowned in concentration. "I never kept count."

"Can you give an estimate of the number of wheelchair races you saw?"

"It had to be dozens."

"Dozens," Livingston repeated.

"Did you observe employees of the Maple Leaf Assisted Living Center watching the races?"

"Oh yes. The employees were cheering the racers on just like many of the residents were. I think the employees bet on the races the way the residents did."

"Objection and move to strike the answer!" Amy Huff exploded out of her chair. "There's no evidence that the witness saw any employee hand out or receive money, and what she thinks is beside the point."

Judge Henderson turned toward Frank. "Did you ever see any employee of the Center give or receive money in connection with a wheelchair race?"

"No," Frank said, and Philly silently bemoaned the fact that the yes answer that would have sunk the Center was not forthcoming. "But I did hear one of the employees say something about betting."

"May we have a side bar, Your Honor?" Huff requested. "We need to discuss whether there needs to be a brief hearing before the witness may testify further before the jury."

Henderson considered Huff's request and quickly dismissed it. "No," he said. "What did you hear?" the judge asked Frank.

"I heard a maintenance man swear because he said that he had lost twenty dollars by betting on someone who had lost a wheelchair race."

Philly's spirits brightened.

"Are you able to name this employee?" the judge asked.

"It was Carlos. I don't know his last name. Everybody knows Carlos. If you need something or want to get something done, go to Carlos."

"Your objection is overruled," the judge informed Huff.

"Objection for the record," Huff said resignedly.

Ernesto Cruz shifted uncomfortably in the witness chair. Amy Huff braced herself for additional bad news. Simon's direct examination had established that Cruz and a fellow maintenance worker, Carlos Ramos, had observed wheelchair races and bet on them on at least one occasion.

"Let me get this straight," Marcia Livingston said in a tone that suggested she didn't require clarification of anything that Cruz had said during direct examination. "Is it your testimony that you and another maintenance man not only saw wheelchair races but also, at least once, bet on one of the races?"

Cruz sighed. "Yes," he said in a voice so soft that Philly entertained the thought that Livingston might end up drawing forth sympathy for the short, wiry worker if she belabored sarcasm.

"Did you report the races to Mr. Mason or to anyone else?"

"No."

"Why not?"

"I didn't want to cause trouble."

"Did you think that it was okay for residents to race their wheelchairs?"

Cruz shrugged. "I guess so," he said. "They had been going on for a long time and nobody stopped them."

"Nobody stopped them," Livingston repeated. "Thank you, Mr. Cruz."

Amy Huff regarded Ernesto Cruz warily. Philly appreciated Huff's predicament and was curious about what she would do.

"Did Mr. Mason ever ask you whether wheelchairs were being raced?" Huff inquired.

"Yes."

"Did you tell Mr. Mason that there was no wheelchair racing?"

"Yes."

"Did you tell him that both before and after Mary Foster's accident?"

"Yes."

"Did you tell him there was no wheelchair racing because you didn't want to cause trouble?"

"Yes. I didn't want trouble. Trouble is no good."

"Of course I remember the accident," Mildred Haynes said in response to a question from Simon. She was a short, thin woman with short, white hair. "It could have been me," she added, as she pushed back the pink-framed glasses perched on her aquiline nose.

"What did you see?" Simon asked.

"I had left the dining room," Haynes said. "I heard noise and looked up and saw two wheelchairs bearing down on me. I moved against one of the walls of the corridor so I wouldn't get hit. There were other residents standing there against the wall. When the wheelchairs got near the dining room door, the door opened outward and Mary Foster came out of the dining room. She turned to the right and that's when the wheelchair knocked her down. It was horrible."

Philly counted five beats as the word horrible hung in the air.

"Who drove the wheelchair that hit Mary Foster?"

"He did," Haynes said, aiming an accusatory forefinger in Harrison Blaine's direction.

"May the record reflect that the witness has identified the defendant, Harrison Blaine?" Simon requested the judge.

"It may," Judge Henderson ruled.

"Who was driving the other wheelchair?"

"Harry Fried," Haynes said in a clear voice.

"No further questions," Simon said, taking his seat.

"Ms. Haynes, I only have a few questions for you," Amy Huff said as she studied the witness. "At the time you saw Mr. Blaine's wheelchair knock down Mary Foster, did Mr. Blaine call out any kind of warning?"

"I didn't hear him say anything."

"What about Mr. Fried? Did he call out any kind of warning?"

"I didn't hear him say anything either."

"At the time Mary Foster was knocked down, did you see Mr. Mason or any other employee of Maple Leaf Assisted Living Center on the scene?"

Haynes gave her glasses another gentle backward push. "I'm pretty sure Mr. Mason wasn't there. I don't remember seeing him there. He's never around much. I don't think any of the other employees were there either. I'm pretty sure I would have remembered seeing them if they were there."

"Thank you, Ms. Haynes. Did you see Mr. Blaine do anything after he knocked Mary Foster down?"

Mildred Haynes flashed an angry look in Blaine's direction. "He didn't stop if that's what you mean. He just kept going. When he went past the dining room door, he raised his hands over his head."

Huff's look of surprise was real in Philly's estimation. She wondered whether Simon had drawn out this information when he interviewed Haynes and had been saving it for redirect examination.

"What did you make of Mr. Blaine's gesture?" Huff asked.

"It looked to me like a victory gesture. It looked to me like he was celebrating winning his race with Mr. Fried."

"Celebrating," Huff repeated. "What about Mr. Fried? Did you see him do any celebrating?"

"No," Haynes replied. "He looked angry. He reminded me of a sore loser."

"No further questions."

"Tell me, Ms. Haynes," Livingston said. "Is it correct based on your observations of Mary Foster when she was knocked down by Mr. Blaine's wheelchair, that Harry Fried never touched Mary Foster with his wheelchair?"

"Yes."

"Did you ever see Mr. Fried's wheelchair come into contact with Mr. Blaine's wheelchair?"

"No."

"No further questions."

Simon had taken Dr. Parker Jones through a description of Mary Foster's injuries. Jones was tall and thin with blond hair close to white. Simon had complained that Jones had only permitted him one telephone discussion to review testimony. On the stand, he had an imperious manner which Philly wished he'd lose; Simon had to repeatedly ask him to explain medical terms to the jury.

Simon paused, studied Mary Foster's treating physician. "What's next for Mary Foster in terms of medical procedures?" he asked.

"When she's finished with this trial, she's going to have hip replacement surgery. That's because less drastic treatment alternatives haven't worked."

"What are the objectives of the hip replacement surgery?"

Jones rolled his eyes as if he had been asked a question too elementary for his consideration. "The surgery is necessary to relieve the pain that she's experiencing and to wean her from the pain medications she's been taking. If the surgery is successful, it should also improve her mobility. Currently she's using a walker. Hopefully, after the surgery, that won't be necessary."

"You said 'if the surgery is successful.' Are you able to assess the likelihood of the surgery being successful?"

"Objection!" Boyd interjected. "The witness is not a surgeon."

"Sustained," Henderson ruled.

"Have you discussed this case with the surgeon who will do the hip replacement surgery?"

"Of course."

"Have you referred other cases to this surgeon for hip replacement surgery?"

"Dozens."

"Have you monitored the outcome of these hip replacement surgeries?"

"Of course."

"What is the likelihood of the surgery to be performed on Mary Foster being successful?"

"Same objection," Boyd said.

"Different ruling," Henderson replied. "The objection is overruled. You may answer the question, doctor."

"In my opinion, seventy-five percent."

"What happens if the surgery is not successful?"

"Then I believe that Ms. Foster's pain and mobility problems will persist."

"No further questions," Simon declared.

After the lunch recess, Ruth Foster assisted her mother to the witness chair. The jury took in Mary Foster's slow progress as she edged her walker forward. There was a step up to the witness chair and Ruth had to grip her mother's elbow to help her reach the chair.

There was a rhythm to Simon's background questions and it quickly became evident to Philly that Simon had established a rapport with their client. Mary Foster directed her answers to Simon and not to the jury, but Philly assessed that drawback as minor. If getting Mary Foster's story out in clearly understood sentences was the price to pay for no eye contact with jurors, Philly believed her client's case came out ahead.

"Why do you need to use a walker?" Simon introduced an abrupt subject change.

"Because I got run over coming out of the dining room. I was badly hurt."

"What do you mean you got run over?"

"I was coming out of the dining room. I opened the door and passed through to the corridor and the next thing I knew I was on the floor in terrible pain."

"Did you see what happened to put you on the floor?"

"No," Foster said. "It all happened in a blur. One second I was walking out the door and the next second I was on the floor in pain."

"So how do you know that you were run down?"

"That's what I was told. Mildred Haynes told me she saw the whole thing and that it was Harrison Blaine who ran me down."

"Objection," the three lawyers for the defendants said in unison.

"Sustained," Judge Henderson said. "The jury is to disregard the witness' last answer.

Philly noticed that Simon did not seem at all distressed to have the jury see a phalanx of lawyers ganging up on a little old lady. "What happened to you medically after you found yourself on the floor in pain?" he resumed without missing a beat.

Foster described her operations in a summary manner, largely tracking the procedures that Dr. Jones had described. She was more descriptive in recounting her therapy sessions.

"Have your injuries prevented you from doing things you used to do before you were injured?"

"Yes."

"What did you used to do before you were injured that you are unable to do now?"

"I can't walk without this damn walker," Foster said pointing at her therapy aid. "I don't get to see my family, especially my grandchildren, a lot. Now they have to come to me. I used to go to visit them all the time, but I can't do that anymore. And it isn't just walking. I need people to help me do basic things like bathing. Even now I sometimes need help cutting up my food." Foster paused. She looked about the courtroom and her gaze settled on Harrison Blaine. "And it's all his fault."

"Objection," Boyd nearly shouted.

"Sustained," the judge ruled. "Ladies and gentlemen. You will disregard the witness' comment on fault. The only people who will decide fault are you."

"What are you going to do once you finish with your court testimony?" Simon asked.

"I'm going to have another operation. I need to have my hip replaced."

Simon paused. "No further questions," he said after Philly counted ten beats.

Philly thought Simon had done well. But cross-examination by three lawyers in a row would be an exhausting gauntlet for Mary Foster.

Amy Huff was first, for the Center. "Before you were injured were you aware of wheelchair races?" she asked Mary Foster.

"I had seen people racing before."

"Did you see them racing around mealtimes?"

"I'm not sure about the times."

"On the day you were injured, did you look right and left before entering the corridor when you came out of the dining room?"

Foster looked bewildered and Philly nudged Simon, whispering to him to request that Huff's question be rephrased. Simon shook his head.

"Why would I do that?" Mary Foster retorted, and Philly was surprised by the abrupt change in Foster, befogged one moment and feisty the next. "I was in my home. I wasn't at a traffic intersection. Do you look right and left when you leave your dining room?"

Philly saw several jurors grin broadly. She decided to shut her mouth and trust Simon's judgment. He knew their client.

"Did you ever complain to the Center about wheelchair races?" Huff asked.

"Why would I do that? My daughter complained. A lot of good that did."

Philly didn't understand where Foster's combativeness was coming from. Before the trial, she had been so demoralized there had been a question whether to have her testify at all. Huff must have realized that Mary Foster was turning into a witness who couldn't be pushed around. Philly glanced at Simon; he had set a photograph against his briefcase facing Foster. Philly leaned forward. There had been a lot of damage to the photograph but there was no mistaking that the photograph was of Harrison Blaine.

"No more questions," Huff announced and promptly sat down.

Then it was the turn of Harrison Blaine's attorney. "You said you found yourself on the floor, is that correct?" Robert Boyd asked.

"Yes," Mary Foster replied.

"Is it also correct that you don't remember how you ended up on the floor?"

"Yes."

"To your knowledge, did the Center ignore your daughter's complaints about wheelchair racing?"

"They didn't do anything about stopping the races if that's what you mean."

"That's exactly what I mean. No further questions."

Marcia Livingston was the last in the parade. "Do you blame Mr. Blaine for the injuries you suffered, Mrs. Foster?" she asked.

Mary Foster nodded. "I do."

"Is that because you believe that he ran into you with his wheelchair?"

"Yes."

"Is it true that in this case you are not claiming Mr. Fried ran into you?"

Mary Foster exhibited the bewildered look that previously had troubled Philly. But her client recovered and answered Livingstone in a strong voice.

"He didn't run into me but if he hadn't raced with Mr. Blaine, there probably wouldn't have been any race."

"Move to strike the answer after 'he didn't run into me,'" Livingston requested the judge.

"Denied," Henderson promptly acted.

"Please note my objection," Livingston said. "No further questions."

"Who's your next witness?" the judge directed at Simon.

"That would be Mr. Mason, the Center's administrator."

The judge looked at his watch. "We'll start with Mr. Mason tomorrow. Court is adjourned for today."

Ruth Foster held the grips at the back of her mother's wheelchair. "How's it going?" she asked her mother's lawyers outside the courtroom.

"Why don't I answer," Carpenter proposed. "I've been observing the trial and perhaps I can offer a fresh perspective."

Philly and Simon nodded gratefully. Carpenter knew that the last thing a trial lawyer wanted to do when a long day of testimony had concluded was confront his client's inquiry as to whether the trial was going well.

"The case is proceeding according to our game plan in my opinion, which is positive. We explained to you that the defendants would do our work for us and would beat up on each other. That's exactly what's happening. Each defendant is pointing fingers at the other defendants. When it comes time for final argument, Simon will pull all that together."

Ruth Foster nodded. Carpenter believed that it was the first time he had seen her in less than warpath mode. If Ruth Foster had nothing to bitch about, maybe the case really was moving in the right direction.

"Tomorrow, when you get Mason on the stand," Ruth Foster said to Simon, "I want you to rip him a new asshole."

Now that's more like it, Carpenter thought.

96

The second day proceeded briskly, and Carpenter considered that witness testimony might conclude before the judge discharged the jury for the day. There was even a chance that closing arguments would conclude today's court session and that the judge would charge the jury tomorrow.

During Simon's direct examination of Richard Mason, Ruth Foster smiled on two occasions. If Simon wasn't cutting Mason a new asshole, he at least was coming close to doing so. Mason came across as an incompetent, out-of-touch administrator. Several jurors had smirked at Mason's attempts to explain why he had failed to credit Ruth Foster's e-mail warning about wheelchair races. Simon had shown Mason to be a hands-off executive who was clueless about what went on in the facility he was supposed to manage. Amy Huff's cross-examination of Mason did little to change that impression, and cross-examination from Robert Boyd and Marcia Livingston reinforced Mason's lack of knowledge about what went on at the Center.

When Simon rested Mary Foster's case after Mason's testimony, Carpenter found his interest picking up. He was genuinely curious whether Robert Boyd would put Harrison Blaine on the witness stand. In Boyd's shoes, he would advise Blaine not to take the stand. And maybe that was Boyd's advice to his client for when Blaine's wheelchair was positioned before the witness chair, Boyd looked uncomfortable. Blaine, however, smiled amiably at his attorney, exuding confidence. He was dressed in a blue pinstriped suit. He had white hair and broad shoulders with musculature that suggested he exercised his upper body even though his legs were compromised. Carpenter guessed he was in his early seventies, still a vigorous man.

Boyd tried to limit Blaine to one-word answers, but Blaine wanted to expound. Whenever Blaine opened his mouth for extended talk, he came across, in Carpenter's opinion, as smug and obviously impressed with himself, unable to comprehend anyone having a lesser opinion of his person. Blaine claimed that Mary Foster had come into the path of his wheelchair unexpectedly, out of nowhere. He said that he tried to stop but wasn't able to—the collision was unavoidable even though his wheelchair wasn't moving all that fast. He denied raising his hands in the air after the collision.

Philly did the cross examination, and she tried to make the most of how off-putting Blaine's manner was. She asked questions that required more than a one-word answer. Carpenter would never forget one exchange between Blaine and Philly, an exchange that caused several jurors to wince.

"Do you see yourself as being at all responsible for the injuries your wheelchair caused Ms. Foster?" Philly had asked.

"Not at all," Blaine had replied immediately. "She should have watched where she was going. She obviously didn't look at all."

Philly had paused to let that exchange resonate with the jury. Then she shifted gears.

"Mr. Blaine, would you please tell the jury how much you weigh?"

Robert Boyd jumped to his feet. "Objection. Mr. Blaine's weigh is not relevant here."

"May it please the court, I intend to show very quickly how it is relevant."

Judge Henderson turned to Boyd. "Overruled."

Philly repeated the question.

"I guess I'd say that I was in the neighborhood of one hundred eighty," Blaine responded.

"And how much does your wheelchair weigh?" Philly continued.

"I can't say I really know."

"Would you be surprised to learn that the manufacturer of your wheelchair says it weighs about two hundred pounds?"

"I really don't know. If you say so."

"So together, you and your wheelchair weigh just under four hundred pounds. Is that right?"

"If you say so." Blaine replied, sounding defensive.

Philly glanced very briefly at Judge Henderson, then turned back to Blaine. "Are you aware, Mr. Blaine, that NFL linemen often weigh around three hundred pounds?"

"I don't really know."

"Are you aware that when you and your wheelchair hit Mrs. Foster, who weighs about one hundred pounds, it was as if an NFL lineman was tackling a junior high school quarterback?" Philly had reached her point.

"I couldn't tell you."

"No further questions."

Amy Huff had grilled Blaine unmercifully. She had obtained manufacturer instructions for Blaine's wheelchair. Prohibited uses included racing. When asked whether he had engaged in that particular prohibited use, Blaine had looked up at Huff and said: "I hardly think going five miles an hour is racing."

"Mr. Blaine, isn't your wheelchair one that is also manufactured for outdoor use, such as on sidewalks?" Huff pursued.

"Yes, I guess so. I do use it outside sometimes."

"And isn't it true that your wheelchair can actually go close eight to ten miles an hour?"

"I wouldn't know," Blaine said acidly. "I never timed it. I don't think I was going that fast at all."

Huff had the Maple Leaf Assisted Living Center's rules and regulations placed in front of Blaine. "Please read rule seventeen," she had requested the witness.

Blaine read the rule silently before reading it aloud. "Residents are prohibited from undertaking or engaging in any activity on Center grounds that is dangerous or poses a danger to any other resident of the Center."

"You engaged in dangerous wheelchair racing, didn't you Mr. Blaine?" Huff had challenged.

"I disagree," Blaine had replied with a stubborn edge to his voice. "I hardly call going five miles an hour racing or dangerous, and no one from the Center ever said it was."

"But you don't know how fast you were really going. Isn't that so?"

Blaine was now clearly cross. "Like I said. I don't know."

"No more questions."

Harry Fried, another white-haired man, denied any wrongdoing when it came to his turn to testify. Marcia Livingston's direct examination lasted ten minutes by Carpenter's count. Fried's wheelchair hadn't struck anybody. The wheelchair races were a matter of common knowledge and no one at the Center tried to put a stop to them.

Philly used her cross-examination of Fried to confirm the testimony of other witnesses, particularly Mildred Haynes. Yes, Fried admitted; he and Blaine were racing their wheelchairs. Yes, Blaine did not stop after the collision. Yes, Blaine raised his hands over his head after he had gone some distance beyond the door to the dining room.

When the defendants' rested their cases shortly after the lunch break, Judge Henderson adjourned for fifteen minutes and announced that on return from the short break counsel were to deliver their closing arguments.

Before Simon rose, each of the defendants' lawyers had presented a closing argument. Everything Marcia Livingston said helped Mary Foster's case. Her client, Harry Fried, hadn't injured anyone. The direct cause of Mary Foster's injuries was Harrison Blaine. And the other negligent culprit in Livingston's view was the Maple Leaf Assisted Living Center. Richard Mason had to be deaf, dumb and blind not to know wheelchair races were going on in the building he managed, and that Center employees bet on them. If the Center had wanted to stop the practice of racing, it should have done so. Ruth Foster had certainly alerted Mason to the practice.

Amy Huff had beaten the only drum she had to bang—Harrison Blaine struck Mary Foster and no one associated with the Center was on the scene. Blaine's denial that he was racing his wheelchair was rebutted by every other witness who testified on the subject. The Center should not be held responsible because a resident, without permission, engaged in a dangerous activity that was prohibited by the Center's rules and regulations.

Robert Boyd hammered away at the Center for being negligent. If the Center regarded any use of wheelchairs as dangerous, it was the Center's responsibility to put a stop to the dangerous practice. In this case, the Center did nothing when it came to wheelchair use and the Center's administrator, Richard Mason, had his head so buried in the sand, he claimed that he didn't even know how wheelchairs were being used in the facility he managed. Carpenter had to hand it to Boyd—the man never once referred to his client as racing his wheelchair.

Now it was Simon's turn. He would have the final say before the jury began deliberations. And once Simon began, the jurors became totally locked into his presentation. Simon played up the defendants' pointing fingers at each other without the sarcasm that Carpenter knew he would have employed. Carpenter realized that Simon's tone was the correct tone—he concluded this portion of his argument by reminding the jurors that the final finger pointing in this case would be done by them. Each of the defendants was responsible for Mary Foster's injuries and each of them should be made to pay.

"As we get older," Simon said, "I think it's true that we tend to treasure more the time we have left. The defendants in this case have taken away Mary Foster's bright hopes for her remaining years. Her medical miseries have yet to conclude. She will again go into the hospital for a hip replacement. And as you heard from her physician, there is no guaranty that will be the last of her surgeries."

Simon detailed the changes in Mary Foster's life following Harrison Blaine running her down. Here again his tone was matter of fact, and Carpenter had to admit the approach seemed to be working for the jurors.

"I want you to do something for me," Simon concluded his argument. "There's an image in this case that I find distasteful and abhorrent. I want you to change that image. The image I'm talking about is of Harrison Blaine raising his hands over his head after viciously running Mary Foster down. Here's a very smug man who had literally just committed a hit and run accident, thinking only of himself and how he had won a wheelchair race. So here's what I want you to do. I want you to make it so that Mary Foster gets to raise her hands over her head in victory. And you can do that by awarding her the damages she's entitled to. And she *should* have her hands raised over her head in victory. The reckless wheelchair racers and incompetent employees of the Maple Leaf Assisted Living Center should be made to pay for their buck passing, negligence, and downright stupidity." Simon raised his hands over his head. "Picture Mary Foster doing what I'm now doing. That picture seems right and just, doesn't it? Of course it does."

As Simon returned to his seat there wasn't a sound in the courtroom. Carpenter had to hand it to Simon. He had zeroed in on the image of a gloating Harrison Blaine and had given the jurors an image of a worthier individual entitled to claim victory—Mary Foster. Carpenter sensed that if a more physically imposing lawyer had made Simon's argument and raised his hands over his head, the gesture might not have been effective. Coming from Simon with his slight, frail build, the gesture made you want to root for and help the underdog.

"Thank you, counsel," Judge Henderson said. "Court is adjourned for the day. Tomorrow I will instruct the jurors on the law and then they will begin their deliberations."

97

Ruth Foster reminded Carpenter of a caged animal as she paced about the small lawyers' conference room they had appropriated. Carpenter wanted to tell her to sit down or get the hell out of the room, but that directive was properly Philly's or Simon's and neither seemed to be as bothered by Foster as he was. True, Ruth Foster had more to worry about than the suspense of the jury returning. This morning, her mother was having her hip replaced. Yesterday, a surgical spot had opened up and Mary Foster insisted on taking advantage of the opportunity. "I wanted her to wait," Ruth Foster related. "After all, she had just testified. But it was if the testimony invigorated her. She said she wanted to try to get her life back as soon as possible."

The morning had already been action packed. Before Judge Henderson charged the jury, the defendants had offered to settle Mary Foster's case for $600,000. "Fuck the lot of them," Ruth Foster had responded to the proposal and although he wouldn't have put it that way, Carpenter agreed that she'd made the right call. This was a case where it made sense to roll the dice for a big score.

An hour after the jury had retired to begin deliberations, the jurors submitted a question to the judge. They wanted the judge to clarify his instructions on damages: if they awarded damages to the plaintiff would the defendants share in the payment or would each be responsible for the damage figure? That question had two immediate consequences: it took away the suspense of who was going to prevail at trial, and it produced an increased settlement proposal of $750,000. Carpenter believed the increased offer at least warranted discussion, but Ruth Foster had nixed that possibility with another, "Fuck them."

Ruth Foster finally left the conference room without a word as to where she was headed. Carpenter studied Philly and Simon. Philly looked drained, as well she might be. Back to back jury trials were wearing under any circumstances. But with a toddler at home, Philly had to have been under incredible stress. In contrast, Simon appeared calm and reflective.

"The two of you did a terrific job no matter how this comes out," Carpenter said.

Philly responded with a weak shrug. "Thanks," Simon said without emotion.

"Let's get out of here for an early lunch," Carpenter suggested. "The jury won't be coming in with a verdict until after lunch. They're going to want at least one free meal today."

"I'm not hungry," Philly said.

"Then watch me eat," Carpenter came back. "Let's get out of here before Foster comes back."

Philly offered up a weak smile. "Now that's a persuasive reason for getting off our asses."

Philly felt guilty for cutting out on Ruth Foster, but as she and Simon and Carpenter slid into a booth at a diner two blocks from the courthouse, she realized that she needed a break from the woman. Ruth Foster was always on, pressing, combative, uncompromising. Being around her was enervating.

A short, stocky waitress distributed menus and silverware wrapped tightly in thin paper napkins. "Drinks?" she asked.

Philly was struck by how badly she wanted a beer. She could taste the foamy liquid course down her throat and the sensation set her tingling. Mercifully the diner didn't serve liquor and she settled for a Coke. She hadn't felt like a drink at the end of Martin Hays' trial, but there must have been something about the Foster case that made her want to indulge in a forbidden release. Philly knew what she needed to do: call her sponsor. Melanie would be both surprised and pleased by the contact.

Carpenter produced a sheet of notepaper and folded it into thirds. He pressed hard along the fold lines and was easily able to tear the sheet into three rectangles. He handed Philly and Simon a slip of paper, reached for his wallet, and extracted a ten-dollar bill which he tossed in the middle of the table. "Ante up," he said.

Philly knew what was coming as she reached for her purse and noted Simon's bemused expression.

"Come on, Simon," Carpenter urged. "We know you can afford it after the Martin Hays payday."

Philly added her ten dollars to the pot and Simon, still looking puzzled, followed suit.

"We're going to write down the figure we think the jury will come back with," Carpenter said. "Whoever is closest wins the pot."

Simon nodded, his expression suddenly serious. "Is it the closest without going over?" he asked, and Philly remembered asking the same question the first time Carpenter had played this game with her.

"Let's say closest period," Carpenter decreed.

The waitress reappeared with their drinks and took their lunch orders. When she left, Philly began to consider Carpenter's wager in earnest. Simon was deep in thought, eyes closed. Carpenter's jaw muscles were working which meant that he was playing to win.

Given their last settlement offer of $750,000, Philly figured that the defendants believed Mary Foster would recover far more than that sum. Her overall impression from watching the jurors during Simon's closing argument was that the jury was going to stick it to Harrison Blaine big time. If that occurred, the verdict would be seven figures.

"We're not figuring in interest are we?' Simon interrupted her train of thought.

"Right," Carpenter said. "Forget interest."

Philly wrote *$1.5M* on her piece of paper, set her initials beside the figure and folded the paper. What the hell, she thought. So what if her number was divisible by three?

Simon sighed deeply and wrote a number on his piece of paper. Carpenter was the last to jot down a figure.

"Show and tell," Carpenter said, and he unfolded his paper.

"A million two," Philly read. She unfolded her paper and set it beside Carpenter's. "I'm at a million five."

"Now who's the pessimist?" Simon said as he revealed his figure, *$1.8M*.

"Interesting," Carpenter said. "There's a pattern here. We each chose a number divisible by three."

Walking back to the courthouse, Carpenter drew abreast of Philly and put an arm around her shoulder. "How are you doing?" he asked, as Simon moved ahead of them.

"I'm beat to shit if you must know," Philly replied. "Is it that obvious?"

"You've looked better."

"Thanks a fucking a lot," Philly said without any heat behind her words since she appreciated his concern.

"Anything you want to talk about?"

Philly shook her head. "Why don't you catch up with Simon? There's a personal call I need to make."

Carpenter gave her one of his probing looks, and Philly tried to keep her expression neutral. He had a way of tuning into what you were thinking, and she didn't want to offer him a clue as to whom she needed to call.

Melanie picked up on the first ring. "Hi, this is Melanie."

"It's Philly."

"Philly! Are you okay?"

"For the first time in a long time I really wanted a beer."

Melanie didn't say anything, and Philly let the silence lengthen. Melanie wasn't a sponsor for anyone else. Perhaps Melanie hadn't thought through how to respond if her one charge called her for help.

"I'm glad you called," Melanie said in a formal way that made it sound to Philly as if she was reading from a script. "Why don't you tell me what made you want a beer?"

The courthouse was coming up on her right, and Philly made a left turn. A stiff breeze met her head-on and she pulled her coat tighter. "I just got through with this trial," she started, and soon she was telling Melanie everything, grateful that her sponsor didn't interrupt.

"I have three things to say to you," Melanie said when Philly had finished talking. "The first is, I want you to think of your daughter. You need to stay sober for her sake. I know how much you love her. Second, if the feeling of wanting a drink returns, I want you to call me. You can call me anytime, it doesn't matter."

"Thanks," Philly said, feeling relief at Melanie's offer.

"Third, I want to see you at Saint Sebastian tonight. It's very important that you come."

Philly doubted that she'd have the energy to leave the house once she got home. "I'll try," she said.

"That's not good enough," Melanie said sharply. "I expect to see you there."

Philly kept silent, not wanting to speak aloud a promise she might not keep.

"You know," Melanie said, "I never thought you'd call me for help. I've always felt that you looked down on me. I'm glad you called and I hope I helped you. I'll see you tonight, okay?"

"You did help me," Philly acknowledged. Perhaps Melanie had done what she had subconsciously wanted Melanie to do: her sponsor had taken charge.

"I need to hear you say you'll come to tonight's meeting," Melanie pressed.

Simon was approaching. "Where did you run off to?" he called out. "The jury's reached a verdict."

"I've got to go," Philly said. "The jury's back."

Carpenter thought you could never relax until a jury had answered all of the questions it had to address. But when the forewoman announced that the jury had found each of the defendants negligent and Mary Foster to be free from negligence, he was conscious that his breathing had returned close to normal and the twisted feeling in his gut had eased.

The court clerk consulted the list of questions that had been presented to the jury. "Was the plaintiff damaged by the defendants' negligence?"

"Yes," the forewoman replied.

"What is the amount of the plaintiff's damages?"

"One million, six hundred thousand dollars."

Holy shit! Carpenter thought. Philly had pulled off the second seven-figure verdict in two months. He glanced at the defendants' counsel table. Amy Huff and Robert Boyd were giving the forewoman hard stares. Marcia Livingston had a weak smile on her lips.

Carpenter refocused his attention on the court clerk's next questions and began to jot down notes. The jury had determined that Harrison Blaine and the Maple Leaf Assisted Living Center were jointly responsible for Mary Foster's damages but that Harry Fried was only on the hook for twenty-five percent of the damage award. The Center and Blaine would soon be involved in a focused negotiation as to how each party would contribute to the damage award. Marcia Livingston would probably try to get Harry Fried out from under any payment obligation.

Ruth Foster had been paying close attention to the forewoman's answers to the clerk's questions. Carpenter was surprised to see her suddenly rise and make a quit exit from the courtroom.

Judge Henderson granted Robert Boyd's request that the jurors be polled. Each juror confirmed that the forewoman's answers were the jury's unanimous decision.

"Thank you, ladies and gentlemen, for your service," Judge Henderson declared. "You are now excused."

The jurors filed out of the courtroom. Carpenter noted that a few directed friendly smiles in the direction of Philly and Simon.

"Do counsel have any other business before we adjourn?" the judge asked. "No? In that case, court is adjourned. Thank you, counsel, for a well-tried case."

Carpenter congratulated Philly and Simon as the lawyers for the defendants made a hasty exit from the courtroom. Robert Boyd held the door while Harrison Blaine and Harry Fried maneuvered their wheelchairs into the corridor. Carpenter noted that Richard Mason was not in attendance.

In the corridor outside the courtroom it took Carpenter a moment to spot Ruth Foster. She was sitting on a bench, head in her hands, obviously weeping. Carpenter nudged Philly and reached for Simon's shoulder. "We have a problem," he said pointing to their client's daughter.

Philly took a deep breath. "I'll handle this."

Carpenter and Simon followed Philly to where Ruth Foster was sitting but kept their distance. Carpenter sensed that their client's daughter needed space. "Ruth, what's going on?" Philly asked.

Ruth Foster looked up red-eyed and ashen. "My cell vibrated and I saw it was the hospital. My mother's dead. Her heart stopped during the surgery. Those fucking wheelchair morons and Mason killed her. She's gone."

Ruth Foster had departed for the hospital after turning down Simon's offer to accompany her. They were standing in the courthouse parking lot, coat collars turned up to protect from the wind, cheeks reddened from standing in the cold trying unsuccessfully to comfort Ruth Foster.

This was one of the times that Carpenter hated the way his mind worked. He should have been focusing solely on Ruth Foster's loss. Instead he'd begun to think about whether the defendants in the just concluded trial could be sued for wrongful death. For all he knew there might be a legal action against the physicians and hospital responsible for Mary Foster's hip replacement surgery. Wasn't hip replacement surgery one of those common surgeries that presented little risk?

Carpenter knew that Philly and Simon were looking to him for guidance. "I don't have anything brilliant to offer," he said and straightaway saw the disappointment in Simon's eyes. Simon seemed more torn up over Mary Foster's death than Philly. Carpenter had thought he'd never see the day when Simon appeared on the verge of tears, but when Ruth Foster had delivered her news, Simon's icy reserve disappeared.

"Look," Carpenter said. "There's nothing any of us can do to change things. Let's plan on meeting tomorrow. If you don't want to come into Boston," he directed at Philly, "we'll patch you into a call."

"I don't fucking believe this," Simon muttered. "It took a lot of guts for her to testify. I thought this was a common medical procedure. What the hell happened here?"

Carpenter had a sudden insight. Simon had been the one to prepare Mary Foster for trial. "I know this is hard on you," he said to the young lawyer. "You obviously got to know her gearing up for the trial. It was clear during her testimony that she liked and trusted you. Right now, it's okay to grieve. Tomorrow is another day. We'll sort through the legal maze tomorrow."

Even Carpenter was surprised to hear himself making that speech. What was he doing—channeling Maxine?

"I'm out of here," Simon said, moving off toward his new car. "I'm going to get stinking drunk. This sucks big time."

Philly started to say something, but Carpenter put a finger to his lips and shook his head. Words would do nothing for Simon.

"Maybe I should join Simon for a drink," Philly said after Simon drove off.

"That's not an option and you know it."

"During lunch," Philly said, "I wanted a beer in the worst way. That personal call I made was to my sponsor. And that was *before* Mary Foster died."

What is it with this goddamn case? Carpenter thought. Philly and Simon were becoming unglued.

"I've got to get out of here," Philly said. "I need to go to a meeting tonight. I can't believe this."

Carpenter nodded, watched Philly head for her car. Was he the only one who felt no urge to get sloshed?

Carpenter settled in behind the wheel of his car and waited for the heater to kick in. Did the defendants have any basis to appeal the jury's recent verdict? By and large he felt that Henderson had run an error-free trial. This might be another case in which the defendants sought a discount if they promised not to appeal.

And then there was Ruth Foster. Her mother's death would likely turn her into a heat seeking missile bent on destroying Blaine, Fried, and anyone involved with the Maple Leaf Assisted Living Center. The verdict in the just concluded trial was a great victory. But chances were that it would be a long time before anyone saw any money.

"I don't know what came over me," Philly said to the sparse crowd in the basement of Saint Sebastian Church. "This was the first time I needed to talk to Melanie, and she was there for me. But I can't figure out why the idea of having a beer was so overwhelming. If someone had put a beer down in front of me, I would have knocked it back in a heartbeat."

At the front of the room, Charlie nodded, and Philly couldn't stop staring at his bobbing ponytail. Not for the first time, she was taken aback by looking to an aged hippy lookalike for direction. Today Charlie's Hawaiian shirt featured a school of colorful fish, bright reds and yellows against a blue background. He looked more likely to light up a joint than deliver a pearl of wisdom.

"You've been under a lot of stress the last couple of months," Charlie said. "I imagine it was a lot of work to prepare for two jury trials."

"It was," Philly responded. "But I had help. Besides, trying cases is what I need to do to make a living. I should have been in heaven especially after winning each case. I just can't get a handle on where the sudden urge to drink came from."

"I always have the urge to drink," a middle-aged man in a red ski parka interjected. "Consider yourself lucky you don't *always* have the sudden urge."

"James has a point," Charlie said. "For some reason, your urge to drink has stayed in the background. Maybe we should be focusing on the period when the urge to drink wasn't front and center for you."

Charlie's read on her situation didn't seem right to Philly. It didn't make sense to examine the times she didn't feel like having a drink. Scrutiny of the recent occasion when she felt the urge to drink seemed a more appropriate direction to pursue.

Melanie raised her hand tentatively and Charlie nodded in her direction. "I've been thinking about this," she said. "I believe we're over-thinking this situation. I think Philly was just worn out. I know that when my daughter runs me ragged and I wish she would go to bed, is when I start thinking about drinking. So maybe Philly just reached the point of tiredness where the urge to drink came to the surface for a time."

Charlie was literally chewing over Melanie's observation; his jaw muscles were working the way Carpenter's did when the geezer was deep in thought.

"Do you think Melanie has a point?" Charlie asked Philly.

"I don't know."

"Let's try out her theory. You're excused. Go home and go to bed. We expect a report a week from today."

"Can I go too?" James asked. "I've also had a hard day."

"No," Charlie decreed. "Your hard day isn't over yet."

Philly was so wound up she couldn't sleep. Paul's breathing had become regular and she knew it was a matter of moments before he dropped off. "Hey," she whispered, giving him a gentle poke in the ribs.

"What's the matter?"

"I can't fucking sleep is what's the matter," Philly said as she nestled against Paul. "My mind keeps racing."

"Turn around," Paul directed, and he began to rub her back. Philly first tensed at his touch, then began to relax.

"I think your sponsor may have figured out what happened if that's what's worrying you," Paul whispered.

"I don't know."

"Think about it. Since we've been together you've dealt with the drinking. It hasn't been an issue. It came up after a particularly brutal two months with a lot of pressure on you. Maybe your defenses were down."

Philly had to admit there was a certain logic to what Melanie had come up with and Paul was now seconding. "It bothers me that the urge to drink came up at all. I thought I had it under control."

"Didn't you tell me once that you'd never have it under control?"

"I did, but I thought I had it under control. I feel like damaged goods, like I have to lug this thing that's wrong with me through the rest of my life."

"You do have to haul this problem around for the rest of your life, but it doesn't make you damaged goods. You've done very well for yourself. You've helped a lot of people along the way and you've ended up with a wonderful daughter and a husband who's willing to put up with you. Stop complaining."

Paul was doing something she was incapable of doing, standing back and looking at her life from a big picture perspective. "I can't help it," Philly said. "I *feel* like damaged goods."

"If I tell you something will you promise not to get angry?"

"Moi? Me get fucking angry? When has that ever happened? What the hell are you talking about?"

"Do you promise?" Paul said when he stopped laughing.

"Okay, I promise."

"You're pissed off and unable to sleep because you can't stand the fact that there's this part of your life you can't control, and it controls you."

"Are you saying I'm some kind of a control freak?"

"The thought has occurred to me."

Philly resisted the urge to turn around and confront Paul face-to-face. Instead she matched her breathing to his and considered what he had said. It was true that she liked to be in charge and that she hated loose ends. In that respect, she was a lot like Carpenter who wouldn't rest until he had mastered everything there was to know about a case. But in the two recently concluded trials she had made a conscious effort to delegate work to Rachel and Simon because she had known that she couldn't prepare both cases alone with Daisy in her life. Maybe that was what had stressed her out—maybe the urge to drink had surfaced because internally she was a wreck over entrusting major portions of each case to another lawyer.

"Earth to Philly. Come in Philly."

"I need to talk to Carpenter," Philly said.

"Okay."

"Thanks," Philly said. "Don't stop," she added when Paul rolled over and ceased to knead her back. "Wait till I drop off."

"Fat chance," Paul said. "I'm giving you three more minutes. Then you're on your own."

98

"You were supposed to keep my proposal confidential," Richard Jenner complained over the phone. "I ought to report you to the Board of Bar Overseers."

Carpenter gave Crystal Queen's lawyer a few second to cool down. "Report away," he said.

"You had no right to copy Brandeis' lawyer on your letter rejecting the proposal I gave you."

"Says who?" Carpenter came back.

"I gave you a settlement proposal. Settlement proposals are supposed to be kept confidential."

"Oops," Carpenter said.

"You're a real fucking comedian," Jenner said. "Maybe I'll write the Brandeis lawyer and say I never made any proposal to you."

"Which is it?" Carpenter asked. "Is it that I shouldn't have passed along a response to a settlement offer you did make? Or is it that I passed along a response to a settlement offer you didn't make."

"That's for me to know and you to find out," Jenner said, and the lawyer's remark took Carpenter back to his childhood when that retort was standard kid banter.

"Here's what I know," Carpenter said. "I copied Beatrice Gold on a letter rejecting a payment you proposed that my client make to your client. You proposed it to me on a telephone call that you initiated and that took exactly six minutes and twenty-two seconds." Carpenter had remembered the time of the call, but he consulted the copy of the telephone record obtained by Barney Freedman just to make sure he hadn't screwed up that detail. The possibility that Jenner would deny making an offer had prompted Carpenter to enlist Freedman and now he was glad that he did.

"I guess this is going to litigation," Jenner said.

"Be my guest," Carpenter said. "You might want to ask your client why her last boyfriend broke up with her. Have a nice day," he added before hanging up his phone.

Carpenter reviewed the just completed call. Freedman had provided him with a further item of intelligence. The white guy Crystal Queen had been dating had broken up with her. The guy had told Freedman there was something off about her. She had asked him too many questions about the trust fund payments he'd be receiving once he graduated.

Carpenter considered whether he'd be in trouble if Jenner reported him to the Board of Bar Overseers. His Barrister friends had split on that issue. If the roles were reversed, he'd be furious if Jenner had revealed the nature of a rejected settlement proposal to anyone. Still, once Bernard Mucowahandi, with Connie's blessing, had made the decision to fight Crystal Queen, Carpenter had decided to push the envelope to get Queen off Bernard's back.

"More aggravation," Carpenter said to the photograph facing his desk, and he received a slight head nod in acknowledgement.

"I'm listening," Philly said, when Amy Huff announced that she was on the line with a proposal to resolve all issues in the Mary Foster case.

"Two million dollars," Huff said, "in return for a release of all claims including future wrongful death claims."

Philly reasoned that Huff and Robert Boyd had decided that their clients had exposure if wrongful death claims were brought on Mary Foster's behalf. Carpenter had run that question by his Barrister buddies, and they were unanimous that wrongful death claims could be brought and likely would be successful.

"Obviously, the recent verdict would not be appealed if this proposal is accepted," Huff elaborated.

"I'll get back to you," Philly said. "We need to think about what you've put on the table, and then we'll have to present it to Ruth Foster. Right now, Miss Foster is not in a position to address something this complicated."

"I understand," Huff said evenly. "I know I also speak for Robert Boyd when I tell you we're very sorry for her loss. As a practical matter, we will file an appeal of the verdict if we cannot work something out before the time to appeal runs out in about another four weeks. I hope you understand."

"I understand," Philly confirmed. "Thank you for your proposal."

Philly set down her phone. Sarah would soon be off duty, so Daisy and she were joined at the hip the rest of the day. With luck, Daisy would crash for an hour in the afternoon and she'd be able to talk to Carpenter on the phone. But the idea of a telephone discussion, even one enhanced by a Skype hookup, seemed inadequate for the occasion. There were some meetings with Carpenter when she needed to look him in the eye. If Carpenter had free time, she and Daisy were heading into Boston. It wasn't just the Mary Foster case that she needed to discuss with him.

Rachel had needed little urging to volunteer for Daisy duty, and Philly now sat across from Carpenter in the conference room relating Amy Huff's proposal. Carpenter received the details without expression, and she had no idea what she would have done if Carpenter were not around to provide advice.

"They're putting another four hundred thou on the table," Carpenter said in a manner that made Philly think he needed to speak Huff's proposal aloud to help his own thinking. "Plus, they haven't said anything about interest on the verdict."

Philly nodded. She'd been remiss in not pinning Huff down on the interest issue.

"Would you be willing to waive attorney fees on the amount above the jury's verdict if we came to an agreement quickly?"

Carpenter's question surprised Philly. Perhaps their contingency agreement with Mary Foster didn't cover wrongful death claims so that they would need a new agreement on fees when it came to those claims.

"I probably would," Philly decided, after a little thought.

"So would I," Carpenter said. "If they made it five hundred thousand and agreed to pay interest, I'd seriously think of recommending it to Ruth Foster. I might even be prepared to provide a slight discount on the interest if that would make a deal happen."

"She's going to want another trial," Philly said. She couldn't shake the image of Ruth Foster sobbing in the courthouse corridor after the jury had been discharged. In all their dealings with Foster, Philly had assessed that the woman's desire for vengeance was stronger than her desire for money.

"You're probably right," Carpenter said. "But that's not our problem. Our problem is to advise Ruth Foster. And we will. Whether she takes our advice is her business."

"Should we involve Simon in these settlement discussions?" Philly asked.

Carpenter shook his head. "Tell him what's going on, but I want the two of us to handle this. Call Huff back and tell her what we'll recommend. If she says that her offer stays where it is, don't tell her whether we'll recommend it or not. Leave her hanging."

"Will we tell Foster not to accept the offer if Huff and Boyd won't up it?"

"We don't have to decide that now," Carpenter said. "Just to be clear: when Huff asks whether you'll recommend her original offer and she will press you on that point, you can tell her to connect the dots. You'd have already told her what you'd recommend."

Philly played out a telephone discussion with Huff. She could see no downside in following Carpenter's approach. "All right," she said. "There's something else I want to talk to you about."

"Give me a minute," Carpenter said.

In the men's room down the hallway from their office, Carpenter splashed cold water on his face, using the moment alone to assess whether to broach with Philly the idea that had begun to make more and more sense each time he kicked it around. He also wanted a moment to collect himself for whatever Philly was about to lay on him. He had been around her long enough to know when she wanted to discuss something in her personal life. He hated those discussions and complained about them to Philly but, in the end, he'd listen to what she had to say and help her if he could. Christ, he thought. Philly had just pulled off two impressive trial wins and he sensed that they would take second fiddle to what he wanted to discuss with Philly and what Philly was about to unload. There was no let up, no time to savor a bright moment or a major victory.

Carpenter stared at Philly across the conference room table. She had just related her recent urge to drink and her husband's theory as to why that had occurred. The Cambridge cop was probably right about Philly being a control freak. Christ, he was more of a control freak than Philly would ever be, so he knew the type. As he thought about what Philly had said, he realized that it provided a natural lead-in to what he wanted to discuss with her.

"I'm going to remind you that I hate these personal discussions," Carpenter began.

"Yeah, yeah, yeah," Philly replied. "What else is new?"

"I'm just reminding you," Carpenter said, hoping he didn't sound defensive. "I have no idea why you got the urge to drink. But I'm proud of you for not giving into the urge and getting help. Good for you. And don't give me this damaged goods crap. You just pulled off a rare feat of seven-figure verdicts in successive months. Damaged goods my ass!"

Philly smiled weakly.

"Do you mind if I change the subject?" Carpenter asked.

"Yeah, I do. This is about me."

"Just listen to me," Carpenter entreated. "I think it ties into what you've been talking about."

Philly looked skeptical but gave a brief nod for him to continue. Carpenter saw no easy way to lead into what he wanted to discuss. "I've been thinking about this a lot lately and I'm leaning toward the four of us forming a firm."

Philly emitted a sharp laugh. "You're kidding right? You're the lone wolf, remember?"

"Hear me out," Carpenter said, his thoughts ordered. "First of all, for young lawyers, Rachel and Simon are terrific. We're beyond lucky to have them. They've made a big contribution to any success we've had this year and last year. We both know we'd have been up shit's creek without them."

Philly nodded. "No dispute there," she said.

"Second, I don't want to lose them. I want there to be a structure that they're invested in. Third, I like them and trust them."

"Would they be associates and the two of us partners?" Philly asked.

"Maybe that's how it would start out," Carpenter said, and he proceeded to fill Philly in on two possible structures he envisioned.

"What tipped you in this direction?" Philly asked.

"A lot of little things and one big thing. The big thing is that you've got a kid to deal with and for all I know another might be on the way. Also, Maxine's been after me to slow down. But I may be way ahead of her because, in fact, I've actually started to do that."

"You could have fooled me," Philly said.

"I've been fooling you for a while now," Carpenter said, his joking half-hearted. "Years ago, I wouldn't have left my office on a workday except for a family emergency. Lately, Christ! I've regularly cut out for exercise and that goddamn spinning you do."

"That just means you've picked up a few good habits from me."

"Yeah, I have. If we do this, it's going to be a big adjustment. In a few years, we won't have absolute control over decisions. For control freaks like us, that is going to be hard to deal with."

"What does this have to do with what I wanted to discuss?"

"Let's say Paul is right about you being a control freak," Carpenter put forward. "If we go with a firm, you won't have to be a control freak. Actually, you wouldn't be able to be a control freak. That would be taken out of your hands. Maybe that would help you with this drinking thing."

Philly slumped in her chair. "This is a lot to take in. Let me think about it and get back to you."

"Fair enough," Carpenter said. "Are you okay with coming into Boston to meet with Ruth Foster?" he changed the subject.

"More than okay. I wouldn't miss that meeting for the world. What do you think she'll do?"

"I don't have a clue," Carpenter said. "But very shortly we're going to find out what she wants."

99

Ruth Foster looked drained as she sat across from Philly, Carpenter, and Simon in the conference room. Simon had been the only lawyer in the office to attend Mary Foster's funeral service, and he reported that Ruth had appeared frail and needed a supporting arm to enter and leave the church service. In advance of this meeting, Amy Huff had agreed that the defendants would pay interest on the jury verdict and that $500,000 would be added to the jury award. Philly had sent Ruth Foster a letter outlining the defendants' settlement proposal and setting forth their recommendation that the offer be accepted.

Carpenter had been chosen to lead this client discussion and he had just gone through the offer and their recommendation, going over in detail the points that had been set forth in Philly's letter. Philly wondered whether anything Carpenter said had registered with Foster. Maybe Foster hadn't even read her letter.

"Do you understand the offer that's been made to you and why we're recommending that you accept the offer?" Carpenter asked, concern in his voice.

"I really can't deal with this right now," Foster complained. "I don't see what the rush is about."

"There really is no rush to make a decision," Carpenter said. "And we're not asking you to make a decision when you're not capable of making up your mind. I want to be clear about that."

"Is there any other family member who can assist you in dealing with this issue?" Philly asked.

Foster shook her head. "Nobody I care to involve. I'm on my own here."

Carpenter paused and Philly took in Foster staring at him with a blank look. She'd hoped that Foster would make a decision at this meeting and now realized that wasn't going to happen.

"Do you have any questions for us?" Carpenter asked.

"Go over that business about your legal fees again," Foster requested.

"We have a contingency fee agreement with you that covers the jury trial that just concluded," Carpenter explained. "Under that agreement, legal fees are a third of the recovery. What we've agreed to do if you accept the offer on the table is to forego any legal fees in connection with the five hundred thousand dollars the defendants have agreed to add to the jury's award of damages. The five hundred thousand dollars goes to you without a legal fee being backed out."

"Why are you agreeing to that?"

"Because it's the right thing to do. If you take the settlement offer and we don't have to go to trial over claims relating to your mother's death, we don't think we should profit by the added settlement amount."

"That's very generous," Foster said. "I appreciate it." She paused for a long moment, lost in thought. "If I take the deal, I can't sue anyone for my mother's death, right?"

"Right," Carpenter confirmed. "Except the hospital and the physicians who operated on your mother if any of them screwed up."

"Do you think I could recover more than five hundred thousand dollars if I did sue?" Foster asked.

"I'm not sure," Carpenter owned up. "If you sued and won there would be legal fees coming out of the award. There's no easy way to predict what value a jury would place on your mother's life."

"I don't know . . ." Foster said in a soft voice that trailed off.

"What's the first thing you thought of when you read our letter explaining the settlement offer?" Simon spoke for the first time.

"I thought they were trying to get off easy," Foster replied. "I said to myself, the hell with them, I'll sue them again."

"You've always wanted to make them pay for what they did to your mother, haven't you?" Simon followed up.

"You bet I did," Foster said, showing animation for the first time since the meeting started.

Philly wondered where Simon was going with his questions, but she didn't see an easy way of interrupting him to find out. Putting up with Simon's approaches would become a given if they formed a firm.

"The thing is, you've already made them pay once," Simon said. "The jury verdict is a large verdict and the defendants are willing to pay the amount with interest if you accept their deal. So what we're really talking about is making them pay again because your mother died."

"Well, I want them to pay again," Foster said. "Why would I not want to make them pay again?"

"Exactly. And they are. Under their proposal, they are paying again—half a million dollars." Simon paused a beat and it seemed to Philly he wanted to allow time for the sum to sink in. "So the only question is whether that amount is sufficient for you."

"You haven't helped me much on that question," Foster groused.

"Actually, we have," Simon said. "We've made a recommendation that you take the offer and we've given you the reasons for our recommendation. Mr. Carpenter is right. We have no way to predict whether you'd do better than their offer by going forward with a second trial. Also, this way you can put it behind you."

"I don't want to put it behind me," Foster shot back. "Those assholes killed my mother." Then she wilted again. Ruth Foster seemed no closer to making a decision than she was when she entered the conference room. Actually, she looked even more conflicted than before.

"I hear what you're saying," Philly said. "It's hard to imagine putting something like this behind you."

The next thing she said brought Carpenter and Foster up short while Simon's expression was neutral. "My fiancé was killed by a drunk teenaged driver." Philly paused, and then went on. "I was devastated, and I was furious. I wanted to sue the driver and I asked Mr. Carpenter to represent me. Mr. Carpenter refused. It's a long story but in the end, I never sued the driver. I ended up forgiving him, instead. I realized that there was nothing that was going to bring back my fiancé. There was a time when I didn't think I could ever let go of my anger over what had happened, but I did. It helped me in the long run. I'm not saying your situation is identical to mine. Your feelings are your own, and your situation is different. But I am saying that there is a value to closing out a situation where something horrible happened to a loved one. We think the extra five hundred thousand dollars in the defendants' offer tips the scales toward accepting the offer. It's a good offer, and it may help you, eventually, to move on. That's what my letter to you tried to get across."

Foster dropped her eyes, studied her hands folded on the conference room table. Carpenter was no longer paying attention to Foster; he was staring at Philly intently, but she couldn't figure out whether he approved of her short speech or was pissed off because she made it. Simon offered up a sad smile that Philly returned.

"I don't think I should make a decision today," Foster said, looking up. "I think I should sleep on it."

"Of course," Philly said. "As we mentioned, take your time. There's no rush."

Simon returned to the conference room after showing Ruth Foster out. Philly and Carpenter weren't exactly glaring at each other, but their looks were far from friendly.

"What did I miss?" Simon asked.

"Nothing," Carpenter said gruffly.

"Carpenter doesn't think personal anecdotes should be shared with a client," Philly countered.

Simon had noticed Carpenter's sour expression when Philly recounted the story of her fiancé being killed. Now he understood its source.

"As a general rule, I guess I agree with Carpenter," Simon said. "But in this case, I'm glad Philly made an exception. I think Ruth Foster needs all the input she can get."

Carpenter and Philly remained silent and Simon figured it was just a matter of time before one of them told him he was a young lawyer who needed to be seen and not heard. If he had to guess, Carpenter would deliver the rebuke. Instead, to Simon's amazement, Carpenter and Philly locked eyes and both began to smile.

"What's going on?" Simon asked.

"Nothing," Carpenter said without his former gruffness. "Tell Rachel she can go off babysitting duty."

"Am I being dismissed?" Simon asked.

"You are," Philly said. "Take over for Rachel with Daisy. Carpenter and I need a minute."

Simon couldn't figure out what he was missing.

"You can go," Philly said. "Now."

100

Carpenter studied his list of active cases. At the top was Martina Glass' personal injury suit. He had advised Philly to take the deposition of the guy who had fallen on Glass, and Philly had turned that task over to Simon. The deposition would take place in January.

Second on his list was the lawsuit by Keith and Jane Spring against Roland Butler, the psychologist who had failed to warn the Springs about their son, Ryan, possessing a gun. Butler's lawyer, Hillary Reese, had just offered to settle the case for $120,000. Carpenter needed to relay the offer to the Springs today. He'd recommend that the offer be rejected. Reese's proposal was predictable; she had put on the table a lowball settlement figure divisible by three which was likely based on what the insurance company she represented pegged as the cost of litigation. The Springs case reminded Carpenter of the wheelchair case in one respect—it was a case that might produce a substantial jury verdict if tried. A settlement in the case would probably be for small dollars.

Third on his list was the upcoming February trial in the case Philly had brought in involving the young woman who had been labeled a killer on a bill-board. The young woman's parents had paid half the legal bill, and Carpenter foresaw a lot of work on the case with no money coming in. He reminded himself not to give Philly a hard time over the lack of payment. Her client had been harmed in a vicious way and needed an advocate.

Carpenter said, "Come in" when he heard a knock on his door.

"Mail," Rachel said, depositing a short stack of letters on his desk before departing.

Carpenter's heartbeat picked up when he saw the Brandeis University letterhead relating to the final item on his list. He used a scissors to slit the envelope and read the brief letter from Beatrice Gold. The University had concluded its complaint investigation and had determined that there were insufficient facts to support the allegations in the complaint. The University was treating the matter as closed. Carpenter breathed a sigh of relief. Bernard Mucowahandi had lucked out. Carpenter knew he should be thinking about Bernard's reaction to this news, but all he could think about was Connie's response. His ex had damn well better be pleased with the result. For that matter, they both better be overjoyed.

Carpenter considered whether Bernard's case might be over. If Crystal Queen wanted to see any money, Richard Jenner would have to bring suit against Bernard. Faced with the prospect of actually having to go to court to get a payday for himself, Jenner might decide he no longer wanted anything to do with the case. Of course, Jenner might also make good on his threat to go to the Board of Bar Overseers in which case Carpenter realized that the only person at risk would be him. His next emitted sigh was not one of relief. How do I get myself into these situations? he mused.

Carpenter used the intercom to reach Philly's office and Rachel picked up. "Is Simon around?" he asked.

"He just walked in."

"Tell him to get his ass down here. I've got some good news he needs to hear."

"Can I come too?"

"Be my guest."

Carpenter put down his phone and considered the list of active matters. They needed more business.

101

Ruth Foster was back in the office suite's conference room. Foster had called, saying that she wanted to tell them what she had decided to do in a face-to-face meeting. That had brought about another wager. Philly had pocketed the initial thirty-dollar pot by coming closest to estimating the jury's verdict. The problem with their second bet was the availability of only two options: either Foster would accept the defendants' offer or she wouldn't. Simon was the only one to bet she would take the offer. Carpenter and Philly were convinced that she'd sue. Now, As Foster sat at the conference room table, Simon was struck by her determination and confidence. Less than a week ago, she had been distraught and tentative. Today she looked more like the woman they'd first met.

"First, I want to thank you all for everything you've done," Foster began. "I'm extremely grateful. I know I haven't been the easiest person to get along with and I appreciate that you were always direct with me." Foster turned to Simon. "I don't know how you did it, but you got my mother to come through when she testified. I thought she was going to be a disaster, but she delivered and I think it was because of you. She liked you, by the way. She said you were a sweet, young man."

"That's me," Simon said, smiling.

"I'm going to take the offer," Foster cut to the chase. "I don't really want to go through another trial. Ms. Piper's comments when we last met helped tip the scales for me. I want this behind me. I don't want to keep living with unhappy images of my mother. I want to keep remembering her at her best. So I'm going to follow your recommendation. I bet there were times when you didn't think that would ever happen."

Carpenter reached across the conference room table and offered his hand. Foster leaned forward and shook hands.

"Those were very kind words," Carpenter said. "We appreciate them. Since you followed our recommendation, we can only say you made the right decision."

Foster smiled. "What now?" she asked.

"We're going to work out a settlement agreement with the lawyers for the defendants. When the lawyers have signed off on the document, we will get it to you and explain the terms. If you agree that the settlement agreement is in order, you will sign the document, the defendants will sign the document, and you will be paid. The settlement check will be deposited into our clients' account and we'll distribute your share and our share and provide you with an accounting before anyone is paid anything."

"Sounds good," Foster said.

"I liked your mother," Simon said. "I'm always going to remember her courage in taking the witness stand to testify."

"So how did you get her to focus?" Foster asked. "There were days when I couldn't even carry on a conversation with her."

Simon opened his case file and produced the battered photograph of Harrison Blaine. "I had her punch Blaine's photograph," Simon said. "It definitely got her to focus. Here. You should have this. Any time you want to remember your mother as the fighter she was, take a look."

Carpenter had been awaiting Connie's call with a mixture of dread and anticipation. He was hoping that she'd thank him for a job well done, but he couldn't shake the notion that she'd find some fault with the way he had handled her husband's case. Bernard had called earlier. His actual client was thrilled with the University's decision and couldn't imagine Crystal Queen bringing a civil suit against him. "Let her try," he had said. "We shall defeat her again."

Carpenter considered a possible link between the contrasting claims he had made on Bernard's behalf, the claim that Crystal Queen had a crush on Bernard and the claim that Queen was setting him up for a sexual harassment charge. Queen probably never had a crush on Bernard, but Carpenter was convinced that she had tried to come on to him in the hope he'd be indiscreet. What had the student called Queen's expression? Goo goo eyes? Maybe Queen was flirting with Bernard to get him to respond. The unexpected encounter at the door to the bedroom might have panicked Queen and accelerated her making a sexual harassment claim before she intended to do so.

Carpenter knew that this reasoning didn't explain Queens's taking the photograph of Bernard and Connie. But what theory was perfect? The photograph was definitely a piece of the puzzle but, in the legal game, not all of the pieces of the puzzle ended up fitting. The fact that a white guy had broken up with Queen was another puzzle piece that had never found a certain home but helped make a case that Queen was out to find a man to fleece.

"I suppose I owe you a big thank you," Connie said.

"There's no suppose about it," Carpenter fired back.

"You're right. Thank you. Do you think it's over?"

"That's not a question I'm going to waste time considering. Queen may bring a civil suit or not. If she sues, we'll decide how to proceed." Carpenter left out Richard Jenner's threat against his law license. There were some subjects better kept to himself.

"We should celebrate," Connie said.

"Give me a break!"

"Right," Connie laughed. "For a moment, I forgot who I was talking to."

"How are you doing?" Carpenter inquired.

"Good. The economy is crazy and markets are all over the place but by and large we are doing well. Raul has been a big help."

"I wasn't asking if your business was doing okay. I was asking whether *you* were doing okay?"

"I am," Connie said. "I'm happy. You just contributed to my happiness."

"That's part of my mission in life."

"What about you?" Connie asked.

"It's turned out to be a good year. Philly and I have these two young lawyers working with us who have been terrific. We're ending the year on a high note. In January, Maxine and I will be moving in together in a condo in Arlington. For the moment, even I can't find anything to bitch about."

"Look at us," Connie said. "Content."

"I wouldn't go that far."

"No, of course not. What was I thinking?"

102

Keith Spring had had his say over the phone and now Carpenter was more convinced than ever that clients were an incomprehensible combination of unpredictability and foolishness. Spring wanted to accept the $120,000 settlement offer Hillary Reese had made on behalf of the psychologist, Roland Butler. To date, Spring had come across as uncompromising, hell bent on seeking vengeance for the shooting of his younger son, Darren. In that respect, he was akin to Ruth Foster. But where Foster had soldiered on through a trial, Spring was ready to pack it in to avoid a trial. Carpenter couldn't decide whether he was more annoyed with Spring turning into a wuss after all his tough talk, than he was irked by seeing a case he had targeted for a big payoff disappearing before his eyes.

"I think you're making a mistake here," Carpenter said. "This offer is extremely low. Why are you even thinking of taking this offer?"

Spring didn't answer right away. Once again Carpenter wondered where the absent Jane Spring fit into the family decision making.

"The truth is I could use the money," Spring said. "Besides, back at the beginning, you weren't impressed with the case."

"I've changed my mind," Carpenter said. "Rudolph Nelson has come up with a way to present the case that makes it easy to understand and a likely winner. You could be passing up a potential million-dollar verdict. And weren't you the guy who said he didn't need money?"

Spring didn't acknowledge his previous statement about money. "I still want to take the offer," he said

"Why don't you at least let me try to get the other side to increase the offer?"

"If you do that, could they take this offer off the table?"

"That's possible," Carpenter said, "but highly unlikely. My read is that the offer on the table represents the other side's guess as to what it will cost them to go to trial even if they win. This is a classic lowball offer."

"I don't like it that they can take the offer off the table," Spring replied.

Christ, Carpenter thought. Spring was all talk and no action. He couldn't account for the client's sudden turnaround.

"Sleep on it at least," Carpenter said. "I don't understand where you're coming from. I don't believe that you're thinking this through correctly."

"All right," Spring said. "Try to negotiate something higher."

"All right," Carpenter parroted. "I'll get back to you."

Carpenter wanted to be immediately put out of his misery, so he called Hillary Reese without taking the time to come up with a game plan as to how to approach her.

"You're going to have to do a lot better than one hundred twenty thousand to make this case go away," Carpenter said when Reese took his call.

"How much better?"

"I'm not going to bid against myself," Carpenter said.

"My client has made an offer. I take it you're rejecting the offer. Unless you're going to make a counteroffer, this case is going to trial."

"One million dollars," Carpenter blurted out before giving reason a chance to kick in.

"That's rejected," Reese said promptly.

"Okay. Then the ball is back in your court."

"No, it isn't," Reese demurred. "Your figure wasn't reasonable. I'm not going to bid against *myself.*"

Carpenter knew that he was handling this negotiation all wrong, but he couldn't stop himself. "We both know that Ryan Spring's producing a gun during a therapy session is an act so off the charts that Butler should have informed the Springs. In this situation, Butler had a duty to warn the Spring family, and he didn't. That fact is not going to go away."

"Save it for the jury," Reese replied. "Butler took possession of the gun. That's a fact that's not going to go away either. Butler removed the threat he witnessed. Also, Ryan has no history of violence."

Reese's comment reminded Carpenter of a loose end. "I have a question for you. We'll find this out in discovery when we take Butler's deposition, but would you tell me whether the gun Ryan Spring handed over to Butler was loaded?"

Reese didn't answer for a long moment. "There were two bullets," she finally said.

Carpenter decided not to comment; they both knew that the fact just revealed helped the Springs' case. And perhaps the fact explained why Reese had proposed a lowball settlement and had never filed a motion to dismiss the Springs' case because of Ryan's lack of a history of violence.

"I guess we're at an impasse," Carpenter said. "The fact that you made an offer got the Springs to think about settlement. But you're simply going to have to do better to get a settlement done."

"We're going around in circles," Reese said. "Tell me what will make this case go away and I'll present it to my client. Until you do that, I don't think we have anything left to say."

"You're probably right," Carpenter replied. "Thanks for your time."

When he hung up his phone, Carpenter realized what he should have done after his talk with Keith Spring. He needed to get Spring and his wife into his office and confront them together. Calling Reese had been a mistake.

103

Getting the Springs to come to his conference room made Carpenter think of moving the mountain to Mohammed. Keith Spring had bitched and moaned about making the trip to Boston and Carpenter had thrown back at him some off-the-cuff bullshit about a lawyer's ethical responsibility to make sure a client fully understood the terms of a settlement. Jane Spring was another unhappy camper. His other client looked like she had renewed the vow of silence she had taken at their initial meeting.

Simon sat to his right and Carpenter was glad to have the young lawyer with him. Simon had drafted a short memo outlining the pros and cons of accepting Hillary Reese's offer. Carpenter refused to begin discussions until each of his clients reviewed Simon's analysis. Keith Spring finished his perusal so quickly that Carpenter was convinced that he hadn't internalized anything. In contrast, Jane Spring took her time and Carpenter sensed that her husband had kept her in the dark about his wanting to accept Reese's settlement offer. Maybe Spring had kept the existence of the settlement offer from his wife.

"Nothing here changes my mind," Keith Spring said when his wife looked up from her reading.

"That's unfortunate," Carpenter said. "What about you?" he directed to Jane Spring.

Jane Spring stared at him for such a long moment that Carpenter wondered whether she had gone into some kind of trance. "Do we both have to agree to settle the case?" she finally asked.

"That's the only way Dr. Butler will settle the case," Carpenter responded. "Each of you is suing for damages for the death of your son."

"I'm not signing the settlement they want us to sign," Jane Spring announced to her husband's surprise.

"What are you talking about? If I tell you to sign, you're going to sign."

"No."

"What the hell has gotten into you?"

Jane Spring faced her husband. "What the hell has gotten into *you*?" she came back. "You were ready to kill Butler the last time we came here. Now you're ready to take the first offer made to us."

"We could use the money," Keith Spring said, but his comeback was so lame sounding that his wife actually smirked.

"As you said before, we don't need the money right now," Jane Smith said. "Why are you giving up without a fight? And why didn't you tell me about this settlement business before?"

"I didn't want to get you all wrought up."

"Well, I'm all wrought up right now over what you want to do."

"You need to listen to me on this," Keith Spring said.

"I know why you're doing this," Jane Spring said.

"I'm doing this to put this behind us so we can move on."

"That's not why you're doing it."

Keith Spring glared at his wife. "So why am I doing this?"

"You know why but I'll spell it out for you anyway. You're caving in because you feel guilty. You've been beating yourself up over not getting the gun away from Ryan before it went off. After your deposition, something changed for you. I read your deposition and I think I know what changed. I think you got scared of going in front of a jury because you thought they'd blame you for Darren's death. I think you're second-guessing yourself for trying to get the gun away from Ryan."

Keith Spring stared at his wife, but Carpenter doubted that he was seeing her. "That's a load of crap," he finally said.

"Maybe it is, maybe it isn't. But I'm not putting a one hundred twenty-thousand-dollar value on Darren's life."

"A jury might not give us anything."

"If they do that, they'll have to look us in the eye when they do it."

"Shit," Keith Spring muttered. "I can't take this anymore."

"I'm not signing that settlement," Jane Spring said with finality.

Carpenter let the silence lengthen. "Is there any amount that you both would be willing to accept in settlement?" he asked, when it seemed the couple had cooled down.

"A million dollars," Jane Spring said.

"I tried that," Carpenter said. "That was rejected."

"Why didn't you say that in this paper you just put in front of us?" Keith Spring asked.

"Because I just threw the number out there when Butler's attorney asked me to make a counteroffer. I knew there was no way the offer would be accepted."

"Five hundred thousand dollars," Jane Spring said. "Go back to them with that and tell them not a penny less."

Keith Spring offered up a despairing shrug.

"That will probably be rejected also," Carpenter said. "But I'll call Butler's attorney and present it."

"Will I be deposed?" Jane Spring changed the subject.

"It's possible," Carpenter said. "I don't know."

"Could *you* depose me?"

"I could. That's unusual, but I could."

"Tell them if they don't take the five-hundred-thousand-dollar offer, you're going to take my deposition."

"Where are you going with this?" Simon interjected.

"I think I'll be a good witness. After you depose me, make them another offer. Make it six hundred thousand dollars. You can tell Butler's lawyer our settlement figure will go up after my deposition."

"You're crazy!" Keith Spring fumed.

Jane Spring shook her head and pointed to Simon's memo. "It says here that Butler will say he took away the gun Ryan had so he thought there was no further danger to anyone. I understand that, but Ryan threatened you before he handed over the gun. True, Butler says that Ryan took back the threat. But Ryan *had* a gun for Christ's sake, something he had never done before and the gun was loaded. I think Butler should have picked up the phone and told us that Ryan had threatened you and had been carrying a loaded gun. If he had done that, you know we wouldn't have let Ryan in the house. Any parent on that jury would have wanted to be told what Butler didn't tell us. That expert we've got is right about this case."

Keith Spring was speechless. Carpenter began to revise in his head the argument he would make to the jury in this case.

Carpenter's discussion with Hillary Reese played out pretty much as he thought it would. Reese rejected the $500,000 counteroffer and made a $200,000 offer in return. Carpenter rejected Reese's revised settlement figure.

"I'm going to depose Jane Spring," Carpenter said. "I've been instructed to tell you that after her deposition, the plaintiffs won't settle for less than six hundred thousand dollars."

"Let me get this straight. You're going to depose your own client?"

"She's insisting on it."

"And after her deposition, the plaintiffs' settlement demand goes up?"

"That's what Jane Spring's position is. I'm just the messenger."

"What's the husband's position on all this?"

"Take his deposition again and ask him."

"What am I missing here?" Reese asked. "This is nuts."

Carpenter recognized that this moment might be the only time when the case was capable of settlement. He decided to be forthright with Reese.

"You're not missing anything," Carpenter said. "This case is not moving forward as either of us probably expected it to move. Jane Spring refused to put a value of one hundred twenty thousand dollars on Darren's life. She valued the life at one million and I told her that you shot that down."

Reese remained silent.

"Jane Spring is willing to roll the dice. She thinks any parent on the jury would have wanted to be told by your client that the parent's child had threatened one of his parents and had shown up at the therapist's office with a loaded gun. She knows that you're going to argue that Butler took the gun from Ryan and that Ryan recanted the threat he made against his father. But she doesn't think that was enough. I think she has a point."

Reese still didn't say anything.

"I guess we each know what the other is going to argue to the jury," Carpenter opted for levity.

"My client absolutely will not settle for five hundred thousand dollars," Reese said. "So I guess it doesn't matter that we know each other's argument."

Carpenter didn't have a read on whether he could move Jane Spring off her $500,000 figure. "Just for the hell of it and off the record, what's the highest you would recommend to your client?"

"I don't play that game," Reese said.

"Make an exception here," Carpenter urged.

"Three hundred thousand."

"I'll be back to you."

Carpenter had Jane Spring on the line and had just finished going over his discussion with Hillary Reese. Jane Spring was now controlling the plaintiffs' case and Carpenter had deliberately decided not to involve her husband in this conversation.

"If Butler's lawyer sells three hundred thousand dollars to the insurance company, we net two hundred thousand dollars, after we pay you," Spring said.

It wasn't a question and Carpenter stayed silent.

"What do you recommend?"

"When your husband was dealing with the negotiations, I told him I recommended taking the case to trial. That would still be my recommendation. But if what you said was true about his being emotionally torn up over the case, you've got to factor that into your decision. He handled himself reasonably well at his deposition, but I do recall him looking uncomfortable when he was asked about failing to get the gun away from Ryan. Now you've got me worried about how he'll do at trial. At trial, in my opinion, you both need to testify."

"Shit!" Spring exclaimed, and Carpenter had never expected that word to leave her lips. "I suppose I should be grateful," she added after a pause. "At least they may be prepared to move a lot higher. The thing is, if I tell Keith about this, it's only going to make him feel bad because he was prepared to take much less."

Carpenter thought of all the times he had to deal with a family dynamic that turned resolving a case into a tangled mess.

"Maybe I need to get off my high horse," Spring said. "But the truth is, I can't see settling for anything that won't put two hundred fifty thousand dollars in our pocket."

Carpenter did the math. The case would have to settle for $375,000 for Jane Spring to realize her bottom-line figure. He and Philly could agree to cut their fee but that was not something he wanted to do.

"Are you saying if they offered three hundred seventy-five thousand you would accept the offer?"

"Right now, I would," Spring said. "Ask me tomorrow, I might be singing a different tune."

Carpenter found himself warming to Spring. He knew what it was like to waver between positions where each had plusses and drawbacks. Spring had to be weighing the size of a payoff against her husband's newly displayed reluctance to do battle because of guilt.

"Why don't you think about it?" Carpenter suggested. "Nobody's going anywhere. Your answer can wait."

"All I've been doing is thinking about it," Spring said. "If you can make the deal happen, do it before I change my mind. If Butler's lawyer says no, go ahead and take my deposition like we talked about before. I'll work on Keith to get him ready for trial."

"Okay," Carpenter said. "I'll see what I can do."

104

Carpenter and Maxine were sipping drinks in the hotel bar, Maxine opting for a cocktail, Carpenter sticking with beer, no glass, an imported brand of dark ale he had never heard of and which had a satisfying, bitter taste. For this New Year's Eve, he and Philly had decided to break with tradition and splurge for a private dining room in one of the five-star hotels on the Boston waterfront. With four lawyers and four guests they would rattle around in the private room, but what the hell. They wanted some privacy when it came to the serious part of the evening. Carpenter thought he'd end up having more beers than were good for him and had splurged a second time by booking a room for the night so he didn't have to drive home.

"This isn't like you," Maxine said. "I'm assuming that you had a good year in spite of yourself."

"Two seven-figure jury verdicts didn't hurt," Carpenter replied. And next year, he thought, would start out with a modest infusion of cash. This morning, Hillary Reese had e-mailed him that they had a deal at $375,000 in the Spring case.

"If I didn't know you better," Maxine said, "I'd say you're happy."

"You really know how to kill a good mood," Carpenter joked. The truth was he felt content. Most of the year had been nerve wracking due to the lack of cash coming in. But the year had ended with two bangs and he had been around long enough to understand that you needed to be grateful for whatever good fortune came your way even if belatedly. Plus, the course he and Philly had opted for had left him . . . not exactly feeling peaceful . . . but settled. It was a course that would require him to let go and he found himself looking forward to that change. He had let go in another way; he had never pressed Camellia Kim on her failure to get back to him on whether her grandmother would agree to have her herbal remedy analyzed. By letting time pass he had accepted Kim's statement that her grandmother wanted nothing to do with a laboratory analysis. He would continue to take the grandmother's concoction and bury the urge to know what was in it.

"That's quite a room you booked for us here," Maxine observed. "Maybe we could swap it for our condo. I think it's bigger."

"The idea of driving home didn't appeal to me. Besides, I was trying to butter you up in the hope of getting some action tonight."

"You don't have to butter me up to get action."

"You can't be too careful; it never hurts to hedge your bets."

Maxine sipped at her cocktail and gave the bar a full circle examination. "This is nice," she said.

Maxine was wearing a black dress that Carpenter liked. She had on very little makeup. The string of pearls at her neck was her only jewelry. "You're nice," he said.

Josh's one sports jacket had seen better days, but Rachel had successfully fought the urge to get him a new one or to suggest that he get a new one. Instead, she'd told him the jacket would do fine. Now that he was dressed for the evening, she wondered whether she'd made the right choice. The sports jacket was gray, and Josh had located a pair of black slacks and a buttoned-down white shirt. His one tie was a mismatch—brightly colored whales, sharks, and assorted other fish swimming upstream toward his neck. The truth was Josh looked like he always looked—somewhat unkempt. "You look nice," Rachel said. After making the decision not to try to make Josh over, she was going to live with it even if it killed her.

For this evening, Rachel had put on the nicest dress she owned—a blue dress with a plunging neckline and a blue sash at her waist.

"Am I dressed up enough?" Josh asked.

"I'd say so," Rachel responded. "I think it's safe to say Carpenter and Simon won't have your look, but that's their problem."

Josh stared at her. "I've decided on a New Year's resolution," he announced. "You're taking me shopping for a wardrobe upgrade. I hope you know what a serious resolution this is for me."

Rachel knew that Josh hated shopping generally but loathed shopping for clothes in particular. "I'll help you get through it," she said.

Philly and Paul were the first to enter the private dining room. Philly was looking forward to this grownups-only evening. Paul's daughter Jenny was babysitting Daisy and Rosalind tonight. Philly smiled as she recalled Jenny's serious look as they gave her final instructions. Raul and Isabella had grown up plans for the night, but Sarah Ferguson was staying home on the holiday eve and had promised not to retire until the adults had returned.

"This is pretty swanky," Paul observed.

"Carpenter and I figured why not. The year ended with two big cases going our way, so we decided to go out on a high, expensive note. Besides, you're looking pretty swanky."

"It's my only suit."

"It just goes to show that we can both dress you up *and* take you out. You look nice." She'd done a double take when Paul emerged from their bedroom in a blue suit, striped blue dress shirt, and red patterned tie. She'd never seen him fully dressed up before.

"You and Carpenter have been on the phone a lot recently. What's going on?"

"You'll find out tonight. There's one serious part of this evening."

"Does Maxine know what's going on?"

"She shouldn't. All will be revealed in good time."

A waiter appeared out of nowhere. "May I get you a drink while you're waiting for the other guests?"

Paul was watching her with concern. "He'll order for both of us," she nodded in Paul's direction.

"What if they don't like me?" Frank Stevens said.

"I don't think that's going to be a problem," Simon said as they walked through the hotel lobby. He wondered whether Frank's question masked a concern about their sexual orientation. On that score, Simon felt completely at ease. Exactly a year ago he had told Carpenter and Philly that he was gay. From their expressions, it was clear that they'd had no clue that he was. But in the past year, the subject simply hadn't come up. Carpenter and Philly had accepted his declaration and treated him as a colleague. And for Rachel, who had known about his sexual orientation for years, his being gay wasn't an issue.

"I'm going to be the youngest one here, right?" Frank asked.

"Right."

"What if I can't think of anything to say?"

"With Carpenter and Philly around, that won't be a problem. Don't expect too many lulls in the conversation."

"I thought you said Carpenter was a crotchety guy who didn't like to socialize."

"I did say that. But tonight I suspect he's not going to be thinking about cases and will actually make small talk."

"I'm nervous," Frank admitted.

"It's okay to be nervous. It's not okay not to have a good time. I'm looking forward to this dinner. We've all had a good year. Don't be a party pooper."

"Easy for you to say."

"Easy for you to do."

Sometime toward the end of the main course, Carpenter was struck by the thought that he liked everyone in the room. The three male guests were a motley crew, but he had conversed with each and had found it easy to do so. He wouldn't have guessed at the pairings. It still took him aback that Philly had married the cop who had broken the news to her about Philip Sizemore's accident. Rachel was the last person he would have predicted to take up with a guy who was laid back beyond mellow. Then there was Simon who looked like he didn't have an athletic bone in his body but had paired up with an obvious jock.

Carpenter made eye contact with Philly and she gave him a nod. Their waiter had been instructed to hold off on the coffee, tea, and desserts. As he tapped his water glass with a spoon, he felt a rush of nervousness. This was as bad as standing up in court.

"You probably wondered why Philly and I asked you all here tonight," Carpenter began, and the uniform serious expressions that greeted his attempt at humor confirmed that he was constitutionally incapable of achieving a light tone. "But there is a reason you're here that's separate and apart from our wanting to have everyone present celebrate what we think was a very good year. Philly and I have a proposal for Rachel and Simon and we're okay with setting it out with everyone who's here."

Rachel was staring at him wide-eyed and Carpenter suppressed a smile. Simon had become even more serious.

"Some history," Carpenter continued. "At the start of 2008, Philly and I discussed forming a firm. For a number of reasons, it never happened. In later years, it also never happened although for all intents and purposes we had pretty much worked together on anything either of us brought in. When Philly became pregnant, we reached out to Rachel and Simon and have never regretted doing so. I'm still trying to figure out how we lucked out getting you two to work with us. You've saved our sorry asses time and again, and perhaps it took a while for that to sink in."

Carpenter was now relaxed. Rachel and Simon had to know what was coming. Maxine certainly knew; her grin gave her away.

"To cut to it, we're proposing that the four of us form a firm. We'd all be partners. For two years we wouldn't be equal partners. For two years Philly and I would have a twenty-six percent interest in the firm and you two would have a twenty-four percent interest. Beginning after two years we'd be equal partners—twenty-five percent interest for each of us."

Josh Horgan and Frank Stevens were staring at their partners.

"Nobody has to decide anything immediately. Philly and I just want you to think about it. If you decide it's a go, we're going to expect a full-time commitment. No more part-time jobs."

Carpenter paused. He tried to clear his head; the beers he had consumed were getting in the way of what he wanted to say next. "For years I've thought of myself as a lone wolf. And Philly has an independent streak in case you didn't notice. We're not always the easiest people to get along with. So you really do need to think about this proposal."

Rachel dabbed at her eyes with her napkin and Josh Horgan put an arm around her shoulder. Frank Stevens reached over and squeezed Simon's shoulder and Carpenter half expected Simon to wince in pain.

"I don't have to think about it," Simon said. "I'm in."

All eyes turned to Rachel, and Carpenter felt her embarrassment.

"This is all so sudden," Rachel said. "I guess I do want to think about it."

Josh leaned over and whispered in Rachel's ear. Whatever message he was conveying, it took him a while to deliver it.

Josh straightened up and leaned back in his chair. Rachel had turned scarlet.

"I was just reminded that I have a habit of over-thinking some things," Rachel said. "So I'm not going to over-think this one since many times this year I hoped we'd end up practicing law together. So I'm in too. But I do have a condition that is non-negotiable."

Carpenter didn't like the sound of that. "What's the condition?" he said guardedly.

"We're getting a website and you're going to be on it."

Maxine and Philly burst out laughing. Carpenter felt himself reddening. He swore by the credo that nothing was easy, and his belief had just been confirmed for the umpteenth time. Christ, he thought, we haven't even signed a partnership agreement and things are out of control. "Sure, what the hell," he said to avoid further unproductive soul searching.

"That was easy," Maxine said, and Carpenter succumbed to an eye roll and a heartfelt sigh.

"Which of you is the oldest?" Carpenter addressed Simon and Rachel.

"I am by two months," Simon said.

"Then it's Carpenter, Piper, Jeffries, and Boyle," Carpenter declared.

"Make that Carpenter, Sullivan, Jeffries, and Boyle," Philly amended before leaning over to give Paul a serious kiss.

"Get a room," Simon said.

"Carpenter and I already have one," Maxine said. "Some of us think ahead."

The waiter peered into the room and Carpenter gave him the signal to start on desserts.

"Do Rachel and I still have to share Philly's office?" Simon asked.

"Yes," Philly said.

Simon shrugged. "Well, you can't have it all."

Philly smiled. "Yes, you can."

Author's Note

The first draft of *All* was written in 2011.

I would like to thank Meredith Larson for her edits, comments, and suggestions. I probably should have made all the changes she suggested.

I am also grateful to Jon Behar for his edits and comments.

While I have visited on Carpenter and Philly clients who are beyond difficult, I have dedicated this book to former clients who were anything but.

Any and all errors are mine.

Made in the USA
Monee, IL
04 November 2026

67385362R00277